Truck Accident Litigation

Fourth Edition

Ashley N. Baker and
D. J. Young, III
EDITORS

AMERICAN BAR ASSOCIATION
Tort Trial and Insurance Practice Section

Cover design by Jill Tedhams/ABA Design

Printed in the United States of America.

29 28 27 26 25 5 4 3 2 1

ISBN 978-1-63905-573-9

Discounts are available for books ordered in bulk. Special consideration is given to state bars, CLE programs, and other bar-related organizations. Inquire at Book Publishing, ABA Publishing, American Bar Association, 321 N. Clark Street, Chicago, Illinois 60654-7598.

www.shopABA.org

Contents

Part II
Investigation and Trial Preparation

Part III
Special Topics Applicable to Truck Accident Litigation

Acknowledgments

The editors, Ashley N. Baker and D.J. Young, III, thank the members of the American Bar Association's Tort Trial & Insurance Practice Section's Commercial Transportation Litigation Committee with entrusting this important project to us, and we would like to give special thanks to Sarah (Sam) Forbes Orwig, PhD, from the American Bar Association, for her encouragement and patient support.

I, Ashley N. Baker, thank my co-editor, D.J. Young, III, for his devotion to this project and for seeing it through to completion. I thank Mark Perkins for his vision to publish a new edition of this book and for trusting me with getting this project underway. I would like to thank my mother, Charlene Baker, and my sister, Lindsey Baker, for their love and support throughout my life and career. I would not be the person I am without them. They have believed in me even when I did not believe in myself. Lastly, I would like to recognize my dear aunt Anna Brown who died in a trucking accident before I was born. It is my hope that my work to improve the trucking industry honors her memory.

I, D.J. Young, III, thank my co-editor, and friend, Ashley Baker, for her vision for this book, her dedication, her teamwork, and her friendship. I thank Michael A. Vercher for his patience with me and for some important insights he gave me about the direction this book should take. I thank Mark Perkins for his enthusiasm and encouragement and willingness to help. I thank Julia C. Young for her countless hours of meticulous diligence in fact-checking hundreds of citations throughout the book. I thank my brother and law partner Andrew R. Young, and my law partners and friends, Michael Leizerman, Rena Leizerman, and Matt Wright, for all they've taught me. I thank my competitors who are friends, Morgan Adams and Danny Ellis. There are a number of other attorneys who, in important and significant ways, contributed to who I am as an attorney, and, without their trust and guidance, I would not be the attorney I am: Roger Petersen, James A. Squires, F. Blair Wimbush, Henry Light, Elizabeth L. Hendershot, Duncan Whitney, David J. Brehm, Robert D. Gary, Jose Angel Flores, Suntrease Williams, Vic Whitney, Scott Wolf, and Roberto F. Ramirez. I also wish to thank Sandy Starr, James Earl Carter Jr., David Flack, Karen Young, Phil Magley, Karen Magley, Kevin Hover, Timothy S. Yoder, and, most especially, my wonderful wife and professional colleague, Melissa Young. There probably are other people I should thank, and I apologize now if I have omitted you. Named or unnamed, I share the credit with you for the success of this project. Thank you, and I am grateful to all of you.

About the Editors

Ashley N. Baker, Esq., M.S., LL.M.

Ashley N. Baker is the 2024–2025 chair of the ABA Tort, Trial, and Insurance Practice Section's Commercial Transportation Litigation Committee. She is a double-barred attorney in Pennsylvania and Washington, D.C. Ashley has been a licensed truck driver for 15 years. She was formerly on the truck driving faculty at Georgia Piedmont Technical College and an over-the-road trainer for a large trucking company. Her combined teaching experience has allowed her to train hundreds of drivers on the rules of the road. She has driven a tractor-trailer through nearly every part of the United States. She is the author of nine authoritative books on the transportation industry, including a series called *The Art of Commercial Trucking®*. She is also the author of *Modeerf's Transportation Law Dictionary*, which was acquired in 2023 by the Executive Office of the President of the United States.

In 2022, she was the recipient of the prestigious Connie Award scholarship from the Containerization and Intermodal Institute. She received her J.D. from Southern University Law Center, her M.A. in international transportation management from the State University of New York, and her LL.M. in trial advocacy from the Temple University Beasley School of Law. Ashley is currently pursuing a Ph.D. in transportation and urban infrastructure systems at Morgan State University. Ashley is a defense attorney handling truck accident and cargo loading claims, defending clients in both state and federal courts.

D.J. Young, III, Esq.

D.J. Young, III, dedicates his legal work nearly exclusively to handling wrongful death and catastrophic injury cases for the victims of truck crashes. He is a partner in The Law Firm for Truck Safety LLP, in its Columbus, Ohio, office. The focus of his legal work is on legal strategy; legal research and analysis and writing complaints, dispositive motion briefs, and appellate briefs; and arguing points of law before state and federal trial and appellate courts. He has successfully taken numerous cases through jury verdict as lead trial counsel. He also has had successful appellate experience in federal and state courts, including the Supreme Court of Ohio. He has spoken on trucking law topics before the Oklahoma Association for Justice, North Dakota Association for Justice, and the Ohio Association for Justice. He has served on the board for the Ohio

Association for Justice, and he has been published (in 2023) in the American Association for Justice's *Trial Magazine*.

He has held a Class A Commercial Driver's License since 2016 and is endorsed to drive CMVs with manual transmissions, air brakes, and double and triple trailers. Much earlier in his career, he was a construction lawyer, real estate development attorney, Assistant United States Attorney for the Southern District of Texas, railroad attorney in house at Norfolk Southern Railway Company, and a general contractor. He was on the law review at the University of Notre Dame Law School. In his free time, he is a part-time seminary student, and he likes to teach at his church. He is a member of the Gideons International, the American Association for Justice, the Academy of Truck Accident Attorneys (ATAA), the Christian Legal Society, and the American Bar Association.

About the Authors

Morgan Adams, Esq.

Morgan Adams is a past chair of the American Association for Justice's (AAJ) Trucking Litigation Group (2009–2010). In addition to trying all types of commercial motor vehicle cases, he works as a national litigation consultant on liability and punitive damage issues for other lawyers. Morgan is a past member of the AAJ Board of Governors, a Life and Board of Governors Member of the Tennessee Association for Justice, and has chaired the Tennessee Trucking Litigation Seminars since 2004. He has been selected repeatedly as a Mid-South SuperLawyer, is a member of the Belli Society, is a member of the Million Dollar Advocates Forum, and was recognized as an AAJ Diplomate in 2011. Fewer than 200 lawyers in the country have the AAJ Diplomate designation. In 2010, West Publishing included his chapter on "Truck Accident Litigation" in its multivolume set *Handling Motor Vehicle Cases,* 2nd edition. He has also had "The New Rules in Trucking Discovery" published in AAJ's Trial magazine in February of 2011 and "Spoliation in Trucking Cases" in the Arkansas Trial Lawyers Association's Docket in the Winter 2012 edition. He is AV rated by Martindale-Hubbell.

Gabriela R. Atkisson, Esq.

Gabriela Ruiz Atkisson, Esq., received her B.A. in communication with a minor in Spanish from Auburn University. After graduation, she attended Samford University's Cumberland School of Law. Gabriela is a member of the Transportation and Insurance Defense practice groups at Christian & Small, LLP, in the Birmingham, Alabama office. She represents clients in civil litigation, focusing primarily on insurance defense, trucking and automobile accidents, and premise liability. She is a member of the Alabama State Bar Association, Alabama Defense Lawyers Association (ADLA), Birmingham Bar Association (Young Lawyers Section and Women Lawyers Section), and Defense Research Institute's (DRI) Diversity and Inclusion Committee.

Sheri E. Belitz, Esq.

Shari Belitz, Esq., is a nationally recognized litigation consultant, keynote speaker, best-selling author, and chief executive officer of Shari Belitz Communications LLC. She is certified by the National Women's Business Enterprise National Counsel (WBENC). She is also the founder of the educational subscription course, EnPSYCHLAWpedia®. Shari Belitz Communications, LLC is a litigation consulting company that helps civil defense lawyers and insurance professionals achieve favorable litigation outcomes using psychology. Shari conducts mock trials, prepares witnesses for depositions and trials, writes theme development reports for mediation and trial, and performs jury selection and other customized trial services.

Riley Laine Brown, Esq.

Riley Laine Brown is currently an associate at Christian & Small, LLP, based in Birmingham, Alabama. Riley received her juris doctor from the University of Mississippi School of Law, with a concentration in business in May 2022. Prior to attending law school, Riley received her undergraduate degree in political science, with a minor in business, from the University of Mobile. Riley's practice primarily involves commercial trucking defense. She is a member of the Transportation and Insurance Defense practice group at Christian & Small, LLP. Riley is licensed to practice law in Tennessee, Texas, and Alabama. Riley is a member of the American Bar Association's Tort Trial and Insurance Practice Section and Young Lawyers Section, Alabama State Bar Association, Texas State Bar Association, Alabama Defense Lawyers Association (ADLA), Birmingham Bar Association (Young Lawyers Section and Women Lawyers Section), and Defense Research Institute (DRI).

Jeffrey A. Burns, Esq.

Jeff has focused his practice on representing truck crash victims and their families for more than 30 years. In addition to representing truck crash victims, Jeff has spent much of his career working to improve laws and regulations to make the trucking industry safer. He has served on the boards of Citizens for Reliable and Safe Highways (CRASH), Parents Against Tired Truckers (PATT), the Center for Truck Safety, and the Brain Injury Association of Kansas and Greater Kansas City. He has been National Transportation Counsel for PATT since 1996 and serves on the Executive Committee of the Truck Safety Coalition. He was appointed by the U.S. Secretary of Transportation to the National Freight Advisory Committee to advise the Secretary on issues relating to the future of freight transportation in the United States and has represented clients in truck crash cases in 38 states. He is a frequent speaker on truck safety issues to both plaintiff and defense lawyer associations and to trucking industry trade groups.

JJ Burns, Esq.

JJ helps truck crash victims and their families hold trucking industry participants accountable for their negligence. He is a trial attorney who focuses almost exclusively on claims against trucking companies, freight brokers, logistics companies, and shippers who cause life-ending and life-altering tractor-trailer crashes. He is currently serving as the chair-elect of the American Association for Justice's Trucking Litigation Group, and regularly teaches other trucking and transportation industry lawyers at seminars and conferences across the country. He serves on the Executive Board of Parents Against Tired Truckers. JJ is licensed to practice in Missouri and Illinois and has litigated cases against motor carriers in 28 states. JJ teaches a personal injury litigation course at the University of Missouri-Kansas City Law School every year, and he spends a substantial amount of time in Washington, D.C., advocating for laws and regulations that will improve safety on our nation's highways.

Alex Celio, Esq.

Alexandra "Alex" Celio is an associate at Simon, Peragine, Smith & Redfearn in New Orleans where she centers her practice around transportation matters of all kinds. She works closely with clients to help mitigate risk and exposure after catastrophic accidents. Frequently involved at the ground level, Alex spearheads gathering and preserving evidence in accordance with federal trucking regulations to guide clients in pre-suit accident investigations. She is a sitting board member of the Association for Women Attorneys New Orleans Chapter and active in both the New Orleans Federal Bar Association and Louisiana State Bar Association. Alex also sits on the programming committee of the Transportation Lawyers Association (TLA) and attends the annual Trucking Industry Defense Association (TIDA) conference. Since admitted to practice in 2019, Alex has been named a Best Lawyer in America Ones to Watch in Commercial Litigation and Transportation Law as well as a Louisiana Super Lawyers Rising Star.

Peter Doody, Esq.

Peter Doody is a California trial attorney specializing in the defense of catastrophic trucking cases. He is a partner in the San Diego law firm of Higgs, Fletcher & Mack. Mr. Doody has litigated over 50 jury trials to verdict as first chair and is a member of the American Board of Trial Advocates (ABOTA). He is past president of the Association of Southern California Defense Counsel (2019) and past president of San Diego Defense Lawyers (2005). Mr. Doody received his law degree from the University of San Francisco School of Law.

Mary Eliasen, Esq.

Mary Eliasen is an associate attorney at Penn, Kestner & McEwen, where she represents plaintiffs who have been injured by commercial motor vehicles. Prior to joining PKM, she was an associate at a North Dakota-based personal injury firm and clerked for the federal judiciary. She currently serves on the board of governors of the Minnesota Association for Justice (MNAJ). She has published articles in the American Association of Justice (AAJ) Trucking Litigation Group (TLG) Journal of Trucking Litigation and the North Dakota Law Review. Mary earned her B.A. in political science at the University of Minnesota in 2005 and graduated first in her class from the University of North Dakota School of Law in 2017. While at UND School of Law, she externed for the Eighth Circuit Court of Appeals and the U.S. Attorney's Office. She also served on the North Dakota Law Review and won numerous academic awards. Mary is licensed to practice in Minnesota and North Dakota state and federal courts.

Danny R. Ellis, Esq.

Danny is an attorney at Truck Wreck Justice, PLLC, a firm that specializes in tractor trailer and commercial bus litigation. In October 2020, Danny received his Truck Accident Law Certification from the National Board of Trial Advocacy. With this firm, Danny utilizes his 20 years of experience, trial skills, and learning to best help those injured by the reckless and negligent acts of these companies and their drivers. In 2021, Danny was named the Tennessee Trial Lawyer of the Year, an award voted on by his peers. Danny has earned the reputation of being willing to try his cases, and for using cutting-edge techniques to achieve full justice. Danny is also known as always willing to lend support and give helpful advice to other lawyers pursing justice. He considers being a dean of the deposition college and a faculty member of the Keenan Trial Institute his greatest professional achievement and has taught hundreds of attorneys trial and litigation skills necessary to hold wrongdoers accountable. Danny has also authored the Tennessee chapter in the book, *Negligence and Purpose, Elements and Evidence, The Role of Foreseeabiity in the Law of Each State*. ISBN 978-0-9980073-3-5 (2018)

Tia Ghattas, Esq.

Tia Ghattas is a supply chain lawyer. She is the co-chair of the Transportation and Logistics industry team at the law firm Cozen O'Connor. Ms. Ghattas is an industry leader for transportation companies faced with supply chain disputes, managing partnerships, navigating large losses, regulatory compliance, contract disputes, and emergency response. She is usually the first call from a general counsel's office or a company safety director seeking legal expertise in the field to provide strategic and efficient counsel. Providing a unique perspective as a first-generation college graduate who was closely affiliated to the industry her entire life (her mother,

her grandmother, and her grandfather made a living as commercial drivers along with several other family members in the industry as drivers, dispatchers, and line workers), her knowledge of the business and its people is an invaluable asset. She is a litigator in jurisdictions across the country; she is also regularly appointed as an arbitrator in disputes and has represented some of the largest companies in the United States including the nation's leading component parts manufacturers as well as both large and small entities in the supply chain industry.

Jordan M. Jones, Esq.

Jordan Jones is a trial attorney based in Los Angeles who only handles catastrophic truck wreck cases. Jordan is licensed in California and Michigan. He is board certified in Truck Accident Law by the National Board of Trial Advocacy (NBTA), he is an executive officer of the AAJ Truck Litigation Group, sits on the Board of Regents for the Academy of Truck Accident Attorneys (ATAA), and he regularly presents as an invited speaker across the United States about truck wreck litigation. Jordan has been recognized by Super Lawyers as a Rising Star, by Best Lawyers as Ones to Watch, and by Michigan Lawyers Weekly as a top Up and Coming Lawyer. Jordan previously served as a litigation advisor for the Institute of Continuing Legal Education (ICLE) in Michigan and sat on the board of a nonprofit legal organization that served indigent clients. In his spare time, he enjoys reading, Peloton, and entrepreneurship.

Peter J. Kestner, Esq.

Pete Kestner has more than 30 years' experience with truck wreck cases. He is a co-founder of the law firm McEwen & Kestner and recently a co-founder of a national trucking practice with Penn, Kestner & McEwen. Pete earned his B.S. from Skidmore College in 1989, and his J.D. from William Mitchell College of Law in 2001. He was among the first group of lawyers in the country to become board certified in truck accident law by the National Board of Trial Advocacy and is the only lawyer in Minnesota with such a designation. Peter is the past chair of the Academy of Truck Accident Attorneys (ATAA) and past chair of the American Association of Justice's (AAJ) Interstate Trucking Litigation Group. He is one of the members of the Amicus Committee for AAJ's Interstate Trucking Litigation Group and he also holds a Chartered Property & Casualty Underwriter (CPCU) professional designation in insurance. He has litigated truck accident cases in 24 different states in both state and federal courts.

Chad C. Marchand, Esq.

Chad Marchand is a national high stakes litigator who focuses on transportation, aviation, and retail cases. He is a former chair of the ABA Tort, Trial, and Insurance Practice Section's Commercial Transportation Litigation Committee and is a current member of the American Board of Trial Advocates,

Transportation Industry Defense Association, Transportation Lawyers Association, and Lawyers Pilot Bar Association. He is licensed to practice in Alabama, Florida, and Mississippi. He received his law degree from Cumberland School of Law of Samford University, cum laude, in 2000, where he also served as the editor in chief for the American Journal of Trial Advocacy, a winner of the 1999 Judge James O. Haley Federal Mock Trial Competition, and a teaching fellow for the Cordell Hull Legal Research and Writing.

Joseph P. Moriarty, Esq.

Joseph P. Moriarty is a partner in the catastrophic loss and tort defense practice group at Willcox Savage, P.C., headquartered in Norfolk, Virginia, with a second office in Tysons, Virginia. Joe has over two decades experience defending commercial transportation, trucking, and logistic claims, often involving potentially high exposure losses. Joe is vice-chair of the ABA's Commercial Transpiration Litigation Committee (CTLC), as well as being a member of the Themis Advocates Group, Trucking Industry Defense Association (TIDA), and Defense Research Institute's (DRI) Trucking Law Committee. He holds Martindale-Hubbell's AV Preeminent© rating—the highest possible—in both legal ability and ethical standards. He has also been peer-recognized for inclusion in the Best Lawyers in America® for Litigation-Insurance. Reach him at jmoriarty@wilsav.com or visit www.willcoxsavage.com.

Amy Papuga, Esq.

Amy Papuga focuses her practice on handling catastrophic injury and wrongful death truck crash cases. She is licensed to practice in Ohio and Washington, D.C. She holds a Class A commercial driver's license and is regularly invited to teach others about truck safety and truck crash litigation. She has taught paralegals and lawyers about various topics related to truck crash litigation, and she regularly teaches new truck driver applicants about safety at a local truck driving school. Prior to becoming an attorney, she worked in the legal field for over 15 years as a legal assistant and paralegal. She worked full-time while obtaining her B.A., M.S., and J.D. She is member of Phi Kappa Phi, the American Bar Association, American Association of Justice, Academy of Truck Accident Attorneys, and the Ohio Association for Justice. She has been recognized as a Rising Star by *Super Lawyers*® from 2023 to 2025. In her free time, she enjoys gardening and training her dogs.

Mark A. Perkins, Esq.

Mark Perkins is the founder and owner of Perkins & Associates, L.L.C., a regional defense firm serving all of North Louisiana and East Texas. The firm has earned the reputation as aggressive, well-prepared litigators. In 1987, he graduated from Paul M. Hebert Law School at LSU Baton Rouge and was admitted to the practice of law in 1987. He began his legal profession as an assistant district attorney, litigating hundreds of bench and jury trials. Before DNA evidence became common-place, Mark was the first to use DNA evidence in North Louisiana in the successful prosecution of a serial rapist. In 1998, Mark opened a boutique law firm, Perkins & Associates, LLC, which focuses on the defense of commercial- and trucking-related matters. Mark is admitted to practice in both Louisiana and Texas, all federal courts in Louisiana, Federal Eastern District of Louisiana, the U.S. Fifth Circuit Court of Appeal, and the U.S. Supreme Court. He is a member of Defense Research Institute (trucking section), Louisiana Association of Defense Counsel, Trucking Insurance Defense Association, Transportation Lawyers Association, and the Louisiana Motor Transit Association. Mark has conducted numerous seminars for trucking and insurance industries regarding the defense of complex litigation claims, particularly trucking claims. He served as the editor in chief for the quarterly newsletter of the Trucking Industry Defense Association from 2017 until 2024.

Megan S. Peterson, Esq.

Megan S. Peterson is a partner at Simon, Peragine, Smith, & Redfearn in New Orleans, Louisiana. Although she handles a variety of civil litigation matters, her practice focuses on defense of business clients in trucking and transportation; premises liability; and retail, restaurant, and hospitality litigation. She is licensed to practice in all state and federal courts of both Louisiana and Mississippi and handles claims from pre-suit investigations through all stages of appeals. Megan enjoys service in various bar organizations. Currently, she has the pleasure of serving DRI, a civil defense bar organization, as the Retail and Hospitality Committee Chair. She has previously enjoyed working on behalf of young lawyers through leadership in DRI and the Louisiana State Bar Association. She has also previously served as a delegate in the American Bar Association's Young Lawyers Division and as the Louisiana Young Lawyer Delegate in the ABA House of Delegates. She helped champion several initiatives, such as a resolution to encourage lactation spaces in courthouses and encouraging judges to allow young lawyer oral arguments when possible. She remains actively involved in the American Bar Association through the Tort Trial & Insurance Practice Section (TIPS) and their Commercial Transportation Litigation Committee. She is also past president of the Association for Women Attorneys in New Orleans and has worked with other national women's bar organizations and their programming, such as the Good Guys Panel with the National Association of Women Lawyers and Raising the Bar with MothersEsquire. In her down time, she enjoys spending time with her husband lawyer, Matt McCluer, their two young children, and their two miniature Australian Shepherds. She also enjoys dancing, live music, a good book, and anything Disney related.

Lauren Pilié, Esq.

Lauren Pilié is a personal injury trial lawyer based in New Orleans, Louisiana. She is the first attorney in Louisiana to become board-certified in trucking law by the National Board of Trial Advocacy. She began her career doing defense work, and she had her first trial two weeks after getting her bar results. Lauren switched to the plaintiff's side three years into her practice, and she enjoys representing injured people and their families. Lauren started focusing on trucking wrecks in approximately 2017, and she has devoted considerable time to learning about truck crash cases. After a lifetime of driving almost every type of vehicle (cars, trucks, motorcycles, ATVs, dirt bikes, etc.), Lauren decided to attend trucking school in 2019 to fully learn what it was like to drive an 18-wheeler. She has been all over the country and traveled internationally to depose trucking company representatives. Lauren hopes at the very least, after leaving the deposition, that she gives the corporate safety rep the desire to increase their company's safety and also to have knowledge of the areas in which to do so.

Roberto Franciso Ramirez, Esq.

Roberto F. Ramirez was born and raised in San Antonio, Texas. He attended Texas A&M University graduating with a B.S. in civil engineering. After graduation, he was commissioned a second lieutenant in the U.S. Marine Corps and served as an infantry officer and recruit training officer. While in the Marine Corps, he attended the University of Texas School of Law under the Funded Law Education Program. After obtaining his J.D., he served the remainder of his twenty-year career as a judge advocate as trial and defense counsel, review officer, legal assistance officer, civil law officer, Special Assistant U.S. Attorney, and deputy staff judge advocate. Upon retirement, he worked for 15 years as an Assistant U.S. Attorney in the Southern District of Texas and in the Eastern District of North Carolina. He returned to San Antonio, Texas, after 39 years and is now enjoying private practice as a solo practitioner. Roberto has been happily married to Louisa LeGwin for 31 years and they have raised six children. They live in Rio Medina, Texas, on the Medina River.

Kevin Rider, Ph.D.

Kevin Rider is a Professional Engineer (PE), Certified Professional Ergonomist (CPE), and a human factors consultant, whose expertise includes investigating driver-related causes of catastrophic truck crashes around the country. He has served as a consultant since 1999, including five years as a professor at West Virginia University; his research includes driver behavior, perception, attention, and distraction. He has a B.A. and M.A. in industrial engineering from the University of Tennessee in Knoxville. He earned his Ph.D. in industrial and operations engineering from the University of Michigan in Ann Arbor.

Iiona D. Scully, Ph.D., CXLT

Iiona D. Scully received her B.S. in psychology from Elmira College. She holds an M.A. in psychology from Towson University and a Ph.D. in psychology from Lehigh University. She is a human factors consultant at Exponent, Inc., where she regularly addresses how the capabilities and limitations of people interact with the products, equipment, and systems in their environment, and how this interaction affects safety. Through her work, she has evaluated issues related to human performance, vehicle operator behavior, visual and auditory perception, attention and distraction, stress and fatigue, human memory and experience, and information processing. She routinely applies this expertise to the investigation of human factors in transportation accidents; product use; compliance with safety information; memory and eyewitness testimony; slips, trips, and falls; and the use of in-vehicle technologies and Advanced Driver Assistance Systems (ADAS). She has published research and presented at professional conferences on a variety of human factors issues, including human memory, cognition, performance, and learning, as well as driver knowledge and behavior regarding in-vehicle technologies. She is a member of the Human Factors and Ergonomics Society, SAE International, the Association for Women in Science, and the Association for Psychological Science.

Peter Shlanta, Ph.D.

Peter C. Shlanta specializes in using a human factors approach to evaluate driver visual behavior, perception response time, pedestrian behavior, situational awareness, visual attention, nighttime visual perception, warning and safety compliance, fatigue, inattentional blindness, and more as a human factors consultant with Exponent, Inc. Dr. Shlanta has applied his evaluations to a variety of real-world situations, including vehicular accidents, pedestrian accidents, slip-and-fall incidents, safety trainings, and product safety scenarios. Dr. Shlanta received his B.A. in psychology from Bloomsburg University, his M.A. in experimental psychology from Towson University, and his Ph.D. in experimental psychology from Central Michigan University. As part of his graduate studies, Dr. Shlanta examined visual attention, eye movements, and how these processes affect text processing and comprehension when applied to a reading context. He is a member of the Psychonomic Society, the Association for Psychological Science, and the Human Factors and Ergonomics Society.

Harrison M. Smith, Esq.

Harrison M. Smith received his B.A. in marketing from the University of Mississippi. After graduation, he attended the University of Mississippi School of Law, where he graduated with high honors. Harrison spent his first year following law school clerking for the U.S. Court of Appeals for the Fifth Circuit. Since then, he has been a member of the Commercial Litigation and Tort, Transportation, and Specialized Litigation groups at Butler Snow LLP in Ridgeland,

Mississippi. Harrison represents clients in civil litigation, focusing primarily on trucking accidents, business disputes, first party insurance defense, and breach of warranty claims brought against manufacturers. He serves as a member of the Mississippi Bar Association, American Bar Association, Capital Area Bar Association, and Jackson Young Lawyers.

Robin Squires, Esq.

Within his transportation, class actions, and defense practice, Robin advises on complex casualty matters and class actions involving multiple parties and inter-jurisdictional and cross border insurance issues. In addition to Robin's court experience, he advises transportation clients on corporate matters and liability and risk management issues, including drafting of service agreements, contracts and bills of lading, governance issues, and labor and employment matters. Robin is the national leader of BLG's Transportation Focus Group.

John C. Steiner

John Steiner earned a B.S. in mechanical engineering in 2001 from California State University, Long Beach. Today he is CEO, principal scientist, and co-founder of Mecanica Scientific Services Corp. His primary duties include overseeing the company's growth, planning management of Mecanica's executive- and director-level leadership teams including support and involvement in director-lead departments. Mr. Steiner has served as chief researcher on government-funded highway safety research projects and manages Mecanica's continued government contracting and government-funded highway safety project endeavors. On a clinical case level, Mr. Steiner specializes in transportation accident reconstruction and analysis including the imaging (download) and analysis of data from SAE J1698 compliant Event Data Recorders (EDR) on equipped passenger vehicles and SAE J2728 compliant Heavy Vehicle Event Data Recorders (HVEDR) found on medium-duty and heavy-duty trucks and buses. Since 2008, Mr. Steiner has served as one of two original third-party vendors authorized by Mack Trucks, Inc. (Volvo Trucks North America) to provide Mack and Volvo truck HVEDR data imaging and analysis services. Mr. Steiner is also one of the original developers and one of four instructors of the SAE Continuing Education Courses on Accessing and Interpreting Heavy Vehicle Event Data Recorders (Course ID # C1022) from December 2010 to present.

Sarah Sweet, Esq.

Sarah's diverse practice focuses on maritime and transportation law as well as insurance coverage and defense. Sarah acts for clients in complex shipping and rail casualty matters, cargo claims, commercial disputes, bills of lading and contracts of affreightment disputes, ship arrest and sale, and cargo arrest. She also advises on transportation agreements, transportation regulatory matters, and transactions in a variety of transport modalities.

Michael A. Vercher, Esq.

Mike Vercher has defended commercial transportation companies for over 25 years in Alabama and across the Southeast with the same law firm, Christian & Small, LLP. Mike helped start the firm and is currently serving his second term on the firm's Executive Committee. He also serves as the chair of the firm's Commercial Transportation Committee. Mike has been recognized by Benchmark, Best Lawyers, and Super Lawyers, and he has been an active member of the American Bar Association (serving as a delegate to the ABA House of Delegates) and ABA TIPS (serving in various leadership roles on Council and as a program chair of the Transportation Megaconference). In his community, Mike is chair of the Planning and Zoning Committee for his city and is active in his church.

Keishunna Webster, Esq.

Keishunna is a member of the Tort Transportation and Specialized Litigation practice group at Butler Snow LLP. Her practice focuses on commercial trucking and transportation accidents, insurance and products defense, and commercial litigation. Keishunna has been recognized by *Super Lawyers*® as a Mid-South Rising Star for her work in personal injury defense.

Introduction

Mark Perkins, Ashley N. Baker, and D.J. Young, III

Trucking litigation is a unique area of law because it deals with predominantly laborers driving as much as 40 tons (and sometimes more) of freight with highly regulated commercial motor vehicle equipment. These vehicles are traveling on interstate highways at no less than 50 miles per hour. When combined with road hazards, distractions, and ever-evolving road conditions, the potential for catastrophic injuries is high.

According to the Federal Motor Carrier Safety Administration 2022 *Pocket Guide to Large Truck and Bus Statistics*, in 2020, of the 35,766 fatal crashes on the nation's roadways, 4,588 (12.8 percent) involved at least one large truck or bus. In addition, there were an estimated 5,215,000 nonfatal crashes, 440,000 of which involved at least one large truck or bus.

Crashes involving large trucks are generally more serious, just like accidents involving trains and planes are more catastrophic. Consequently, lawyers involved in prosecuting or defending trucking accidents require more sophistication and expertise in handling trucking accident cases. It requires not only extensive knowledge, like that of the authors of this book, but also fundamental principles of advocacy like listening to your client, asking the right questions, and being analytical.

For trucking cases, analysis typically starts with applying the facts of your case to the detailed regulations governing the trucking industry. This is what makes trucking lawyers so unique. These regulations are substantially different from standard automobile accidents, involving a concentration of proficiency. Truck accident cases involve federal statutes, the Federal Motor Carrier Safety Regulations (FMCSRs), state-specific laws and regulations, and numerous industry-specific customs and practices, as well as most common law negligence doctrines. Trucking lawyers must be well-versed in the FMCSRs and can expertly traverse their intricacies.

Truck accident cases are rarely simple. There are multiple components and parties involved that may have some percentage of liability for an accident, including the truck driver, the trucking company, and other parties involved in interstate and/or international transportation. These parties are vast and can extend beyond the parties present at the scene of the accident. Trucking lawyers initiate comprehensive investigations, and collaborate with experts, specialists, and investigators to find decisive evidence. This data may involve witness statements, analysis of the accident site, retrieval of electronic controlled data from the large truck and other vehicles, and much more. By thoroughly studying the evidence, trucking lawyers prove or disprove responsibility while constructing convincing cases for their clients.

Almost every truck crash case facing the prospect of significant damages warrants the use of expert witnesses, and all truck accident attorneys know that, for that reason, these cases can very quickly become very expensive to litigate. Plaintiffs or their attorneys must be able to advance $50,000 to $150,000 (as valued in 2024) to fund the costs of engineers, crash reconstruction experts, human factors experts, medical experts, life-care planners, economists, video-recorded depositions, transcription costs, and travel costs. Defense attorneys will, in many cases, have similar experts, and their clients must be able and willing to fund their cases similarly.

Evaluation of damages is fundamental. A small error severely impacts the monetary consequences. Because of the potential severity of the injuries, trucking lawyers are educated in life-care analysis, economics, psychology, traumatic brain injury, orthopedic injuries, and a host of other body parts and damages.

Although most trucking accident cases are resolved through negotiations, for the catastrophic cases, negotiated resolutions are unlikely until after the completion of investigations, written discovery, depositions, dispositive motion practice, and mediation. A skilled trucking lawyer is a skilled trial lawyer, and a skilled trial lawyer is one who begins advocating at the first notice of an accident. Trucking lawyers prepare, study the recent techniques implemented by their adversaries, and counter with precise presentation of evidence, accomplished examination of fact witnesses and experts, careful legal analysis, and persuasive argumentation before judges and juries. Trucking lawyers persistently argue for their clients' rights, just as if the client's life and reputation were on the line, because in some cases they are. Lawyers who have never been in a trial, or who are reticent to go to trial, may be more likely to fail to achieve favorable outcomes for their clients.

This is why the publication of this book is so important. It has been more than 12 years since the third edition of this book was published, and since then there have been changes in the law, changes in strategy, and changes in truck technology, all of which warrant an update to the prior edition. *Truck Accident Litigation 3rd Edition* is still an excellent resource. There are some topics in that edition that for various reasons we chose not to include in *Truck Accident Litigation 4th Edition*, and there are topics that were not addressed in the third edition—or were not addressed in the third edition in as much detail—that are addressed more fully in this edition. In some ways, therefore, the fourth edition is completely new, and in other ways this fourth edition is a supplement to the third edition.

It is important to note that anyone using this book or prior editions of it should understand that this is a practice handbook. It is meant to help attorneys become generally aware of factual and legal issues that can be expected in truck crash litigation. It is no substitute for your own legal research and factual analysis, using the law of your jurisdiction. In other words, this book (like its predecessor) is more likely to help you spot the issues so that you can more efficiently investigate the facts and engage in legal research and analysis than it is likely to solve your unique factual and legal problems. The editors and chapter authors have worked hard to be as accurate as possible while maintaining the brevity necessary for consolidation of many topics in one book. Yet, none of us are perfect, and, undoubtedly, like every law book published, there may be places where the reader disagrees with the chapter author's assertions and legal conclusions. Indeed, you may have a new or better argument that displaces or contradicts something in this book. Such is the nature of the practice of law and effective advocacy. One can never blindly rely on another lawyer's work, even if published in print, and a competent lawyer always fact-checks and conducts his or her own legal research and analysis. That is the best practice and it is necessary because the law is constantly changing. Statutes and regulations are amended, and new court decisions are always forthcoming.

This book is divided into three parts. Part I has to do with subjects that are involved in almost every case. For attorneys of any experience level who are new to truck crash litigation, this is essential reading. Part II has to do with special practical problems that occur in many cases and that, in many cases, warrant the use of expert witnesses. Part III addresses some important legal issues that arise in some cases.

This book is written by a number of different authors. Several of the authors are expert witnesses, and they have interesting things to say about their topics. The prior edition of this book was more expert-intensive and there is much to be learned from the experts who contributed to both editions. Most of the authors in this fourth edition are attorneys. Most of these attorneys primarily only work either on the plaintiff's side of the case or only on the defense side of the case. If you are a plaintiff's attorney reading this book, do not overlook the chapters written by the defense attorneys. They have much to teach you about how they approach their cases and what they find to be important in their work. Similarly, if you are a defense attorney reading this book, it will be worth your time to consider the chapters written by the plaintiffs' attorneys to have a closer look at how they approach their cases. You can see from their contributions to this book that these attorneys are very passionate about their work. The fact that all of the authors have taken time out of their deadline-packed schedules to contribute to this book demonstrates their commitment to the mission they share with the publisher—that of defending liberty and pursing justice.

PART I

Subjects All Truck Accident Attorneys Should Understand

CHAPTER 1
The Business of Trucking

Tia Ghattas, Esq.

If You Bought It, a Truck Brought It: A Passion Project of Resiliency and Adaptability

Tia Ghattas, Esq.

"To deliver the world's leading transportation system, serving the American people and economy through the safe, efficient, sustainable and equitable movement of people and goods."

—The Department of Transportation Mission Statement

Introduction

Trucking plays a critical role in the U.S. supply chain. America's truck drivers deliver goods to every corner of this country, from large cities to remote areas. In some communities, trucks are the only form of delivery. Often referred to as the backbone of the American economy, trucking companies not only "deliver the goods" but also employ 3.54 million truck drivers and 8.4 million people in industry-related jobs,[1] including mechanics, managers, dispatchers, and workers in other occupations.[2] In addition, vehicle manufacturers, equipment suppliers, component part manufacturers, technology developers, and others in the commercial vehicle space are all part of the trucking industry.

The trucking industry is heavily regulated in the United States. Safety regulations are always at the forefront. The Federal Motor Carrier Safety Administration (FMCSA) is a subdivision of the United States Department of Transportation (USDOT). Its mission is to prevent commercial motor vehicle–related fatalities and injuries.[3] The federal regulations are promulgated by the FMCSA and are published in title 49 of the Code of Federal Regulations (C.F.R.). Largely, these regulate interstate trucking operations. Big or small, whether

1. (Excluding the self-employed,) *see* Am. Trucking Ass'ns, Economics and Industry Data (2022), https://www.trucking.org/economics-and-industry-data.

2. Jennifer Cheeseman Day & Andrew W. Hait, *Number of Truckers at All-Time High*, Census.gov (June 6, 2019), https://www.census.gov/library/stories/2019/06/america-keeps-on-trucking.html.

3. Fed. Motor Carrier Safety Admin., https://www.fmcsa.dot.gov/mission (last visited Sept. 12, 2024).

a trucking business owns or leases one or 1,000 tractors, each motor carrier is required to follow federal and/or state regulations.[4]

It may be surprising to learn that trucking remains a small business industry. The American Trucking Associations reported that out of 750,000 active U.S. motor carriers, 95.8 percent operate ten or fewer trucks, while 99.7 percent operate 100 or fewer trucks.[5]

The FMCSA regularly develops campaigns to remind the general public that safety on the roadways is a shared responsibility for pedestrians, bicyclists, car drivers, motorcyclists, and truck and bus drivers alike.[6] Enforcement authorities include the USDOT, and its sub-agencies, namely, the National Highway Transportation Safety Administration (NHTSA) and the FMCSA as well as other organizations like the National Transportation Safety Board (NTSB), the U.S. Environmental Protection Agency (EPA), U.S. Customs and Border Protection (CBP), and applicable state authorities. FMCSA, in 2022 and 2023, conducted approximately 12,000 carrier investigations per year as well as reported an annual average of three million roadside truck and bus inspections performed by state or federal officers.[7]

Road safety is everyone's responsibility. However, while navigating the complexities of an accident involving a truck, this area requires an attorney to know trucking regulations. There are generally two essential sources of rules: federal trucking regulations and state trucking regulations.

With that background, the following are some tips for evaluating a trucking accident involving damage. Know the details and the operating authority. Additional specifics are more fully covered in other chapters in this book.

Know the Following

In the event of loss or damage, be it property or personal, establish the following:

- Who owns the tractor and trailer.
- Who employs the driver.
- What type of freight is on board, if any.
- Who owns the freight.

It is likely that law enforcement has been involved by the time an attorney is evaluating the accident. The report from law enforcement or information provided by law enforcement will provide a good starting point.

4. An intrastate carrier may be subject to regulation by other state agencies, like the relevant state's public utilities commission or equivalent agency.

5. Am. Trucking Ass'ns, https://www.trucking.org/economics-and-industry-data#:~:text=According%20to%20the%20U.S.%20Department,operate%20100%20or%20fewer%20trucks (last visited Jan. 15, 2025).

6. Fed. Motor Carrier Safety Admin., About the Our Roads, Our Safety® Campaign, https://www.fmcsa.dot.gov/ourroads (last visited Jan. 15, 2025).

7. U.S. Dep't of Transp., Motor Carrier Safety Progress Report (as of March 31, 2024), https://www.fmcsa.dot.gov/sites/fmcsa.dot.gov/files/2024-07/March%202024%20progress_report_20240426%20508.pdf (last visited Jan. 15, 2025).

Know the Authority

One of the issues to be evaluated following an accident is the type of operation the carrier was engaged in at the time of the incident and whether the carrier was legally authorized to conduct that type of operation. A motor carrier generally must have "authority" from a federal or state government to operate commercially utilizing our public road system. Consider this as permission from regulatory agencies to carry cargo or people commercially on public roads.

There are many types of authority depending on the type of business being run. For example, carrier operations can be interstate, intrastate, private, for-hire, and can involve commercial motor vehicles (CMVs) or non-CMVs. A single motor carrier may apply for multiple authorities. A motor carrier may have both for-hire and private authority, as well as passenger authority. A private motor carrier may obtain authority to take additional paying loads or obtain passenger authority so it can transport its employees from site to site. For example, a trucking company that hauls other people's property for a fee or a hotel that provides transport to and from the airport may require different authority credentials. The Code of Federal Regulations Title 49, or C.F.R. 49, contains regulations for all forms of surface transportation. The type of authority granted will dictate the regulations that must be followed, and also impacts the type and level of insurance required by FMCSA.[8]

Whether or not freight crosses state lines or national borders should also be part of your investigation. Intrastate carriers may not require federal operating authority for intrastate commerce but still must comply with applicable state codes and regulations. About 40 states have adopted the Federal Motor Carrier Safety Regulations (FMCSRs) for their intrastate rules, while others use only a portion.[9] Regulatory compliance depends on several factors, including the types of vehicles operated, whether passengers are transported, whether hazardous materials are transported, and whether the operation is "for-hire" (compensated). Each state has different regulations for operating authority so check with the appropriate state agency. Check the state codes and regulations.

For any motor carrier transporting passengers or hauling cargo in interstate commerce, the motor carrier must be registered with the FMCSA and is required to comply with the FMCSRs. A registration number is issued to the motor carrier from the USDOT.[10] The assigned DOT number is required to be posted on the side of the truck with the company name. This DOT number is a unique identifier that allows regulators to, among other things, collect and monitor safety data information on the carrier. Data associated with the carrier's DOT number can be collected during audits, compliance reviews, crash investigations, and inspections. This data is compiled and publicly available

8. Fed. Motor Carrier Safety Admin., https://www.fmcsa.dot.gov/registration/types-operating-authority (last visited Jan. 15, 2025).

9. Brian Straight, *Intrastate vs. Interstate: The Subtle Differences That Matter for Motor Carriers*, Freightwaves (Apr. 29, 2021), https://www.freightwaves.com/news/intrastate-vs-interstate-the-subtle-differences-that-matter-for-motor-carriers.

10. FMCSRs can be found at 49 C.F.R. pts. 350–399.

on the FMCSA website. A "company snapshot" contains information about the particular entity associated with the DOT number. A motor carrier must ensure its employees also comply with the FMCSRs.[11]

Know the Agreement(s)

A motor carrier will typically have some contractual agreement with the entity that hired it. This contract may outline the understanding and agreements between the entities for transport including their respective roles and responsibilities and may be referred to as a Motor Carrier Agreement. Some motor carriers may have extensive and detailed contracts, while other arrangements are much less formal.

Know the Operational Documents

Along the supply chain, many operational documents are key to understanding the transport's movement. One of the key documents to start with is the Bill of Lading (BOL).[12] A BOL serves as a contract entered into between two parties identifying the carrier, the shipper, the consignee, and the delivery location. These details appear on the face of the BOL along with other information typically required for the transportation of the freight—for example, details about the shipment, the rate for transport, and possessor of the title of the goods, that is, whether it is negotiable or nonnegotiable. On the backside there are usually terms and conditions of the carriage. This governing document is a good place to start your analysis as it can provide information as to when the load was picked up, where it was picked up, and who may have been responsible for the load.

The BOL can also reflect a shipper's representations to the carrier of the terms of the service, carrier's notes from its own inspection of the goods prior to taking ownership of the cargo, and the consignee's notes of its inspection upon delivery of the goods.

Let's start with a basic and standard scenario. The carrier accepts an assignment from a shipper to carry the freight from coast to coast. The carrier provides a copy of the BOL to the shipper and carrier then transports the cargo to the consignee. As the cargo changes hands—from the shipper to the carrier to the consignee—ownership interests of the cargo also transfer.

Understanding ownership interests during the shipment may be necessary in the event the actual shipment has a relation to the personal injury. It also is important when evaluating a cargo claim, as discussed in the next section.

---

11. *See, e.g.*, 49 C.F.R. §§ 390.3(e), 392.1.
12. *See, e.g.*, *id.* § 373.101.3(e).

Cargo Claims

If cargo is damaged during the course of the interstate movement (shipments that move between two states or between a state and foreign country), federal law supersedes state laws under the Carmack Amendment.[13] The Carmack Amendment establishes a uniform national system of liability in interstate cargo claims affecting either the carrier or the shipper. Generally, the Carmack Amendment provides that the carrier is responsible for any damage to goods that it has transported, and no proof of negligence is necessary. Be mindful of the limited period for filing claims. The Carmack Amendment provides nine months from the date of loss. In response to a claim, the carrier can defend with one of five exceptions: act of God, public enemy, an act or default by the shipper, public authority, or inherent vice or nature of the goods shipped. Again, the Carmack Amendment is a federal law that applies to interstate shipments of cargo.[14] For intrastate shipments (within a state) that result in a cargo claim, state law causes of action like fraud, negligence, or breach of contract are remedies to consider.

For a trucking accident involving damage to property, state law causes of action are all remedies to consider. Liability scenarios may be developed by identifying the entities involved and the details about the cause of the damage and who is responsible. Other avenues of recovery and defenses are discussed in other chapters in this book.

Know the Entities along the Supply Chain

Before starting operations, any entity subject to FMCSA regulations needs to register with the FMCSR using the Unified Registration System (URS). The applicant will describe its operations to obtain the correct registration including all of the necessary applicable operating authorities. The FMCSA then evaluates the application.

The entity's operations are evaluated by the FMCSA before issuing authority. Motor carriers, freight forwarders, shippers, brokers, and third-party logistics providers (3PL) alike also may apply for operating authority, since they manage different aspects of freight as it moves along the supply chain.

Generally speaking, a broker arranges the transport but is not involved in the physical transport of the cargo,[15] and a freight forwarder organizes shipments, which can include assembling and consolidating shipments, and provides for break-bulk and distribution of shipments. Unlike brokers, freight forwarders may assume responsibility for the transportation and may transport the freight itself. Therefore, they may be involved directly or indirectly with the cargo.[16]

13. 49 U.S.C. § 14706.

14. The chapter in this book on intermodal transportation contains additional information about the Carmack Amendment and cargo loss claims in other transportation contexts.

15. Evaluate the entities in the supply chain and review applicable case law where an entity exercises significant control over the motor carrier an agency relationship may exist.

16. 49 U.S.C. §§ 13102, 13901–13904.

The operations will also dictate the level of required insurance. The FMCSRs prescribe the minimum levels of financial responsibility required to be maintained by motor carriers of property operating motor vehicles in interstate, foreign, or intrastate commerce.[17] "The purpose of these regulations is to create additional incentives to motor carriers to maintain and operate their vehicles in a safe manner and to assure that motor carriers maintain an appropriate level of financial responsibility for motor vehicles operated on public highways."[18]

Know the Lingo

To understand the trucking industry well, you need to know some of the lingo that is unique to the industry. It will help you communicate well with clients and witnesses if you can speak their language. Most of the key definitions that you will need to litigate trucking cases can be found in various parts of United States Code Title 49 and Code of Federal Regulations Title 49. But there are some that are not contained in these sections and you still need to know them.

Here are some common industry terms and acronyms:

- **For-Hire Motor Carrier.** Motor carriers that transport people or products owned by another entity from one place to another for compensation.
- **Hours of Service (HOS).** "Hours of service" refers to the maximum amount of time drivers are permitted to be on duty, including driving time, and specifies the number and length of rest periods to help ensure that drivers stay awake and alert. In general, all carriers and drivers operating commercial motor vehicles (CMVs) must comply with HOS regulations found in 49 C.F.R. part 395.
- **Intermodal.** Moving goods in shipping containers through different modes of transport—from an aircraft or a ship to a truck to a rail car. The term intermodal shipping is used to refer to moving freight by two or more forms or modes of transport.
- **Intrastate motor carrier.** A company that hauls freight solely within a single state, thus is subject to individual state laws.
- **Interstate motor carrier.** A company that crosses state lines during the course of business, thus is subject to the FMCSRs.
- **Over the Road (OTR).** Also known has long-haul trucking and typically are drivers traveling from one coast to the other coast.
- **Owner-Operator (O/O).** An individual who owns his or her own commercial vehicle or small fleet, typically truck tractors. If this individual has his or her own operating authority, he or she may haul loads for hire.

---

17. 49 C.F.R. § 387.1. Please refer to the chapter in this book on the financial responsibility and insurance requirements on motor carriers for more information.

18. 49 C.F.R. § 387.1.

- **Private motor carrier.** A company that transports freight that it manufactures or owns, or the commodities used to make the product.

Conclusion

The pre-litigation steps discussed in this chapter serve for a high-level overview of a personal injury or cargo loss involving a commercial carrier. It is a high-level list but certainly not a fully exhaustive list. Trucking is a complex universe of regulatory compliance and when there is an accident, a detailed review of facts requires a level of expertise in this industry. An attorney should know and understand the equipment, the operations, and the industry, as each case presents a unique set of circumstances. A sophisticated evaluation early on will provide you with guidance for your client, on either side of the case, and invaluable insight to help manage the outcome of the litigation.

CHAPTER 2
Motor Carrier and the Driver

Ashley N Baker, Esq., LL.M.

The relationship between a motor carrier and its driver may seem like an ordinary employer–employee relationship, but in trucking that is not that case. The relationship may be employer–employee, but it may be a situation where the driver and the equipment are contracted by the carrier in an owner–operator scenario. When the driver is an owner–operator the truck is owned or leased by the driver, who then operates under the operating authority of the motor carrier. The motor carrier is simply the entity that has authority from the U.S. Department of Transportation (USDOT) to operate in the transport of property or person in interstate commerce. The requirements of the carrier in relation to its oversight of the operations of the owner–operator are the same as if the driver were an employee. This chapter will focus on the motor carrier's selection of drivers, the driver qualification file, training, dispatching, audits, and carrier duties.

Selection

Regardless of the type of driver the carrier is acquiring, the process of selecting qualified drivers is the same. The Federal Motor Carrier Safety Regulations (FMCSRs) require that motor carriers ensure that their drivers meet a set of basic qualifications.[1] These include being at least 21 years old, possessing the ability to read and speak English sufficiently to converse with the general public and understand highway traffic signs, having the skill and experience to operate a commercial vehicle safely, and holding a valid commercial driver's license (CDL). Additionally, it is the motor carrier's responsibility to make sure drivers are physically qualified to operate a commercial motor vehicle. This includes making sure their drivers have the required medical certifications.[2]

The Federal Motor Carrier Safety Administration (FMCSA) also requires that the carrier conduct a background investigation process.[3] Within 30 days

1. 49 C.F.R. § 391.11.
2. *Id.* § 391.41–391.49.
3. *Id.* § 391.23.

of hiring a driver, motor carriers must delve into the individual's employment history, reaching out to all employers from the preceding three years. They must also obtain a comprehensive motor vehicle record, reviewing the driver's history on the road for the same period. This inquiry also includes a determination of whether the driver was subject to the Substance Abuse Professional (SAP) program following a failed test for alcohol or drugs. This background check serves a dual purpose: it verifies the information provided by the driver and uncovers any red flags that might indicate a risk to safety.

Driver Qualification File

Once a driver is selected, the motor carrier's obligations shift to maintaining a record of the driver's qualifications and performance. The driver qualification file is a crucial document that must contain a variety of items. These include drivers' application for employment, a copy of their CDL, their road test certificate (or an acceptable equivalent), annual reviews of their driving record, a list of violations of motor vehicle laws, and their medical examiner's certificate.[4]

Training

Some carriers double as both trucking companies and training programs. These carriers are subject to the entry level driving training (ELDT) requirements for training providers. Motor carriers are not under any additional general obligation to provide their drivers with training, but it is best practice to do so. Ongoing training programs that cover topics such as defensive driving techniques, updates to the Hours of Service (HOS) regulations, proper cargo securement procedures, and vehicle inspection and maintenance protocols are usually a part of the orientation process conducted at the time of onboarding a new driver. This training includes an assessment of the driver's ability to operate the carrier's equipment. Carriers typically have an employee handbook that outlines company policy on safety and driver expectations. Carriers can impose more restrictive policies on its drivers than are required by the FMCSA, but it cannot apply less restrictive policies that would allow noncompliance with the FMCSA or state regulations.

Dispatching

Truck dispatching is traditionally performed in-house where the motor carrier is the employer of the dispatcher and the driver. However, in smaller trucking companies that have limited ability to hire employees or operations with only a single driver, dispatching may be outsourced to a third-party company. In this nuanced relationship, brought on by the needs of the industry, these dispatching companies handle the communications between the broker or shipper

4. *Id.* § 391.51.

and the driver. These third-party companies could be located anywhere around the world. This third-party dispatcher, similar to an owner–operator would be operating under the authority of the motor carrier. Prior to 2022, the FMCSA had no guidance or regulations regarding dispatchers. In 2022, the FMCSA published interim guidance, which it did finalize in 2023, distinguishing between a third-party dispatcher and a broker. Brokers are required to have authority with the FMCSA, whereas dispatchers are not. The guidance released by the FMCSA denotes which activities would be considered brokering and which would be considered dispatching and draws a line between the two practices.

Whether the dispatcher is in-house or a third party, the role of the dispatcher is essentially the same. The dispatcher works on behalf of the motor carrier to acquire work for the carrier from brokers or shippers. Dispatchers do not take possession of such work, but communicate to the carrier the work, and allow them to either accept or decline it. The dispatcher also communicates to the driver the pertinent information for the load so that it can be picked up and delivered in a timely fashion.

Responsibilities

The relationship between carrier and driver requires ongoing monitoring and assessment. For example, the FMCSA mandates annual reviews of each driver's record.[5] Additionally, carriers must monitor their drivers for compliance with alcohol and controlled substances and Hours of Service regulations.[6] The driver must submit to the employing motor carrier each record of the driver's duty status within 13 days following the completion of each record.[7] This allows the carrier unfettered access to the driving record. It is important to note that the carrier cannot alter the driving record, as the record can only be made by the driver.[8] In addition to keeping records of their drivers' HOS, carriers are responsible for the equipment operated under its authority. This includes making the necessary repairs to vehicles placed out of service and to remedy defects the driver reports to the carrier via their inspection report.

5. *Id.* § 391.25.
6. *Id.* pts. 382, 395.
7. *Id.* § 395.15(h)(1).
8. *Id.* § 395.15(h)(3).

CHAPTER 3

Driver Licensing and Responsibilities

Ashley N. Baker, Esq., LL.M.

Introduction

The Motor Vehicle Safety Act of 1986 mandates that all drivers of commercial vehicles obtain a state commercial driver's license (CDL) as a prerequisite to operate commercial motor vehicles (CMVs). The purpose of this regulation was to enhance safety in the trucking industry.[1] The requirement forced drivers to learn not only how to operate the desired CMV but also to learn how to inspect and spot potential mechanical issues. A driver could do this by attending a training program, which could be as long as 16 weeks or as short as two weeks. Alternatively, a driver could choose to forego formal training altogether and learn under the guidance of another licensed driver.

However, in 2022, the U.S. Department of Transportation (DOT) implemented the Entry Level Driver Training (ELDT) program, which requires drivers to attend a training program that adheres to specific training guidelines and for training programs to certify that their curriculum complies with the DOT guidelines. This chapter will address the licensing requirements of commercial drivers, the ELDT program, and driver responsibilities.

Licensing

The type of license a commercial driver is required to have largely depends on the type of vehicle he or she intends to operate. There are three types of CDL: Class A, Class B, and Class C. The Class A CDL is required to operate any combination vehicle with a gross weight rating of 26,001 pounds or more, where the vehicle(s) being towed is/are in excess of 10,000 pounds. A combination vehicle

1. Fed. Motor Carrier Safety Admin., Motor Carriers (2022), https://www.fmcsa.dot.gov/registration/commercial-drivers-license/motor-carriers#:~:text=To%20improve%20CMV%20safety%2C%20in,unsafe%20drivers%20from%20the%20roads; 49 C.F.R. § 383.23(a)(1).

is one that has a powered unit, like a tractor, and a towed unit, like a trailer. The operator of a traditional tractor-trailer would be required to have a Class A CDL.[2]

The Class B CDL is required to operate any single vehicle rated in excess of 26,001 pounds. Typically, a Class B CDL is required to operate a bus or a large box truck. The Class C CDL is required to operate vehicles under 26,001 pounds. The operator would be able to tow vehicles under 10,000 pounds and carry up to 16 passengers, including the driver.[3]

It is important to understand that simply because a driver possesses a CDL in a specific class does not mean that the driver can operate any vehicle that falls into that class without appropriate endorsements for that type of vehicle. For example, even if a driver has a Class A CDL, that driver would not be able to haul over 1,000 pounds of hazardous material or pull a tanker trailer unless the driver has the applicable endorsements. There are six endorsements available for commercial driver's licenses:

- T: Double/Triple Trailers (Knowledge test only)
- P: Passenger (Knowledge and Skills Tests) (ELDT)
- N: Tanker vehicle (Knowledge test only)
- H: Hazardous materials (Knowledge test only) (ELDT)
- X: Combination of tank vehicle and hazardous materials endorsements (Knowledge test only) (ELDT)
- S: School Bus (Knowledge and Skills Tests) (ELDT)

Training

The ELDT established minimum training standards for entry-level drivers, and some established drivers that are seeking updates to their CDL. The ELDT requirements apply to first-time CDL applicants, applicants upgrading their CDL to a different class, and those seeking specific endorsements. For example, a driver who held a Class B CDL prior to the implementation of ELDT would now need to take additional training to acquire a Class A CDL. Likewise, a CDL driver trying to acquire a hazmat, passenger, or school bus endorsement would be required to complete an approved training course prior to applying for the endorsement.

The ELDT also established specific curriculum requirements for applicants. This curriculum is divided into theory and behind-the-wheel training. The theory portion includes topics like pre- and post-trip inspections, hours of service, fatigue awareness, hazard perception, speed management, and distracted driving. Drivers are required to be tested on each subject in the required curricula and obtain a passing grade of 80 percent before moving forward to behind-the-wheel training.[4]

---

2. 49 C.F.R. § 383.91 (2021).
3. *Id.* § 383.91.
4. U.S. Dep't of Transp., ELDT: Entry Level Driver Training Minimum Federal Curricula Requirements, (2021), https://tpr.fmcsa.dot.gov/content/Resources/ELDT-Curriculum-Summary.pdf.

In addition to requirements for CDL applicants, there are also requirements for CDL training programs. These CDL training programs, which include trucking companies, colleges, and independent training schools, are required to register and self-certify via the Training Provider Registry (TPR) that their curriculum complies with the federal requirements and any state requirements in which they operate, if applicable. Additionally, they are subject to audit by the Federal Motor Carrier Safety Administration (FMCSA). Upon successful completion of the training program, the training provider must upload a certificate of completion to the TPR for each driver that completes the program. This certification will be required for the applicant to apply to be tested for licensing in his or her respective state.

Qualifications

Before applying for any type of CDL the prospective driver must obtain a medical certification that he or she is fit to operate a commercial motor vehicle over 10,000 pounds.[5] In 2014, the FMCSA established a self-certification requirement for operators requiring all CDL holders to declare to their state licensing agency that they only operate or expect to operate commercially in one of four possible categories with their CDL. These for categories are:

- **Interstate non-excepted.** Driver must meet the federal DOT medical card requirements.
- **Interstate excepted.** Driver does not have to meet the federal DOT medical card requirements.
- **Intrastate non-excepted.** Driver must meet the medical requirements for his or her state.
- **Intrastate excepted.** Driver does not have to meet the medical requirements for his or her state.[6]

The excepted categories do require medical certification but are limited to operating a commercial vehicle in specific situations. For example, a driver in the interstate excepted category would need to be engaged in transporting school children and/or staff between home and school, transporting migrant workers, government employment operations, transporting corpses or sick and injured persons, responding to pipeline leaks or ruptures, responding to fire emergencies, and other limited and rare situations to qualify.[7]

---

5. Fed. Motor Carrier Safety Admin., Medical (2023), https://www.fmcsa.dot.gov/registration/commercial-drivers-license/medical.

6. *Id.*

7. Fed. Motor Carrier Safety Admin., How Do I Determine Which of the 4 Categories of Commercial Motor Vehicle (CMV) Operation I Should Self-certify to with My State Driver Licensing Agency (SDLA)? (2023), https://www.fmcsa.dot.gov/faq/how-do-i-determine-which-4-categories-commercial-motor-vehicle-cmv-operation-i-should-self.

Drivers can apply for limited waivers of the medical certification requirements. Only the FMCSA can grant a waiver of the medical certification requirement for drivers in interstate commerce.[8]

Examination

The FMCSA requires states to administer certain tests for the licensing of CMV operators.[9] The CDL exam itself consists of three parts: a general knowledge test, a vehicle inspection, and a road test that includes a backing test.[10] The general knowledge test is different depending on the type of CDL being acquired and the type of endorsements, if any, that are being applied for. The general knowledge test includes a basic driver's license test where the applicant is not a licensed driver. In most places, this test is administered in a testing center via computer. Once the applicant scores satisfactorily on the written test, he or she is eligible for a CLP, which is a type of CDL learner's permit. This allows the applicant to drive a commercial motor vehicle in the class for which he or she applied with a licensed operator in the vehicle overseeing the driving.

The inspection, backing, and road test are the second portion of the CDL exam. Similar to how a driver would begin his or her workday, the CDL exam requires that the road test begin with a vehicle inspection. For a Class A CDL, this would require a full inspection of the tractor and trailer, identifying parts of the vehicle and examining them to see whether they are properly mounted and secured; whether they are cracked, bent, or broken; or whether there are any cuts or frays to hoses and cords. This test is conducted to determine whether the applicant has enough knowledge of how the truck and trailer operate to become a licensed driver. This portion of the test also includes a brake test performed in the cab of the truck by the applicant. The applicant must pass this test to move on to the backing test.

The backing test consists of a series of maneuvers such as straight-line backing, parallel parking, alley docking, and offset backing. Each maneuver mimics common ways drivers would "back up" in real life situations at loading docks, truck stops, and other parking facilities. It is worthy to note that the alley docking maneuver is done where the driver is backing into a space he or she can see from the driver's side (sight side). This is because drivers should avoid backing from their blind side (passenger side), where possible, because of the limited sight the driver has on the side of the vehicle once the 45-degree angle is formed with the tractor and trailer. The examiner may also check to see whether the driver uses the Get Out And Look (GOAL) method while backing. This method is self-explanatory and should be used in all backing situations to check the positioning of the truck and neighboring vehicles and objects when backing. This method should also be used to determine whether conditions have

---

8. Fed. Motor Carrier Safety Admin., Driver Exemptions (2023), https://www.fmcsa.dot.gov/medical/driver-medical-requirements/driver-exemption-programs.

9. 49 C.F.R. § 383.1(b)(7).

10. *Id.* § 383.1(b)(6).

changed since the driver was last able to see both sides of the truck during an angled backing maneuver.

The next test is a road test, which is similar to that of a road test taken by a regular driver's license applicant, except a few of the requirements are different. For example, a regular driver's license applicant may be required to perform a test where the car needs to reach a specific speed and is then stopped suddenly by the driver. This is not a test a CDL applicant would undergo. Another example is where a CDL applicant is seeking a passenger or school bus endorsement; the applicant may be required to stop at railroad tracks and open his or her door to listen before crossing. This portion of the exam would look different for a Class A CDL applicant, where they would simply listen and look without stopping, similar to a driver's license applicant. The test examines the driver's ability to control the vehicle, make turns at appropriate speeds, accelerate, and decelerate.

Responsibilities

Commercial drivers have specific responsibilities that include a self-assessment of their fitness to operate a CMV, safely operating the CMV, recordkeeping, and honesty.[11] Under the Federal Motor Carrier Safety Regulations (FMCSRs), a driver must be fit to operate a CMV before beginning to drive. This includes ensuring that they are properly licensed to operate the CMV that they plan to drive and that they have a medical certification, if applicable. The driver has an obligation to ensure they hold only one CDL, in one state.[12] They also have a duty to provide the medical provider conducting the medical exam with accurate information as to their medical history. The driver also must provide his or her employer with accurate information as to driving and employment history; this will be discussed further is subsequent chapters.[13]

Their obligation to be honest is not the same general obligation as that of an attorney or similar professions, but there are certain documents such as medical certification forms that require drivers to attest that the information they provide is accurate. The driver should operate the CMV safely and adhere to safety practices. These practices will be discussed in subsequent chapters.

The driver has an obligation under the FMCSRs to make and retain certain records in the operation of the CMV. The first is a driver logbook for recording the driver's hours of service (HOS). The HOS will be discussed more in-depth in a subsequent chapter. The driver is required to retain a copy of his or her driver log for the current day and the prior seven days. The HOS regulations have multiple restrictions on the time a driver is allowed to operate a CMV. One of those mandates is that a driver must stop driving after reaching 60 hours in a seven-day period or 70 hours in an eight-day period, depending on the

11. *Id.* § 383.1(b).
12. *Id.* § 383.1(b)(1).
13. *Id.* §§ 383.1(b)(3), 383.1(b)(2).

operations of the motor carrier.[14] This is why the FMCSA requires drivers to have driver logs for the previous seven days as well as the current day. The driver has an obligation to certify the correctness of the driver log.[15] Drivers also have an obligation to report to the motor carrier citations received while operating the CMV and any accidents that occur, regardless of fault. Drivers must conduct daily inspections of their equipment and report any defects to the motor carrier.

14. Most trucking carriers fall under the 70-hour rule, where they operate CMVs every day. *Id.* § 395.3(b).

15. 49 C.F.R. § 395.8(f)(7).

CHAPTER 4

Drug and Alcohol Testing and Impairment

D.J. Young, III, Esq.

Introduction

It is well known that many motor vehicle crashes are the result of impaired driving due to alcohol or drug intoxication. There are extensive regulations binding on motor carriers and drivers, and the purpose of these regulations is "to help prevent accidents and injuries resulting from the misuse of alcohol or use of controlled substances by drivers of commercial motor vehicles."[1] This chapter serves as a survey of these legal requirements so that truck crash attorneys can understand what substances are regulated, when testing is required, what records to request in discovery, and how these might relate to the question of whether the driver was impaired.

Legal Overview

A driver shall not drive (or perform any other "safety-sensitive functions") while under the influence of controlled substances or alcohol, and the driver's employer is prohibited from allowing or requiring the driver to drive (or perform any other safety-sensitive functions) if the employer knows that the driver is under the influence of controlled substances or alcohol or has otherwise violated the drug and alcohol regulations.[2] In furtherance of these legal principles, the Federal Motor Carrier Safety Regulations mandate extensive drug and alcohol testing requirements. All drivers and employers of drivers of commercial motor vehicles are bound to comply with these testing regulations, subject

1. 49 C.F.R. § 382.101.

2. *Id.* § 382.501. "Safety-sensitive functions" includes driving, waiting to be dispatched to drive, inspecting motor vehicles, serving motor vehicles, sitting at the controls of a motor vehicle, loading, unloading, supervising loading or unloading, repairing a disabled vehicle, and attending a disabled vehicle. *Id.* § 382.107.

to limited exceptions.[3] All testing must be conducted in accordance with the requirements of 49 C.F.R. Part 40,[4] which addresses every detail from regulations over urine collection, regulations of testing laboratories, drug concentration "cutoff concentrations," the requirements for "medical review officers" to review tests, failure of the driver to provide a sufficient quantity of urine, driver refusals to test,[5] other testing problems, and countless other details to ensure the integrity of the testing system. Employers of drivers must train the people who supervise the drivers about alcohol misuse and drug use.[6] Employers are required to explain the drug and alcohol testing requirements to their drivers and provide them a policy on such testing.[7] The attorney should obtain these policies during discovery when drug or alcohol use is a suspected cause of the accident.

Rules Specific to Alcohol

Drivers shall not report for duty nor remain on duty in the performance of safety-sensitive functions (including driving) "while having an alcohol concentration of 0.04 or greater," and employers shall prohibit them from driving when the employer has knowledge of a violation.[8] Use of any amount of alcohol within four hours of performing any safety-sensitive function is prohibited.[9] After a motor vehicle accident, alcohol use is prohibited for the next eight hours, or until after a post-accident alcohol test, whichever comes first.[10]

Rules Specific to Controlled Substances

Drivers shall not report for duty nor remain on duty in the performance of safety-sensitive functions (including driving) "when the driver uses any drug or substance" listed in 21 C.F.R. 1308.11 Schedule 1.[11] Schedule 1 lists numerous opiates, including their "isomers, esters, ethers, salts, and salts of isomers, esters and ethers"; opium derivatives, including their "salts, isomers, and salts of isomers"; hallucinogenic substances, including their "salts, isomers, and salts of isomers"; depressants, including "any material, compound, mixture, or preparation which contains" any of the listed depressants; stimulants including "any material, compound, mixture, or preparation which contains any quantity" of the listed stimulants; and cannabimimetic agents, including "their salts, isomers, and salts of isomers." Hundreds of substances are listed on Schedule 1, including familiar names like fentanyl, marihuana, peyote, mescaline, morphine, and

3. *Id.* §§ 40.11, 382.103(A).
4. *Id.* § 382.105.
5. Refusals are addressed both in 49 C.F.R. pt. 40 and in 49 C.F.R. § 382.211.
6. 49 C.F.R. § 382.603.
7. *Id.* § 382.601.
8. *Id.* §§ 382.201, 382.205.
9. *Id.* § 382.207.
10. *Id.* § 382.209.
11. *Id.* § 382.213(a).

heroin. And, unless medical approval has been obtained,[12] a similar rule applies to Schedule 2 substances such as codeine, amphetamine, and methamphetamine; Schedule 3 substances such as ketamine, lysergic acid, anabolic steroids, and various narcotic drugs; Schedule 4 narcotics, depressants, and stimulants; and Schedule 5 narcotics, depressants, and stimulants.[13] The use of any drug on Schedules 2 through 5 on duty in the performance of safety-sensitive functions (like driving) is prohibited "except when the use is pursuant to the instructions of a licensed medical practitioner . . . familiar with the driver's medical history and has advised the driver that the substance will not adversely affect the driver's ability to safely operate a commercial motor vehicle."[14] Employers shall not allow drivers in violation of these provisions to drive.[15] Employers are permitted to require drivers to report therapeutic drug use.[16] A driver shall not report for duty for safety-sensitive functions if the driver has tested positive for controlled substances, and the employer shall not permit the performance of such work if the employer has knowledge of the positive test results.[17]

Pre-employment Testing

Subject to limited exceptions, prior to the first time performing a safety-sensitive function, like driving, the employer must attempt to obtain drug and alcohol test information from prior employers of the driver during the previous three years,[18] the employer must require the driver to take a pre-employment controlled substance test, and the employer shall not allow that driver to drive until the employer has received legally satisfactory test results.[19] It is mandatory to test for these classes of substances: marijuana metabolites, cocaine metabolites, amphetamines, opioids, and phencyclidine (PCP).[20] It is permissible for employers to test for alcohol, but that is not mandatory.[21] Employers have the authority to test for other controlled substances.[22]

---

12. *Id.* § 382.213(b).
13. *Id.* § 382.213(b); 21 C.F.R. §§ 1308.11–1308.15.
14. 49 C.F.R. § 382.213(b).
15. *Id.* § 382.213(c).
16. *Id.* § 382.213(d).
17. *Id.* § 382.215.
18. *Id.* §§ 40.25(b), 382.413(a). There is now a "Drug and Alcohol Clearinghouse" that employers must, as of January 6, 2023, use for purposes of compliance. *Id.* §§ 382.413(b), 382.701(a). The medical review officers that review the drug test results pursuant to the protocols in 49 C.F.R. pt. 40 must report positive tests and refusals to the Drug and Alcohol Clearinghouse. *Id.* § 382.705. Similarly, employers must also report. *Id.* Drivers have the right to review the information in the Drug and Alcohol Clearinghouse (49 C.F.R. § 382.709) and, consequently, attorneys should require the driver to do so and report the results for purposes of civil discovery.
19. *Id.* § 382.301.
20. *Id.* §§ 40.82 (list of drugs), 382.301 (pre-employment test), and 382.107 (definition of "controlled substance"). The cutoff concentrations for urine tests are found in § 40.85, and for oral fluid tests, the cutoff concentrations are in § 40.91.
21. *Id.* § 382.301(d).
22. *Id.* § 382.111.

If information gathered from prior employers indicates that the driver has violated drug and/or alcohol regulations, then the current employer must not allow the driver to drive or perform other safety-sensitive functions until the driver complies with all "return-to-duty" regulations, which include substance abuse professional treatment.[23] An employer is not required to provide a driver an opportunity to receive substance abuse professional treatment, but if an employer does do so, the employer must verify satisfactory completion of the treatment requirements.[24]

Post-Accident Testing

If the commercial driver is in a crash involving the loss of human life, then "as soon as practicable," the employer shall cause the driver to be tested for alcohol and controlled substances.[25] In a circumstance in which the crash involves bodily injury to any person requiring treatment away from the scene of the crash or the crash involves disabling damage to one or more vehicles requiring such vehicle to be towed away, if within eight hours of such a crash the driver is cited for a moving traffic violation arising out of the crash, then the employer shall cause the driver to be tested for alcohol as soon as practicable.[26] If, within 32 hours of such a crash, the driver is cited for a moving traffic violation arising out of the crash, then the employer shall cause the driver to be tested for controlled substances as soon as practicable.[27] If any required alcohol test is not taken within two hours following the accident, the employer must create a record of why the alcohol test was not taken, and if any controlled test is not administered within 32 hours, the employer must create a record of why it was not taken.[28] To facilitate post-accident testing, the driver must remain readily available for such a test,[29] and if the driver fails to do so, the driver will be deemed to have refused to test, in which case the driver's employer shall not permit the driver to drive or perform other safety-sensitive functions.[30] If law enforcement requires and administers a test, then that test satisfies the mandatory post-accident testing requirements.[31]

---

23. *Id.* § 40.25(e). *Id.* pt. 40, subpt O, contains information about substance abuse professionals and return-to-duty procedures.
24. 49 C.F.R. § 40.289.
25. *Id.* § 382.303(a)(1), (b)(1). For the list of drugs that must be tested for, *see id.* §§ 40.82 and 382.107 (definition of "controlled substances").
26. *Id.* § 382.303(a)(2).
27. *Id.* § 382.303(b)(2).
28. *Id.* § 382.303(d).
29. *Id.* § 382.303(e).
30. *Id.* § 382.211. When a test is lawfully required or permitted, and the driver refuses, then the employer shall not permit the employee to drive. This applies to pre-employment tests, post-accident test, random tests, and reasonable suspicion tests.
31. *Id.* § 382.303(g).

Random Testing

All employers of CDL-licensed drivers must implement random alcohol testing procedures that test at least 10 percent of their drivers annually, and they must implement random controlled substance testing procedures that test at least 50 percent of their drivers annually.[32] Random tests shall be unannounced and shall be spread out throughout the year, and, when an employee is chosen for random testing, the employer shall cause the employee to proceed immediately to the test collection site.[33] If a driver refuses to test, then the employer shall not permit the driver to drive or perform other safety-sensitive functions.[34] Similarly, if the driver fails the test, the employer shall prohibit further driving or performance of other safety-sensitive functions.[35]

Reasonable Suspicion Testing

If the employer has reasonable suspicion to believe that the driver has violated any of the alcohol or controlled substance regulations, the employer "shall require" the driver to submit to a test.[36] Reasonable suspicion "must be based on specific, contemporaneous, articulable observations concerning the appearance, behavior, speech or body odors of the driver" and, with respect to controlled substances, the "observations may include indications of the chronic and withdrawal effects of controlled substances."[37] The observations for purposes of developing and proving reasonable suspicion must be made by a supervisor or other official who is trained on alcohol misuse and controlled substance use.[38] With respect to alcohol reasonable suspicion testing, the observation must have been made just before, during, or immediately after the scheduled time for work, and the employer shall not permit the driver to drive until the driver's alcohol concentration is less than 0.02 or, alternatively, until 24 hours after the test have elapsed.[39] The employer shall maintain written records describing the observations that gave rise to the reasonable suspicion test.

Return to Duty

If a driver has a verified positive drug test, or a positive alcohol concentration test of 0.04 or greater, adulterates a test, substitutes a specimen, or otherwise refuses to test when required to do so, that "constitutes a DOT drug and alcohol

32. *Id.* § 382.304. For the list of drugs that must be tested for, *see id.* §§ 40.82 and 382.107 (definition of "controlled substances").
33. *Id.* § 382.305(k).
34. *Id.* § 382.211.
35. *Id.* §§ 382.201, 382.213.
36. *Id.* § 382.307. For the list of drugs that must be tested for, *see id.* §§ 40.82 and 382.107 (definition of "controlled substances").
37. *Id.* § 382.307.
38. *Id.* § 382.307(c).
39. *Id.* § 382.307(d), (e). *See also id.* § 382.505.

regulation violation."[40] A driver who has committed any DOT drug and alcohol use regulation is prohibited from driving or performing other safety-sensitive functions until having received substance abuse professional evaluation, referral, and education and/or treatment.[41] As noted earlier, once a driver has committed a DOT drug and alcohol regulation violation, the driver's employer is prohibited from allowing the driver to drive, and, furthermore, is not required to allow that driver to return to any safety-sensitive function, including driving.[42]

Records Retention and Discovery

Drug and alcohol testing records must be retained for the time periods established by law.[43] Generally, employers of drivers must retain records of positive alcohol tests, positive drug tests, and refusals for five years.[44] They are discoverable in personal injury and wrongful death litigation.[45] According to an example in the discovery regulation, "in personal injury litigation following a truck or bus collision, the court could determine that a post-accident drug test result of an employee is relevant to determining whether the driver or the driver's employer was negligent."[46]

Proving Impairment

It is important to remember that many more controlled substances are listed as prohibited than are tested in the various tests just identified. The fact that some substances are not tested does not change the illegality of their usage without compliance with applicable doctor's prescriptions. Moreover, the legality of the usage of a substance does not negate negligence when the substance, even if lawfully used, impairs the driver under the circumstances of the case.

Drug or alcohol use can be proven by a driver's admission. A driver's medical records may reveal the usage of drugs or alcohol. Post-crash tests may prove the usage of drugs or alcohol. An expert on the validity of the drug or alcohol test, itself, may be necessary. In the absence of a post-crash test, the driver's medical records or other testing records might shed light on the driver's usage history. Sometimes the only evidence of substance usage is evidence of drugs (paraphernalia or pills) found in the post-crash search of the vehicles. Such unlabeled substances will have to be sent to a lab for testing and identification. Attorneys for each side of the case should work together to develop mutually

---

40. *Id.* §§ 382.309, 383.311, 40.285(b).
41. *Id.* §§ 40.285(a), 382.501, 382.503, 382.701(d).
42. *Id.* § 40.289.
43. *Id.* § 382.401.
44. *Id.*
45. *Id.* § 40.323(a)(2).
46. *Id.*

satisfactory protocols for lab-identification of the unknown substances or pills if law enforcement has not done so.

It is not enough to prove that the driver was under the influence of a potentially intoxicating substance. Without evidence of impairment (or intoxication), the driver's attorney likely will file a motion in limine to avoid unfair or undue prejudice or confusion of the issues. If not barred by an order in limine the attorney still must prove that it is more likely than not that the driver was impaired by the intoxicating substance at the time of the crash.[47] Some jurisdictions may allow eyewitnesses to testify about a person's level of impairment.[48] This approach utilizes the lay opinion evidence rules and circumstantial evidence. Sometimes, though, that approach is insufficient, especially when impairment is not obvious to the lay witness. Depending on the severity of the impairment, the truck crash attorney may need to retain an expert witness with expertise in toxicology, pharmacology, impairment, and/or the diagnosis and treatment of addictive substances to demonstrate impairment.[49]

---

47. For an introduction to toxicology, *see* Bernard D. Goldstein & Mary Sue Henifin, *Reference Guide on Toxicology, in* Federal Judicial Center's Reference Manual on Scientific Evidence 633 (3d ed. 2011).

48. *See, e.g.*, City of Seattle v. Levesque, 12 Wn. App. 2d 687, 460 P.3d 205 (Wash. App. 2020).

49. *See, e.g.*, Smith v. Stone, 2013 IL App (5th) 110541-U, 2013 Ill. App. Unpub. LEXIS 588, 2013 WL 1197781 (Ill. App. 2013) for an example of an appellate court's analysis of such issues. For another example of a court fully explaining the issue, *see* Coughlin v. Massaquoi, 542 Pa. 212, 220–30, 170 A.3d 399 (Pa. 2017) (explaining that evidence of consumption of alcohol can be greatly prejudicial unless there is evidence that the person was intoxicated).

CHAPTER 5
Inspections and Maintenance

Amy Papuga, Esq.

The Role of Inspections in Truck Crash Litigation

Proper inspections and maintenance of commercial motor vehicles keep commercial drivers and other road users safe. The Federal Motor Carrier Safety Regulations (FMCSRs) provide guidance for the minimum standards to keep commercial motor vehicles (CMVs) in safe operating condition.[1] Many, but not all, states have codified the minimum standards of the FMCSRs. Thus, if the Federal Motor Carrier Safety Administration (FMCSA) lacks jurisdiction over the truck, check state law. The same standard may be in effect.

While the FMCSRs arguably do not specifically require motor carriers (including owner operators) to establish a maintenance program, they do require motor carriers to regularly and systematically inspect and conduct maintenance of the CMV.[2] A CMV is not to be operated if it is in a condition that is likely to cause an accident or breakdown of the vehicle.[3] Proper inspection and maintenance procedures ensure that CMVs are in safe operating condition so not to pose an increased risk or danger to the CMV driver and other road users.

Inspection reports and maintenance records assist in establishing or rejecting a claim for negligent maintenance. Review the information in the inspection reports and maintenance records to determine if there is a pattern and practice of maintenance violations or problems or an overall lack of a preventive

1. *See* 49 C.F.R. §§ 396.3(a), 396.7.

2. *See id.* § 392.7; *id.* § 393, generally; and *id.* § 396.3(a), which provides that a motor carrier and intermodal equipment provider *must* systematically inspect, repair, and maintain, or cause to be systematically inspected, repaired, and maintained, all motor vehicles and intermodal equipment subject to its control (2008). This includes parts and accessories *shall be in safe and proper operating condition at all times* (*id.* at § 396.3(a)(1) (emphasis added).

3. *Id.* § 396.7. Further, additional equipment or accessories may be used in commercial motor vehicles (CMVs), but any such equipment or accessories cannot decrease the safe operation of a CMV in interstate commerce. *Id.* § 393.3.

maintenance program.[4] Inspection reports are also regularly utilized in indicating the cause of a truck crash. This chapter provides an overview of common inspections, their roles within the trucking industry, and minimum maintenance requirements.

Roadside Inspections

Roadside inspections are a fact of life in the trucking industry. Roadside inspections serve the purpose of enforcing compliance with the FMCSRs (and applicable state laws).[5] Roadside inspections also ensure unsafe CMVs or their drivers are not on the roadway.[6] These inspections can occur at truck inspection areas, on the road at random locations (such as pulling over a truck), and at motor carriers' facilities.

Only qualified individuals are permitted to conduct roadside inspections of CMVs. On the federal level, these are individuals appointed by the FMCSA as special agents.[7] On the state level, these individuals are either certified by the FMCSA or certified through the Commercial Vehicle Safety Alliance (CVSA). At the state level, these individuals' titles vary from state to state, but they are usually associated with a state department of public safety or department of transportation of the state where the inspection occurs.[8]

There are eight levels of inspections that may occur during a roadside inspection.[9] The standards or protocols for each inspection are developed and updated by the CVSA.[10] Litigators should review and understand the inspec-

---

4. Preventive maintenance (PM) encompasses periodic, scheduled, or systematic maintenance, such as oil changes, tire rotation, lubrication, brake system checks, and so on. For a discussion on PM *see generally* J.J. Keller & Assoc., Inc., Elements of a Successful Preventive Maintenance (PM) Program, https://www.jjkeller.com/learn/preventive-maintenance-program (last visited June 2, 2024). Preventive maintenance programs should be designed and implemented so defects are discovered, and repairs are made before a violation or accident occurs. *Id.*

5. If violations of the FMCSR minimum standards referenced in 49 C.F.R. §§ 393 and 396 are found during an inspection, drivers are issued a violation citing the specific regulation violated.

6. CVSA, Inspections, https://www.cvsa.org/inspections/ (last visited May 22, 2024).

7. *See* 49 C.F.R. Appendix B to Part 390(1-3); 49 C.F.R. § 396.9(a).

8. It is important to identify the state entity responsible for enforcement of regulations and state laws, and the entities responsible for or certified to perform inspections on a state-by-state basis. For example, in Ohio, the Motor Carrier Enforcement Investigation unit is the entity that is certified and performs most CMV inspections. The MCEI unit is a branch of the Ohio State Highway Patrol, which is a branch of the Ohio Department of Public Safety. However, oversight of regulatory and state law compliance of motor carriers is under the Public Utilities Commission of Ohio (PUCO) (https://puco.ohio.gov/transportation). All records concerning inspections in Ohio then are sent to PUCO for enforcement of any fines, penalties, or further action. Other states certified inspectors, enforcement officers, and records may be under one entity such as the state police or the state's department of transportation. Therefore, it is important to verify each state's procedure where a crash may have occurred.

9. CVSA, All Inspection Levels, https://www.cvsa.org/inspections/all-inspection-levels/ (last visited May 22, 2024).

10. *Id.* The CVSA annually publishes a handbook that specifies how to conduct inspections and specifics of out-of-service criteria in North American Standard Out-of-Service Criteria, Handbook and Pictorial (Commercial Vehicle Safety Alliance rev. April 2024).

tion levels and what occurs at these inspections. Roadside inspection results are recorded in a roadside inspection report usually referred to as a Driver Vehicle Examination Report (DVER).[11] The DVER will contain any violation discovered on the CMV at the time of the inspection.[12] Most drivers strive to receive zero violations during an inspection. However, inspections may result in a driver receiving violations, citations, fines, or being declared out of service.[13] Drivers must deliver a DVER to their motor carrier within 24 hours of report.[14] DVERs can indicate and provide valuable information into whether a motor carrier maintains its trucks.[15]

Post-Crash Inspections

Post-crash inspections occur following a crash.[16] Post-crash inspections are performed by an authorized inspector who records any violations on a DVER.[17] Violations recorded on a post-crash DVER will note any violations found post-crash and specify which violations are a result of the crash or not. However, many law enforcement agencies, such as municipal or local law enforcement, are not certified as CMV inspectors. So, if a certified inspector is not called to conduct a post-crash inspection of a vehicle, then there will be no DVER.

Pre-Trip Inspections

Drivers are required to perform a pre-trip inspection of their CMVs before they begin operation.[18] Under the FMCSRs, a driver shall "be satisfied the CMV is in safe operating condition."[19] A proper pre-trip inspection should find deficiencies that would make the truck unsafe, present a danger to the public, or cause a breakdown.

A review of a driver's electronic logging device or record of duty status should note whether a pre-trip inspection was performed. There is no mandated

---

11. 49 C.F.R. § 396.9(b).

12. There are many violation citations that a CMV could receive for violating the FMCSRs or state laws (not counting criminal charges). These violations are not limited to CMV maintenance but could list other violations such as driver violations, hours of service, drugs and alcohol, and/or hazardous materials, and operating authority violations. *See* North American Standard Out-of-Service Criteria Handbook and Pictorial (Commercial Vehicle Safety Alliance rev. April 2024).

13. Out-of-Service standards are established and compiled by the CVSA and published in the North American Standard Out-of-Service Criteria Handbook, which is updated annually.

14. 49 C.F.R. § 396.9(d)(1).

15. DVERs can help identify the inspection and maintenance practices (or lack thereof) at a particular motor carrier. However, reliance on DVER data alone is likely not a strong indication that negligence maintenance claims will survive in litigation.

16. Fed. Motor Carrier Safety Admin., Definitions, *Crash Causal Factors Program*, https://www.fmcsa.dot.gov/CCFP/definitions (last updated Sept. 19, 2023).

17. 49 C.F.R. § 396.9(b).

18. *Id.* §§ 396.13, 392.7, 392.8, 392.9.

19. *Id.* § 396.13(a).

form that a driver must complete. There is no timeframe specified in the regulations to complete a pre-trip inspection. However, understanding what is involved in conducting a pre-trip inspection may offer guidance. A proper pre-trip inspection requires checking all fluid levels, steering and suspension, brakes,[20] tire condition, tire pressure, chassis and frame condition, all lights, any air or fluid leaks, trailer coupling, locking and safety devices, and other vehicle parts.[21] A pre-trip inspection should also include checking that cargo is properly secured,[22] and the vehicle contains the proper emergency equipment, such as a fire extinguisher, reflective triangles, and fuses.[23]

A driver is also required to review any Driver Vehicle Inspection Report (DVIR) prepared by the prior operator of the CMV, or if it is the same driver, then that driver must be satisfied that the deficiencies previously noted were repaired.[24] This is discussed next.

Post-Trip Inspections

Drivers are required to perform a post-trip inspection of their CMVs and record defects or deficiencies of any parts or accessories that may affect safely operating the CMV.[25] A post-trip inspection should occur at the end of each shift, or anytime a driver switches trucks.[26] A driver is required to submit a report to the motor carrier if a defect is found.[27] This form is generally referred to as a Driver Vehicle Inspection Report (DVIR). Prior to a driver resuming driving a truck that had a DVIR prepared, the driver taking the truck must sign off on that DVIR that the repairs were completed as a part of that driver's pre-trip inspection.[28] Alternatively, the motor carrier can make a determination that the defect reported on the DVIR would not present a safety issue.[29] DVIRs are required to be retained for three months.[30]

---

20. This includes not only the condition of the brakes but also performing an air brake check to ensure there is no air leak and proper air pressure. *See* Section 11 of the AAMVA 2005 CDL Testing System, CDL Driver's Manual (July 2014), https://www.fmcsa.dot.gov/sites/fmcsa.dot.gov/files/docs/2005%20CDL%20Driver%20Manual%20-July%202014%20-%20FINAL.pdf, or Section 11 of any state CDL manual for detailed instructions on performing an air brake check.

21. *Id.* Section 11 of most state CDL manuals provides a detailed example of items drivers are trained to inspect and should inspect while conducting a pre-trip of a commercial motor vehicle. *See also* the inspection protocol for a Level 1 inspection by the CVSA for the parameters of what trained inspectors will look for during an official inspection of a CMV (Commercial Vehicle Safety Alliance and https://www.cvsa.org/inspections/all-inspection-levels/).

22. 49 C.F.R. § 392.9.

23. *Id.* §§ 392.8, 393.95.

24. *Id.* § 396.13(b).

25. *See id.*§ 396.11, generally.

26. *See id.* §§ 396.11(a)(1), 396.11(a)(2)(i), 396.13.

27. *See id.* § 396.11(a)(2)(i). If no defect was found, then no report needs to be completed.

28. 49 C.F.R. § 396.13(b) and (c).

29. *Id.* § 396.11(a)(3)(ii).

30. *Id.* § 396.11(4).

Annual and Periodic Inspections

Motor carriers and intermodal equipment providers that operate in interstate commerce are required to have their CMVs inspected every year.[31] At a minimum, such inspections must include the parameters found in Appendix A to Part 396 of the FMCSRs. These inspections must be performed by a qualified inspector.[32] A motor carrier or intermodal equipment provider may perform the annual inspection on its own equipment subject to proper authorization.[33] Some states have mandatory inspection programs as well.[34] A CMV inspected under a state inspection program approved by the FMCSA does not need a separate annual inspection.[35]

Upon passing the required annual inspection, a form is prepared[36] and a decal or sticker is affixed to the outside of the equipment (truck, trailer, or chassis) that indicates passage of the required inspection.[37] The annual inspection form must be kept by the motor carrier or intermodal equipment provider for 14 months.[38]

Maintenance of Commercial Motor Vehicles

Motor carriers and intermodal equipment providers that operate in interstate commerce are required to maintain their CMVs at the minimum standards set forth in Appendix A to 396.[39] While a preventive maintenance program is not required under the rules, it is nearly impossible to meet this requirement unless a maintenance schedule is in place and adhered to, to ensure a CMV is in safe operating condition. A CMV should not be inspected only when it breaks down or undergoes an annual inspection. Motor carriers or owner operators should ensure their CMVs undergo a planned maintenance program to ensure that the CMV is in a "safe and proper operating condition at all times."[40]

---

31. *Id.* § 396.17. If the motor carrier you are investigating is operating in intrastate commerce only, consult the requirements for that state to determine the inspections required for operation in intrastate commerce of that state.

32. *Id.* § 396.19.

33. *Id.* § 396.23.

34. *See* Inspection, Repair, and Maintenance; Periodic Inspection of Commercial Motor Vehicles, 73 Fed. Reg. 63040 (Fed. Motor Carrier Safety Admin., Oct. 22, 2008). *See also* 49 C.F.R. § 396.23.

35. 49 C.F.R. § 396.23.

36. *Id.* §§ 396.17(c)(1), 396.21(a).

37. Usually, this decal is found on the cab of the truck, the front or rear of the trailer, or on the chassis of intermodal equipment.

38. 49 C.F.R. § 396.21(b).

39. *Id.* § 396.17(g).

40. *Id.* § 396.3 provides that a motor carrier and intermodal equipment provider must systematically inspect, repair, and maintain, or cause to be systematically inspected, repaired, and maintained, all motor vehicles and intermodal equipment subject to its control. This includes parts and accessories shall be in safe and proper operating condition at all times. *Id.* at 396.3(a)(1). *See also* J.J. Keller & Assoc., Inc., Vehicle Inspections & Maintenance, https://www.jjkeller.com/learn/vehicle-inspection-maintenance-compliance (last visited June 2, 2024); and Elements of a Successful Preventive Maintenance (PM) Program, *supra* note 4.

Many motor carriers, such as large national or international motor carriers or intermodal equipment providers, may have maintenance facilities they operate. Motor carriers may also utilize outside mechanics or heavy vehicle maintenance garages. These facilities generally keep maintenance files on the CMVs, along with the motor carrier. These maintenance files may be useful sources of information on negligent maintenance practices. Sometimes the parts that they use for repair might not meet industry standards or FMCSRs or both. Anytime maintenance is performed on a CMV, the work performed should be documented. Motor carriers are required to keep maintenance records for a CMV for one and a half years after the CMV leaves the motor carrier's control.[41]

Systematic Maintenance

Under the FMCSRs, motor carriers and intermodal equipment providers are required to systematically inspect their CMVs.[42] The FMCSA mandates that this includes all parts and accessories on the CMV including those identified in 49 C.F.R. § 393. Broadly, this includes any part, accessory, or component on a CMV that may "affect safe operation of the CMV."[43]

As discussed earlier, an effective maintenance schedule, such as a preventive maintenance schedule, should aim to keep the truck in safe operating condition, not just to avoid accidents but also to avoid breakdowns.[44] In considering systematic maintenance, a motor carrier should consider the location of operation of the CMV; the use of the CMV; the loads, the hours, and miles; and the conditions the CMV may be subjected to in relation to time. Not all CMVs are run on interstate highways. Not all CMVs run for just 11 hours before a rest. Therefore, the location, terrain, miles traveled, time the motor runs, loads, among other considerations, should be understood and considered when developing a maintenance program. For just one example of many possibilities, if a CMV is regularly running dirt roads in the Bakken (off-road North Dakota oilfields), a maintenance schedule to clean and ensure all parts and accessories are free from debris and properly lubricated is especially important to ensure breakdowns do not occur.

Regardless of whether a motor carrier has a maintenance program, the litigator should consider the maintenance requirements specified in the CMV's owner's manual (original equipment manufacturer's (OEM) manual), service manual, or parts manual. Failure to comply with the OEM manual's recommendations may be evidence of negligence. A maintenance expert can assist in developing or refuting a claim of negligent maintenance.

41. 49 C.F.R. § 396.3(c) (2008). So, motor carriers are required to maintain maintenance records on each CMV under their control for the entire time it "controls" the CMV and for one and a half years after the CMV leaves its "control." However, this requirement only begins or takes effect after the CMV is within the "control" of the motor carrier for 30 days. *Id.* § 396.3(b).

42. 49 C.F.R. § 396.3.

43. *Id.*

44. See footnote 4. Additionally, conducting an online search of PM generally can produce additional recommendations or common practices from CMV leasing companies and motor carriers.

Additionally, research any state requirements for an inspection program. For example, California requires motor carriers to submit to its BIT Program.[45] Researching specific state requirements for inspections may assist in developing a successful negligent maintenance claim.

Conclusion

The inspections referenced throughout this chapter can indicate to a litigator whether there is a maintenance issue or claim of negligent maintenance. If there are violations recorded on a DVER, the violations can identify patterns of unsafe behavior that the motor carrier should improve upon.[46] Therefore, it is important to review any inspection forms available for the CMV, any history of the CMV's maintenance, a motor carrier's maintenance practices, or a lack thereof, to determine the patterns and practices of maintenance of the CMV involved in the litigation, whether those patterns and practices indicate the CMV is in safe or unsafe operating condition, and whether a claim for negligent maintenance can be established.

---

45. California's BIT Program provides for highway patrol to conduct inspections at motor carrier terminals to determine if the motor carrier has a scheduled maintenance program and whether that maintenance program is "adequate to prevent collisions or mechanical breakdowns." Welcome to BIT, The Basic Inspection of Terminals (BIT) Program, Dep't Cal. Highway Patrol (2016), https://www.chp.ca.gov/CommercialVehicleSectionSite/Documents/O%20chp800h.pdf.

46. Violations are recorded in the vehicle maintenance category in the Behavioral Analysis Safety Improvement Categories (BASICs) of the Compliance, Safety, Accountability (CSA) enforcement program the FMCSA *See generally* Vehicle Maintenance BASIC Factsheet, U.S. DOT, FMCSA CSA, https://csa.fmcsa.dot.gov/Documents/FMC_CSA_12_009_BASICs_VehMaint.pdf (Dec. 2012). Patterns of unsafe vehicle maintenance can be found by looking up a motor carrier's USDOT number in the FCMSR Safety Measurement System at https://ai.fmcsa.dot.gov/SMS.

CHAPTER 6

Recordkeeping Requirements for Trucking Businesses

Roberto F. Ramirez, Esq. and D.J. Young, III, Esq.

Complete mastery of the relevant facts rests at the heart of any litigation. This is especially the case with truck accident litigation. For each given truck crash, the attorney must be capable of untangling the records pertaining to ownership of the commercial motor vehicle (CMV), daily operations of the CMV, insurance, maintenance of the CMV (including tractor and, if applicable, trailer), and the status and fitness of the driver. The attorney must obtain discovery and thoroughly research the records that may support claims, often against multiple parties.

This records analysis is crucial because much of the litigation has to do with whether one truck company (or someone else) is vicariously liable for the negligence of the driver (either pursuant to the "statutory employer" doctrine or pursuant to the common law *respondeat superior* doctrine), and it takes records to support or refute such a claim. This records analysis also is crucial to determining whether the trucking company is directly liable for its own negligence in hiring, training, or supervision of the driver, and whether the truck driver was unhealthy, unfit, or whether the driver was over the driver's regulatory maximum drive time. These records may reveal other negligent parties, such as third-party trainers or third-party truck maintenance shops, and other negligent acts.

This analysis should start at the beginning stages of the intake of the case because the statutes of limitations will bar being able to bring into the litigation additional responsible parties once the limitations period runs. It should start early, too, for the reason that records may cease to exist before requested if records retention laws or policies allow the destruction of such evidence. Civil discovery often is slow due to scheduling orders, attorneys' schedules, and problems with clients, and, to allow for enough time to fully investigate, prosecute, and defend the facts, without surprises, you need to obtain all applicable records. As the records begin to come in, make sure to cross reference records received from different sources for consistency. The truth is in the details. The falsification of one record may be revealed by the information contained in another record.

For the truck crash plaintiff's attorney to conduct effective discovery from transportation defendants, the attorney must know what records are required to be available. For the attorney representing the motor carrier, the attorney also must know this information in order to satisfy duties to the court and adequately and thoroughly defend the case. Two main bodies of law having records creation and/or retention requirements that could be useful to the attorney investigating a truck crash are (1) the Internal Revenue Code applicable to accounting and tax records and (2) the Federal Motor Carrier Safety Regulations (FMCSRs)[1] applicable to a multitude of aspects related to the operation of ground transportation businesses.

Accounting and Tax Records

In many serious truck crash cases, the effective plaintiff's attorney will seek records showing the date, time, and amount of expenditures from the business. These might include financial statements, expense receipts, invoices, and/or payroll records (including W2s and 1099s). The records might corroborate travel times and travel locations, or they might be circumstantial evidence of who supervised and controlled the transportation. Fortunately, such records normally are available and discoverable.

Businesses are required to be able to record and substantiate all of their business expenses if they desire to deduct those expenses against income for federal income tax purposes.[2] Federal tax law requires businesses to implement and use an accounting system that clearly reflects taxable income by accounting for all items of income and expense.[3] The business must retain "permanent books of accounts or records . . . as are sufficient to establish the amount of gross income, deductions, creditors, or other matters required to be shown by such person in any return of such tax or information."[4] "The books or records required by this section shall be kept at all times . . . and shall be retained so long as the contents thereof may become material in the administration of any internal revenue law,"[5] which ranges from a minimum of three years or six years to ten years and beyond.[6] Often receipts, statements, and other records of income and expenditures are necessary for the effective maintenance of that accounting system and to meet the requirements for deductibility. Many of these same business records are also required by the FMCSRs to be retained.[7]

The tax records and the accounting records, including expense records, are discoverable (assuming the requirements of the discovery rules are satisfied).

---

1. 49 C.F.R. pts. 300–399.
2. 26 U.S.C. §§ 162(a), 274.
3. 26 U.S.C. § 446 and 26 C.F.R. § 1.446-1(a)(2).
4. 26 U.S.C. § 6001 and 26 C.F.R. § 1.6001-1(a).
5. 26 C.F.R. §1.6001-1(e).
6. 26 U.S.C. §§ 6501, 6502, 6511. The audit period is three years from the filing of the return, except that it is extended to six years for certain understatements and overstatements. § 6501(a) and (e)(1)(A).
7. 49 C.F.R. § 379.3 and Part 379 Appendix A.

The party in possession of the records might attempt to avoid production by denying their relevance, denying their existence, or claiming confidentiality. Given the record retention requirements, it would be disingenuous for the party to deny the existence of the records, and, if they no longer exist, it would raise questions of the unlawful spoliation of evidence. While an argument can be made that the tax returns are confidential, that argument lacks merit in litigation between private parties because the statutory confidentiality provision is limited to information in the hands of the IRS and does not apply to identical information in the hands of private parties.[8] Moreover, in the event a party claims that it does not have such information (which seems unlikely given the accounting recordkeeping requirements) there is a statutory procedure for disclosure of such information directly from the IRS while protecting their confidential nature, which is binding on the recipient of the information.[9]

FMCSR-Mandated Records

Owners and operators of a trucking company in the United States are required to maintain extensive records under the regulations promulgated by the Federal Motor Carrier Safety Administration (FMCSA). These regulations are known as the FMCSRs, which will be summarized later in the chapter. Major categories of records required by the FMCSRs include driver training records, drug and alcohol screening records, financial responsibility (insurance) records,[10] accident records, registration records, driver's employment records, the driver's hours of service records, truck and trailer inspection and repair records, brokers' records, and freight forwarders' records. These records requirements are extensive and detailed, and they are summarized in the tables at the end of this chapter.[11] There are significant fines for noncompliance with the recordkeeping requirements of the regulations.[12] The retention periods for each type of record varies, as noted in these tables. Some of the records retention periods are less than one

---

8. 26 U.S.C. § 6103; Jade Trading, LLC v. United States, 65 Fed. Cl. 188 (Ct. Fed. Claims 2005); Baskin v. United States, 135 F.3d 338, 342–43 (5th Cir. 1998); United States v. Six Hundred Forty-Four Thousand Eight Hundred Sixty and 00/100 Dollars, 2007 U.S. Dist. LEXIS 28820, at *2–3, 99 A.F.T.R.2d (RIA) 2007-2386 (C.D. Ill. Case No. 05-cv-4055, Apr. 19, 2007). These cases demonstrate that the records are discoverable through normal civil discovery channels. Confidentiality rules apply, to some extent depending on the facts, on discovery sought directly from the IRS and other applicable government agencies.

9. 26 U.S.C. § 6003(c).

10. Interestingly, "[t]he proof of minimum levels of financial responsibility required by this section shall be considered public information and be produced for review upon reasonable request by a member of the public." 49 C.F.R. § 387.7(e); *see also* § 387.31(e). Motor carriers domiciled in Canada and Mexico must carry their proof of financial responsibility aboard the vehicle. 49 C.F.R. §§ 387.7(f–g), 387.31(f–g).

11. The summary tables are not intended to be completely comprehensive of every type of record, but are meant to summarize the requirements for the major record types. For example, records related to hazardous materials shipments are not included on these tables. Another chapter in this book addresses hazardous materials transportation and records related to it.

12. *See* 49 C.F.R. Part 386, Appendix B.

year—like hours of service records and driver vehicle inspection reports—and, therefore, evidence preservation letters (spoliation letters) should be used to demand and require the preservation of those (and other) records. The attorney should review these tables, and the applicable regulations, to analyze which records might be relevant to the issues involved in the case, seek them through discovery, and use them at trial.

Other Sources of Mandatory Records

In addition to discovery from the parties to the litigation, the attorney should also consider attempting to obtain, through the use of public records requests and subpoenas, records from other sources such as state agencies regulating transportation businesses, the U.S. Department of Transportation (records of carrier registration and safety),[13] the U.S. Department of Labor (for reporting of retirement and health benefits programs),[14] secretaries of state or state corporation commissions that retain corporate-related filings, the respective state department of motor vehicles, and (for some businesses) the U.S. Securities and Exchange Commission.[15] This is not intended as an exhaustive list but to suggest that there are collateral sources of transportation company records.

Conclusion

In some cases, the parties to the litigation and their respective financial responsibility will become clearly defined early on, while in other cases, the named owner of a trucking company may later show to be a shell for another possibly financially responsible entity. Only a thorough identification, request for, obtaining, and reviewing of the relevant records will tell the story of who owns what, who is responsible, and what was the status and safety record of the driver and the truck and trailer at the time leading up to the crash. Request and use the kinds of records described in this chapter to help you prosecute or defend your trucking case.

---

13. Records may be requested pursuant to Freedom of Information Act procedures.

14. The "EFAST Form 5500 Search" database can be quite helpful in providing information about which entity actually employs the driver, the dispatcher, and other management-level persons. *See* https://www.efast.dol.gov/5500Search/. There are other types of filings and searches here that may yield helpful information. https://www.dol.gov/agencies/ebsa/employers-and-advisers/plan-administration-and-compliance/reporting-and-filing.

15. Publicly traded and some other businesses that rely on investors for capitalization are required by the securities laws to file a variety of reports with the U.S. Securities and Exchange Commission (SEC). The SEC's database, known as EDGAR, can be a mine of interesting information about the legal and organizational structure of such businesses.

FMCSR Part 380, Special Training Requirements

Record	Retention Period	FMCSR Subsection
Training Providers' Records	3 years from date record is generated	§ 380.725(c)
Longer Combination Vehicle (LCV) Certificate of Grandfathering maintained by the Motor Carrier (MC) in individual Driver's Qualification File	Unspecified	§ 380.111(d)
LCV Driver-Training Certificate in Driver's Qualification File	Term of employment	§ 380.401(b)

FMCSR Part 382, Drug Screening and Alcohol Misuse Testing Program Records[16]

Record	Retention Period	FMCSR Subsection
Driver's alcohol test results showing an alcohol concentration of .02 or higher	5 years	§ 382.401(b)(1)(i)
Driver verified positive controlled substance test result	5 years	§ 382.401(b)(1)(ii)
Refusals to take controlled substance or alcohol tests	5 years	§ 382.401(b)(1)(iii)
Driver evaluation and referrals	5 years	§ 382.401(b)(1)(iv)
Calibration documentation	5 years	§ 382.401(b)(1)(v)
Records relating to controlled substance and alcohol testing program, including documentation of all driver's violations	5 years	§ 382.401(b)(1)(vi)
A copy of each annual calendar summary required under § 382.403 (Reporting of Results in a Management Information System)	5 years	§ 382.401(b)(vii)
Related to the alcohol and controlled substance collection process (except related to calibration of evidential breath testing devices)	2 years	§ 382.401(b)(2)
Negative and canceled controlled substances test results and Medical Review Officer (MRO) reversal of canceled controlled substances test results (as defined in part 40)	1 year	§ 382.401(b)(3)
Alcohol test results with a concentration of less than 0.02	1 year	§ 382.401(b)(3)
Education and training of breath alcohol technicians, screening test technicians, supervisors, and drivers	While individual performs functions and 2 years after ceasing to perform functions	§ 382.401(b)(4)

16. These are discoverable in injury and wrongful death litigation. 49 C.F.R. § 40.323.

FMCSR Part 387 Financial Responsibility—Proof of the required financial responsibility shall be maintained at the motor carrier's principal place of business.

Record	Retention Period	FMCSR Subsection
Form MCS-90 Endorsements for Motor Carrier Policies of Insurance	Current	§ 387.7(d)(1), § 387.31(d)(1)
Motor Carrier Surety Bond for Public Liability Under Section 30 of the Motor Carrier Act (MCS-82)	Current	§ 387.7(d)(2), § 387.31(d)(2)
A written decision, order, or authorization of the FMCSA authorizing a motor carrier to self-insure under § 387.309	Current	§ 387.7(d)(3)

FMCSR Part 390, General Safety Regulations and Requirements

Record	Retention Period	FMCSR Subsection
Bill of Lading containing names of consignor and consignee, origin and destination, and other details of the freight, and other freight records, records of agents	1 year	§ 373.101, § 379.3 & Part 379 App. A
Corporate organizational records and meeting minutes	Various legal requirements	§ 379.3 & Part 379 App. A
Annual reports to stockholders, accounting records (stock records, debt record, ledgers, journals, cash books, vouchers, accounts receivable records, accounting codes, equipment ownership and cost records, equipment maintenance records)	Minimum 3 years	§ 379.3 & Part 379 App. A
Miscellaneous contracts	Various legal requirements	§ 379.3 & Part 379 App. A
Payroll Records	Minimum 1 year	§ 379.3 & Part 379 App. A
Claims Records, claims registers of injuries, etc.	Minimum 1 year after settlement of the claim	§ 379.3 & Part 379 App. A
Dispatcher's sheets, registers, and other records related to movement of transportation equipment	3 years	§ 379.3 & Part 379 App. A
Import/export and loading records	2 years	§ 379.3 & Part 379 App. A
IRS (tax) and Securities Exchange Commission records, and records required by state and local and other agencies	Various legal requirements	§ 379.3 & Part 379 App. A
Equipment leases and receipts for equipment	Unspecified	§ 376.11(d), § 376.12
Accident register containing date, location, by city or town and state, driver, number of injuries, number of fatalities, and whether hazardous materials other than fuel spilled were released	3 years from date of accident	§ 390.15(b)(1)(i)–(vi)

Record	Retention Period	FMCSR Subsection
MSCA-1 and/or State Performance and Registration Information Systems Management (PRISM) program filings	Biennially	§ 390.201(d)(2) & § 390.203(a)
Requirements of states or local laws relating to safety, the compliance with which are not pre-empted by FMCSA Regulations	Unspecified	§ 390.9
Bill of Lading containing names of consignor and consignee, origin and destination, and other details of the freight		§ 373.101

FMCSR Part 391, Driver's Records

Motor Carrier's Driver Qualification File Contents	Retention Period	FMCSR Subsection
Driver Qualification File (may or may not include personnel file)	Current plus 3 years	§ 391.51(a–d)
Application for employment	Current plus 3 years	§ 391.51(b)(1) & (c)
Copy of motor vehicle record from each driver's licensing authority	Current plus 3 years	§ 391.51(b)(2) & (c)
Certificate of driver's road test issued to the driver, a copy of the license or certificate accepted as equivalent, or the original of the written statement providing that the motor carrier determined the driver is not required to complete a road test and the original, or a copy, of the driver's certification	Current plus 3 years	§ 391.51(b)(3) & (c)
Motor vehicle record received from each driver's licensing authority to the annual driver record inquiry	3 years from execution	§ 391.51(b)(4) & (c–d)
A note relating to the annual review of the driver's driving record to include consideration of any evidence that the driver has violated any applicable FMCSA Regulations or Hazardous Materials Regulations, with great weight given to any violations such as speeding, reckless driving, and operating under the influence of alcohol or drugs	3 years from execution	§ 391.51(b)(5) & (c–d)
Medical examiner's certificate or a legible copy MCSA-5876	3 years from execution	§ 391.51(b)(6)(i) & (c–d)
For CDL holders, if the Commercial Driver's License Information System (CDLIS) motor vehicle record contains medical certification status information, the motor carrier employer must meet this requirement by obtaining the CDLIS motor vehicle record.	3 years from execution	§ 391.51(b)(6)(ii) & (c–d)
Copy of medical variance certification documentation if certification was obtained via a medical variance	3 years from execution	§ 391.51(b)(6)(iii) & (c–d)
Skill Performance Evaluation Certificate issued by FMCSA or Federal medical program for drivers with missing or impaired limbs	3 years from execution	§ 391.51(b)(7) & (c)

Motor Carrier's Driver Qualification File Contents	Retention Period	FMCSR Subsection
For drivers not required to have a CDL, a note relating to verification of medical examiner listing on the National Registry of Certified Medical Examiners under § 391.23(m)(1)	3 years from execution	§ 391.51(b)(8)(i) & (c–d)
Through June 22, 2025, for drivers required to have a CDL, a note relating to verification of medical examiner listing on the National Registry of Certified Medical Examiners under § 391.23(m)(2)	3 years from execution	§ 391.51(b)(8)(ii) & (c–d)
Driver Investigatory History File[17]—safety performance histories and drug and alcohol histories received from previous employers for a driver who is hired including responses received, good faith efforts to contact, and former employers' information	Current plus 3 years	§ 391.53(b)(1)–(2), (c), & (d)
For previous employers, each request for safety performance inquiry and the response including the date, the party to whom it was released, and a summary identifying what was provided	1 year	§ 391.23(g)(4)
Qualification file for each Long Combination Vehicle (LCV) driver-instructor it employs or uses	Term of employment	§ 391.55(a) & (b)

FMCSR Part 395, Hours of Service (HOS) of Drivers Records

Record	Retention Period	FMCSR Subsection
Motor carrier records of duty status for each of its drivers and supporting documents which include bills of lading, dispatch record, electronic mobile communication (phone) records, expense receipts, and each payroll record, settlement sheet, or equivalent document	6 months from date of receipt	§ 395.8(k)(1) § 395.11(c)(1)(i)–(v)
Driver's copy of each record of duty status	7 days	§ 395.8(k)(2)
Electronic Logging Device (ELD) records (which may be in the ELD device service's records and/or the motor carrier's records)	6 months	Appendix A to Subpart B of Part 395 4.9.2(a) & (b)

FMCSR Part 396, Inspection, Repair, and Maintenance Records

Record	Retention Period	FMCSR Subsection
Roadside inspection reports of motor vehicles and intermodal equipment in operation	12 months from date of inspection	§ 396.9(d)(3)(ii)
Driver vehicle inspection report, the certification of repairs, and the certification of the driver's review	3 months from date of written report	§ 396.11(a)(4), (b)(4)

17. The driver qualification file required by 49 C.F.R. § 391.51 should not be confused with the driver investigation history file required by 49 C.F.R. § 391.53.

Record	Retention Period	FMCSR Subsection
Periodic (annual) inspection reports	14 months from date of inspection report	§ 396.21(b)(1)
Systematic inspection, repair, and maintenance records	1 year; 6 months after the motor vehicle leaves the MC's control	§ 396.3(c)
Evidence of individual's qualifications to perform annual inspections	While performing inspections and 1 year thereafter	§ 396.19(b)

FMCSR Part 371, Summary of Records of Brokers

Record	Retention Period	FMCSR Subsection
Each transaction record	3 years	§ 371.3(a)
Name and address of the consignor	3 years	§ 371.3(a)(1) & (b)
Name and address of the originating motor carrier	3 years	§ 371.3(a)(2) & (b)
Bill of Lading (or related documentation)	3 years	§ 371.3(a)(3) & (b)
Amount of brokerage compensation and the name of the payer	3 years	§ 371.3(a)(4) & (b)
A description of any non-brokerage service performed in connection with each shipment or other activity, the amount of compensation received for the service, and the name of the payer	3 years	§ 371.3(a)(5) & (b)
The amount of any freight charges collected by the broker and the date of payment to the carrier	3 years	§ 371.3(a)(6) & (b)

FMCSRs Specific to Freight Forwarders

Record	Retention Period	FMCSR Subsection
Application for Registration as Freight Forwarder must include § 387 evidence of financial responsibility	Unspecified	§ 390.205(a)(1) & (2)
Agent designated for service of process	Unspecified	§ 390.205(a)(1) (3)
Surety bond or trust fund, certificate of insurance, qualifications as self-insurer, or other securities agreements	Maintained in effect	§ 387.403(b) & (c)
Each freight forwarder must issue the shipper a receipt or through bill of lading, covering transportation from origin to ultimate destination, on each shipment for which it arranges transportation	Upon shipment	§ 373.201

PART II

Investigation and Trial Preparation

CHAPTER 7

The Lawyer's Role in Pretrial Investigation

Keishunna R. Webster, Esq. and Harrison M. Smith, Esq.

Preparation and investigation are crucial for properly handling trucking cases, and without an understanding of the laws and motor carrier regulations that govern the trucking industry, an attorney is automatically at a disadvantage in protecting the interests of his or her client. Regardless of which side of the bar counsel is on for a particular accident, effective trucking litigation *must* start with the regulations. Every transportation litigation matter ultimately drills down to regulatory compliance and the causal connection between such compliance and the accident. This means that success in a trucking litigation case requires developing the facts immediately after an accident, if possible.

Because of the high stakes involved in truck accident litigation, sophisticated trucking defendants often hire defense attorneys who offer rapid response teams so that early investigation efforts are properly targeted, and further to protect the information that may be obtained by consulting experts if litigation is reasonably anticipated. A rapid response team is a group of specialized individuals who are trained to respond immediately when a catastrophic accident occurs. Their involvement and work at the scene are vital in controlling key evidence that will have a material effect on litigation management—key evidence that often can disappear. This is very important to the development of an effective defense strategy. Additionally, with the rise in spoliation claims, preservation of key evidence is necessary to protect a company from the increased exposure caused by missing or destroyed evidence. The most assertive plaintiffs will hire attorneys who have their expert witnesses on scene, for similar reasons, as soon as possible after being retained. Whether representing the plaintiff or the defendant, these processes are expensive and worth the time, money, and resources. Acting immediately after an accident places your client in the best position to understand the value of a potential claim and its strengths and weaknesses. One of the first things to accomplish is to have all pertinent witnesses thoroughly interviewed.

Witness Statements and Reports

Witness Statements

Witness interviews are critical to trucking accident investigations and should be taken as quickly as possible after the accident, when the information is fresh. Having a seasoned investigator with a law enforcement background is a huge help during the investigation. Allowing the investigator to take statements from fact witnesses helps to ensure that their testimony is not influenced by potential claimants, preserves a record of their observations, and provides for a more thorough evaluation of liability. Ultimately, the investigator needs to know who was involved, what they were doing, what was happening at the time, and when and where the accident occurred.

Client's Interview

The truck driver is at the heart of any trucking accident. He or she is going to be the one who provides notice to the company. He or she, along with the claimant, will know the most about what happened. Thus, the truck driver must undergo a through debriefing as soon as he or she is emotionally able to do so. The driver interview should be conducted by the attorney who is going to handle the case.

All aspects of the driver's memory must be probed regarding the facts and circumstances of the accident as well as the events leading up to the accident. This is also the time to discuss how the truck or trailer was operating at the time of the accident, any pre- or post-trip inspections of the truck or trailer, a review of the driver's logs, and any U.S. Department of Transportation (DOT) issues with the driver, depending on the circumstances. The driver interview provides valuable insight into what was going through the driver's mind as the accident unfolded, the driver's credibility, and what type of impression he or she is going to make at deposition and at trial.

Investigating Officer Interview

The investigating officer is usually the first person on the scene to investigate and determine the cause of the collision. For this reason, he or she should be interviewed as early in the process as possible. The investigating officer is usually the first person to interview after meeting with the client. Conversations with the investigating officer should be recorded by your investigator, if possible. The investigating officer can provide valuable information, including statements from drivers and witnesses; scene measurements; points or areas of impact; skid, yaw, and gauge mark locations; vehicle points of rest; scene photographs; sight distance measurements; weather conditions; and other contributing factors. Without this information, the reconstructionist may have difficultly forming accurate opinions regarding causation and fault.

Other Witnesses

It is beneficial to also speak with first responders, emergency personnel, and tow truck drivers for important information ranging from the rate of speed at which the vehicles were traveling to any verbal admissions possibly made at the scene of the accident while emotion still trumped reason. Interviewing everyone who was even tangentially connected to the accident is helpful so that the attorney can develop a detailed overview of the case and then target possible weaknesses. Counsel should always attempt to interview the following people following a trucking accident: eyewitnesses to the accident, including the truck driver; law enforcement officers; firemen; first responders; EMS workers; post-accident bystanders; any individuals who stopped to render aid or assistance or who spoke with anyone who was involved in the collision; tow truck drivers; helicopter air medical personnel, if applicable; and media (including photographers, reporters, and cameramen). For any of these likely to have records, you should request or subpoena their files.

Collision Report

Following a trucking accident, everyone involved will likely remember the event differently. To sort out the details, an objective account of what happened is crucial. The police report of the accident at issue will contain relevant evidence. It includes the time, date, and location of the accident, the names and contact information of all parties involved, and statements from witnesses, which can be crucial in establishing what happened. The report often contains a diagram of the scene and photographs of the damage incurred. Often these reports are not available for several days or weeks following an accident; thus, it is important that the attorney interview the investigating law enforcement officer as soon as possible after the accident.

Investigating Officer's File

Obtaining a copy of the investigating officer's file is warranted in every trucking case. In most instances, you can obtain a copy of the file by simply requesting it.[1] If you are dealing with a local police department, the city or town may not release the investigating officer's file without a court order.

The investigating officer's file typically contains the officer's hand-drawn diagram of the scene, tire impression measurements, the location and size of any gouge marks, and miscellaneous notes. Within the file, you may also find written and/or recorded statements from drivers and witnesses, photographs, video, dispatch records, and 911 call records.[2]

1. Be aware of how the public records request law works in your jurisdiction, as compliance with it may be the key to rapidly obtaining the information you need.

2. 911 emergency tapes can provide valuable insight into how and why the crash occurred. Counsel should always attempt to obtain copies of any and all recordings made to 911 operators. The calls placed to the 911 Emergency Services are recorded, and the telephone number from which the call was placed is logged. Therefore, obtaining these records can also lead to the identification of witnesses to what was going on in the moments leading up to a crash.

Data Collection and Experts

In trucking litigation, motor carriers must maintain driver's logs, maintenance records, driver qualification files, medical qualification forms, and other data. Most of this information is mandated to be preserved under the Federal Motor Carrier Safety Regulations (FMCSRs). Additional information, such as electronically stored data found in electronic control modules (ECMs), may also have to be preserved, particularly if a spoliation letter is sent by the claimant's attorney.

Data Collection

Defense counsel should act quickly to assist the motor carrier in preserving the following potentially relevant materials:

- Inspection, maintenance, and repair records for the tractor and trailer
- Driver's personnel, qualification file, safety file, and DOT file
- Driver's logs for day of the accident and six months preceding the accident
- Post-accident alcohol and drug screen, if applicable
- Daily inspection report for the tractor and trailer
- Lease agreement or document showing ownership of tractor and trailer
- Trip documents including GPS records, dispatch records, bills of lading, weight tickets, and delivery records
- Photographs or video recordings of the accident scene or things located near the accident site
- Photographs or video recordings of the tractor and trailer before or after the accident
- Company accident report form and complete accident file
- Cellular phone records of driver for the date of the accident, if possible

Prudent counsel should send an early spoliation letter in certain cases to the adverse parties and their insurers. A demand that the party's vehicle, electronic data, cell phones, and cell phone data from the day of the accident be preserved is appropriate and can help with discovery strategy and evidentiary issues later in the litigation.

Issues of spoliation are raised frequently because, in many instances, the "spoliated" evidence would not have been relevant evidence. However, the threat of receiving a negative inference instruction during trial—an instruction to the jury that they are to assume the spoliated evidence would have been unfavorable to the party who lost it—is real and can impact a case. Therefore, whether a party is a plaintiff or defendant, early efforts to preserve information, or to request it be preserved, can be critical down the road in litigation.

Experts

It is especially important that you retain your experts early in truck accident cases.[3] If liability is an issue, then having someone on your team from the

3. All experts are expensive. The best qualified experts can be very expensive. If you or your client cannot afford the necessary experts, it will negatively impact your ability, as an attorney, to

very beginning to help you identify the more scientifically technical issues is essential. Identifying these issues early will allow you to develop effective case themes and strategies. Having your experts involved early will also decrease the chance that you will miss an important issue or piece of evidence. Having an experienced investigation team of your own, whose members will drop what they are doing and immediately respond to your request for help, also increases your chances of obtaining valuable evidence before it disappears. In many trucking accident cases, you may need to hire the following experts as soon as possible: (1) an accident reconstruction engineer, (2) a truck safety expert, and (3) an electronic control module expert.

Accident Reconstruction Engineer

The accident reconstructionist should be an engineer who is experienced in investigating trucking accidents. He or she is the person who will help you figure out how and why the crash happened. His or her role is to be the technician—the on-the-scene expert—who determines how the accident happened by documenting, photographing, and measuring the scene and the vehicles involved.

The accident reconstructionist will collect the electronic data from the truck, and, if possible, other vehicles involved in the accident. If at all possible, the data should be extracted at the scene before the vehicles are moved and key data is overwritten. If the data cannot be extracted on scene, the vehicle should be towed and secured, because the data will be overwritten as soon as the vehicle is operated, or the engine is engaged. The reconstructionist should determine the truck's manufacturer, model, and VIN number, as well as the engine's manufacturer, model, and build date. A visual inspection will confirm the tractor's and the engine's specifications. If the event data recorder (EDR) seems to be destroyed, it is important for the accident reconstructionist to remove the EDR recorder before the vehicle is scrapped. Chain of custody is key in these circumstances. Even if the accident reconstructionist does not think that the EDR contains any data, there is still a duty to preserve it so that any potential claimants can make that determination themselves.[4] After extraction, the EDR needs to be secured and proper notice given to ensure all concerned have had an opportunity to observe and test the EDR before it is destroyed.

The attorney should visit the site of the crash with the reconstructionist as soon as possible. Active participation in the investigation is critical because visiting the site, hearing the engineer's initial analysis, viewing the physical evidence, and observing the vehicles will provide the attorney insight into the dynamics of the accident and any potential liability of the truck driver.

---

be successful in the litigation. It is important for attorneys to educate their clients about the value that the best experts can add to the case.

4. In some cases, even if the device containing the data appears to be destroyed, the memory chip in the device may not necessarily be destroyed. In such a case, a "chip swap" can be accomplished by some forensic data experts so that the data may be retrieved.

Truck Safety Expert

A truck safety expert focuses on the driver and the motor carrier. He or she specializes in understanding the intricacies of commercial truck operation and regulations. The truck safety expert will want to review all compliance documents, including all of the driver's daily logs, daily inspection sheets, log audit reports, dispatch records, Global Positioning System (GPS) data, and supporting trip documents, among others. The trucking safety expert can professionally identify safety violations, driver negligence, or equipment failures that may have contributed to the accident.

ECM Expert

An ECM expert is one who is certified by the engine's manufacturer and familiar with accident reconstruction. An ECM is a device that is mounted to the engine of most commercial tractors manufactured after 2005, and it controls various engine functions and records data that is relevant to an accident. ECMs, the data they store, and the length of time the ECM retains the data varies by engine model and manufacturer. Depending on the ECM, it may have data that includes the VIN number, the engine serial number, speed, cruise control, transmission style, hard stops, and various other engine performance data. Your expert should obtain the ECM data and provide it to you. Your expert should be capable of interpreting all of the data in the EMC relevant to the accident.

The extraction and interpretation of ECM data should include all available reports. More than one extracted report is often necessary to establish the complete picture of what occurred during an accident. If at all possible, the expert extracting the data should be the same person interpreting it. In cases with older ECMs, only a certified ECM expert may know how to extract all the available data.

Depending on the type of ECM involved, the way that the data is downloaded can mean the difference between getting the data you need and not getting it at all. A qualified ECM expert will understand the subtle differences between the various ECM models produced by the manufacturer in your specific case. He or she will also know how to maneuver within the ECM system and locate the information you need. The best scenario for downloading the ECM data is to have your ECM expert on-site and involved in the actual downloading of the data. If that is not possible, then it is important to have your ECM expert talk with the download technician so that everyone is on the same page regarding the information being sought before the download is attempted.

Because ECM data can make or break your case, it is important to properly extract and read the data. In some cases, it may be the only source of precise information about the accident. It also provides a record that may eliminate unpleasant surprises in discovery, such as when the defense suddenly produces ECM records that refute all or most of the claimant's arguments.

In many cases, ECM data can accurately pinpoint what happened during an accident and provide details that might otherwise be unavailable. The point is that if the tractor has an ECM, then the attorney should retain an ECM expert, not simply an accident reconstruction engineer who claims to know, or can learn, how to interpret ECM data. If you need an ECM expert, you must do your homework on the front end and make sure the expert is qualified to interpret the data.

Items to Inspect as Soon as Possible

Tractor and Trailer

The tractor-trailer analysis is potentially the single most important piece of information that can be obtained within the entire case. A thorough analysis of the tractor-trailer in question will be necessary. Just as your reconstructionist surveyed the crash site using a total station device, he or she should also complete a total station survey of the crush damage on the tractor-trailer. This data may be critically important when the expert begins calculating the speed of the tractor-trailer. The tractor and trailer should also be documented (inside and out) using high quality digital photography. If the claimant has retained counsel, it is always better to arrange to have everyone present when the tractor-trailer is inspected.

A specific protocol should be followed in photographing the tractor-trailer. The following list is an example of the items that should be documented:

- Photograph the tractor and trailer from each angle, walking all the around the vehicle
- Photograph the logos, placards, DOT, and tractor and trailer unit numbers
- Photograph each mirror on the tractor
- Photograph the inside of the tractor, and the sleeper berth if it has one
- Photograph any items that might prove driver fault or a violation of the FMCSRs, such as radar detectors and urine jugs
- Photograph the inside of the trailer, including its cargo, restraints, and any damaged goods
- Photograph all tractor and trailer tires such that you can see the manufacturer's name, the model number, the side, and any other writing located on the tire (tractor tire information is critical when calculating speed based on ECM data)
- Photograph any inspection plates or stickers
- Photograph the side and rear guards, be sure to place a measuring device from the bottom of the rear guards to the ground to document their height in a photograph
- Photograph the fifth wheel
- Photograph the kingpin
- Photograph all damage to the tractor and the trailer, including the undersides of the vehicles
- Photograph the condition of the tractor and trailer's brakes
- Photograph all lights and reflectors

- Photograph the filaments of any damaged lights or signals
- Photograph interior and compartments of the tractor and trailer and catalog the contents

Everything that is located in the driver's cab needs to be documented and cataloged. This documentation is not limited to work-related materials such as logs, a bill of lading for the load on the freight, weight tickets, or fuel receipts. Counsel should also include the driver's personal items. The cab of the truck is the driver's home and office. The personal information in the cab is just as important as the work-related materials because it will provide an understanding of the driver and may be used for or against him/her later during litigation. Knowing this information immediately after the accident will provide further information to factor into the defense strategy.

Tractor's Electronic Evidence

While ECM data can be very important in a trucking case, additional electronic data may exist in the truck. Many of the larger motor carriers use GPS and mobile tracking systems to track vehicles along their route. This technology allows the motor carrier and the driver to communicate, and the motor carrier can gather vast amounts of data about the way the driver is operating the vehicle at any point during the trip. The types of data include speed, RPMs, accelerator position, brake position, steering wheel position, and so on. This data is available in real time while the truck driver is on the road, as well as after the trip is completed. The length of time that the data is retained varies by brand. The import of this type of data is obvious in the post-collision scenario.

GPS and Mobile Communication Systems

The motor carrier can use the GPS data to determine the location of a truck driver and/or the rig at a particular time. The motor carrier can use this data to cross check the truck driver's daily log entries to see if the driver is falsifying his hours of service (HOS). Some GPS-based tracking systems, like Qualcomm, also have the ability to record vehicle data in the event of a crash, much like an event data recorder (EDR) on a passenger car's airbag system.

Mobile communications systems are interactive management systems that include two-way mobile communications between the company and its driver. Following a wreck, the truck driver will often communicate with the dispatcher about what happened while waiting on the highway patrol or emergency workers to arrive. These communications are saved on the dispatch end and are retrievable.

EDRs and ELDs

Electronic data recorders (EDRs) and electronic logging devices (ELDs) are electronic devices attached to a commercial motor vehicle that is used to record the amount of time a vehicle is being driven. These devices record a truck driver's hours of service.

Passenger vehicles may be equipped with EDRs or event data recorders. The EDR can be found inside the control module for the vehicle's airbag system. The control module is the electronic device that causes the airbag to deploy. The EDR makes a record of the information available for a short period before, during, and after any crash where the airbag is triggered or there is an excessive rate of vehicle deceleration. The information available from an EDR depends on the make, model, and year of the vehicle at issue, and may include the following:

- Vehicle speed five seconds prior to impact
- Engine speed five seconds prior to impact
- Brake status five seconds prior to impact
- Throttle position five seconds prior to impact
- Steering wheel position in degrees
- Delta-V (change in velocity) for up to three-tenths of a second after event
- Time from vehicle impact to max Delta-V
- Maximum Delta-V
- Ignition cycle count information
- Driver's seat belt switch position
- Seatbelt pretensioner activation
- Airbag deployment
- Passenger's airbag (enabled/disabled)[5]

Claimant's Motor Vehicle

With regard to the inspection of the claimant's vehicle, the accident reconstructionist should follow the same protocol as was followed for the tractor and trailer. The reconstructionist should gather total station data regarding the vehicle crush damage. The expert should also document the inside and outside of the vehicle by still photographs and video.

As it relates to totaled vehicles, the claimant's vehicle and/or the tractor-trailer should not be destroyed until counsel advises that it is okay. This is usually only done after all parties have had the opportunity to inspect the vehicle. All potential parties to the suit, including those that might be added to the case for comparative fault purposes, should be notified of an opportunity to inspect the vehicle before it is destroyed. Counsel should provide these individuals and entities ample advance notice to avoid a later spoliation claim. This prevents them from later arguing that they are prejudiced because they were not allowed to inspect and test the vehicle.

---

5. Andrew Askland, *The Double Edged Sword That Is the Event Data Recorder*, 25(1) TEMPLE ENV'L L. & TECH. J. 25 (2006).

Roadway

Prompt investigation of the roadway is necessary because evidence left behind can disappear quickly due to passing traffic, wind, and other weather issues. Investigators document all skid, gouge, scrape, and yaw marks on the roadway. Counsel should make sure that each mark is measured for future analysis and/or reconstruction. Counsel should also ensure that all debris left in the roadway is documented. This debris includes materials from the collision, as well as any other materials that may have been left in the roadway. Debris in the roadway includes fluid stains or leaks, blood, glass from broken windshields, cargo separated from the vehicle, and damage to guardrails, telephone poles, trees, or other objects. Proper documentation ensures that the experts do not rely on evidence unrelated to the crash in their analysis.

The reconstructionist must document the physical features of the roadway starting with the type of road surface and weather conditions. The expert must also document and diagram the road layout at the area of the impact (AOI) and leading up to the collision site, including any straight and curved sections. He or she must also photograph all traffic control devices at and leading up to the collision site such as signs, lane markings, speed limits, or traffic signals. Any other obstructions present should be photographed and diagrammed. All diagrams must include the location of all vehicles and/or pedestrians involved. Here is a checklist for evidence that should be gathered by the reconstructionist at the accident site:

- Locate the AOI and photograph it from all angles
- Photograph the line of sight for vehicles approaching the AOI
- Photograph evidence from the AOI to the location of final rest for each vehicle
- Photograph the final rest areas from all angles
- Capture aerial photos and videos
- Measure geometry using 3D scans and/or an aerial photo grid
- Record vehicle approach videos
- Obtain original video footage for security cameras that may show the collision or the approach of any vehicle
- Document construction zone signage and traffic controls

Internet Resources

Following are some useful internet sources that can assist with the investigation, prosecution, and defense of trucking accidents. Internet information can prove invaluable immediately after an accident or during the early stages of a dispute. Intelligence gained from the internet and social media can assist in making liability decisions and even gathering evidence that can be used to prosecute or repudiate claims.

Federal Motor Carrier Safety Administration

A key online source is the Federal Motor Carrier Safety Administration's (FMCSA) webpage. The site includes links to several databases yielding information of significant value. The FMCSR site includes up-to-date FMCSRs[6] and various other federal laws affecting or regulating trucking transportation. A regulatory guidance section provides plain-English translations of official regulations that are helpful as you try to determine the regulations that may apply to a particular situation. The site also lists carriers who have been taken out of service for regulatory violations and failures to pay fines. Whether you are defending a trucking company or representing a plaintiff injured in a trucking accident, it is helpful to know whether the FMCSA considers the trucking company to have a poor safety rating.

The Safety and Fitness Electronic Records System (SAFER)

The FMCSA implemented the Safety and Fitness Electronic Records or the "Safer System" to provide the trucking industry and the public with detailed safety information concerning interstate trucking companies.[7] Entering the name of a company in the search bar yields information on inspections, accidents, and the company's safety rating. At the top right corner of the Company Snapshot, you can click on "Licensing and Insurance" to obtain information concerning the company's insurer for the past several years, the policy limits, and the agents of service of process in various states. Since the availability of trucker's insurance can ensure the collection of any potential judgment, this information can be of strategic importance.[8] Some states have similar websites for carriers registered in those states.[9]

Compliance, Safety, and Accountability System (CSA)

The FMCSA's webpage contains a section devoted to Compliance, Safety, and Accountability (CSA). An integral part of CSA is the Safety Management System (SMS), which evaluates the safety performance of a trucking company. The SMS then utilizes this data to calculate the safety of drivers and carriers based on seven line items called BASICs (behavior analysis and safety improvement categories):[10]

- **Unsafe driving.** Operation of CMVs by drivers in a dangerous or careless manner. *Example violations*: speeding, reckless driving, improper lane change, and inattention.
- **Hours-of-service violations.** Operation of CMVs by drivers who are ill, fatigued, or in noncompliance with the HOS regulations. This category involves violations of regulations pertaining to logbooks as they relate to HOS requirements and the management of CMV driver fatigue. *Example violations*: HOS, logbook, and operating a CMV while ill or fatigued.

6. The Federal Motor Carrier Safety Regulations also can be found at www.ecfr.gov in Title 49 of the Code of Federal Regulations.

7. Currently, this is located at https://safer.fmcsa.dot.gov/CompanySnapshot.aspx.

8. Currently, this is located at https://li-public.fmcsa.dot.gov/LIVIEW/pkg_carrquery.prc_carrlist.

9. See the chapter in this book by Pete Kestner and Mary Eliasen about insurance for interstate and intrastate motor carriers.

10. *See* 49 C.F.R. pt. 385.

- **Unfitness of driver.** Operation of CMVs by drivers who are unfit to operate a CMV due to lack of training, experience, or medical qualifications. *Example violations*: failure to have a valid and appropriate commercial driver's license and being medically unqualified to operate a CMV.
- **Controlled substances/alcohol.** Operation of CMVs by drivers who are impaired due to alcohol, illegal drugs, and misuse of prescription or over-the-counter medications. *Example violations*: use or possession of controlled substances/alcohol.
- **Vehicle maintenance.** Failure to properly maintain a CMV. *Example violations*: brakes, lights, and other mechanical defects, and failure to make required repairs.
- **Hazardous materials compliance.** Failure to properly prevent shifting loads, spilled or dropped cargo, overloading, and unsafe handling of hazardous materials on a CMV. *Example violations*: improper load securement, cargo retention, size and weight, and hazardous material handling.
- **Crash indicator.** Histories or patterns of high crash involvement, including frequency and severity based on information reported by the state to FMCSA.

Preemployment Screening Program (PSP)

The FMCSA's PSP is a voluntary program available to all trucking companies at a minimal cost. The PSP allows the motor carrier and drivers to purchase their driving record from the FMCSA's motor carrier management information system (MCMIS). The MCMIS will contain a five-year history of crash data and a three-year history of safety inspections. The FMCSA believes that making this information available to trucking companies will help them make an informed decision before hiring a truck driver.

Social Media

In today's digital age, there is always the possibility that the parties involved in a motor vehicle accident and/or those who witnessed it may post about it. Sites like Facebook, Instagram, X, and NextDoor may assist with gathering information about the parties involved in the trucking accident. Screenshot anything interesting you find. These posts can inform the initial investigation. It is true that social media can dramatically impact a claim if it is used incorrectly. But the reverse is also true. When it is used wisely, it can support the prosecution and/or defense of a claim.

Conclusion

In all catastrophic transportation cases, it is important that a protocol is developed to rapidly respond to and investigate these accidents immediately after they happen. Accidents leave behind troves of evidence that might be critical to defending a trucking company and its driver. But just as quickly as the evidence appears, it starts to disappear; vehicles are moved, debris and glass are swept up, tire marks begin to fade, and witnesses filter away. A rapid response team can not only gather this evidence but also take the steps necessary to make sure that the evidence is collected, preserved, and ultimately admissible in a trial.

CHAPTER 8

Identifying All Potentially Liable Parties

D.J. Young, III, Esq.

Introduction

Everyone involved in a commercial motor vehicle (CMV) crash has an interest in determining (1) who the potentially responsible parties are and (2) who the potentially liable parties are. For plaintiffs, this is about suing someone who can pay. For some defendants, shifting the blame and cost elsewhere is a defense strategy.

Distinction must be drawn at the outset between and among the four following different categories of claims that might arise out of a CMV crash: (1) the CMV driver's workers compensation claims, (2) freight damage claims, for which the remedy is pursuant to federal law, (3) vehicle property damage claims, and (4) third-party claims related to the injuries and deaths of persons other than the CMV driver. This chapter does not address workers compensation claims or freight damage claims.[1] For vehicle property damage claims, personal injury claims, and wrongful death claims, which are the focus of this

1. Worker compensation claims are governed by state law and vary by state. Most freight damage claims arising out of transportation in interstate commerce are exclusively governed by what is commonly known as the Carmack Amendment to the Interstate Commerce Act, currently codified at 49 U.S.C. § 11706 (rail) and 14706 (motor carriers and freight forwarders). It preempts most state law damages claims, but there are exceptions. For greater understanding of this unique body of law, *see* Kawasaki Kisen Kaisha Ltd. v. Regal-Beloit Corp., 561 U.S. 89 (2010), Adams Express Co. v. Croninger, 226 U.S. 491 (1913), Royal & Sun Alliance Ins. PLC v. Ocean World Lines, Inc., 612 F.3d 138 (2d Cir. 2010), REI Transport v. C.H. Robinson Worldwide, Inc., 519 F.3d 693 (7th Cir. 2008), White v. Mayflower Transit, L.L.C., 543 F.3d 581 (9th Cir. 2008), Hall v. N. Am. Van Lines, Inc., 476 F.3d 683 (9th Cir. 2007), Ward v. Allied Van Lines, Inc., 231 F.3d 135 (4th Cir. 2000), North Am. Van Lines v. Pinkerton Security Sys., Inc., 89 F.3d 452 (7th Cir. 1996). *See also* David N. Nissenberg, The Law of Commercial Trucking: Damages to Persons and Property Vol. 2, Chs. 15 & 17 (4th ed., New York: Matthew Bender, 2023). As to freight damage claims arising out of inland transport originating in ocean transit, see Chapter 26 in this book by D.J. Young, III, concerning claims arising out of inland transport.

chapter, the extent of the search for potentially responsible and potentially liable parties will correlate to the magnitude of the damages and injuries. From the plaintiff's perspective, if there is enough insurance coverage applicable to the tortfeasor driver, there is little justification for finding other potentially liable parties. From the defense perspective, third-party claims against other potentially liable parties might be warranted so that the named defendant is not required to shoulder all responsibility.

This chapter describes a systematic chronological approach that can be expected of a reasonably competent attorney in identifying all tortfeasors and all potentially liable parties in cases in which a jury verdict reasonably could exceed the amount that could be collected from the CMV driver or the CMV driver's insurance carrier.[2]

Legal Theories of Liability Inform the Identification of Potentially Liable Parties

A very large proportion of truck crashes are caused by underinsured, undercapitalized trucking businesses. For plaintiffs who have suffered tragic losses, the search for other potentially liable parties is imperative. Yet, this task is difficult because many participants in the trucking industry organize their legal relationships in ways that have the effect of obfuscating responsibility and shifting or avoiding liability. Consequently, lawyers for plaintiffs must be well-versed in the various legal doctrines that lead to liability for the persons who share responsibility for the crash so that all such persons are sued. This can lead to much better results for plaintiffs. Lawyers for defendants, therefore, must also be well-versed in these legal doctrines to defend the cases well. It is not the purpose of this chapter to explain the various legal theories of liability, but simply to remind attorneys of them so that they research and investigate correctly for potentially liable parties.

The category of people "directly" liable for their own negligence frequently includes vehicle drivers, supervisors (both dispatch and safety), mechanics, vehicle owners, and, in many jurisdictions, the truck companies.[3] Sometimes

2. "The proof of minimum levels of financial responsibility required by [49 C.F.R. § 387.7] shall be considered public information and be produced for review upon reasonable request by a member of the public." 49 C.F.R. § 387.7(e)(1). Sometimes the insurance policy identifies affiliated companies and/or additional insured parties—information that could be helpful in identifying all responsible parties. *See* Chapter 17 in this book by Mary Eliasen and Peter Kestner for an explanation of the insurance requirements for truck drivers and motor carriers.

3. Different courts view the merits of direct negligence claims beyond the truck driver differently, with some courts endorsing the concept and others folding them all into vicarious liability claims. Several state supreme court cases illustrate the complexity. Martin v. Thomas, 346 So. 3d 238 (La. 2022), McQueen v. Green, 2022 IL 126666 (Ill. 2022), JTL Grp., Inc. v. Gray-Dockham, 2022 WY 67 (Wyo. 2022), Sheppard v. Geneva Rock, 2021 UT 31 (Utah 2021), Ramon v. Nebo Sch. Dist., 2021 UT 30 (Utah 2021), Quynn v. Hulsey, 850 S.E.2d 725 (Ga. 2020), Community Health v. McKenzie, 185 N.E.3d 368, 377 (Ind. 2017), Sedam v. 2JR Pizza Ent. LLC, 84 N.E.3d 1174 (Ind. 2017), Fox v. Mize, 428 P.3d 314 (Ok. 2018), MV Transport, Inc. v. Allgeier, 433 S.W.3d 324 (Ky. 2014), Diaz v. Carcamo, 51 Cal. 4th 1148 (2011), James v. Kelly Trucking, 377 S.C. 628 (S.C. 2008), McHaffie v.

this category can include safety compliance businesses, brokers, and shippers.[4] The failure to properly qualify a driver as fit to drive can lead to a negligent hiring or negligent supervision claim.[5] If a dispatcher ordered a driver to meet a delivery schedule that was impossible without speeding,[6] that person's negligence could be a proximate cause of the crash that resulted. Similarly, a safety manager may be personally liable for negligent training that, had the training been correct, would have prevented the crash. Sometimes groups of high-ranking management officials enact and enforce company policies that contribute to unsafe business practices. Try to think of the matter from the perspective of the truck driver. Who else made decisions that contributed to the crash? Consider, also, negligent hiring or negligent selection claims. If the truck driver or truck company was unfit, did the person or entity who selected the truck driver or company choose negligently?

In addition, some people are "vicariously" liable (not directly liable) for the direct negligence of others. The most common legal theory of vicarious liability is *respondeat superior*—that the master or employer is liable for the negligence of the employee or servant.[7] Some defendants will argue that a master cannot be vicariously liable for a servant's negligence if the servant is not named as a defendant and found liable, so, in some jurisdictions, naming the servant (or the servant's estate) as a defendant may be a procedural and practical requirement.[8] Keep in mind that a party can be deemed a "master" or "employer" for purposes of negligence law even if not in fact treated that way for purposes of tax law, labor law, or workers compensation law, and vice versa. Stated another way, the Internal Revenue Service and the U.S. Department of Labor have their own definitions of who counts as an "employee" for purposes of the laws they administer and, while those agencies' policies and regulations may be helpful to understanding the issues at stake in different contexts, they are not

---

Bunch, 891 S.W.2d 822 (Mo. 1995), Clark v. Stewart, 126 Ohio St. 263 (1933). See Chapter 9 in this book by J.J. Burns on this subject. *See also* D.J. Young, III, *Override the "Business Immunity Rule,"* TRIAL MAGAZINE 21 (Feb. 2023); MICHAEL J. LEIZERMAN & RENA LEIZERMAN, LITIGATING TRUCK ACCIDENT CASES §§ 8.2–8,3, 9.8, 10.9 (Thomson Reuters, 2021); J.J. Burns, *Respondeat Superior as an Affirmative Defense: How Employers Immunize Themselves from Direct Negligence Claims*, 109(4) MICH. L. REV. (2011).

4. MICHAEL J. LEIZERMAN, ET AL., LITIGATING TRUCK ACCIDENT CASES §§ 9.4–9.8 (Danvers, MA: AAJ Press/Thomson Reuters: Danvers, MA, 2022).

5. *See* 49 C.F.R. pts. 380 and 391. *See also* the driver qualification file required by 49 C.F.R. § 391.51 and the driver investigation history file required by 49 C.F.R. § 391.53. Driver disqualification regulations appear in various places, including 49 C.F.R. Part 382 and 49 C.F.R Part 383 Subpart D, including Tables I through IV to 49 C.F.R. § 383.51.

6. 49 C.F.R. § 392.6.

7. There are other possibilities that do not depend on a traditional master–servant relationship. *See* RESTATEMENT OF THE LAW, TORTS 2D §§ 410–429.

8. *See, e.g.*, Clawson v. Heights Chiropractic Physicians, LLC, 2022-Ohio-4154, 170 Ohio St. 3d 451, 214 N.E.3d 540 (Ohio 2022). This decision explains the nature of the legal debate. It has resulted in plaintiffs' attorneys filing suit against numerous employee defendants in order to avoid a procedural defect. This, in turn, has resulted in an amendment to the law in 2024 as a solution. *See* OHIO REV. CODE § 2307.241.

determinative in tort law.[9] Similarly, the fact that two parties to an agreement have labeled their relationship as that of hirer and independent contractor is not determinative of whether, in fact, the relationship is that of employer and employee—a question that turns on an analysis of the facts and circumstances. On the other hand, the definition of "employee" and "employer" for purposes of the Federal Motor Carrier Safety Regulations tends to impact the state tort law outcome on vicarious liability of trucking companies for the negligence of their drivers—even those that are "independent contractors" for purposes of contract law or tax law. This is because the statutory and regulatory definitions of "employee" specifically include "independent contractors" within the definition of "employee."[10]

9. When hirers "misclassify workers," the result can be under-collection of income and employment taxes, avoidance of the provision of worker benefits and workplace labor law protections, and other problems. For tax and labor definitions and tests of who is an "employee," *see, e.g.*, 26 U.S.C. § 1402(d), 26 U.S.C. § 3121(d), 26 C.F.R. § 31.3121(d)-1 for purposes of tax law; 29 U.S.C. § 203(d), (e), and (g) and 29 C.F.R. §§ 795.105(b) and 795.110 (89 FR 1638 effective Mar. 11, 2024) in the context of the Fair Labor Standards Act (focusing on the economic reality of whether the worker is "economically dependent" on the hirer for work). When deciding the line between "employees" and "independent contractors" in some contexts the Supreme Court has favored an "economic reality" of the relationship versus wooden common law factors. *See* NLRB v. Hearst Publications, 322 U.S. 111 (1944), U.S. v. Silk, 331 U.S. 704 (1947), Rutherford Food Corp. v. McComb, 331 U.S. 722 (1947), Bartels v. Birmingham, 332 U.S. 126 (1947), Goldberg v. Whitaker House Co-op, Inc., 366 U.S. 28 (1961); Nationwide Mutual Ins. Co. v. Darden, 503 U.S. 318 (1992).

10. 49 U.S.C. §§ 31101 and 31132, and 49 C.F.R. §§ 390.5 and 390.5T. In the context of federal motor carrier transportation, the definition of a "motor carrier" can include any individual person or corporations, companies, or partnerships. 49 U.S.C. § 13102(14) and (18) and 1 U.S.C. § 1. Thus, coupled with the definition of "employee," there arises the "statutory employment doctrine" in trucking negligence cases. *See* Michael J. Leizerman, et al., Litigating Truck Accident Cases §§ 3.1-3.2 (Danvers, MA: AAJ Press/Thomson Reuters: Danvers, MA, 2022). As a matter of state law, the general rule that employers are not liable for the negligence of independent contractors does not apply when the duty is imposed by statute or franchise. Pusey v. Bator, 94 Ohio St. 3d 275, 278, 762 N.E.2d 968, 2002-Ohio-795; Restatement of the Law, Torts 2d, § 411(b), *cf.* §§ 417 and 424 (both of which are related to § 411(b)). Motor carriers registered with the U.S. Department of Transportation must comply with commercial vehicle safety regulations. 49 U.S.C. §§ 31134(a) and 14101(a). Motor carriers must either use their own or leased vehicles, have control over them, and be responsible for them, even as to leased-on drivers and equipment. 49 U.S.C. §§ 13902(i) and 14102, 49 C.F.R. § 376.12. *See* Puga v. RCX Sols., Inc., 922 F.3d 285, 292 (5th Cir. 2019), Simpson v. Empire Truck Lines, Inc., 571 F.3d 475, 476 (5th Cir. 2009), Zamalloa v. Hart, 31 F.3d 911, 917 (9th Cir. 1994), Puga v. About Tyme Transp., Inc., 227 F. Supp. 3d 760, 763–64 (S.D. Tex. 2017), *aff'd on proc. grounds,* 922 F.3d. 285 (5th Cir. 2019), Edwards v. McElliotts Trucking, LLC, 268 F. Supp. 3d 867, 879 (S.D. Va. 2017), Bays v. Summitt Trucking, LLC, 691 F. Supp. 2d 725, 732 (W.D. Ky. 2010). Not all courts agree about the existence or extent of this doctrine. This is explained in *Morales v. OK Trans. Inc.*, 2024 U.S. Dist. LEXIS 57475, 2024 WL 1348405 (S.D. Tx. 2024). The policy reasons for the federal laws that form the basis of the statutory employment doctrine favor recognition of the statutory employer doctrine in multi-business cases. "By eliminating the common law employee/independent contractor distinction, the definition ['employee'] serves to discourage motor carriers from using the independent contractor relationship to avoid liability exposure at the expense of the public." Consumers Cnty. Mut. Ins. v. PW & Sons Trucking Inc., 307 F.3d 362, 366 (5th Cir. 2002). When analyzing this subject, keep in mind that in the context of labor law, "employ" is defined to include "to suffer or permit to work." 29 U.S.C. § 203(g).

In the ground-transportation industry, it is very common for the businesses reaping the financial rewards of trucking transactions to attempt to shield themselves through creative layers of corporate entities and contractual relationships. The key word here is "attempt." There are valid uses of such entities and relationships, and there are invalid uses. The law does not reward the invalid uses. Doctrines like "borrowed servant," "loaned servant," "piercing the corporate veil," "alter ego," "joint venture," "joint employer," "dual employer," "common law partnership," "aiding and abetting," "civil conspiracy," "entity," and "enterprise" liability may be applicable. Think about which corporate entity or collection of entities comprise the "business" that received the financial benefits of the driver's labors. The "business" that is vicariously liable could be a collection of corporate entities under one corporate umbrella or could be a set of contractually related companies each of which could not logically exist without the teamwork of other entities comprising the "business."[11] It is naïve for counsel on either side of the case to assume that each separate limited liability company or each separate corporation necessarily is a separate business. As much as we are trained in law school to believe that liability stops within the boundaries of a separate limited liability company or separate corporation, there are exceptions to that rule that may apply in your case. This area of corporate law is complicated, varies by state, and is developing.[12] It is time-consuming and expensive to litigate. Significant legal research is necessary. Significant discovery is required. When faced with these claims, defendants will risk losing credibility with the judge and jury if they attempt merely to elevate corporate formalities over business realities.

In analyzing scenarios where vicarious liability might be involved, if there is going to be a legal battle, it likely will be over the meaning of words like "master," "servant," "employer," "employee," "employ," "control," and "business" or "enterprise." Statutory and case law definitions of these words may be helpful.

Step 1: Identify Drivers and Owners Using Police Reports and/or News Articles

For attorneys on both sides of the case, it is important to ascertain who was driving each of the vehicles, and who owns each of the vehicles. While police reports often are the first and best sources of this information, sometimes the news is reported before the law enforcement reports are available. You should

11. State law varies significantly on this subject. Whether this situation could apply in your case depends on the status of applicable law, the facts of your case, and whether you can persuade the court of the merits of your argument. Do not make an argument for an application or extension of the law unless you have a sound good-faith basis. Similarly, do not make arguments against the same unless you can do so in good faith.

12. An entire treatise is dedicated to liabilities arising by and through intercorporate relationships. Blumberg, Strasser et al., Blumberg on Corporate Groups 2d. (Wolters Kluwer, 2024). *See also* David N. Nissenberg, The Law of Commercial Trucking: Damages to Persons and Property, 4th ed. Vol. 1 §§ 7.01–7.15, 9.04 (New York: Matthew Bender, 2023).

check both sources whenever you have both because, sometimes, one or the other is incorrect or incomplete.

News reports can be helpful for identifying witnesses, drivers, and the owner of the commercial motor vehicle. Even if the news reports do not state the names in the narrative, they do often contain sufficiently good photographs of the CMV that one can identify the business responsible for the CMV's operations from the name and numbers posted on the side of the CMV. Specifically, almost every CMV used in interstate commerce must have a "USDOT Number" posted on the front sides of the vehicle. Often there is an "MC" or "Motor Carrier" number, too. You can search these numbers on the Federal Motor Carrier Safety Administration's website.[13] Trailers, especially intermodal trailers, have identifying information, too.[14] Some websites allow searching of the intermodal trailer identification numbers. Some vehicles have the license numbers of state regulatory agencies posted on them, and the identity of the owners or operators of those vehicles can be ascertained from those state agencies.

Police reports[15] must be requested in accordance with applicable public records requesting procedure governing the jurisdiction that created the police reports. This is different in different places. A call to the local law enforcement agency that has jurisdiction over the location of the crash is one way to start. Frequently more than one law enforcement agency responds to a crash scene. You need to obtain the reports from each such law enforcement agency. Police reports usually contain the name and address of the driver and passengers of each vehicle involved in the crash. They usually contain the identification of the owners of the vehicles involved in the crash. They usually contain information about whether the vehicles were insured and the identity of the insurance companies. If the CMV has a trailer, it frequently is owned by and insured by different parties than the CMV tractor, so look for this in the police reports. If the other kinds of emergency responders prepared reports, like EMS and fire departments, you should obtain them.

Step 2: Issue Notices of Representation and Evidence Preservation Letters

The issuance of notices of representation and evidence preservation letters to the driver and businesses identified in Step 1, and their insurance companies, sometimes results in communications that point to other parties that may be liable.

13. https://safer.fmcsa.dot.gov/CompanySnapshot.aspx.

14. For intermodal equipment, *see* 49 C.F.R. § 390.21T.

15. These include those of local law enforcement, state highway patrols, and "Driver Vehicle Examination Reports" prepared by special agents of the Federal Motor Carrier Safety Administration. *See* 49 C.F.R. § 396.9 and Pt. 390 App. B.

Step 3: Search for Related Parties

If the tortfeasor driver was driving in furtherance of the employer's business, the business is vicariously liable for the driver's negligence. The business identified in Step 1 might not be the only possibility, nor is it always the correct party. Taking the names that you have obtained in Steps 1 and 2, conduct a significant internet search. The CMV may be held in an entity that is a sham attempt to compartmentalize liability in that entity. Who owns the sham entity? Who controls it? Who benefits from it? Take the names that you have and search the applicable secretaries of state or state corporation commissions' records. Consider using a relational database service like Lexis, or having a licensed private investigator conduct a search. The Security and Exchange Commission database can be a wealth of information that shows relationships between and among companies under one corporate umbrella. Use the Federal Motor Carrier Safety Administration's SAFER online database to obtain addresses of possible defendants. Regular case law searches on Westlaw or Lexis sometimes turn up helpful leads. Check Pacer.gov and major state court websites of the place where you think the defendants can be found. Sometimes there are extensive records in court online docket systems that expose related liable parties. If you can obtain motor vehicle registration information based on license plates or vehicle identification numbers, you should obtain that information in your search for liable parties.

Once you have identified the names of parties from this step and the previous two steps, check the websites for each entity. Often, they share their website with all of their corporate affiliates. Often, the websites of the corporate affiliates are linked. Often, you will find common names used by all the various entities—a sign that they might not be truly separate legal entities for purposes of tort liability. Always use internet mapping services to obtain sky views and street views of the defendants' business locations. It is not uncommon for the signage at such locations to be different from the information obtained in Steps 1 and 2. These other names may be the truly liable parties.

Step 4: Crash Vehicle Inspection

Once the plaintiff's attorney sends the evidence preservation letter, usually the defendant retains an attorney who contacts the plaintiff's attorney. This is the time to schedule the inspection of the crash vehicles—before they have been released from the impound lots. When inspecting the CMV, it is important to reconcile the information gathered in Steps 1 through 3 with the physical evidence. Do the records match the ownership information marked on the CMV? If there is a trailer, does anything on it identify its owner? Also, obtain all paperwork and electronic records found in the vehicles during the vehicle inspections.

Obtain the bill of lading. Most CMVs contain paperwork concerning the freight that the CMV was transporting, or the freight that an empty CMV either recently delivered or is about to pick up. Usually, the relevant document is called a "bill of lading"[16] or "manifest," but other types of documents are sometimes

16. *See* 49 C.F.R. pts. 373 and 1035, 49 U.S.C. § 14706, and 49 U.S.C. ch. 801.

used, like a "freight bill" or "expense bill." Be sure to obtain copies of all such documents found in the truck during the crash inspection. The police often do not gather this information during their investigation. These documents identify the owner of the freight and the name of the carrier that was hired to transport the freight. These documents sometimes identify other potentially liable parties like shippers, third party logistics companies, or freight brokers. Often there are other kinds of documents, like paper time sheets (hours of service logs), instructions, notes, vehicle maintenance information, human resources manuals, safety manuals, and repair receipts. Any of these papers could reveal the identities of potentially liable parties. All labels on the truck and trailer should be noted to the extent they identify parties involved in the ownership, maintenance, and operation of the vehicle. All items having possible useful information should be photographed or scanned during the inspection.

Obtain all electronic records from the vehicles. Most vehicles have computer equipment on board that records pre-crash information. For automobiles, some of this information is contained within the vehicle's own computer systems, including the engine control module or engine control unit and the air bag control module. Sometimes additional information is contained within the vehicle information or entertainment system. For CMVs, the engine control module should be downloaded, as should the electronic logging device and the vehicle telematics system. Trailers may have their own tracking devices. Driver and company cell phones may be found in the vehicles during the inspections. While the electronic information contained within all of these devices can be useful for proving negligence, contributory negligence, or comparative fault, it has several possibilities for identifying other potentially liable parties. First, some of the information may include video—video that could show the acts of other drivers. Second, if there was a vehicle mechanical failure of some kind, it could open up the possibility for a products liability case against the vehicle manufacturer. Third, it can lead to the identification of persons supervising or controlling the truck driver.

Normally, attorneys send expert witnesses to the vehicle crash inspections. The attorneys should send someone capable of accessing and copying the electronic records stored in the various vehicle systems.

Step 5: Use Discovery to Identify Other Liable Parties

Once suit is filed, discovery can be used to identify additional liable parties, but this only works if the lawsuit is filed early enough to allow for discovery and adding additional defendants before the expiration of the statute of limitations.

Discovery abuse is a real and growing problem. Do not assume that parties will cooperate with discovery in good faith. While it is unethical and sometimes illegal, some attorneys will aid and abet their clients or collude with their clients to stonewall the discovery process. Ironically, this can lead to attorney liability or discipline[17] for interfering with the case. Even if those consequences do not

17. *See* American Bar Association's Model Rules of Professional Conduct, rules 3.2 (expediting litigation), 3.3 (candor toward the tribunal), 3.4 (fairness to opposing party and counsel).

arise, attorneys involved in discovery abuse can lose credibility with the judge. Regardless of the presence or absence of misconduct, discovery takes time, and lawsuits filed earlier are more likely to result in discovery that identifies other tortfeasors and other vicariously liable parties.

Discovery should be used to identify every person involved in the movement of the CMV and the freight within it. Anyone involved in the supervision of the transportation of the freight, or the safety of the operations can be directly liable to the extent of that supervisor's own share of the negligence.

Discovery often reveals related parties because the names of related parties are contained within discovery responses—either in interrogatory answers, on documents produced, or in deposition answers. The related parties might have significant control over the tortfeasor or may derive significant financial benefits from the business of the tortfeasor. Sometimes the true motor carrier in control of the CMV and driver are intentionally obscured. The true motor carrier, however, is the one that should bear the financial risk of the crash because it reaps the profits of the transportation.

Sometimes insurance policies are discoverable. Frequently they name multiple persons or entities as insured under the same policy. The fact that these parties share an insurance policy can be strong evidence that one or more of them has some role in the "business" that placed the CMV driver on the road. These other entities may be directly or vicariously liable for the negligence that occurred.

Use depositions to clarify the identity and roles of potentially additional liable parties so that the complaint can be amended in good faith to include all such persons.

A Word of Caution

While there may be sound reasons for suing everyone whose conduct was a proximate cause of the crash, there may be strategic reasons that are unique to some jurisdictions for not doing so. For example, if the applicable comparative fault rule requires the plaintiff's negligence to be less than any of the defendants' fault in order to avoid being contributorily barred, the mathematical consequences of such a rule will lead to a decision to keep the number of defendants to a minimum when there are concerns about the plaintiff's fault.[18] Another consideration is whether one desires the case to be heard in state court or federal court.[19]

---

18. *See, e.g.*, Hansen v. St. Paul Metro Treatment Center, Inc., 609 N.W.2d 625, 627 (Minn. App. 2000). *See also* Victor E. Schwartz, Comparative Negligence Ch. 3 (6th ed., Matthew Bender, 2019).

19. *See* 28 U.S.C. §§ 1332 and 1441(b)(2). Note that if there is both an in-state and out-of-state defendant, some federal courts allow what is colloquially known as "snap removal" from the state court. If you represent the plaintiff, it is important to know how your jurisdiction handles the "snap removal" situation before the case is filed in state court. If you represent the defendant, it is important to know whether and when "snap removal" might allow the case to be removed to federal court.

Conclusion

The identification of the potentially responsible parties is much more complicated than simply identifying and suing the truck driver and the driver's employer. Everyone whose conduct fell below the standard of care for a person in that position under the circumstances who was a proximate cause of the crash may be held liable. The identification of potentially liable parties is concerned with who has financial liability as a matter of tort law, statute, or contract for the negligence of those whose conduct fell below the standard of care.

The identification of other responsible and/or liable parties can be beneficial to either or both sides of the case. Plaintiffs can add defendants. Defendants can file crossclaims and third-party claims to bring the newly discovered parties into the litigation. The search for justice is enhanced when each party that played a role in the crash is held accountable for that party's own share of the liability.

CHAPTER 9

Motor Carrier Liability for Failure to Properly Hire, Train, and Supervise Drivers

J.J. Burns, Esq.

Introduction

A significant number of truck crashes are caused by driver "errors" that are a direct result of a motor carrier failing to follow reasonable hiring, retention, training, and supervision practices.

While it may certainly be true that the individual truck driver should know better than to commit the error(s) that may have contributed to cause a crash, an individual driver making an unreasonable mistake or a poor decision is typically not the root cause of the problem; such driver error is frequently a symptom of a much larger problem that reflects an industry that has become overcompetitive, makes unrealistic demands of its employees, and cuts too many corners. The reality is that most truck drivers are salt-of-the-earth-type people who are working very hard to try to put food on the table for their families. Individual truck drivers lack the economic power to have a real say in job conditions and are usually just following the lead of the management of their motor carrier employer.

Crashes caused by truck driver error are frequently predictable and preventable. Some of the more responsible members of the trucking industry have acknowledged the responsibility of the industry to deal squarely with the issues by incorporating responsible practices such as comprehensive driver qualification, training, sleep apnea screening, payment for all time worked, sincere driver log auditing protocols, establishment of crash prevention as a company goal from the top down, measurement of driver health and wellness, assessment of risk factors, and involvement of the drivers and their families in solving the pervasive problem of truck driver fatigue.

The reality is that the truck driver is not solely to blame in the circumstances of many truck crashes. Often the truck driver's employer has its own fault. Underlying factors contributing to the employer's fault include structural problems in the trucking industry like diminishing profit margins, fragmentation in the industry, and insufficient regulation. The problem continues to be fed by companies that are desperately chasing an ever-diminishing profit margin, and an industry in denial. This is not to say that there are no "enlightened" trucking companies. There are several industry leaders that participate in safety conferences and are setting "best practices" standards; but the industry itself is so fragmented that no one company has enough market power to effectively set standards on its own. Unfortunately, for far too long, government regulators have failed to address the issues, and when they have tried, the political force of the industry has stopped most significant safety efforts.

In a particular claim, of course, the industry cannot be put on trial, but the involved trucking company can and should be. In addition to the "best practices" that have been set by the more reasonable, responsible companies as reasonable industry standards, various regulations require motor carriers to take steps to make sure their drivers are operating safely. For example, in the fatigue context, there is a regulation that requires a company to take reasonable steps to make sure that it does not allow its drivers to operate commercial motor vehicles when they are too tired to drive safely. 49 C.F.R. § 392.3 provides in part:

> No driver shall operate a commercial motor vehicle, and a motor carrier shall not require or *permit a driver to operate a commercial motor vehicle, while the driver's ability or alertness is so impaired, or so likely to become impaired, through fatigue,* illness, or any other cause, *as to make it unsafe for him/her to begin or continue to operate the commercial motor vehicle.*[1]

Other regulations require a variety of safety checks by motor carriers. For example, § 391.11(b)(3) prohibits a motor carrier from "require[ing] or permit[ing] an unqualified driver from operating a commercial motor vehicle." In order for a driver to be "qualified," the motor carrier must establish that the driver "can by reason of experience, training, or both, safely operate the type of commercial motor vehicle he/she operates."

The question in these kinds of regulations becomes: what does it mean when a regulation says a company shall not "permit" a driver to operate a commercial motor vehicle in violation of the regulation? The answer is found in the interpretations to another regulation. 49 C.F.R. § 395.3 is the regulation regarding the maximum driving time for semi drivers. That regulation also prohibits a company from "permitting or requiring" its drivers to operate a commercial motor vehicle in violation of the regulation. In the Department of Transportation Interpretations to this regulation, under question 8 of the Interpretations is the following:

> Question 8: Are carriers liable for the actions of their employees even though the carrier contends that it did not require or permit the violations to occur?

1. Emphasis added.

> Guidance: Yes. Carriers are liable for the action of their employees. Neither intent to commit, nor actual knowledge of, a violation is a necessary element of that liability. *Carriers "permit" violations* of the hours of service regulations by their employees *if they fail to have in place management systems that effectively prevent such violations.*[2]

That is the answer: a company "permits" its drivers to operate in violation of the regulations when the company "fail[s] to have in place management systems that effectively prevent such violations."[3]

What management system(s) actually will effectively prevent a driver from driving in violation of a particular regulation? It is clearly not enough to give drivers a copy of the regulations and tell them never to drive in violation of the regulations. The "management system(s)" motor carriers must have in place concern the motor carrier's hiring, training, and supervision policies and practices.

In a variety of states, negligent hiring, training, and/or supervision claims against a motor carrier are subject to dismissal where the motor carrier employer admits that it is responsible for the negligence of its driver.[4] This "rule" is sometimes called the "*McHaffie* rule," the "*Armenta* rule," the "business immunity rule," or the "claim preemption rule." The *McHaffie* rule is problematic for a number of reasons. Fortunately, its application is being rejected more and more by courts;[5] unfortunately, it still poses a significant threat to legitimate claims against motor carriers in a number of jurisdictions.

"Direct" Negligence Claims against an Employer

Conceptually, the most important aspect of claims like negligent entrustment, hiring, retention, supervision, and training is that they concern allegations of the employer's negligence that is related to, but *separate from*, the negligence of the driver in causing the crash. The principal negligence asserted in this kind of claim is not imputed from the driver to the employer; instead, the focus of the cause of action is the separate breach of an independent duty of the motor carrier.[6] This is in stark contrast to claims based on vicarious liability, where the

---

2. https://www.fmcsa.dot.gov/regulations/hours-service/are-carriers-liable-actions-their-employees-even-though-carrier-contends (emphasis added).

3. *Id.*

4. *See, e.g.*, Diaz v. Carcamo, 51 Cal. 4th 1148 (Cal. 2011); Wise v. Fiberglass Sys., 718 P.2d 1178 (Idaho 1986); Community Health v. McKenzie, 185 N.E.3d 368 (Ind. 2022); Houlihan v. McCall, 197 Md. 130 (Md. 1950); McHaffie v. Bunch, 891 S.W.2d 822 (Mo. 1995); Johnson v. Lamb, 273 NC 701 (N.C. 1968); Bogdanski v. Budzik, 408 P.3d 1156 (Wy. 2018).

5. *See, e.g.*, Bruck v. Jim Walter Corp., 470 So. 2d 1141 (Ala. 1985); Brown v. Romero, 2021 CO 67 (Col. 2021); McQueen v. Green, 2022 IL 126666 (Ill. 2022); Marquis v. State Farm, 265 Kan. 317 (Kan. 1998); MV Transport, Inc. v. Allgeier, 433 S.W.3d 324 (Ky. 2014); Martin v. Thomas, 346 So. 3d 238 (La. 2022); Clark v. Stewart, 126 Ohio St. 263 (Ohio 1933); James v. Kelly Trucking, 377 S.C. 628 (S.C. 20008); Roman v. Nebo School Dist., 2021 UT 30 (Utah 2021).

6. *See, e.g.*, Allen v. Toledo, 167 Cal. Rptr. 270, 274 (Cal. App. 1980); Connes v. Molalla Transp. Sys., Inc., 831 P.2d 1316 (Colo. 1992); Ridgeway v. Whisman, 435 S.E.2d 624, 626 (Ga. Ct. App.

employer need not have breached any duty to be held responsible.[7] In vicarious liability situations, the employer is liable for the misconduct of its driver because courts have made a "public policy determination that liability for acts committed within the scope of employment should be allocated to the employer as a cost of engaging in that business."[8] Alternatively, in what we call "direct" negligence claims, the employer is liable because of its own misconduct.[9] In other words, liability for these direct claims "is not based upon any rule of the law of principal and agent or master and servant. It is a special application of the general rules stated in the Restatement of Torts."[10] If a plaintiff cannot demonstrate independent negligence on the part of the employer, the plaintiff cannot prevail in a direct negligence action.

Nevertheless, many courts occasionally treat direct negligence claims as if they were vicarious claims. This seems to happen most frequently when courts are presented with the situation where a plaintiff alleges both a vicarious liability claim and a direct negligence claim against an employer.[11] In these cases, some courts assert that claims like negligent entrustment and negligent hiring simply represent alternative avenues for holding an employer vicariously liable for a driver's conduct (and these courts often assert that these claims are, therefore, superfluous in those instances).[12] These courts reason that since claims like negligent entrustment are vicarious, and "[t]he fault of the employer for negligent entrustment . . . [is] derived from the negligence of the employee,"[13] the negligence of the employer cannot exceed the negligence of the employee. Put differently, this view recognizes that the negligence of the employer may be relevant, but once it is established, the fact of such negligence simply means that the employer stands in the shoes of the negligent employee. The difference between the two positions in some cases can be quite subtle—indeed, in some circumstances, there will be no practical difference—but in other cases, the difference can be critical. The main point of disagreement centers on whose

---

1993); Kansas State Bank & Trust Co. v. Specialized Transp. Servs. Inc., 819 P.2d 587, 598 (Kan. 1991); Neale v. Wright, 585 A.2d 196, 199 (Md. App. 1989); Lim v. Interstate Sys. Steel Div., 435 N.W.2d 830, 832 (Minn. App. 1989); Plummer v. Henry, 171 S.E.2d 330, 332 (N.C. App. 1969); Williamson v. Eclipse Motor Lines, Inc., 62 N.E.2d 339, 341 (Ohio 1945); Ferry v. Fisher, 709 A.2d 399, 403 (Penn. Sup. Ct. 1998); Ali v. Fisher, 145 S.W.3d 557, 564 (Tenn. 2004); Green v. Tex. Electrical Wholesalers, Inc., 651 S.W.2d 4, 6–7 (Tex. App. 1982).

7. The common law principle of *respondeat superior* makes an employer vicariously liable for torts committed by its employees in furtherance of the employer's business. *See, e.g.*, Rosenthal & Co. v. Commodity Futures Trading Comm'n, 802 F.2d 963, 966 (7th Cir. 1986) ("[I]n legalese, it 'imputes' the employee's negligence to his employer. . . .").

8. Fahrendorff v. North Homes, Inc., 597 N.W.2d 905, 910 (Minn. 1999).

9. *See, e.g.*, Kansas State Bank & Trust Co. v. Specialized Transp. Serv's, Inc., 819 P.2d 587, 598 (Kan. 1991).

10. Restatement (Second) of Agency § 213, cmt. a (Am. L. Inst. 1958).

11. *See, e.g.*, Willis v. Hill, 159 S.E.2d 145, 151 (Ga. Ct. App. 1967), *rev'd on other grounds*, 161 S.E.2d 281 *Ga. 1968); McHaffie v. Bunch, 891 S.W.2d 822, 826 (Mo. 1995).

12. *Id.*

13. Campa v. Gordon, 2002 U.S. Dist. LEXIS 15032, at *3–4 (N.D. Ill. Case No. 01 C 50441, Apr. 14, 2002).

negligence is to be compared. The direct view focuses on the negligence of the employer; the vicarious view focuses on the negligence of the driver.

The view that any of these direct negligence claims are vicarious is problematic for several reasons. First of all, many of the same courts that treat direct negligence claims as vicarious claims in those cases where a plaintiff alleges both vicarious and direct liability turn right around and recognize them as non-vicarious where a plaintiff alleges only direct liability.[14]

Second, this kind of analysis generally ignores the reality that negligence on the part of the employee is actually not required for a successful direct negligence action against the employer. It is certainly true that employee negligence is an essential element of claims like negligent entrustment and hiring most of the time; however, there are a variety of fact patterns where an employer may be found to be negligent even where its employee was not. We will address some of these possibilities later in the chapter; for now, it is necessary to point out that since an employer can be found negligent absent negligence on the part of its employee, it simply cannot be that the employer's negligence is necessarily derived from the employee driver's negligence in a direct negligence action.[15]

A similar complication arises where there exists the possibility of punitive damages.[16] The vicarious view either has to deny such damages (unless the employee also acted with gross negligence or recklessness)[17] or create another exception in some instances for this class of torts.[18] If courts deny the possibility of punitive damages based on the employer's own gross negligence or recklessness, the core purposes of punitive damages are thwarted.[19] If they create another exception that is comparatively preferable, they make the litigation unnecessarily complex and practically difficult. Of course, the direct view has no problem contemplating the possibility of punitive damages where such conduct by an employer was a proximate cause of a plaintiff's injury.

Third, when courts and commentators argue that direct negligence actions are vicarious, they are probably simply confusing the imputation of negligent conduct with the general requirement of proximate cause. This confusion is likely the result of the nature of direct negligence claims in that they are almost

---

14. For example, *compare Willis*, 159 S.E.2d at 151, *with Ridgeway*, 435 S.E.2d at 626. Also, *compare* Rosell v. Cent. W. Motor Stages, Inc., 89 S.W.3d 643, 657 (Tex. App. 2002), *and* Loom Craft Carpet Mills, Inc. v. Gorrell, 823 S.W.2d 431, 432 (Tex. App. 1992) *with Green*, 651 S.W.2d at 6, and Bedford v. Moore, 166 S.W.3d 454 (Tex. App. 2005).

15. For those situations where the employee may not be found to be negligent, but where the employer is nonetheless negligent and a proximate cause of the plaintiff's injury, proponents of the vicarious view—where they recognize the viability of these torts in these situations at all—have to develop a strange exception to the general rule that negligence in these cases is imputed from the employee to the employer. Essentially, they have to say, "where the employee is negligent, only that degree of negligence is imputed to the employer; but where the employee is non-negligent, the employer is responsible for his own negligence." This seems unnecessarily complicated and underscores the error of the "vicarious" view.

16. We will revisit this issue later in this chapter.

17. *See, e.g.*, Hood v. Dealers. Transp. Co., 459 F. Supp. 684, 686 (N.D. Miss. 1978).

18. *See, e.g.*, Clooney v. Geeting, 352 So. 2d 1216, 1220 (Fla. Dist. Ct. App. 1977).

19. *See* notes 123–25 and accompanying text in this chapter.

always *causally* dependent on employee conduct. Crucially, however, "[t]he employer's *negligence* . . . is independent of the employee's misconduct and the employer's liability under *respondeat superior*."[20] In other words, the driver-employee's action or omission may be a necessary condition of the employer's liability, but only because some conduct on the part of the employee is required to establish proximate cause. Admittedly, absent special circumstances, direct negligence claims are usually difficult to prove absent negligent conduct on the part of the employee. But, "this is not because non-negligence on the employee's part results in no imputed negligence; rather, the direct negligence claim is difficult in those circumstances because a finding of employee non-negligence [usually] means that there is no proximate cause, no connection that links the employer's independent negligence with the plaintiff's injuries."[21] All things considered in these cases, it seems more reasonable that the employer is responsible for its own negligence in entrusting, hiring, retaining, supervising, or training, not simply for the negligence of another.

It appears that the view that direct claims are superfluous when the "scope of employment" issue is admitted is an unfortunate anachronism. The view (and attendant rule that excludes "direct" claims) was developed under a related principle of law (contributory negligence) which principle later developed so as "to have left the old rule no more than a remnant of abandoned doctrine."[22] Although there have always been problems with the logic, fairness, and consequences of the rationale of the rule (excluding direct claims when "scope of the employment" is admitted by a driver's employer) the rule at least made some degree of sense when, under contributory negligence principles, a defendant was either 100 percent liable or 0 percent liable to the plaintiff, no matter what. Under more modern principles of tort liability (such as comparative fault), the rule makes no sense whatsoever, is blatantly unfair to the truck driver and to the victim, and runs 180 degrees counter to our tort and judicial systems' policies of holding negligent wrongdoers accountable for the damages they cause and discouraging wrongful conduct that causes harm to others. While a number of courts have abandoned this position recently, this anachronism is still present in numerous jurisdictions.

Some courts and commentators seem to split the difference on the question of whether claims like negligent entrustment are direct or vicarious. According to them, claims like negligent entrustment are neither direct nor vicarious: "The liability is *derivative* because it depends upon a subsequent wrongful act or omission."[23] Such cases are said to "involve wrongful conduct both by the

20. Brent Powell, Note, *Submitting Theories of Respondeat Superior and Negligent Entrustment/Hiring*, 61 Mo. L. Rev. 155, 159 (1996) (emphasis added).

21. J.J. Burns, Note, *Respondeat Superior as an Affirmative Defense: How Employers Immunize Themselves from Direct Negligence Claims*, 109 Mich. L. Rev. 657, 668 (2010–2011).

22. *See* Planned Parenthood of Southeast Pennsylvania v. Casey, 505 U.S. 833, 855, 112 S. Ct. 2791, 2808, 120 L. Ed. 2d 674 (1992) (cited as a reason to reconsider precedent).

23. William D. Underwood & Michael D. Morrison, *Apportioning Responsibility in Cases Involving Claims of Vicarious, Derivative, or Statutory Liability for Harm Caused by the Conduct of Another*, 55 Baylor L. Rev. 617, 619 (2003) (emphasis added).

person who is derivatively liable and the actor whose wrongful conduct was the direct cause of injury to another."[24] Confusingly, courts in this camp differ on how negligence should be apportioned in such cases, and whether "derivative" claims may accompany a *respondeat superior* claim.[25]

As is often the case, labels such as "vicarious," "direct," and "derivative" can be far more misleading than they are helpful, and they can mean very different things depending on one's jurisdiction, one's judge, and one's particular case. The unclear meanings allow for unclear reasoning and have allowed the perpetuation of legal positions that have outlived their initial rationales. In any event, attorneys need to know how their jurisdictions treat these claims before they file their first pleadings.[26] In some states, torts like negligent entrustment, hiring, and retention have been more clearly defined by courts and/or statute; in other states, the contours of these claims are still vague and unsettled. The casual use of an imprecise label could result in the loss of a claim. Therefore, in briefs, attorneys should clearly define these terms to reduce the risk of confusion.

The Claims

Any clear analysis recognizes that "direct" claims are based on the separate negligence of the employer. In addition to the characteristic of independent employer negligence, these direct negligence claims all share some other features. First, while *respondeat superior* holds employers liable only for employees' wrongful acts committed within the course and scope of employment, direct negligence claims may be pursued even where the driver was not acting within the scope of employment at the time of the wrongful act.[27] Furthermore, the driver need not necessarily be a technical "employee" of the employer.[28] Second, punitive damages may be available in a direct negligence claim.[29] Third, certain defenses that are applicable to *respondeat superior* actions—guest statutes or assumption of the risk—may not be applicable to these claims.[30] And fourth,

24. *Id.*

25. We address these issues later in the book.

26. For example, an allegation of *respondeat superior* by the plaintiff could result in the dismissal of a plaintiff's direct negligence claim; conversely, a defendant's admission of *respondeat superior* could be a strategic move in some states, and a misstep in others.

27. *See* Rodolfo A. Camacho, *How to Avoid Negligent Hiring Litigation*, 14 WHITTIER L. REV. 787, 790–92 (1993); Donald K. Armstrong, Note, *Negligent Hiring and Negligent Entrustment: The Case Against Exclusion*, 52 OR. L. REV. 296, 303 (1972–1973).

28. *See* RESTATEMENT (SECOND) OF TORTS § 409, cmt b (1965) (explaining the exceptions to the general rule that the employer of an independent contractor is not liable for harm caused to another by the negligence of the independent contractor). *But see* Reeves v. Kmart Corp., 582 N.W.2d 841, 846 (Mich. App. 1998) (holding that Michigan has not recognized a duty requiring an employer to exercise care in the selection and retention of an independent contractor).

29. *See, e.g.*, Breeding v. Massey, 378 F.2d 171 (8th Cir. 1967).

30. *See* Armstrong, *supra* note 27, at 304–05.

evidence of a driver's prior bad acts or character is often admissible in these cases to prove negligence on the part of the employer.[31]

More Problems with Labels

Just like shorthand descriptions such as "direct" and "vicarious" can be confusing, ambiguous, and unhelpful, the specific appellations for different kinds of direct negligence claims can be problematic as well.

Regardless of what a direct negligence claim is called, all of them are just ordinary negligence causes of action; the labels (hiring, training, supervision, etc.) simply describe the specific duty at issue. All these claims have the same core negligence requirements: the defendant owed a legal duty to the plaintiff, the defendant breached that duty, the plaintiff suffered damages, and the damages were proximately caused by the defendant's breach.[32] Neither courts nor parties should get too caught up in labels. If a court asserts that its jurisdiction does not recognize the torts of "negligent training" or "negligent supervision," what that actually means (or what it should mean) is that the jurisdiction has not come to recognize the particular duty the plaintiff claims the defendant has. In such a situation, if all the plaintiff needs to do is change the label on the negligence action (or change the description of the defendant's alleged duty), he or she should do just that.

On the other hand, defendants in these cases should pay special attention to the labels plaintiffs use for their claims. A motion to dismiss filed at the pleading stage based on the jurisdiction's rejection (or nonrecognition) of a particular negligence claim label could be an easy win. Even if it does not result in the dismissal of the entire case, the dismissal of a particular unrecognized claim very likely impacts the overall nature of the case and the scope of discovery.

Certainly, some research and analysis is necessary at the pleading stage. Some jurisdictions do not recognize all of these direct claims[33] (or, at least, their labels); a plaintiff may be forced to pursue a negligent hiring claim in a state where negligent entrustment is either not recognized or has been very narrowly interpreted. In particular jurisdictions, one claim may offer tactical or legal advantages that the other does not. Additionally, a plaintiff may lack knowledge of precisely *when* the entrustor/employer breached his duty: if it did not properly screen applicants, a negligent hiring claim is appropriate; if it did not terminate a driver's employment after a series of preventable accidents or incidents, a negligent retention claim may be more fitting. Finally, the direct negligence label that a plaintiff chooses should best fit the facts of the case and thematic elements the plaintiff desires to emphasize. A plaintiff should carefully

31. *See* Camacho, *supra* note 27, at 792–93; Stephen M. Blitz, *Conduct Evidencing Negligent Entrustment Is Provable Despite Admission of Vicarious Liability*, 17 Stan. L. Rev. 539, 542 (1965). This scenario likely will require the use of special jury instructions in order to avoid unfair prejudice to the driver under Evidence Rule 404.

32. Zarzana v. Ashley, 218 S.W.3d 152, 158 (Tex. App. 2007).

33. *See, e.g.*, Gomes v. Univ. of Maine Sys., 304 F. Supp. 2d 117, 133 (D. Maine 2004) (explaining that Maine has not yet recognized the independent tort of negligent supervision).

examine the employer's duty and breach and choose the characterization(s) that is (are) most capable of capturing the story the plaintiff wants to tell.

Negligent Entrustment

The Restatement (Second) of Torts describes negligent entrustment as:

> One who supplies directly or through a third person a chattel for the use of another whom the supplier knows or has reason to know to be likely because of his youth, inexperience, or otherwise, to use it in a manner involving unreasonable risk of physical harm to himself and others whom the supplier should expect to share in or be endangered by its use, is subject to liability for physical harm resulting to them.[34]

Generally, to hold an employer liable for negligent entrustment, a plaintiff must prove that (1) there was entrustment of a chattel; (2) the entrustee was incompetent, inexperienced, or reckless; (3) the entrustor knew[35] or should have known of the incompetence, inexperience, or recklessness of the entrustee; (4) the entrustee's conduct caused the plaintiff's injury; and (5) the entrustee's injurious conduct was the result of the entrustee's incompetence, inexperience, or recklessness.[36]

As is mentioned earlier, the focus of this kind of claim is the employer's negligence that is separate from the driver's negligence. The plaintiff must establish that the entrustor knew or should have known of the driver's incompetence, inexperience, or recklessness. In many cases, this is done in two steps. First, a plaintiff introduces evidence of the driver's character; criminal history; bad judgment; sensory, physical, or mental deficiencies; drug and/or alcohol abuse; previous accidents; and/or other prior bad acts.[37] Alternatively, plaintiff can show that the driver lacked experience, was unlicensed, was underage, or was otherwise incompetent. Second, the plaintiff establishes that the employer actually knew, or should have known, of the driver's character, history, inability, inexperience, and/or lack of capacity. In cases where there is entrustment of a tractor-trailer, a motor carrier has many duties: to inspect the driver's past driving record and previous employment, to determine the driver's driving skills with respect to operating that kind of vehicle, to screen the driver for drugs and alcohol abuse, and/or to examine the driver for other relevant health issues.[38]

---

34. RESTATEMENT (SECOND) OF TORTS § 390. The majority of jurisdictions use this definition of negligent entrustment. *See* West v. East Tennessee Pioneer Oil Co., 172 S.W.3d 545, 555 n.7 (Tenn. 2005).

35. Some jurisdictions require actual knowledge. *See, e.g.*, Pryor v. Brown & Root USA, Inc., 674 So. 2d 45 (Ala. 1995); White v. Inbound Aviation, 82 Cal. Rptr. 2d 71 (Cal. App. 1999); Arkwright v. Taulbee, 546 S.E.2d 335 (Ga. App. 2001); Andes v. Lauer, 399 N.E.2d 990 (Ill. App. 1980); Downs v. Panhandle Eastern Pipeline Co., 694 N.E.2d 1198 (Ind. Ct. App. 1998).

36. *See, e.g.*, Bettis v. United States, 635 F.2d 1144, 1148 (5th Cir. 1981).

37. While the use of this kind of evidence to prove that the driver acted negligently in causing the accident in question is generally barred, it *is* admissible to establish what the entrustor knew or should have known. *See generally* FED. R. EVID. 404(b).

38. *See* Kandel v. Smoker, 783 F. Supp. 948 (D. Md. 1991); Big 3 Motors, Inc. v. Hawie, 895 So. 2d 349 (Ala. Civ. App. 2004); Boyd v. L.G. DeWitt Trucking Co., 405 S.E.2d 914 (1991); North

As is pointed out in more detail later, where the entrustment of a tractor-trailer takes place in an employment setting involving interstate commerce, the Federal Motor Carrier Safety Administration (FMCSA) Regulations—also discussed in more detail later—provide the *minimum standards* for the employment of drivers.[39] Additionally, each state may impose additional requirements (by statute or common law), so long as they are not inconsistent with the federal regulations.[40] If a driver is found to be unfit, and if the employer would have known about such unfitness had they complied with federal and state regulations, this will likely be enough to satisfy the element that the employer knew or should have known that the driver was incompetent, inexperienced, or reckless.

The fifth element of the tort—that the entrustee's injurious conduct was the result of the entrustee's incompetence, inexperience, or recklessness—is a proximate cause requirement, and is shared by the other direct negligence claims as well. In the case of negligent entrustment, this element requires a sufficient nexus between the entrustment (the owner's negligence) and the resulting collision. If the owner entrusts his truck to one the owner knows to be a habitual drunk, and the entrustee gets intoxicated, crashes his truck into another automobile, and injures someone, the resulting injury was clearly within the scope of the risk that was foreseeable (and preventable) by the owner. Proximate cause is satisfied. On the other hand, if the owner entrusted his truck to one with a reputation as a drag racer with a long history of speeding tickets, and the entrustee crashed the truck and injured someone because he or she had a seizure at the wheel (due to a medical condition that the owner had no reason to know of), the resulting injury was likely not within the scope of the foreseeable risk. Proximate cause is not satisfied. Of course, precisely what the "scope" of the risk is in any given case may be subject to interpretation and argument.

In the truck crash context, the chattel in question will almost always be the truck; the entrustee will always be the driver whose alleged incompetence, inexperience, or recklessness contributed to the accident. Most of the time, the entrustor is the motor carrier. The reason these "universals" are important is that they mean that—in the truck crash context—a negligent entrustment claim (depending on how narrowly such a claim has been interpreted by the jurisdiction) is often available when a negligent hiring, retention, supervision, or training claim is available, and vice versa.[41] When a driver is *hired* (or *leased*), it is generally the case that he is *entrusted* with a truck; the entrustment is an essential part of the driver's job (note: even a leased driver who owns his own truck is "entrusted" with the truck under the mandatory provisions of 49 C.F.R.

Houston Pole Line Corp. v. McAllister, 667 S.W.2d 829 (Tex. App. 1983); Go Int'l, Inc. v. Lewis, 601 S.W.2d 495 (Tex. App. 1980); Montgomery Ward & Co. v. Marvin Riggs Co., 584 S.W.2d 863 (Tex. App. 1979).

39. *See generally* 49 C.F.R. pts. 382 & 391. Violation of the regulations may result in civil and criminal penalties. 49 C.F.R. § 390.37.

40. 49 C.F.R. § 390.9.

41. Obviously, an exception arises if the entrustor and the entrustee do not share any kind of employment relationship; in that case, negligent entrustment may be the plaintiff's only viable option.

§ 376.12(c), as the motor carrier is deemed to have exclusive possession and control of the leased equipment). This does not mean, however, that plaintiffs should not allege more than one of these claims in some situations; it also does not mean that they should be chosen indiscriminately. Plaintiffs should allege claims that fit the facts, tell a compelling story, and are cognizable in the jurisdiction. Early on—when information is incomplete or unclear—plaintiffs have to take special care to ensure that their claims are comprehensive and cover the reasonable universe of possibilities; however, if a plaintiff alleges every single claim he or she can imagine, the plaintiff could lose credibility with opposing counsel and the court.

An interesting aspect of this tort that deserves special note is that, in some jurisdictions, the entrustee herself may bring the action against the entrustor.[42] This is known as "first-party negligent entrustment."[43] In *Casebolt v. Cowan*,[44] Susan Casebolt brought a negligent entrustment action against Milco Construction Company, seeking damages for the wrongful death of her husband.[45] She asserted that her husband's employer breached a duty to its employee by failing to prevent him from driving a vehicle owned by the company after learning that he had been drinking and was intoxicated.[46] At trial, the company moved for summary judgment, asserting that it had no duty to protect Casebolt from the consequences of his own intoxication. The trial court granted the motion, and the Colorado Court of Appeals affirmed.[47] The Colorado Supreme Court reversed the decision and determined that summary judgment was improper:

> We recognize that voluntary intoxication is socially undesirable conduct and that individual responsibility to refrain from such conduct should be promoted. These considerations, however, *cannot be permitted to obscure the fact that a vehicle owner who has the right and ability to control the use of the vehicle and takes no action* to prevent the continued use of the vehicle by a borrower who the owner knows is likely to operate the vehicle while intoxicated *is also engaged in morally reprehensible behavior that should be discouraged.* Comparative negligence provides the appropriate framework for examining any negligence on the part of the individual who drives after consuming alcoholic beverages.[48]

Fortunately, Casebolt did not injure anyone else when he crashed. Imagine, however, that Casebolt had injured a third party. Traditionally, plaintiffs tend to view their negligent entrustment lawsuits as cases against the driver

---

42. *See, e.g.*, Blake v. Moore, 208 Cal. Rptr. 703 (Ct. App. 1984); Gorday v. Faris, 523 So. 2d 1215 (Fla. App. 1988); King v. Petefish, 541 N.E.2d 847 (Ill. App. 1989); Greenwood v. Gardner, 366 P.2d 780 (Kan. 1961); Snyder v. Bergeron, 501 So. 2d 291 (La. App. 1986); Shepard v. Barber, 174 N.W.2d 163 (Mich. App. 1969); Axelson v. Williamson, 324 N.W.2d 241 (Minn. 1982).

43. Kayce H. McCall, *Lydia v. Horton: You No Longer Have to Protect Me from Myself*, 55 S.C. L. Rev. 681, 681 (Spring 2004).

44. Casebolt v. Cowan, 829 P.2d 352 (Colo. 1992).

45. *Id.* at 353.

46. *Id.*

47. *Id.*

48. *Id.* at 362.

and the company, but in a situation where the driver-entrustee is injured as well, the driver-entrustee and the injured third party's interests become curiously aligned. In many cases, the entrustee has practical reasons not to sue his entrustor, but in cases where the entrustee's negligence was minimal (or even nonexistent), the entrustee and the injured third party are probably better characterized as (strange) allies than as adversaries.

Beyond the manner in which an entrustee might complicate a traditional suit with a claim of his or her own, the entrustee's right to sue provides additional support for the proposition that the negligence at issue in such a claim is the separate negligence of the entrustor. Obviously, the negligence of the entrustee is not imputed to the entrustor in an action brought by the entrustee; instead, the negligence of the entrustor is compared to the negligence of the entrustee in order to determine the recovery of the entrustee.[49]

Negligent Hiring and Retention

Section 213 of the Restatement (Second) of Agency is regularly cited as the authority for negligent hiring and retention claims. It provides that "[a] person conducting an activity through servants or other agents is subject to liability for harm resulting from his conduct if he is negligent or reckless: . . . (b) in the employment of improper persons."[50] In the comments to the section, it is explained that "[i]f liability results it is because, under the circumstances, the employer has not taken the care which a prudent man would take in selecting the person for the business in hand."[51]

Generally, to hold an employer liable for the negligent hiring or retention of a driver, a plaintiff must show the following: (1) some kind of employment relationship existed between the employer and the driver at the time of the injury, (2) the driver was somehow unfit for the position, (3) the employer knew or should have known of the driver's unfitness, (4) the driver's conduct caused the plaintiff's injury, and (5) the plaintiff's injury was within the scope of the risk of the driver's unfitness,[52] or "the harm is caused by the quality of the [driver] which the employer had reason to suppose would be likely to cause harm."[53]

The elements of this tort are almost identical to those of negligent entrustment. Here, however, instead of an act of entrustment, some kind of employment relationship must exist between the employer and the driver (see 49 C.F.R. § 390.5, definition of employee). While some kind of employment relationship must exist, however, the elements of the tort do not require that the employee's injurious conduct took place within the course and scope of his or her employment.[54] If a plaintiff can establish that the employee's negligence was foreseeable, he or she could make out a case for negligent hiring even though the driver

49. *Id. See also* Hoag v. Paul C. Chapman & Sons, Inc., 233 N.W.2d 530 (Mich. App. 1975).
50. Restatement (Second) of Agency § 213 (1958).
51. *Id.* at cmt. d.
52. Camacho, note 26, at 795.
53. Restatement (Second) of Agency § 213, cmt. d (1958).
54. Camacho, *supra* note 27, at 790–92.

was not working at the time of the injury or at the time the negligent conduct may have taken place.

Most jurisdictions hold that employers have a "duty to exercise reasonable care in view of all the circumstances in hiring individuals who, because of the employment, may pose a threat of injury to members of the public."[55] Importantly, the "nature of the employment directly pertains to the obligations of the employer."[56] In other words—and of special note in situations involving those employed to drive tractor-trailers—"[o]ne can normally assume that another who offers to perform simple work is competent[;] *[i]f, however, the work is likely to subject third persons to serious risk of great harm, there is a special duty of investigation*."[57] As such, trucking companies have a special duty to investigate and screen applicants.

In addition to common law precedent, the FMCSA has promulgated regulations that prescribe driver qualifications and the steps that must be taken by those employers hiring commercial drivers. General qualifications require that all drivers be at least 21 years old, literate and sufficiently fluent in English, and appropriately licensed, and all drivers must complete a driver's road test and be issued a certificate.[58] More recently, the FMCSA has promulgated additional regulations related to a motor carrier's responsibility to verify that drivers have undergone the minimum training requirements set out in 49 C.F.R. Part 380.[59] A driver's application for employment must contain, among other things, the issuing state, number and expiration date of each unexpired commercial motor vehicle operator's license or permit that has been issued to the applicant; the nature and extent of the applicant's experience in the operation of motor vehicles; a list of all accidents in which the applicant was involved in the past three years; a list of all violations of motor vehicle laws or ordinances of which the applicant was convicted during the past three years; statements setting forth the circumstances of any denial, revocation, or suspension of any license, permit, or privilege to operate a motor vehicle; and a list of the names and addresses

---

55. Ponticas v. K.M.S. Invs., 331 N.W.2d 907, 911 (Minn. 1983).

56. Camacho, *supra* note 27, at 796.

57. Restatement (Second) of Agency § 213, cmt. d (1958) (emphasis added).

58. 49 C.F.R. § 391.11. *See also* 49 C.F.R. § 391.31 ("As a minimum, the person who takes the test must be tested, while operating the type of commercial motor vehicle the motor carrier intends to assign him/her, on his/her skill at performing each of the following operations: (1) The pretrip inspection required by § 392.7 of this subchapter; (2) Coupling and uncoupling of combination units, if the equipment he/she may drive includes combination units; (3) Placing the commercial motor vehicle in operation; (4) Use of the commercial motor vehicle's controls and emergency equipment; (5) Operating the commercial motor vehicle in traffic and while passing other motor vehicles; (6) Turning the commercial motor vehicle; (7) Braking, and slowing the commercial motor vehicle by means other than braking; and (8) Backing and parking the commercial motor vehicle. . . . The motor carrier shall retain [the certificate] in the driver qualification file of the person who was examined.").

59. *See* 49 C.F.R. § 380.113.

of the applicant's employers for the past three years.[60] The regulations also prescribe physical qualifications for drivers.[61]

Additionally, federal regulations require each motor carrier to investigate each applicant's motor vehicle record and safety performance history.[62] The motor carrier must investigate applicants' previous employment, obtain the medical examiner's certificate for the applicant,[63] and must conduct pre-employment testing for controlled substances.[64] Motor carriers are also required to maintain a driver qualification file[65] and a driver investigation history file[66] for each driver.

Remember, the requirements of the regulations are the minimum requirements below which a motor carrier is in violation of federal law. A reasonable motor carrier may well be required by state negligence law to do screening, training, or supervision in excess of the established minimums. The regulations do not exhaust the duties that a motor carrier may have in any given situation, but they provide an excellent starting point. If an employer was negligent in hiring a driver (or entrusting a chattel to that driver), it is very likely that the employer was or is in violation of federal regulations, and that records required by those regulations may help establish the employer's negligence.

Negligent hiring and negligent retention claims are virtually identical and are usually treated exactly the same. The only difference between the two concerns *when* the employer knew or should have known about a driver's unfitness. Generally, the negligent hiring claim is appropriate where the employer knew or should have known about a problem with a driver *before* the driver was actually hired and put to work. If the employer finds out (or should have found out) about a problem with a driver's fitness *after* he was hired, and the employer does not terminate the driver's employment or temporarily remove the driver from any work where the driver poses a risk to the public, the negligent retention claim may be better suited to the facts of the case. Many of the duties articulated in the federal regulations are ongoing. That is, motor carriers have a duty to make sure that their drivers are fit throughout their employment.

---

60. 49 C.F.R. § 391.21. Even more information is required for those drivers applying to operate a commercial motor vehicle as defined by Part 383 of this subchapter. *Id.*

61. 49. C.F.R. § 391.41.

62. *Id.* § 391.23.

63. *Id.* Various previous employers also have duties to furnish information to the motor carrier pursuant to the regulations. *Id.*

64. *Id.* § 382.301.

65. *Id.* § 391.51. The file must include the driver's application, a copy of the motor vehicle record received from each state, the applicant's road test certificate, the motor vehicle record received from each state driver licensing agency, a note relating to the annual review of the driver's driving record, a list or certificate relating to violations of motor vehicle laws and ordinances, and the medical examiner's certificate. *Id.*

66. *Id.* § 391.53. The file must maintain records relating to the investigation into the safety performance history of a new or prospective driver. *Id.*

Some regulations are quite specific about what is required.[67] As such, they are useful in negligent retention claims as well.

Negligent Supervision and Training

The same restatement section that courts in many states cite as authority for negligent hiring and retention claims also provides the basis for negligent supervision and negligent training claims:

> A person conducting an activity through servants or other agents is subject to liability for harm resulting from his conduct if he is negligent or reckless: (a) in giving improper or ambiguous orders of in failing to make proper regulations; or . . . (c) in the supervision of the activity; or (d) in permitting, or failing to prevent, negligent or other tortious conduct by persons, whether or not his servants or agents, upon premises or with instrumentalities under his control.[68]

In some jurisdictions, "negligent supervision and training" is often treated as if it constitutes a single tort.[69] Similarly, some jurisdictions often comment on an employer's duty to "adequately hire, train and supervise employees" in general terms.[70] Several jurisdictions assert that the elements of negligent supervision are the same as those required to prove negligent hiring (and negligent retention).[71] Still others occasionally treat negligent supervision and negligent training as individual and independent torts.[72]

That being said—and as mentioned earlier—these labels can be helpful in crafting a case, and can provide parties with alternative means of thinking about the motor carrier's specific duties. Negligent supervision and training are claims that seem especially ripe for use in truck accident litigation precisely because they frequently capture particular fact situations so well. Furthermore, the articulation of a negligence claim in terms of an employer's breach of its duty in supervising or training its employees can focus the negligence at issue on the employer and can serve to mitigate the misconduct of the individual employee.

The Federal Motor Carrier Safety Regulations contain far more driver qualification-related requirements for motor carriers than training or supervision requirements for motor carriers. However, many of a motor carrier's ongoing driver qualification requirements require a nonnegligible level of supervision. Additionally, the aforementioned "management systems" (that are required to effectively prevent violations of the regulations) impose a baseline requirement

---

67. *See, e.g.*, *id.* § 382.303 (requiring post-accident alcohol and controlled substances testing after particular kinds of accidents).

68. Restatement (Second) of Agency § 213 (1958).

69. *See, e.g.*, Knight v. Weise, 2010 WL 5188779, 2010 Conn. Super. LEXIS 3143 (Conn. Sup. Ct. Case No. CV095012638, Dec. 3, 2010).

70. *See, e.g.*, Allen v. AT&T Transp. Co., 79 S.W.3d 65, 70 (Tex. App. 2002).

71. *See, e.g.*, Cooke v. Montgomery Cnty., 814 N.E.2d 505, 509 (Ohio App. 2004).

72. *See, e.g.*, Dragomir v. Spring Harbor Hosp., 970 A.2d 310, 315 (Me. 2009); Waffle House Inc. v. Williams, 313 S.W.3d 796, 804 n.27 (Tex. 2010).

for training and supervision. Furthermore, in order for most motor carriers to obtain operating authority in the first place, they were required to certify (and verify under penalty of perjury) that they (1) had in place a system and an individual responsible for ensuring overall compliance with the Federal Motor Carrier Safety Regulations (FMCSRs); (2) could produce a copy of the FMCSRs and the Hazardous Materials Transportation Regulations; (3) had in place a driver safety training/orientation program; (4) had prepared and maintained an accident register; (5) were familiar with U.S. Department of Transportation (USDOT) regulations governing driver qualifications and had in place a system for overseeing driver qualification requirements; (6) had in place policies and procedures consistent with USDOT regulations governing driving and operational safety of motor vehicles, including drivers' hours of service and vehicle inspection, repair, and maintenance; and (7) were familiar with, and would have in place on the appropriate effective date, a system for complying with USDOT regulations governing alcohol and controlled substances resting requirements.[73] In other words, before the government even allowed the company to operate as an interstate motor carrier, it was required to meet a variety of training/supervision requirements, including a "driver safety training/orientation program." If a motor carrier does not have such a program, that sometimes can be shown to be a proximate cause of a crash.

These direct claims can be relatively straightforward negligence actions against owners of trucks and/or employers of truck drivers. Virtually any complication results from the fact that the principal negligent conduct at issue usually takes place in a different time and space than "the accident" and its resulting injuries. That we (parties, courts, and commentators) are sometimes distracted from the faraway actions and omissions of owners and employers is simply a function of provincial and occasionally faulty human perception. Ultimately—as is the case in all negligence actions—the question in these cases is whether the owner/employer's breach proximately contributed to cause the plaintiff's injury. If so, the owner/employer is liable for its negligence, and may also be vicariously liable for the negligence of its driver.

Other Direct Negligence Claims

Most direct claims against motor carriers are likely best characterized as negligent hiring, supervision, or training claims. Again, however, these are simply labels that tend to describe the legal duty at issue. Other potentially available direct claims against a motor carrier might be related to the motor carrier's vehicles and/or equipment (negligent maintenance), the directions provided to the driver by the motor carrier (negligent routing/dispatch), and/or the arrangement and securement of the freight being transported (negligent securement).

The interesting feature of this particular "class" of direct claims is that they tend to concern themselves less with the conduct of the driver-employee, and more with the conduct of the trucking company itself and/or other employees

73. Form OP-1, https://www.fmcsa.dot.gov/registration/form-op-1-application-motor-property-carrier-and-broker-authority (last updated July 20, 2024).

(e.g., mechanics, dispatchers, loading bay/warehouse personnel). While the FMCSRs do place significant responsibility for the condition of the vehicle, the safety of the route, and the securement of freight on the driver, there are a variety of facts that might serve to mitigate the driver's level of responsibility (practically, if not technically) and focus the attention on the motor carrier's independent negligence in causing a crash.

Apportioning Negligence

How apportionment of negligence in direct negligence actions is performed is related to the characterization or nature of the claim *and* the particular jurisdiction's rules regarding comparative fault. There are three main approaches: (1) the employer is apportioned the employee's negligence, (2) the employer is apportioned the employer's negligence, and (3) the employer is apportioned the employer's negligence *and* the employee is apportioned the employee's negligence.

The Motor Carrier Is Apportioned the Driver's Negligence

Unsurprisingly, this method is used in those jurisdictions that (at least occasionally) recognize direct claims against the motor carrier as "vicarious" claims. In these states, the negligence comparison the fact finder is to perform considers only the parties actually involved in the physical accident:

> The comparative negligence doctrine must be directed to a comparison between the [plaintiff]'s negligence and the driver-employee's negligence—that is, between the negligence of the two drivers of the vehicles actually involved in the collision. It is self-evident that in a case such as this, where the sine qua non of the employer's liability under any theory is the negligence of the employee-driver in the operation of the employer's truck, it is the negligence of the employee-driver which must be compared and not that of the employer. If, as all of our cases hold, there could be no liability on the part of the master-entrustor without proof of actionable negligence against the driver-entrustee, regardless of how negligent the master-entrustee may have been in employing the driver, it must follow as night the day that it is the negligence of the two drivers that is to be compared.[74]

We have already discussed why the vicarious view is problematic on theoretical and policy grounds,[75] but states are relatively free to define their causes of action as they see fit (so long as they are within constitutionally permissible boundaries). This approach also ignores the policy benefits of holding negligent actors accountable for their negligent acts instead of insulating them from such

74. *Willis*, 159 S.E.2d at 159–60.

75. *See* the first section in this chapter. For the policy argument that the consideration of the owner/employer's independent negligence in these kinds of cases can potentially be harmful to plaintiffs in particular cases, see Underwood & Morrison, *supra* note 23, at 645–47.

liability. What is particularly peculiar about the failure to examine the owner/employer's own fault in such situations—from a practical apportionment perspective—is that some of the very same courts have no problem in permitting (or requiring) the fact finder to consider the direct negligence of the owner/employer in cases where the entrustee/worker is an independent contractor or in situations that do not give rise to vicarious liability.

Take, for example, *Fields v. Yellow Cab Co.*[76] In that case, plaintiff alleged that as he was getting in the back seat of the cab the driver accelerated before plaintiff was completely inside the vehicle. As a result, plaintiff fell onto the street and suffered a cartilage tear and a herniated disk.[77] The plaintiff alleged that the driver, an independent contractor of Yellow Cab Company, was negligent, and that Yellow Cab was negligent in its entrustment of the cab to the driver.[78] The jury assessed 90 percent of the proportionate responsibility for plaintiff's damages against the company, and 10 percent of the proportionate responsibility for plaintiff's damages against the driver.[79] If the vicarious view is accurate, Yellow Cab's negligence *is* the independent contractor's negligence, period. That is, the entrustee's negligence fixes the negligence of the entrustor. However, in this case, the negligent entrustor's negligence was treated as if it was distinct from the negligence of the entrustee. Indeed, in this case, the jury determined that the entrustee's negligence was a proximate cause of the plaintiff's injuries and that the entrustor was more at fault in proximately causing the plaintiff's injuries, and apportioned the negligence accordingly. If the entrustor's negligence is distinct and can be considered where the entrustee is an independent contractor, it is very difficult to understand how the entrustor's negligence is purely vicarious when the entrustee is an employee. (Another practical problem with this approach is that it can significantly distort the allocation of fault amongst the parties. We will address this issue later.) This case illustrates a recurring issue in truck crash cases. In many situations, the negligence and disregard for public safety evidenced by the failure of the motor carrier far exceeds the fault of the individual driver in making a driving error.

In states that have expressed the vicarious (or "derivative") view but have since adopted forms of comparative fault that require negligence to be apportioned to all proximate causes of harm (with some states even including nonparties at fault), there is strong potential for a good amount of confusion regarding the allocation of fault in direct negligence cases.[80] At the very least, changes in

---

76. *Fields v. Yellow Cab Co.,* Trial Order, No. 04-01-00005-CV, 2006 WL 6021443 (Tex. Dist. Case No. 04-01-00005-CV, Aug. 18, 2006), *rev'd on other grounds,* 249 S.W.3d 741 (Tex. App. 2008). *See also* Ali v. Fisher, 145 S.W.3d 557 (Tenn. 2004).

77. Houston Cab Co. v. Fields, 249 S.W.3d 741, 743 (Tex. App. 2008).

78. *Id.*

79. *Fields,* Trial Order, No. 04-01-00005-CV, 2006 WL 6021443 (Tex. Dist. Aug. 18, 2006).

80. Texas, specifically, has had its fair share of confusion on this issue ever since the Texas legislature amended its comparative fault statute. The statute requires the factfinder to apportion negligence to all persons causing or contributing to the harm for which recovery of damages is sought, including "responsible third parties." For a decent explanation of the disagreement and confusion in Texas state courts on this issue, see Williams v. McCollister, 671 F. Supp. 2d 884 (S.D. Tex. 2009). In 2023, Texas adopted a statute that specifically permits defendant motor carriers to bifurcate the

a state's comparative fault rules provide strong support for the argument that the vicarious approach is no longer appropriate. The net effect of not allowing consideration of the separate negligence of the employer is that the employer is never held accountable for its own negligent actions, and the aims of the tort system are seriously compromised. A horribly negligent motor carrier is, essentially, given a "free pass," is never held accountable for its own negligence, and is treated in the same way an extremely diligent and careful motor carrier is treated.

The Motor Carrier Is Apportioned the Motor Carrier's Negligence

This approach is generally used by those jurisdictions that treat direct claims like what they are: claims regarding the breach of the motor carrier's independent duty to exercise reasonable care. Under this approach, the motor carrier is liable for its own conduct in proximately causing the plaintiff's injury. If there is a separate claim against the commercial driver, the jury will likely be permitted to apportion negligence between the motor carrier and driver.

The Motor Carrier Is Apportioned the Motor Carrier's Negligence and the Driver Is Apportioned the Driver's Negligence

In some states, the direct negligence claim, by itself, in addition to permitting an apportionment of negligence to the employer, appears to require apportionment of negligence to the employee. States that use this method do so for two distinct reasons. First, in some states, the requirement for apportionment to both motor carrier and driver in direct negligence actions seems to be built into the tort itself. That is, the courts of some jurisdictions have interpreted the negligent entrustment claim as a claim against both the entrustor and the entrustee: "The nature and extent of negligence of the [entrustor] and of the entrustee are separate and distinct. The percentages of fault may be different in amount and should be determined separately."[81]

Second, courts have held that the jurisdiction's comparative fault rules require allocation of fault to nonparties and therefore require allocation between the owner/employer and the entrustee/employee (even if the nature of the tort does not so require). Arizona's statute abolishing joint and several liability requires that "the trier of fact . . . consider the fault of all persons who contributed to the alleged injury . . . regardless of whether the person was, or could have been named as a party to the suit."[82] In *Ogden v. J.M. Steel Erecting, Inc.*,[83] the Court of Appeals of Arizona held that the statute required the jury to allocate some degree of fault to a nonparty employee in a negligent entrustment

---

trial in such a way that the jury must make a finding that the employee driver was negligent in operating a commercial vehicle prior to the "second phase" of the trial on a claim (such as negligent entrustment) against the motor carrier defendant. *See* Tex. Civ. Prac. & Rem. § 72.052.

81. McCart v. Muir, 641 P.2d 384, 389 (Kan. 1982). *See also Ali*, 145 S.W.3d at 564 ("[W]e hold that negligent entrustment does not create vicarious liability and that the jury must allocate the fault between the defendants.").

82. Ariz. Rev. Stat. Ann. § 12-2506.

83. *Ogden v. J.M. Steel Erecting, Inc.*, 31 P.3d 806 (Ariz. App. 2001).

action against the employee's employer.[84] As already suggested, the adoption of these types of comparative fault rules have and/or likely will have a significant impact on how courts tend to think about, and how fault will be allocated in, these kinds of claims.[85]

As discussed next, irrespective of whether a court requires the consideration of fault of nonparties, when a direct claim accompanies a *respondeat superior* claim, and the crash was within the scope of employment, once the separate percentages of fault are determined between the employee and the employer, the fault of the employee should be added to the percentage of fault of the employer by the court, post-verdict, to determine the employer's total liability. The employer is responsible for its own negligence (in hiring, entrustment, supervision, etc.), and the employer is also liable (vicariously) for the negligence of its driver/employee.

Direct Negligence Claims Accompanied by a Claim Based on Agency

In cases in which a direct negligence claim is made against a motor carrier, a plaintiff often pursues a claim against the driver and asserts that the motor carrier employer is vicariously liable under the doctrine of *respondeat superior* as well. As mentioned earlier, in a number of jurisdictions that have considered the issue, courts have dismissed the plaintiff's direct negligence claims if the employer admits that the driver was its employee and that the driver was acting within the course and scope of his employment at the time of the crash.[86] Put differently, once an employer admits that it is vicariously liable to the extent its driver is found to be liable, claims of negligence entrustment, hiring, retention, supervision, and training are no longer available to the plaintiff in many jurisdictions.[87]

---

84. *Id.* at 810.

85. Some recent cases out of Texas illustrate the impact that the state's comparative fault rules have had. *See Williams*, 671 F. Supp. 2d at 890–92; *Bedford*, 166 S.W.3d at 461–63; F.F.P. Operating Partners, L.P. v. Duenez, 237 S.W.3d 680, 681–86 (Tex. 2007).

86. Approximately 15 jurisdictions seem to use some version of the rule at the present time (though a number of the only decisions on the matter in some jurisdictions are federal court decisions, which, while ostensibly applying state law, are not binding on the states): California, Georgia, Idaho, Indiana, Maryland, Missouri, Montana, North Carolina, Nevada, New Jersey, New York, Texas, Washington, Washington, D.C., and Wyoming. For a slightly outdated survey and breakdown of the case law on this issue (and for an argument in support of the *McHaffie* rule), see Richard A. Mincer, *The Viability of Direct Negligence Claims against Motor Carriers in the Face of an Admission of Respondeat Superior*, 10 Wyo. L. Rev. 229, 235 & n.20 (2010). For an in-depth analysis of the history of the *McHaffie* rule and its flaws, see generally Burns, *supra* note 21.

87. *See, e.g.*, Armenta v. Churchill, 267 P.2d 303, 308–09 (Cal. 1954); *Willis*, 159 S.E.2d at 157; Houlihan v. McCall, 78 A.2d 661, 664–65 (Md. 1951). Of course, even in contributory negligence states, the rule had—and has—inherent problems when considering the potential claim of the employer against its employee for indemnity or the right of the employee for contribution against the employer if the employer failed to pay.

The rationales for the *McHaffie* rule, although flawed, are not difficult to understand, and the courts employing the rule tend to be the same courts that understand direct negligence claims to be vicarious in nature. Those applying the rule argue that the direct negligence claims impose no additional liability above and beyond the *respondeat superior* liability. Since the direct claims impose no additional liability and "merely allege a concurrent theory of recovery, the desirability of allowing these theories is outweighed by the prejudice to the defendants."[88] The prejudice at issue is that potentially caused by the evidence of prior bad acts of the driver-employee that is often considered by the jury in direct negligence cases.[89]

The *McHaffie* rule has been outdated and wrongheaded for decades. The reasoning of the rule is based on principles of contributory negligence that do not apply in jurisdictions that have adopted some form of comparative fault. Additionally, the rule is sometimes applied even where there is no danger of any unfairly prejudicial evidence. Furthermore, some states do not account for situations where a *respondeat superior* admission actually fails to establish employer liability for an employee's injurious conduct. And finally, while some states recognize an exception to the rule where an employer's conduct in entrusting or hiring was reckless—as opposed to merely negligent—other states insulate an employer's reckless conduct from any scrutiny in these situations.

History of the Rule

In contributory negligence jurisdictions, the application of the majority rule at least has some basis in logic: a plaintiff's direct negligence claim theoretically adds nothing to the plaintiff's case once the driver's employer admits that it is liable for any of the driver's negligence. If the jury finds that the defendant driver-employee was negligent, the plaintiff may collect all of the damages from the driver's employer; but, if the jury finds that plaintiff was at all negligent, the plaintiff recovers nothing.

> The reasoning for the rule . . . loses much of its force, however, under comparative negligence. Under comparative negligence, it is necessary for a trier of fact to determine percentages of fault for a plaintiff's injuries attributable to the negligence of plaintiff, the negligence of each defendant and [depending on the jurisdiction] the negligence of other non-parties.[90]

An example may be the best way to demonstrate the potential injustice of the rule. Imagine that Peter Plaintiff is traveling to work on the interstate. A tractor-trailer, driven by Doug Driver, negligently crashes into Peter and injures him. Immediately after the truck hits Peter's sedan (without sufficient time to establish the second crash as a superseding cause), another commuter, Carla, negligently fails to keep her automobile from crashing into Peter's. Peter sues

88. *Clooney*, 352 So. 2d at 1220.
89. *Id.*
90. Lorio v. Cartwright, 768 F. Supp. 658, 660 (N.D. Ill. 1991).

(1) Doug, (2) Doug's employer, Edna, and (3) Carla. Peter claims Doug was negligent in his operation of the truck and that Edna is liable under *respondeat superior*. Peter claims Carla was negligent in her operation of her automobile. *And* Peter claims that Edna is independently negligent in its entrustment of the truck to Doug (and/or its hiring of Doug).

No matter how one slices it, Peter's damages are the same, but the apportionment of fault that takes place under a comparative negligence scheme will likely be affected by a claim that Edna was independently negligent. Comparative negligence requires that all of the alleged proximate causes of the collision be considered.[91] If a reasonable jury finds that Edna's independent negligence was a proximate cause of Peter's injuries, this will affect the allocation of fault, and Peter's recovery whether or not he is found to be negligent at all.[92] If, on the other hand, the direct claim is dismissed, the only negligence the jury is allowed to consider is that of the drivers in the collision, and the employer is provided with a pardon for her actions that contributed to cause the plaintiff's damages.[93]

For a moment, let us assume that the direct claim is dismissed as per the rule and that the jury finds that Carla's conduct was not a proximate cause of Peter's injuries. In this situation, the jury considers only Peter's and Doug's negligence and might well determine that both were 50 percent negligent. Alternatively, if the direct claim is not dismissed, and the jury finds that Edna's conduct was a proximate cause of Peter's injuries, the jury might find that each party was, for example, 33 and 1/3 percent at fault. Obviously, the addition of another proximate cause can make a big difference:

> Indeed, in some jurisdictions, plaintiffs who are assigned 50% of the fault are unable to recover any damages. A plaintiff found to be 50% negligent recovers nothing, while a plaintiff who is found to be 33.3% negligent recovers 66.6% of her damages. And considering the appeal of 50-50 allocations in situations where juries find it difficult to assign percentages of fault with any precision, the rule can have drastic effects on recovery.[94]

Of course, we should not forget about Carla. Let us now assume that the jury found that Carla's conduct was a proximate cause of Peter's injuries, and, for simplicity's sake, let us also assume that there have been no allegations that Peter Plaintiff was negligent. In the situation where the direct claim is dismissed and the jury is not allowed to consider the negligence of Edna, then Carla will likely be held responsible for a much larger share of Peter's damages than if the

---

91. Christiansen v. Silfies, 667 A.2d 396, 399–401 (Pa. Super. Ct. 1995); Amend v. Bell, 570 P.2d 138, 142 (Wash. 1977).

92. Absent any fault on the part of the plaintiff, one might argue that the comparative fault issue is not implicated because, regardless of how the fault is apportioned, plaintiff's actual recovery is not affected. However, if Edna is judgment-proof, the "amnesty" given the employer for its own fault can drastically reduce a plaintiff's recovery. Of course, the plaintiff is even the slightest bit negligent, the rule is almost certain to have a negative effect on the plaintiff's recovery.

93. *See* Burns, *supra* note 21, at 665.

94. *Id.*

jury was allowed to consider all proximate causes of Peter's injuries. Put simply, the application of the rule can also adversely affect defendants.[95]

Obviously, many of the arguments that proponents of this rule make are the same as those we encountered at the start of the chapter, when we discussed the vicarious views. For the most part, courts and commentators that support the rule assert that the negligence of the employer cannot affect the allocation of fault:

> [I]f [the employee]'s negligence was a proximate cause of the accident, it really does not matter whether the direct negligence claims have merit or not. If [the employee] is negligent, whether or not the master is also negligent can neither increase nor decrease the percentage of fault attributable to [the employee].[96]

Precisely this logic was used in the case of *Bedford v. Moore*.[97] Interestingly, the court recognized that the independent negligence of the employer should be considered by the jury in its allocation of fault.[98] However, the court held that the trial court's failure to include the employer's fault in the comparative negligence question was harmless error.[99] The error was deemed harmless because

> the submission of the acts of "other parties" whose actions preceded the actions of [the driver-employee] at the time of the accident could only have contributed to [the driver-employee's] actions at the accident scene. . . . What led up to those actions at the time of the accident does not change those actions at the accident scene but can only be subparts of those respective responsibilities.[100]

The argument is that the omitted negligence of the employer was necessarily included in the jury's apportionment of the employee's negligence. The plaintiff was found to be 60 percent at fault, and the employee was found to be 40 percent at fault. Because of the state's comparative fault rules, the plaintiff recovered nothing.[101]

This kind of apportionment reasoning is inherently illogical and fails to recognize the right of a jury to determine the extent to which particular conduct contributed to cause a particular event. The wrongful actions of a motor carrier employer who has greater knowledge of the risks of its driver employees may easily be determined to involve greater fault than the fault of a driver who, because of poor training, was not aware (or not as aware) of the risk he or she was creating by his or her actions. The question is one of proximate cause:

95. For the argument that an employee might ultimately be held responsible for both her own negligence and the negligence of her employer in situations where the rule is applied, see *id.* at 670–71, n.86.

96. Mincer, *supra* note 86, at 233.

97. *Bedford*, 166 S.W.3d at 454.

98. *Id.* at 462–63. This is departure from the treatment of such torts by Texas state courts. *See, e.g.*, *Rosell*, 89 S.W.3d at 643.

99. *Bedford*, 166 S.W.3d at 464.

100. *Id.*

101. *Id.* at 458.

if the employer is deemed a proximate cause of the plaintiff's injury, then the principles of comparative fault require that the jury be allowed to allocate some percentage of fault to the employer. This same issue was identified earlier in the chapter: if this is not how apportionment works, how do we rationalize the allocation of fault in direct negligence claims that involve an independent contractor?[102] "The reality is that fault allocation is a relative and comparative process: if a party's negligence is taken out of the equation, the other parties necessarily have to fill in the vacuum that is left by the absent party."[103]

Unsurprisingly, the rule was first formed and adopted in an environment of contributory negligence.[104] In fact, most states that have adopted the rule did so under contributory negligence regimes, or borrowed the rule from states that had done so.[105] Nevertheless, some state courts have affirmed the rule even after consideration of the requirements of comparative fault.[106] The rationales of these cases, however, fail to recognize or justify the consequences of their rulings.

Prevalence of the Rule

The *McHaffie* rule is not nearly as prevalent as it used to be. In a previous version of this article, the rule was repeatedly identified as the "majority rule." That is no longer the case.

Rulings in Alabama, Delaware, Kansas, Kentucky, Michigan, Minnesota, New Hampshire, North Dakota, Ohio, South Carolina, South Dakota, Utah, Vermont, and Virginia indicate that courts in those jurisdictions have permitted direct negligence claims against employers to proceed where the defendant employers have admitted agency.[107]

The Colorado state legislature actually rejected the rule by statute.[108]

Rulings in Connecticut, Iowa, Hawaii, Massachusetts, New Mexico, Rhode Island, Tennessee, and Wisconsin all contain language that suggests that courts

---

102. In a footnote to his article supporting the majority rule, Mincer (a proponent of the vicarious view) admits that "negligent entrustment does not *necessarily* impose vicarious liability on an entrustor who is not the entrustee's employer." Mincer, *supra* note 86, at 234 n.16 (citing *Ali*, 145 S.W.3d at 564). Mincer's seemingly insignificant admission demonstrates that the vicarious view and majority rule assertion that negligent entrustment is just another method of imputing the negligence of one person to another is simply wrong.

103. Burns, *supra* note 21, at 671. *See also* Armstrong, *supra* note 27, at 310.

104. Burns, *supra* note 21, at 662–63.

105. *Id.* at 664.

106. *See, e.g.*, Diaz v. Carcamo, 253 P.3d 535 (Cal. 2011).

107. Poplin v. Bestway Express, 286 F. Supp. 2d 1316 (M.D. Ala. 2003); Smith v. Williams, 2007 WL 2677131, 2007 Del. Super. LEXIS 266 (Del. Super. Ct. 2007); Marquis v. State Farm Fire & Cas. Co., 961 P.2d 1213 (Kan. 1998); MV Transp. Inc. v. Allgeier, 433 S.W.3d 324 (Ky. 2014); Perin v. Peuler, 130 N.W.2d 4 (Mich. 1964); Lim v. Interstate Sys., 435 N.W.2d 830 (Minn. App. 1989); Zibolis-Sekella v. Ruehrwein, 2013 WL 3208573, 2013 U.S. Dist. LEXIS 88312 (D.N.H. 2013); *Burckhard*, 2014 WL 6807214 (D.N.D. 2014); Clark v. Stewart, 185 N.E. 71 (Ohio 1933); James v. Kelly Trucking Co., 661 S.E.2d 329 (S.C. 2008); Finkle v. Regency CSP Ventures Ltd., 27 F. Supp. 3d 996 (D.S.D. 2014); Ramon v. Nebo Sch. Dist., 493 P.3d 613 (Utah 2021); Brueckner v. Norwich Univ., 730 A.2d 1086 (Vt. 1999); Fairshter v. Am. Nat'l Red Cross, 322 F. Supp. 2d 646 (E.D. Va. 2004).

108. See C.R.S.A. § 13-21-111.5.

in those jurisdictions would reject the rule.[109] Oklahoma and Oregon employ the rule sometimes, but not others, seemingly based on what labels are used for the direct claims in question.[110]

There are conflicting decisions in Arizona, Arkansas, Florida, Illinois, Mississippi, Pennsylvania, and West Virginia.[111] The application of the rule in Mayland, North Carolina, and the District of Columbia is largely irrelevant, as those jurisdictions still practice contributory negligence. And where there have been no rulings on the issue (like in Alaska or Maine), the default position is that an admission related to one claim does nothing to preclude the pursuit of another.

The application of the rule remains a problem, but it is not as big a problem as it once was. Many courts who adopted the rule after their jurisdictions had embraced comparative fault models did so primarily on the basis that it was the so-called majority rule. At the very least, practitioners should be ready to explain to courts that the tide has turned, and that a majority of states do not dismiss direct negligence claims in the face of a *respondeat superior* or agency admission.

Additional Problems with the Rule

In support of the rule, some states focus on the potentially prejudicial evidence that usually accompanies direct negligence claims.[112] Such an emphasis might reasonably lead one to believe that, absent such evidence, the direct negligence claims should be permissible even where pursued alongside a *respondeat superior* claim. However, some courts' articulations of the rule seem to treat it as if its main purpose is to promote efficiency.[113]

---

109. Doe v. Jacome, 1999 WL 329799, 1999 Conn. Super. LEXIS 1237 (Conn. Super. Ct. 1999); Shiga v. Hawaiian Mission Acad., 2007 WL 2422138, 165 P.3d 1049 (Haw. App. 2007); Hardwick v. Bublitz, 119 N.W.2d 886 (Iowa 1963); Or v. Edwards, 818 N.E.2d 163 (Mass. App. 2004); Frederick v. Swift Transp. Co., 616 F.3d 1074 (10th Cir. 2010); Mainella v. Staff Builders, 608 A.2d 1141 (R.I. 1992); Ali v. Fisher, 145 S.W.3d 557 (Tenn. 2004).

110. *Compare* Jordan v. Cates, 935 P.2d 289 (Okla. 1997) *with* Fox v. Mize, 428 P.3d 314 (Okla. 2018); and *compare* Tuite v. Union Pacific, 284 P.2d 333 (Or. 1955) *with* Leonard v. Moran Foods, Inc., 343 P.3d 693 (Or. 2015).

111. *Compare* Quinonez v. Anderen, 696 P.2d 1342 (Ariz. App. 1984) *with* Ford v. Barnas, 2018 WL 5312912 (D. Ariz. 2018); *compare* Elrod v. G & R Constr. Co., 628 S.W.2d 17 (Ark. 1982) *with* McLane v. Rich Transp. Inc., 2012 WL 3257658, 2012 U.S. Dist. LEXIS 111885 (E.D. Ark. Case no. 2:11-cv-00101, Aug. 9, 2012); *compare* Clooney, 352 So. 2d 1216 (Fla. Dist. Ct. 1977) *with* Trevino v. Mobley, 63 So. 3d 865 (Fla. Dist. Ct. 2011); *compare* Gant v. L.U. Transp., 770 N.E.2d 1155 (Ill. Dist. 2002) *with Lorio*, 768 F. Supp. 658 (N.D. Ill. 1991); *compare* Hopson v. Slay Transp. Co., Inc., No. 3:04cv976WS, 2006 WL 8454639 (S.D. Miss. 2006), *with* Cole v. Alton, 567 F. Supp. 1084 (N.D. Miss. 1983); *compare* Pineda v. Chromiak, 2019 WL 175135, 2019 U.S. Dist. LEXIS 5597 (E.D. Pa. Case No. CV17-5833, Jan. 10, 2019) *with* Keifer v. Reinhart Foodservices, 2012 WL 368047, 2012 U.S. Dist. LEXIS 12209 (W.D. Pa. 2012); *compare* Evans v. Snachez Rubio, 2007 WL 712291, 2007 U.S. Dist. LEXIS 15940 (S.D. W. Va. Case No. 2:06-0995, Mar. 6, 2007) *with* Taylor v. Cabell Huntington Hosp., 538 S.E.2d 719 (W. Va. 2000).

112. *See, e.g.*, *Clooney*, 352 So. 2d at 1220; Tindall v. Enderle, 320 N.E.2d 764, 768 (Ind. App. 1974); *Houlihan*, 78 A.2d at 665; Nehi Bottling Co. v. Jefferson, 84 So. 2d 684, 686 (Miss. 1956).

113. .*See, e.g.*, *McHaffie*, 891 S.W.2d at 826; Connelly v. H.O. Wolding, Inc., 2007 U.S. Dist. LEXIS 14426, 2007 WL 679885, at *2 (W.D. Mo. Case No. 06-5129-CV-SW-FJG, Mar. 1, 2007).

The justification for the claim can make a significant difference. For example, in *Wise v. Fiberglass Systems, Inc.*,[114] the plaintiff actually offered to withdraw evidence of the employee's prior bad acts and submit only evidence that the employer permitted its employee to drive without proper instruction or experience.[115] Regardless of the plaintiff's offer, the Idaho Supreme Court held that the trial court properly dismissed the direct negligence claim.[116]

Regardless of the Idaho decision, in other jurisdictions it may be helpful for plaintiffs to make a special argument for their direct negligence claims if they do not require the admission of what is likely to be misunderstood by a jury as propensity evidence. Since many courts that still apply the rule discuss concerns with the introduction of prior acts of negligence by the driver-employee, a strong case can likely be made for those direct negligence claims that do not necessitate such evidence.

For those direct negligence claims that do require arguably prejudicial evidence, courts already have at their disposal a variety of devices that can mitigate and even eliminate the effects of any prejudice without disposing of the plaintiff's claim.[117] A special jury instruction is the most obvious and practical. The fact of the matter, however, is that all negligence claims involve the introduction of evidence that the defendant does not like and wishes the jury would not be allowed to hear. The greater the negligence, the more distasteful the evidence will be to the defendant. It is a strange rule indeed that exonerates a negligent actor merely because his negligence was so bad that the jury will become angry when they hear the evidence that establishes the wrongdoing.

In addition to the moving target that is the justification for the rule, another problem is the possibility of an "ignorant intermediary"—a nonnegligent driver involved in a crash proximately caused by a negligent motor carrier. One supporter of the vicarious view and the rule at issue has argued that "[i]t is difficult to imagine a case where an employer's negligence in the hiring, training, or supervising of his employee is truly a proximate cause of harm to a third party in the absence of a wrongful act committed by the servant."[118] No, it's not. This is exactly the kind of shallow thinking that has allowed the rule to outlive its rationale.

The fact of the matter is that an employer's negligence *can* be a proximate cause of a plaintiff's injuries even if its employee's conduct may be found to be nonnegligent. There are many aspects of a truck driver's job that require specialized knowledge or training in order to allow the driver to operate safely. This may be the result of carrying specialized loads that require unusual weight distribution during loading, or that require special load securement devices with particular load limits; operating specialized types of equipment

---

114. Wise v. Fiberglass Sys., 718 P.2d 1178 (Idaho 1986).

115. *Id.* at 1185 (Bistline, J., dissenting).

116. *Id.* at 1181–82. The dissent pointed out the flaw in the court's reasoning. *Id.* at 1185 (Bistline, J., dissenting). For a hypothetical example of this kind of case, see Burns, *supra* note 21, at 673.

117. Blitz, *supra* note 31, at 544. *See also* Burns, *supra* note 21, at 677–80.

118. Mincer, *supra* note 86, at 233.

that handle very differently from a "normal" tractor-trailer; hauling hazardous materials; and so on.

If a driver is unaware of the special handling requirements of the equipment or the load they are hauling, and the employer-company fails to train the driver with respect to such handling requirements, and the truck driver causes a crash due to the lack of such training, a jury could very well find that the driver, who had no knowledge of the special characteristics of the equipment or the load, was not negligent in any way. A jury could find that the driver acted reasonably and used that degree of care that a reasonable person would use under the same or similar circumstances. Under the *McHaffie* rule, there would be no liability on the part of the motor carrier, even though the crash was directly caused by the motor carrier's negligence in failing to train its employee/driver with regard to the dangers inherent in its operation and the ways to mitigate those damages.

This circumstance is not just limited to situations involving specialized loads or equipment. Trucking is big business, with many risks and dangers that may not be readily known to the general public (or some drivers) that are well known to motor carrier managers. For example, for years there has been a widespread debate within the industry as to whether motor carriers should screen their drivers for sleep disorders because of the risks of falling asleep at the wheel that drivers with sleep disorders such as sleep apnea present. Knowledge of sleep apnea and its effects and simple initial screening mechanisms have become common knowledge to trucking managers across the country over the past ten years such that a jury could find that a reasonable motor carrier should screen its drivers for this dangerous condition. A driver, however, may not have ever heard of disorders such as sleep apnea. If a driver who has severe sleep apnea (and who does not know he has the disorder) is hired by a company that is very familiar with sleep apnea (and could easily screen for the disorder), predictably falls asleep at the wheel, it is possible that a jury could find that the driver acted reasonably because he did not know about his medical disorder, even though the company did know about it, or certainly should have known about it. Of course, a jury could find that the driver was negligent because he was driving when he was too tired to drive safely, but what a jury may end up doing with its verdict will not be known until after the verdict is returned, long after the legal ruling on whether a concurrent claim can be made against the motor carrier.

The bottom line is that modern trucking is a sophisticated business and motor carriers have access to and utilize a great deal of information and technology regarding risk management, crash reduction, and driver risk assessment. Motor carriers are in a much better position to implement policies and procedures that will reduce the number of crashes on our highways than individual drivers. While it is true that, ultimately, there is a driver behind each truck's steering wheel (except in the case of autonomous trucks being driven by computers in some cities), it is not even remotely true that the negligence of a motor carrier in causing a crash is limited to the degree of negligence of its driver immediately preceding a crash. Any ruling that protects negligent motor carriers from being held accountable for their own negligence in failing to operate safely and in failing to make sure their drivers operate safely is a ruling that encourages the ongoing death and destruction on our highways.

Fortunately, some courts that apply the *McHaffie* rule have addressed these possibilities: "Should the [employer] seek to insulate himself from such performance . . . or should his [*respondeat superior*] admission be ineffective to subject him to liability to the same extent as could be imposed upon him as a 'negligent entrustor,' a plaintiff may proceed under the entrustment theory."[119] Some courts, however, do not seem to recognize that the rule is completely inappropriate in these situations.[120] In either case, plaintiffs need to be very careful when they make their allegations: if the facts of the case fit into this "ignorant intermediary" category, that should be made especially clear in *McHaffie* rule jurisdictions. These situations underscore the weakness of the rule and point to the fact that it really has no logical basis.

Those courts and commentators that espouse the vicarious view and promote the *McHaffie* rule either unjustly fail to account for these situations or are forced to create an awkward exception to their own "logic." Rather than create an artificial exception for these situations, courts should abandon the rule and hold that each entity can be held responsible for its own negligence.

Reckless Employers

Some *McHaffie* rule states recognize an exception where a plaintiff alleges that the employer was *reckless* in its entrustment or hiring.[121] Others, incredibly, do not.[122]

> Some courts allow the claim to survive on the rationale that it imposes liability above and beyond that admitted by an employer's *respondeat superior* admission . . . it makes the award of punitive damages possible where the *respondeat superior* admission, by itself, does not. In other jurisdictions, the employer is liable for punitive damages only if its employee would be liable for such damages.[123]

The recognition of an exception certainly mitigates the potentially harsh effects of the rule, but it does not make the rule acceptable. Furthermore, the application of the exception is problematic: in states that have a high bar for pleading punitive damages, the exception only becomes relevant in "the most extraordinary cases,"[124] and in those states that have a low bar for pleading

---

119. *Willis*, 159 S.E.2d at 159. *See also Clooney*, 352 So. 2d at 1220.

120. *See, e.g.*, Rodgers v. McFarland, 402 S.W.2d 208 (Tex. Civ. App. 1966).

121. *See, e.g.*, *Clooney*, 352 So. 2d at 1220; Estate of Arrington v. Fields, 578 S.W.2d 173, 178–79 (Tex. Civ. App. 1979).

122. *See, e.g.*, *Hood*, 459 F. Supp. at 686; *Rodgers*, 402 S.W.2d at 210.

123. Burns, *supra* note 21, at 675.

124. Scroggins v. Yellow Freight Sys., 98 F. Supp. 2d 928, 933 (E.D. Tenn. 2000); *see also* Durben v. Am. Materials, Inc., 503 S.E.2d 618, 620 (Ga. Ct. App. 1998) (holding gross negligence insufficient as a matter of law to support a triable claim for punitive damages).

punitive damages, the exception may apply in every case where the rule is implicated.[125]

Regardless of the problems associated with the exception, the failure to recognize the exception is far more problematic. In these jurisdictions, once an employer admits to *respondeat superior* liability, the employer's wanton disregard, willful misconduct, malice, and/or conscious indifference cannot even be examined: "No matter how culpable the conduct of one who entrusts to another the means of injury to third persons, such entrustor cannot incur direct liability for punitive damages and can prevent evidence of wanton misconduct from being considered by the jury by the simple expediency of admitting agency."[126]

The failure to recognize the exception thwarts the very purpose of punitive damages, which are imposed to punish the "creation of an unwarranted risk, not [just] the actual harm that results from the risk."[127] As such, punitive damages are intended to address the potential but unrealized harm to others. In any given case, the employer's recklessness may result in actual injury to an unlucky few, but the potential harm and the unwarranted risk created by a reckless motor carrier is massive. The punitive damages exception does not solve all of the problems that the majority rule creates, but its recognition is absolutely necessary in those states that do impose the rule.

Dealing with *McHaffie*

When litigating in a *McHaffie* rule jurisdiction, a plaintiff should consider a number of options that might permit him or her to maintain a direct negligence claim(s) against the motor carrier. Arguably, the easiest way to avoid the rule is to avoid any allegations regarding the motor carrier's vicarious liability. Admittedly, this is likely a very frightening proposition for a plaintiff (and his or her attorney). A vicarious liability allegation may be a party's best and most reliable bet for holding a company accountable for an employee's negligence. And certainly, this route is not advisable for those cases where the employee's negligence is solely or primarily his or her own, cases where the plaintiff's direct negligence theory will be difficult to establish, or, frankly, any other cases where such a tactic is just too risky to attempt a novel legal strategy. Nevertheless, such a move might make perfect sense in a situation where a strong direct liability case can be made against the employer and/or where the defendant employee in question is an insured under the motor carrier's insurance policy. In such a case, the defendant company should not be able to invoke the rule because no vicarious liability has been alleged. It is conceivable, and perhaps likely, that in response to such a move, a defendant employer might actually try to assert (rather than admit) the agency relationship in particular cases just so that it may take advantage of the *McHaffie* rule. While such a tactic may prove

125. *James v. Kelly Trucking Co.*, 661 S.E.2d 329, 332 (S.C. 2008); *see also* Porter v. Erickson Transp. Co., 851 S.W.2d 725 (Mo. Ct. App. 1993).

126. *Elrod v. G & R Constr. Co.*, 628 S.W.2d 17, 20–21 (Ark. 1982) (Hays, J., concurring and dissenting).

127. Ayala v. Washington, 679 A.2d 1057, 1069 (D.C. 1996) (citing TXO Prod. Corp. v. Alliance Res. Corp., 509 U.S. 443, 459–60 (1993)).

effective in some courts, such an approach at least puts plaintiffs in a powerful rhetorical position to expose the motor carrier's true purpose in "admitting" *respondeat superior* liability—the obscuring and concealment of its independent negligence and recklessness.

Instead of foregoing a vicarious liability allegation, plaintiffs could also attempt to avoid some of the implications of the *McHaffie* rule by making a claim against the *individual(s)* responsible for hiring, training, or supervising the employee (in addition to the employee) rather than the company employer. In such a situation, the evidence that typically becomes a casualty of the imposition of the rules stays in the case, and the reasoning commonly applied by courts in these kinds of cases—that the suit in addition to the driver-employee is merely an alternative way to establish the employer's liability—loses much, if not all, of its force. Just to be safe, plaintiffs could follow this course *and* sue the company as well: in the worst-case scenario, the direct claim against the *company* might be dismissed pursuant to *McHaffie*. The other claims, however, would remain viable, and the company's negligence could still be show cased via the nondriver employee's actions and omissions.

Finally, more and more claims against trucking companies also include claims against double-brokering motor carriers, freight brokers, freight forwarders, shippers, and other participants in the freight chain. In cases involving such defendants, one of the claims against freight brokers (and other entities responsible for selecting or using motor carriers) concerns the incompetence and/or recklessness of the motor carrier. In these cases, even where the *McHaffie* rule is applied and the plaintiff's direct claims against the motor carrier are dismissed, a significant portion of the evidence related to those dismissed direct claims may still be admissible as evidence related to plaintiff's negligent selection claim against the freight broker and/or other entities. Nevertheless, in such situations, dismissal of the direct claims is still probably in the motor carrier defendant's best interests. First, the dismissal may remove the motor carrier (in its own, independent capacity) from the verdict form and eliminate the possibility of additional fault (and potentially increase the plaintiff's comparative fault). And second, a plaintiff may ultimately settle her claims against the other entities in the freight chain, thereby eliminating the potential relevance of the evidence at issue.

Conclusion

A truck driver's individual error that caused a crash may sometimes be found to be a result of a simple driving mistake, and nothing more. The unfortunate truth is that it is far more likely that the driver's error was predictable and completely preventable had the motor carrier that employed the driver implemented reasonable practices and procedures for proper driver selection, training, and supervision. In order to address these problems, it is essential that motor carriers be held accountable for their own negligence in failing to implement reasonable and safe policies to prevent these crashes.

The trucking defense bar calls direct claims "the bane of [their] existence." There is a good reason they feel that way. Direct claims against motor carriers identify the root causes of dangerous conduct and crashes and allow for the presentation of evidence that makes reasonable juries carefully consider the nuances of proximate cause.

The *McHaffie* rule is no longer the majority position, but direct claims remain under threat. Numerous courts still follow this rule, which permits motor carriers to remain immune from accountability for their own failures. The exclusion of direct claims against an employer when the employer has admitted an agency or employment relationship with the driver was never as well-thought-out as it should have been. As various forms of comparative fault have entered the legal landscape, the logical basis of the already-flawed rationale has eroded to the point that there remains no sound reason for following the *McHaffie* rule. Courts should examine the conceptual underpinnings of the prior decisions and refuse to apply a rule that is a vestigial "remnant of an abandoned doctrine."[128]

Practitioners should continue to argue against the application of the *McHaffie* rule and should continue to find ways around the practical consequences of the rule. Direct claims against motor carriers are still the best way to hold trucking companies accountable for their own negligence.

---

128. *See* fn. 20 and accompanying text in this chapter.

CHAPTER 10
Standard Defenses in a Trucking Case

Joseph P. Moriarty, Esq.

Overview

The focus of this chapter is on defenses to claims arising from accidental injury, death, and damage to property involving the use and operation of commercial trucks and trailers. We start with identifying procedural issues that may impact trucking cases, including the statute of limitations defense and jurisdiction and venue selection. Then we examine factual and legal defenses to the plaintiff establishing a prima facie negligence claim when the defendant denies liability for lack of duty, breach, proximate cause, and/or damages. Next, we look at defenses that apply even when the defendant is negligent under comparative fault and contributory negligent systems, where the plaintiff's recovery is barred or limited by apportioning fault on the plaintiff. In addition, we look at other situations, where the defendant may point the finger at a codefendant or third-party for causing the crash for contribution toward the damages. In other instances, the best defense is to admit liability and defend the claim on damages to attempt to exclude from evidence bad facts and to gain credibility with the jury. We also look at defenses applicable to the plaintiff's claimed damages, including disputing the medical causation of the plaintiff's injuries, arguing the plaintiff's injuries were caused by preexisting conditions, or raising the plaintiff's failure to mitigate damages. Lastly, this chapter ends with a discussion relating to special defenses that arise in cargo claims involving the trucking business.

Procedural and Technical Defenses: Statute of Limitations, Removal to Federal Court, and Transfer to More Favorable Venue

One of the first things you should consider when evaluating a trucking claim is whether the action is time-barred by the applicable statute of limitations. In general, the statute of limitations is a law passed by a legislative body to set the maximum time after an event to file a lawsuit. Thus, the prescribed time period may vary depending on the applicable law and type of claim. For example, in Virginia there is a two-year statute of limitations for personal injury and wrongful death claims,[1] and a five-year statute of limitations for property damage claims.[2] Typically, the statute of limitations begins to run on the date of the trucking accident. However, most jurisdictions toll or delay the start of the limitations period when there are special recognized circumstances. For instance, where the claimant is a minor, the accrual or starting of the limitations period is tolled, in most jurisdictions, until the claimant reaches the age of 18 years old. It is important to determine the applicable accrual date and statute of limitations for filing a lawsuit to avoid being time-barred if you are bringing the claim. If you are defending against the claim, it is similarly important because you could waive the statute of limitations bar if you fail to assert the defense in your initial responsive pleadings.

Another procedural issue to consider in a trucking case is whether to litigate in state or federal court. Federal court jurisdiction arises when there is a federal question, that is, the action arises under the U.S. Constitution or laws of the United States,[3] or diversity of citizenship between the plaintiffs and defendants.[4] Federal question jurisdiction is rare in trucking cases. This is because the alleged violation of the Federal Motor Carrier Safety Regulations, 49 C.F.R. Part 390 (FMCSR), does not create a viable federal claim.[5] Consequently, the ability to litigate in federal court likely depends on establishing diversity jurisdiction based on the citizenship of the parties. Claims against trucking companies often

1. *See, e.g.*, VA. CODE §§ 8.01-243(A) and 8.01-244(B) (Virginia's two-year statute of limitations for personal injury and wrongful death actions). Most states also have two-year limitations periods for personal injury and wrongful death actions. *See, e.g.*, W. VA. CODE § 55-7-6(d); N.C. GEN. STAT. § 1-53(4) (wrongful death actions only, personal injury actions have a threat-year limitations period under N.C. GEN. STAT. § 1-52(16)). But three states have a one-year limitations period. *See* KY. REV. STAT. § 413.140; LA. CIV. CODE art. 2315.2 (wrongful death actions only, personal injury actions have a two-year limitations period under LA. CIV. CODE art. 3493.11); TENN. CODE § 28-3-104. And others have a three-year limitations period. *See, e.g.*, ARK. CODE § 16-62-102(c); MD. CODE CTS. & JUD. PROC. § 5-101.

2. *See, e.g.*, VA. CODE § 8.01-243(B) (Virginia's five-year statute of limitations for property damage actions). Limitations period for property damage actions vary greatly by state. *See, e.g.*, ARIZ. REV. STAT. § 12-542 (two years); CAL. CIV. PROC. CODE § 338(c)(1) (three years); GA. CODE § 9-3-30 (four years); IOWA CODE § 614.1(4) (five years); ME. STAT. tit. 14 § 752 (six years); R.I. GEN. LAWS § 9-1-13 (ten years).

3. 28 U.S.C. § 1331 (providing federal question jurisdiction).

4. 28 U.S.C. § 1441(b) (providing removal based on diversity of citizenship).

5. *See, e.g.*, Lipscomb v. Zurich Am. Ins. Co., 2012 U.S. Dist. LEXIS 72955, 2012 WL 1902595 (E.D. La., May 25, 2015).

involve an in-state claimant against an out-of-state truck driver and trucking company and damages more than $75,000. Such claims may be heard in federal court instead of state court because of diversity jurisdiction.

If there is federal court diversity jurisdiction, then the plaintiff has the choice to file in state court or federal court. If the plaintiff files in state court, and there is diversity jurisdiction, then defendants may elect to remove the case to federal court.[6] The decision to file in, or remove to, federal court versus filing or remaining in state court depends on the legal and factual issues in dispute in the specific case. Factors to consider, among others, include the potential differences in state court and federal court in the applicable jurisdiction as to summary judgment, gatekeeping on expert testimony, enforcement of discovery and evidentiary rules, expected timing for setting a jury trial, assignment of judges, jury pools, and appellate avenues. Additionally, federal courts presiding over an action under diversity jurisdiction will apply federal procedural law and the forum state's substantive law. In general, the plaintiffs' bar prefers state court, and the defense bar prefers federal court, but there are exceptions to this rule of thumb depending on the issues in the case and specific jurisdiction.

Another important procedural issue to consider is the proper and preferred venue. Venue is the court, that is, the city or county in state court and district or division in federal court where the case is litigated. Venue impacts the potential judges and jury pools. A claimant may have the choice to file in several different courts under the applicable venue statute. For example, when the trucking accident occurred on a stretch of interstate in a rural county and the claimant was transported by ambulance to a nearby large city for medical treatment, the rural county and large city could be proper venues to file the action. In other situations, the claimant may select a favorable venue that has no nexus to the claims involving the case. In those instances, the defendants may consider objecting to venue and asking the court to transfer to a proper venue.[7] Moreover, if the claimant filed in a venue that is far away from the factual witnesses in the case, the defendant may consider filing a motion to transfer venue to a more convenient venue.[8] Selecting and challenging the venue could mean a favorable or unfavorable judge and jury pool, thus impacting the outcome of the trucking claim.

Plaintiff's Primary Burden of Proof

To establish a prima facie case for negligence the following elements must be proved: (1) a legal duty to use reasonable and ordinary care toward the plaintiff; (2) a breach of such legal duty through unreasonable conduct; and (3) such breach was both the cause in fact and the proximate cause of plaintiff's injury;

---

6. 28 U.S.C. § 1446 (providing procedure for removal of civil actions).

7. *See* Norfolk & Western Railway Co. v. Williams, 389 S.E.2d 714, 715 (Va. 1990) (quoting Gulf Oil Corp. v. Gilbert, 330 U.S. 501, 507 (1947)); Livingston v. Gregurek, 650 S.W.3d 721, 722 (Tex. Ct. App. 2022).

8. *See* 28 U.S.C. § 1404(a) (providing "[f]or the convenience of parties and witnesses, in the interest of justice, a district court may transfer any civil action to any district or division where it might have been brought").

and (4) plaintiff suffered actual harm and damages in the form of physical injury to plaintiff's person or property.[9] Negligence as a matter of law, also known as negligence *per se*, is based on the breach of a statutory duty and conclusively establishes both duty and breach.[10] Negligence *per se* "is not a finding of liability *per se* because the plaintiff will also have to prove proximate cause and damages."[11]

The primary defense to trucking cases is to argue that the truck driver was not at fault in causing the crash. It is the plaintiff's burden to prove negligence, not the defendant's burden to prove lack of negligence.[12] The no-fault defense is best illustrated by a side-swipe accident where the truck driver denies changing lanes or drifting into the plaintiff's lane of travel before the crash. Another classic example is the red light, green light scenario where the plaintiff and defendant each claim they had the green light when entering the intersection before the crash. Under these situations, the plaintiff has the burden to prove by a preponderance of evidence, that is, a more likely than not standard, that the truck driver was at fault in causing the crash. When the defendant's fault is in dispute, the jury's decision at trial on whether the plaintiff met the burden of proof is typically determined by the credibility of the parties, independent witness testimony, and other evidence, such as the point of impact shown by the property damage to the vehicles. When there is a dash camera in one of the vehicles involved in the crash, often from a forward-facing dash camera in the tractor, liability disputes may be resolved by the video.

In addition, most jurisdictions provide jury instructions for finding no fault in certain instances when the truck driver was confronted by a sudden emergency, mechanical failure, or medical emergency before the crash. These defenses require the circumstances to be sudden and unexpected. Further, typically these defenses may not be invoked by one who creates or contributes to the emergency by that person's own negligence.[13] For example, a driver knowingly driving during adverse weather conditions typically cannot rely on the sudden emergency defense.[14] Similarly, a medical emergency, such as blacking out, and mechanical failure, such as defective brakes, must be unforeseen.[15]

Even if the truck driver breached a duty owed to the plaintiff, the plaintiff must prove that the breach was a proximate cause of the crash. "The proximate

---

9. Kaltman v. All American Pest Control, Inc., 706 S.E.2d 864 (Va. 2011).

10. *See, e.g.*, Sikora v. Wenzel, 727 N.E.2d 1277, 1280 (Ohio 2000).

11. *See, e.g.*, Chambers v. St. Mary's Sch., 697 N.E.2d 198, 201 (Ohio 1998), citing Pond v. Leslein, 647 N.E.2d 477, 479 (Ohio 1995).

12. Davoudlarian v. Krombein, 418 S.E.2d 868, 870 (Va. 1992); Bauer v. J.B. Hunt Transp., 150 F.3d 759, 763–64 (7th Cir. 1998) (quoting Leonardi v. Loyola Univ. of Chicago, 658 N.E.2d 450, 455 (Ill. 1995)).

13. *See* Hancock-Underwood v. Knight, 670 S.E.2d 720 (Va. 2009), citing Bloxom v. McCoy, 17 S.E.2d 401, 403 (Va. 1941); Thibodeau v. Vandermark, 360 S.E.2d 171, 173 (Va. 1987).

14. *See* Herr v. Wheeler, 634 S.E.2d 317, 320 (Va. 2006) (hydroplaning of vehicle held not to constitute sudden emergency).

15. *See* Hancock-Underwood v. Knight, 670 S.E.2d 720 (medical emergency); McGinn v. New York City Transit Auth., 658 N.Y.S.2d 121, 379 (N.Y. App. Div. 1997) (medical emergency); Culberson v. McCloud, 315 S.E.2d 219 (Va. 1984).

cause of an event is that act or omission which, in natural and continuous sequence, unbroken by an efficient intervening cause, produces the event, and without which that event would not have occurred."[16] The "but for" rule of proximate causation is followed, so that defendants are not liable "unless the harm would not have occurred but for the defendant's act."[17] While proximate cause is most often a question of fact for the jury, the court may resolve the question as a matter of law where "reasonable persons could not differ as to its existence or absence."[18] "[I]f the cause of the event is left to conjecture, guess, or random judgment, the plaintiff cannot recover."[19] For example, a truck traveling at a substantial speed over the speed limit is breaching a duty of care owed to other drivers. However, if the truck's speed did not contribute to the crash, then the speeding is not a proximate cause of the accident. At times this is clear and such evidence is excluded by the judge, but more often the proximate cause of the crash is a factual issue resolved by the jury.

Affirmatively Proving Plaintiff's Fault, Comparative Fault, and Contributory Negligence

There are four comparative fault systems that involve some method of dividing damages between the plaintiff and defendant when the plaintiff has been contributorily negligent.[20] "The first is the so-called Mississippi, or 'pure,' form—in which a plaintiff may recover from a defendant who was to some extent negligent, irrespective of the extent of the plaintiff's own negligence."[21] For example, if the plaintiff is 75 percent negligent in causing the crash, then the damages award would be reduced by 75 percent. This allows injured parties compensation even when they are at fault, but reduces damages attributable to that fault, and renders "each tortfeasor responsible for paying for his or her percentage of fault *and no more*."[22]

The modified comparative fault systems—which has been adopted in most jurisdictions—permits the plaintiff to recover if his or her fault is relatively small in contrast to that of the defendant. The modified comparative fault systems are divided into three general types: (1) the 50 percent rule; (2) the 51 percent rule, and (3) the "slight/gross negligence" system.[23] In the modified form

16. McCauley v. Purdue Pharma L.P., 331 F. Supp. 2d 449, 461 (W.D. Va. 2004) (quoting Beale v. Jones, 171 S.E.2d 851, 853 (Va. 1970)).

17. *Id.* at 461 (citing Sugarland Run Homeowners Ass'n v. Halfmann, 535 S.E.2d 469, 474 (Va. 2000)).

18. McCauley v. Purdue Pharma L.P., 331 F. Supp. 2d 449, at 461 (W.D. Va. 2004) (citing Atkinson v. Scheer, 508 S.E.2d 68, 71 (Va. 1998)).

19. Hodge v. Wal-Mart Stores, Inc., 360 F.3d 446, 451 (4th Cir. 2004) (quoting Town of West Point v. Evans, 299 S.E.2d 349 (Va. 1983)).

20. 3 American Law of Torts § 13:8 (Dec. 2023 Update).

21. *Id.* at 691 (chapter contributing editor George E. Abdo, III, Esquire).

22. State Farm Ins. Cos. v. Premier Manufactured Sys. Inc., 172 P.3d 410, 413 (Ariz. 2007) (quoting Dietz v. Gen. Elec. Co., 821 P.2d 166 (1991)).

23. American Law of Torts, *supra* note 20 (citations omitted).

of comparative negligence, a plaintiff may recover in proportion to the percentage of negligence attributed to the plaintiff, but only if the plaintiff's negligence either (1) does not exceed (50 percent rule jurisdictions) or (2) is less than (49 percent jurisdictions) the defendant's negligence.[24] The last modified comparative fault system—the "slight negligence" system—is only followed in South Dakota. There, the plaintiff may recover a proportionate fault share of the plaintiff's damages only so long as the trier of fact finds the plaintiff's negligence to be "slight" in comparison to the negligence of the defendant.[25] "Whether a plaintiff's negligence is slight compared to that of the defendant is a question of fact and varies with the facts and circumstances of each case."[26] In practice, a jury may find it difficult to place a high percentage of negligence on a seriously injured plaintiff against a corporate defendant in a trucking case.

Lastly, there are a few states that do not apply comparative fault. Instead, these states apply a pure contributorily negligence rule, which, if applicable, acts as a complete bar to the plaintiff's recovery of damages. Thus, a plaintiff is barred from recovery if the plaintiff is only 1 percent contributorily negligent. In practice, juries generally require a higher degree of negligence on the part of the plaintiff before returning a defense verdict (particularly in serious cases), and instead return compromise verdicts. If the defendant was willfully and wantonly negligent, then to bar the plaintiff's recovery the plaintiff must also be guilty of willful and wanton conduct.[27] In addition, contributory negligence will not bar plaintiff's recovery if the last clear chance doctrine applies. For example, the last clear chance doctrine may apply when (1) the plaintiff's negligence placed the plaintiff in peril that the plaintiff could not cure or did not realize, (2) the defendant realized or should have realized plaintiff's peril, and (3) the defendant could have prevented injuring the imperiled plaintiff by using ordinary care.[28]

Following is a breakdown for the 50 states and District of Columbia on comparative fault and contributory negligence standards as of January of 2024.[29] This is just a summary. Laws change and some states have unique nuances that must be considered.

---

24. McIntyre v. Balentine, 833 S.W.2d 52, 57 (Tenn. 1992). In multiple defendant situations, some jurisdictions may require the plaintiff's negligence to be less than the negligence of each such defendant. Thus, if there are two defendants and each are only 30 percent at fault, if the plaintiff is 40 percent at fault, the plaintiff will be denied any recovery.

25. S.D. Codified Laws §§ 20-9-1, 20-9-2 (2004).

26. Estate of Largent v. United States, 910 F.2d 497, 499 (8th Cir. 1990).

27. Wolfe v. Baube, 403 S.E.2d 338, 339 (Va. 1991).

28. Williams v. Harrison, 497 S.E.2d 467, 470 (Va. 1998).

29. Morton F. Daller & Nicholas Daller, Tort Law Desk Reference—A Fifty-State Compendium (2024 ed.) (providing a survey of the tort laws of the 50 states and the District of Columbia).

Pure Comparative Fault (12):	AR, AZ, CA, FL, KY, LA, MS, MO, NM, NY, RI, and WA
50 Percent Bar Rule (10)	AK, CO, GA, ID, KS, ME, NE, ND, TN, and UT
51 Percent Bar Rule (23)	CT, HI, IL, IN, ID, IA, MA, MI, MN, MT, NV, NH, NJ, OH, OK, OR, PA, SC, TX, VT, WV, WI, and WY
Slight Negligence (1)	SD
Contributory Negligence (5)	AL, DC, NC, MD, and VA

Pointing Finger at Other Parties Codefendants, Third-Party Claims, and Empty Chair

A defendant may avoid liability or reduce the amount of damages the defendant is responsible for by pointing the finger at a codefendant or third party. States differ on what form of liability to apply when multiple parties are responsible for causing an injury or damage. There are three general forms of joint and several liability with some variations for specific states.[30] The first group is "pure joint and several liability" systems, where a tortfeasor whose negligence proximately contributed to causing an injury may be held liable for the entire resulting loss.[31] The second group is "modified joint and several liability" systems, where a tortfeasor is responsible for the entire verdict only if that tortfeasor is found to be at or above a specified percentage of fault.[32] The third group is "pure several liability" systems, where a tortfeasor is only liable for that tortfeasor's assigned portion of damages based on that tortfeasor's percentage of responsibility.[33]

The jurisdiction's joint and several liability law on the allocation of fault and damages amongst tortfeasors may impact the plaintiff's target defendant and a defendants' decision to point the finger at others. Sometimes this results in a deep-pocket defendant who is only nominally involved being the primary target of the plaintiff's case, especially if the other tortfeasors have already settled (in which case the joint tortfeasor may get a credit for the monies paid in settlement), or are immune from liability, bankrupt, insolvent, uninsured, or otherwise judgment-proof. This also means that defendants may want to use a joint defense agreement and expert sharing agreement to ensure that a codefendant does not settle out early, fund the plaintiff's case, and harm the other defendants by taking a key expert out of play late in the litigation. Earlier is always the best time to look at liability of others and deciding how that could impact the plaintiff's claim and the defendants' defenses.

30. *See, e.g.*, Themis Advocates Group's State Resources—Overview of Court Systems, https://www.themisadvocatesgroup.com/state-resources (last visited Jan. 28, 2024).

31. Holcim (US), Inc. v. Ohio Cas. Ins. Co., 38 So. 3d 722, 729 (Ala. 2009).

32. *See* Iowa Code § 668.4 (applying joint and several liability only for defendants 50 percent or more at fault and for plaintiff's economic damages only).

33. *See* Sowinski v. Walker, 198 P.3d 1134 (Alaska 2008).

Admitting Liability to Sanitize the Evidence at Trial

When liability against a defendant is likely but not certain, the defendant may consider admitting liability. This allows the defendant to focus solely on damages with the jury and moving to exclude harmful evidence that is material solely to the issue of fault. "This, of course, does not mean that an admission of liability precludes a plaintiff from showing how an accident happened if such evidence is material to the issue of damages."[34] "In an action for personal injuries, where liability is admitted and the only issue to be tried is the amount of damage, the force of the impact and the surrounding circumstances may be relevant and material to indicate the extent of plaintiff's injuries."[35] However, in an action for wrongful death where the relevant damages are the loss to the statutory beneficiaries, the details of the crash could have no bearing on the elements of damages.[36] Further, in states where punitive damages are capped, the defendant may consider admitting to punitive damages to exclude evidence unrelated to compensatory damages to the plaintiff.[37] On the motion in limine, the judge may rule on what facts come in and what facts stay out of trial depending on the scope of the admission and damages at issue in the case. The defendants may decide that the concession on negligence in causing the crash takes the sting out of the plaintiff's claims or, at least, allows the defendant to gain some credibility with the jury on the damages at trial.

Damages Defenses—Preexisting Injuries or Medical Conditions and Failure to Mitigate Damages

In many trucking cases, the main dispute on damages is the medical causation of the plaintiff's injuries and damages. In general, the recoverable damages in a personal injury case include the following:

- The injuries' effect on health, degree, and probable duration
- Physical pain and suffering
- Disfigurement or deformity and any associated humiliation
- Inconvenience
- Medical expenses
- Lost earnings and diminished earning capacity[38]

Under the "eggshell skull" rule, defendants must take the plaintiffs as they find them.[39] In other words, a defendant would be liable in negligence for damages to a plaintiff with a thin skull who suffered death, when an ordinary person

34. Fuentes v. Tucker, 187 P.2d 752 (Cal. 1947).

35. *Id.* (citation omitted).

36. *Id.*

37. There are other ramifications of choosing to admit liability, depending on the jurisdiction. See Chapter 9 in this book by J.J. Burns.

38. *See* Va. Model Jury Instr. No. 9.000; *see also* N.C. Pattern Civil Jury Instr. No. 810.02.

39. Fuller v. Merten, 22 P.3d 1221 (Or. 2001).

would only have suffered a mild bump on the head.[40] Thus, the defendant cannot avoid liability because the extent or particular manner of harm was unforeseeable.[41] There are, however, two defenses that may act to limit the plaintiff's claimed damages: (1) the plaintiff's preexisting conditions and (2) the plaintiff's failure to mitigate damages.

The plaintiff has the burden to prove the plaintiff's claimed damages were proximately caused by the crash. Preexisting injuries may be relevant to showing whether a claimed injury was proximately caused by the defendant.[42] It is common sense that the plaintiff is not entitled to recover for the preexisting condition. However, when the plaintiff had a preexisting condition that was aggravated by the accident or that treatment for the condition became more difficult, then the plaintiff may recover for the aggravation and/or increased difficulty of treatment.[43] When there are prior issues documented in the medical records and diagnostic films, then this often becomes an issue for the jury to decide by considering the plaintiff's testimony on onset and aggravation of injuries after the crash, and any evidence on the plaintiff's pre- and post-crash activities.

The second defense arises when the plaintiff fails to mitigate damages. The defendant has the burden to prove the plaintiff's failure to mitigate damages. A jury instruction on mitigation of damages is appropriate when there is evidence of negligence on the part of the plaintiff in not consulting a doctor, not consulting a doctor as soon as a reasonable person would, not following a doctor's advice, or not properly caring for and treating injuries that do not require the attention of a doctor.[44] However, the plaintiff is required only to undertake reasonable efforts to avoid the consequences of injury.[45] If there is sufficient evidence to persuade a jury on this defense, then damages caused by the plaintiff's failure to exercise such care cannot be recovered.[46]

Defenses to Cargo Claims

Liability for the loss or damage of cargo being transported in interstate commerce is governed by the Carmack Amendment to the Interstate Commerce Act

---

40. *Id.*

41. *See* Restatement Second of Torts § 435(1).

42. *See* 6 Wash. Prac., Wash. Pattern Jury Instr. Civ., WPI 30.18 (7th ed) (Apr. 2021 update).

43. *See* Va. Model Jury Instr. No. 9.030.

44. Harris Cnty. v. Smoker, 934 S.W.2d 714 (Tex. App. Houston 1st Dist. 1996), *writ denied* (Oct. 2, 1997).

45. *See, e.g.*, McCalla v. Nusight Vision Centers of Pennsylvania, P.C., 2004 U.S. Dist. LEXIS 2993, 2004 WL 384991 (E.D. Pa. Feb. 25, 2004) (court instructed jury that the law doesn't require an injured person to undergo a medical procedure that doesn't have a reasonable chance of improving the plaintiff's condition or is too risky or has some unusual risks or burdens); Seagers v. Pailet, 656 So. 2d 700 (La. Ct. App. 5th Cir. 1995) (plaintiff failed to have corrective surgery because she could not afford cost, and insurance company refused to pay for it; plaintiff did not fail to reasonably mitigate her damages).

46. Karahodzic v. JBS Carriers, Inc., 881 F.3d 1009 (7th Cir. 2018).

(Carmack Amendment).[47] The Carmack Amendment, which preempts state and common law claims,[48] creates a system of fault distribution and damage recovery, allowing the innocent shipper and consignees to recover for loss or damage to their goods without having to prove where the loss occurred, how the loss occurred, or which carrier was the actual wrongdoer in causing the loss.[49] To make a case against a common carrier, a shipper must show that (1) the shipper delivered the goods to be transported free of damages; (2) that the goods were damaged in some way prior to delivery; and (3) the amount of damages that the goods suffered.[50]

There are also affirmative defenses for carriers, who are without fault if they prove that the sole cause of the loss or damage was due to (1) the act of the shipper, (2) an Act of God,[51] (3) the public enemy (i.e., foreign nation at war with the carrier's government, pirates at the high seas, insurrectionist against their own government, but not robbers, hijackers, or striking employees), (4) the public authority (i.e., seized goods by legal authority, such as writ of attachment), or (5) the inherent vice or nature of the cargo.[52] In order for a carrier to be excused from liability for loss due to one of these five exceptions, it must be the proximate cause of the damage to the cargo, and the carrier must prove it was free from negligence. In addition to the Carmack Amendment, defenses to cargo claims may arise from the Uniform Bill of Lading,[53] limitation of carrier's liability,[54] and notice and claim filing provisions.[55]

In summary, the Carmack Amendment for interstate transport, and state law for intrastate transport, sets forth the liability and recoverable damages for cargo claims. It is important to carefully review the agreements between the carrier and the shipper to determine if an exception applies, or if the terms of the Carmack Amendment were properly modified by contract between the shipper and carrier. For example, the shipper and carrier may agree to exclude certain types of damages from the carrier's liability, or to limit the carrier's liability to a specific amount (see 49 U.S.C. § 14706(f)), or to require a claim be made by the

47. 49 U.S.C. § 14706. The liability of a carrier for damage to property that was transported in intrastate commerce is governed by the law of the state in where the loss occurred.

48. *See* Hughes v. United Van Lines, Inc., 829 F.2d 1407 (7th Cir. 1987) (causes of action for negligence, breach of insurance contract, breach of contract of carriage, conversion, intentional misrepresentation, negligent misrepresentation, and negligent infliction of emotional distress are all preempted by the Carmack Amendment).

49. *Id.; see also* Missouri P. R. Co. v. Elmore & Stahl, 377 U.S. 134 (1964) (holding that the liability of a carrier for damage to an interstate shipment is a matter of federal law controlled by federal statutes and decisions).

50. 49 U.S.C. § 14706.

51. The trucking company will not be relieved of liability if the trucking company's negligence contributed to the loss. *See* Bernstein v. Illinois Cent. R.R., 208 N.W.679 (Mich. 1926) (finding a jury issue whether negligent delay combined with Act of God defense in causing spoiled cargo).

52. 49 U.S.C. § 14706.

53. *Id.*

54. *Id.* § 14706(f) (limiting liability of household goods to declared value).

55. *Id.* § 14706(e) (providing a carrier may, by contract, require that a claim be made to it by a shipper within nine months of the shipment and that a civil action be instituted within two years after the denial of such a claim).

shipper within nine months of the shipment and that civil suit be filed within two years after the denial of such a claim (see 49 U.S.C. § 14706(e)). Lastly, when a carrier is held liable to the shipper or consignee for negligence of another connecting carrier, the Carmack Amendment provides indemnification so that the innocent carrier may recover from the at-fault carrier.[56]

56. *See, e.g.*, United States v. Savage Truck Line, Inc., 209 F.2d 442 (4th Cir. 1953).

CHAPTER 11

Evidence: Data Collection, Analysis, Evidence Preservation, Essential Discovery, Investigation, Spoliation

Alex Celio, Esq., Megan S. Peterson, Esq., and Mark A. Perkins, Esq.

This chapter will focus on evidence gathering, essential discovery, investigation, and spoliation of evidence specific to commercial vehicles. The goal is to provide you with the basics of what attorneys and claims professionals should be aware of. This will not be a deep dive into science, but more of a reference guide so you can proceed in more depth.

Data Collection, Analysis, and Preservation of Evidence

When a commercial vehicle accident occurs, the sophisticated defendant truck company will immediately assemble a team comprised of an experienced trucking defense attorney, a qualified field adjuster, and an accident reconstructionist experienced in investigating truck accidents, and officials from the defendant company. For purposes of attempting to protect the work under the attorney's work product privilege, the claim adjuster and the reconstructionist should receive instructions and communicate directly through the assigned defense attorney. The attorney will instruct them that they are specifically being retained in anticipation of litigation. In order to attempt to prevent the plaintiff from obtaining discovery of his or her work, all formal communication sent to counsel should be conspicuously marked that the investigation is being conducted in anticipation of litigation and that the work product delivered to the attorney is intended to be privileged.

There are two primary goals:

Determine what happened

Each member of the team serves a role.

Dispatcher's Role

The driver likely will call the dispatcher after the accident.

1. Preserve all evidence (favorable or not). A properly trained dispatcher will immediately instruct the driver to:
   a. Place triangles or other warning devices immediately.
   b. Direct traffic to prevent a subsequent accident. If not already done, the driver should politely check on the condition of the other people at the scene of the accident.
   c. If there has been any leakage or spillage of a hazardous substance, to keep people away from the hazard.
   d. Not discuss the accident facts with anyone except the investigating officer unless there is a possibility that the driver is being investigated for a crime, in which case the driver may invoke his Fifth Amendment rights against self-incrimination.
   e. Avoid guessing or speculating when answering police questions about the accident, particularly regarding questions of time, speed, and distance of vehicle movement.
   f. Move the vehicles if there are serious injuries or deaths. And, if they must be moved, to mark the locations of the vehicles on the pavement prior to moving them
   g. Not remove the commercial vehicle from the scene, even if it is capable of being driven and, instead, that it must be towed so that data in the engine control module and other equipment is preserved.
   h. Not tamper with any of the evidence.
   i. Report for the mandatory drug and alcohol test.
2. The dispatcher should obtain the following information from the driver:
   a. Whether or not the driver is injured
   b. Whether or not there are any injuries or fatalities in the other vehicle or to others
   c. Whether the unit is drivable as well as the extent of damage to the unit, if any
   d. The precise location of the accident
   e. Contact information for return calls to the driver
   f. The type of cargo and whether or not the cargo is a hazardous material
   g. Whether there has been any spillage, leakage, or other type of release or damage to the cargo

3. The dispatcher should also do the following:

   a. Contact police to report the accident
   b. Inform the police about the cargo if it is hazardous, and report spills or leaks to the HAZMAT unit of the state police
   c. Inform the police about any known injuries and request that they summon medical assistance if it is obviously needed
   d. The dispatcher should contact the person within the company who has been designated as the person to make decisions on whether and/or

who to immediately send out to the accident scene. The dispatcher should give that person all information obtained by the dispatcher to that point.

Field Claim Adjuster's Role

Because everyone at the scene must cooperate with the police and refrain from interfering with the police investigation, the ability of the field claim adjuster to perform actual accident investigation at the scene is limited. The adjuster can be expected to prevent the driver, who may be in an extremely emotional condition, from saying or doing ill-advised things.

Field adjusters and commercial vehicle drivers sometimes speak about the accident facts to others on scene. Whether this is a good idea or bad idea depends on the circumstances and what actually is said. Admissions of liability can occur in such conversations. The field adjuster will attempt to secure adverse admissions from the driver and occupants of the noncommercial vehicle because the field adjuster will immediately be working on defending the commercial vehicle driver. It is lawful for the field adjuster to do so, but it can be problematic during discovery and trial. The adjuster can be expected to obtain the name and contact information of all persons involved and all witnesses. The field adjuster can be expected to gather evidence if the police are not doing so or if the police have ignored evidence. Some field adjusters can be expected to be completely honest in this process, but others less so. In this process, the field adjuster will take photographs, measurements, and gather information about the vehicles involved, including what electronic data may be recorded by them or the devices in them. The field adjuster will gather all paper evidence from the commercial vehicle, as well as vehicle identification numbers, license plate information, make and model of vehicles, and placard information. The field adjuster might attempt to take statements from occupants of the other vehicles, and sometimes the truck driver, but seasoned field adjusters will avoid taking statements from the truck driver because it is their goal to avoid the truck driver's liability and, instead, point to admissions of liability from the others. The ethical integrity of the field adjuster likely will be a subject for cross-examination and impeachment. The field adjuster will obtain the logistical information from the truck driver about the origin and destination of the commercial vehicle and dispatching information.

Accident Reconstructionist Role/Expectations

Both the plaintiff and the defendant will, in many serious cases, need to hire crash reconstruction experts. This should be done as early as possible by each side because evidence disappears from the scene as time passes. If the expert's first visit to the scene occurs months or years after the accident, the value of his or her testimony will be greatly diminished. Skid marks fade within a day or two and other marks may appear, which will confuse the issues.

The reconstructionist may also be helpful to law enforcement. Often law enforcement personnel inadequately identify physical evidence and other evidentiary facts, which are of great significance in making their final determinations concerning an accident. Obviously, the reconstructionist should never attempt to coerce or manipulate law enforcement personnel with respect to their findings. Any such attempts will be exposed during cross-examination and it will be extremely damaging, if not fatal, to the party's case.

In addition to the investigation of the scene, the crash reconstructionist must have access to the damaged vehicles involved. Often, one or all of the vehicles will have been repaired or salvaged within days of the loss. If you retain a reconstructionist who uncovers damning evidence, you can always choose not to call the reconstructionist as a witness at the trial. In most states, this election will allow the insurer to protect any adverse opinions from discovery.

Your reconstruction expert will make appropriate measurements and record them in an appropriate format and determine whether a survey of the scene would be helpful. Most experts now have computer-surveying equipment that can accurately survey an accident scene in the matter of a few hours. This can be important since accident scenes often change. Roads can be altered. Lighting can change, and any number of other physical changes can occur.

In addition to an inspection of the accident site, the reconstructionist should carefully inspect the vehicles. The expert should check the brakes and tread on the tires and event data recorded all devices in all vehicles involved. A party's failure to extract and preserve electronic data can lead to spoliation issues at trial. For nighttime accidents, the expert should check all appropriate lights and retro-reflective conspicuity tape. Photographs documenting this tape should be done in all nighttime accidents.

Assigned Attorney to Oversee the Investigation/Defense

In many cases, the truck company will arrange for an attorney to arrive at the crash site even before the vehicles and evidence is cleaned up. The ability to protect the accident investigation from discovery is increased by having the investigation conducted by a lawyer. Typically, the truck company will attempt to make sure that only the defense attorney obtains a statement from its driver. Statements taken by any person involved, of course, may be influenced by the adverse effects of trauma—which sometimes can make the statements unreliable. Statements that deviate from the physical evidence can be problematic for either party to the case. Good interviewers of witnesses are aware of this reality and are courteous and respectful of the emotional condition of the eyewitnesses.

The Truck Accident Investigation and Spoliation of Evidence

Initial Accident Response

Preliminary Investigation

The trucking company's goal is to assess liability, prepare a preliminary claim evaluation, and identify any potential experts needed. These experts may be engineers, accident reconstruction experts, or independent adjusters. These professionals will help determine the strength of any potential liability argument through vehicle inspections and aid in any pre-litigation discovery and evidence preservation by conducting witness interviews and scene inspections.

Along with retention of experts, the focus of preliminary accident investigation is gathering all documentation stemming from the investigation itself. Police reports will usually be available within a few days of the accident unless it was a complex multi-vehicle accident requiring more intense liability investigation. Along with the report itself, there may be photographs and body cam footage from the officer's investigation of the scene. The police report will also aid in making the preliminary determination of liability based on who was ticketed for the accident. This is not to say that a ticket or citation will solely decide liability; however, it may create a presumption of fault that will need to be overcome through discovery and expert retention. In the preliminary discovery, it may be fruitful to consult local businesses to determine whether security cameras captured the accident. This is also time sensitive, as these cameras are routinely overridden if not specifically preserved.

Evidentiary Concerns

Preservation of Evidence

In conjunction with the initial accident response, a case can be won or lost over preservation of evidence—or lack thereof. Once a company is alerted of an accident, the immediate concern should be to preserve internal documents that could be useful in discovery down the road. Aside from records required by the Federal Motor Carrier Safety Regulations,[1] companies should prioritize preserving all internal and external dash cam footage, GPS records, driver logs, maintenance records, and accident reports. Dash cam footage can simplify a case by showing video of the accident itself. It can be especially helpful when the accident descriptions from the drivers have any discrepancies. The dash cam footage will either confirm or contradict the accounts to help prove liability. Other internal documentation like event data recorder (EDR) data, GPS records, driver logs, and maintenance records will confirm the location of the truck, the hours of service of the driver, and the upkeep of the truck involved.

A truck company should preserve all driver-specific documents. A truck driver's employment application, personnel file and driver qualification file will be both relevant and discoverable in litigation. These records will be especially important if the case includes claims of negligent hiring, retention, and supervision of the trucking company. They also are relevant to the *respondeat superior* analysis. If a truck driver has a history of citations, hours of service violations, or an extensive criminal background, claimants will focus on these issues to prove the trucking company should not have hired the driver. Knowledge of these issues at the beginning of a claim can help dictate the strategy for defense.

---

1. These records are discussed in Chapter 6 in this book by Roberto Ramirez and D.J. Young about recordkeeping.

While a trucking company should work with defense counsel to maintain all records and electronic data just discussed, counsel should also send a letter of representation and preservation of evidence to claimant's counsel once notified of retention. Similarly, the claimant's counsel should do the same to the truck company and its insurance company, or their lawyers if represented. The trucking company must preserve all electronic and paper records about the truck, the driver, and the crash. The claimant must do the same. Both drivers' cell phone data should be preserved. The claimant's medical records should be preserved. The vehicles involved in the crash should be preserved. A good preservation of evidence letter will include all such things and anything else that might be evidence of the crash. This will set the scene for any spoliation claim down the road if the claimant fails to preserve the requested information. This can also lead to pre-suit resolution if either counsel has definitive information regarding liability.

Spoliation of Evidence

Spoliation of evidence rules vary by jurisdiction and depending on whether your case is in state or federal court. Spoliation can at times involve an independent cause of action or can present as an adverse inference at trial or sanctions. But spoliation cannot exist unless there was first a duty to preserve. Spoliation of evidence occurs when a party that is charged with the obligation to preserve evidence fails to do so.[2] The duty to preserve will arise whenever litigation is reasonably foreseeable and it is apparent that the potential evidence is relevant to the matter.[3] There is no bright line rule for when the duty arises: "When litigation is 'reasonably foreseeable' is a flexible fact-specific standard that allows a

---

2. Klipsch Grp., Inc. v. ePRO E-Com. Ltd., 880 F.3d 620, 628 (2d Cir. 2018) ("The party seeking discovery sanctions on the basis of spoliation must show by a preponderance of the evidence: (1) that the party having control over the evidence had an obligation to preserve it at the time it was destroyed; (2) that the records were destroyed with a culpable state of mind; and (3) that the destroyed evidence was relevant to the party's claim or defense such that a reasonable trier of fact could find that it would support that claim or defense."); Chin v. Port Auth. of New York & New Jersey, 685 F.3d 135, 162 (2d Cir. 2012) ("[A] party seeking an adverse inference instruction based on the destruction of evidence must establish (1) that the party having control over the evidence had an obligation to preserve it at the time it was destroyed; (2) that the records were destroyed with a culpable state of mind; and (3) that the destroyed evidence was relevant to the party's claim or defense such that a reasonable trier of fact could find that it would support that claim or defense.").

3. *See* Van Winkle v. Rogers, 82 F.4th 370, 375 (5th Cir. 2023) (holding that a serious accident was sufficient notice to create a duty to preserve a defective tire which allegedly caused the accident); Zeng v. Texas Tech Univ. Health Sci. Ctr. at El Paso, 836 F. App'x 203, 215 (5th Cir. 2020) (holding that company did not have an obligation to preserve without notice that prior employee intended to file suit); *In re* Rembrandt Techs. LP Pat. Litig., 899 F.3d 1254, 1269 (Fed. Cir. 2018) (Duty to preserve arises when litigation has begun or is reasonably foreseeable.); Hynix Semiconductor Inc. v. Rambus Inc., 645 F.3d 1336, 1345 (Fed. Cir. 2011) (Litigation need not be "imminent, or probable without significant contingencies" in order to be "reasonably foreseeable."); Guzman v. Jones, 804 F.3d 707, 713 (5th Cir. 2015).

district court to exercise the discretion necessary to confront the myriad factual situations inherent in the spoliation inquiry."[4]

To determine the potential consequences of a failure to preserve, look first to the court where the case is pending. Federal courts will apply the substantive laws of the states in which they sit, including any potential tort causes of action that may arise due to spoliation.[5] However, federal courts apply their own procedural rules for admission of evidence and imposition of sanctions.[6] Several states have recognized a separate tort of intentional spoliation.[7] Other states have expressly declined to extend intentional spoliation claims to separate causes of action. California, for example, refused to find a tort remedy for spoliation "when the alleged intentional spoliation is committed by a party to the underlying cause of action to which the evidence is relevant and when the spoliation is or reasonably should have been discovered before the conclusion of the underlying litigation."[8] California reasoned "that existing remedies will

---

4. Micron Tech., Inc. v. Rambus Inc., 645 F.3d 1311, 1320 (Fed. Cir. 2011) (citing Fujitsu Ltd. v. Fed. Express Corp., 247 F.3d 423, 436 (2d Cir. 2001).

5. Erie R.R. v. Tompkins, 304 U.S. 64 (1938); Garcia v. Chiquita Brands Int'l, Inc., 48 F.4th 1202, 1210 (11th Cir. 2022), *cert. denied sub nom.* Doe 8 v. Chiquita Brands Int'l, Inc., 143 S. Ct. 2659, 216 L. Ed. 2d 1237 (2023) ("Under *Erie* and its progeny, federal courts sitting in diversity apply state substantive law and federal procedural law. But as every first-year law student quickly discovers, the distinction between substance and procedure is often hazy."); Guzman v. Jones, 804 F.3d 707, 712 (5th Cir. 2015) (When making an "Erie guess" federal courts may look to intermediate appellate state courts for guidance).

6. Sherman v. Rinchem Co., 687 F.3d 996, 1006 (8th Cir. 2012) ("We now hold, in accordance with our sister circuits, that federal law applies to the imposition of sanctions for the spoliation of evidence."); Adkins v. Wolever, 554 F.3d 650, 652 (6th Cir. 2009) ("a spoliation ruling is evidentiary in nature and federal courts generally apply their own evidentiary rules in both federal question and diversity matters"); Martinez v. Brink's, Inc., 171 F. App'x 263, 269 (11th Cir. 2006) ("we note as an initial matter that *federal* law governs the imposition of spoliation sanctions, such as the adverse inference instruction given here"); King v. Ill. Cent. R.R., 337 F.3d 550 (5th Cir. 2003); U.S. v. Wise, 221 F.3d 140, 156 (5th Cir. 2000) (citing Higgins v. Martin Marietta Corp., 752 F.2d 492 (10th Cir. 1985)).

7. *See, e.g.*, State *ex rel.* W. Virginia Univ. Hosps., Inc. v. Scott, 246 W. Va. 184, 196, 866 S.E.2d 350, 362 (2021) (recognizing tort of intentional spoliation in West Virginia); Herster v. Bd. of Supervisors of Louisiana State Univ., 887 F.3d 177, 189 (5th Cir. 2018) ("Spoliation of evidence may not be based on the negligent destruction of evidence."); Rizzuto v. Davidson Ladders, Inc., 280 Conn. 225, 243, 905 A.2d 1165, 1178 (2006) (Connecticut Supreme Court concluding "that recognition of an independent cause of action for intentional spoliation of evidence is necessary to fulfill the public policy goals of the tort compensation system."); Burge v. St. Tammany Par., 336 F.3d 363, 374 (5th Cir. 2003) ("The Louisiana tort of spoliation of evidence provides a cause of action for an intentional destruction of evidence carried out for the purpose of depriving an opposing party of its use."); Hannah v. Heeter, 584 S.E.2d 560, 563–64 (W. Va. 2003) (recognizing tort of intentional spoliation in West Virginia); Oliver v. Stimson Lumber Co., 297 Mont. 336, 993 P.2d 11 (Mont. 1999) (recognizing torts of intentional and negligent spoliation in Montana); Smith v. Howard Johnson Co., Inc., 615 N.E.2d 1037 (Ohio 1993) (recognizing both first-party and third-party tort of intentional spoliation).

8. Cedars-Sinai Med. Ctr. v. Superior Court, 18 Cal. 4th 1, 4; 954 P.2d 511 (Cal. 1998). *See also* City of Los Angeles v. PricewaterhouseCoopers, LLP, 17 Cal. 5th 46, 71, 553 P.3d 1194, 1210 (2024) (recognizing intentional spoliation tort is unnecessary, where statute provides for sanctions for misuse of discovery); Goff v. Harold Ives Trucking Co., Inc., 342 Ark. 143, 150; 27 S.W.3d 387, 391 (Ark. 2000) (declining to find tort for spoliation and noting that "[a]mong those states refusing

in most cases be effective at ensuring that the issues in the underlying litigation are fairly decided."[9]

Next, consider the level of intent necessary to prove spoliation: is negligence sufficient or must there exist some sort of bad faith or malice? Many jurisdictions require that the "culpability" rise to the level of *intentional* conduct.[10] However, there are those that simply require a showing of negligence for spoliation claims.[11] Some states still will recognize a spoliation claim within traditional negligence principles.[12] Others have expressly refused to recognize a claim for negligent spoliation of evidence.[13]

Thus, to assess the level of risk in failing to preserve certain evidence, be aware of the potentially applicable spoliation rules. While the trucking company

---

to acknowledge the tort, in addition to California, are Alabama, Arizona, Georgia, Iowa, Kansas, Pennsylvania, and Texas"); Downen v. Redd, 367 Ark. 551, 557, 242 S.W.3d 273, 277 (Ark. 2006) (declining to recognize a tort for intentional spoliation by a third party).

9. *Cedars-Sinai Med. Ctr.*, 18 Cal. 4th at 17; *see City of Los Angeles*, 17 Cal. 5th at 71.

10. *Quinn v. RISO Investments, Inc.*, 869 So. 2d 922, 927 (La. Ct. App. 2004) (requiring destruction of the evidence with intention to prevent the opposing party's use at trial); Tomlinson v. Landmark Am. Ins. Co., 192 So. 3d 153, 160 (La. App. 4 Cir., 2016) (absent evidence of intent, tort claim for spoliation could be dismissed on summary judgment); Buchanan v. Wal-Mart Stores, Inc., 834 F. App'x 58, 61 (5th Cir. 2020) (noting that intent is a necessary element of a cause of action for spoliation); Rizzuto v. Davidson Ladders, Inc., 905 A.2d 1165, 1178 (Conn. 2006) (recognizing intentional spoliation tort cause of action). Others frame culpability in the context of "bad faith," akin to a form of intentional conduct. Guzman v. Jones, 804 F.3d 707, 713 (5th Cir. 2015) ("We permit an adverse inference against the spoliator or sanctions against the spoliator only upon a showing of 'bad faith' or 'bad conduct.'"); *see also* Herster v. Bd. of Supervisors of Louisiana State Univ., 887 F.3d 177, 189 (5th Cir. 2018) ("Spoliation of evidence may not be based on the negligent destruction of evidence."); *compare* Bunn Builders, Inc. v. Womack, 2011 Ark. 231, at *11 (Ark. 2011) (recognizing that the Eighth Circuit requires intention with the desire to suppress the truth but that holding that "under Arkansas law, a circuit court is not required to make a specific finding of bad faith on the part of the spoliator prior to instructing the jury...."); Russellville Holdings, LLC v. Peters, 2017 Ark. App. 561, *9, 533 S.W.3d 119, 125 (2017) ("a finding of bad faith is not necessary").

11. *See* Martino v. Wal-Mart Stores, Inc., 908 So. 2d 342, 346–47 (Fla. 2005); Rosario v. Miami-Dade Cnty., 490 F. Supp. 2d 1213, 1226 (S.D. Fla. 2007) (holding that there is no cause of action for spoliation in Florida, but that negligent spoliation can result in an adverse inference in favor of the party prejudiced by the spoliation); Reinsdorf v. Skechers U.S.A., Inc., 296 F.R.D. 604, 627 (C.D. Cal. 2013) ("In the Ninth Circuit, 'a party's destruction of evidence need not be in "bad faith" to warrant a court's imposition of sanctions.'") (quoting *In re Napster, Inc. Copyright Litigation*, 462 F. Supp. 2d 1060, 1066 (N.D. Cal. 2006)).

12. *See* Zubulake v. UBS Warburg LLC, 220 F.R.D. 212, 220 (S.D.N.Y. 2003) ("In this circuit, a 'culpable state of mind' for purposes of a spoliation inference includes ordinary negligence."); Smith v. Atkinson, 771 So. 2d 429, 438 (Ala. 2000) (finding that "liability may be imposed on a third party liable for negligent spoliation of evidence" under the existing principles of negligence); Boyd v. Travelers Ins. Co., 166 Ill. 2d 188, 194, 652 N.E.2d 267, 270 (Ill. 1995) ("An action for negligent spoliation can be stated under existing negligence law without creating a new tort.").

13. *Matter of Lasala*, No. CV 18-11057, 2020 WL 6938807, at *3, 2020 U.S. Dist. LEXIS 221055 (E.D. La. Nov. 25, 2020) (holding that recognizing negligent spoliation claims would not deter future harmful action because negligent spoliation is an unintentional act); Reynolds v. Bordelon, 172 So. 3d 589 (La. 2015) (abrogating previous law and finding no cause of action for negligent spoliation in first or third party claims); Lueter v. State of California, 94 Cal. App. 4th 1285; 115 Cal. Rptr. 2d 68 (Cal. Ct. App. 2002) (abrogating previous law and finding no cause of action for negligent spoliation).

is typically only obligated to retain records for as long as the FMCSA requires, it may be in the best interests of the company to set aside and preserve accident- and driver-related records to avoid unintentional purging in routine data or documents, particularly once a letter of representation has been received or an adverse claim made by another party. Negligent failure to preserve could be sufficient for a finding of spoliation when records are not preserved and then lost in the routine course of business. A claimant, too, can be responsible for spoliation. Perhaps a litigant had but then deleted certain text messages or social media posts that were relevant to the accident. *Any* evidence that is relevant can be subject to spoliation, not just evidence in the hands of the defendant.

Witnesses

Initial Driver Interview

In all accident investigations, the initial driver interview should be taken as quickly as possible after the accident is reported. As time goes on, the details of the accident will become clouded. The driver will likely be speaking to an insurance company representative and/or the investigating police officer; however, counsel should conduct their own driver interview. While the insurance company or police officer will likely only discuss the accident itself, the driver interview should include more in-depth questions regarding the driver's best contact information, driving history, and employment history as well as accident details.

During this initial interview, it is important to discuss the exact details of the accident, including speed, trip details, point of impact, and any potential witnesses. At this point, it is imperative to make the driver feel comfortable to ensure he or she tells the truth about the accident and/or any potential issues in the driver's past. Sometimes, a truck driver may be tentative to speak with a lawyer so a call to the driver's safety manager first will be helpful. This way, the driver feels confident and empowered during the initial interview to provide all necessary details. But, as the attorney representing multiple defendant parties, often the trucking company, the driver, and the insurance company, it is important to be clear about the scope of representation and decision-making on handling the defense of the claim.[14]

Traffic Crash Reports and Official Evidence

After interviewing the driver, the next statement to collect is that of the investigating police officer. While investigating officers likely did not see the accident occur, they gather essential evidence at the accident scene that could support any liability arguments and identify any eyewitnesses. A police officer's

14. When representing both the trucking company and the driver, the attorney's loyalty is owed equally to both. Many attorneys fail to recognize when the truck driver's interests in the litigation are adverse to that of the employer's interests. This may especially be so when direct negligence claims are brought against the trucking company in a comparative fault jurisdiction because the truck company and the driver each will have a personal financial interest in shifting as much of the comparative fault to the other.

investigation may provide insight into how the account occurred and who was at fault. The officer will also have first-hand knowledge about the injuries.

Along with the police report, police officers may also have photographs of the scene and property damage of the vehicles. Some officers will even measure skid marks or tire tracks at the accident scene. While the officers write their findings in a report, these interviews can illuminate officers' impressions on liability outside of their report and any recollection of alleged injuries claimed at the accident scene. The officers' body cam footage will also be helpful to determining the extent of the property damage and validity of any alleged injuries. This footage may not come automatically with the police report but is readily available if requested.

Other Witness Statements

Some of the most important testimony to determine liability comes from witnesses who saw the accident take place. This information is especially persuasive in trial when the witness is unrelated to either party involved. It is critical to identify and interview these witnesses as soon after the crash as possible. That way, the recollection of the accident is fresh in their minds. If not, the witness may only remember the accident generally and lose many of the details.

Essential Discovery in Trucking Cases

Initial Discovery

Interrogatories and Requests for Production

Once discovery has commenced you should promptly issue interrogatories and requests for production to the opposing party. For plaintiffs, you will want to issue discovery not only to the defendant driver but also to the trucking company. Consider the scope of the claims being made, the applicable burden of proof, and the information and documents you will need to evaluate and prove that claim. As against the driver, you will want all essential background information, both at the time of the accident and in the present day. Inquire about employers, other accidents or lawsuits, licensure issues, and any medical treatment related to the accident. If the truck driver was an owner–operator, request information about damage or repairs to the truck. As against the trucking company, request all information and documents pertaining to the driver, the accident, and the load at issue. In addition, request any insurance information, so that the potential scope of coverage is identified and placed on notice.

Medical History and Treatment

In every personal injury matter, the full scope of treatment and damages needs to be evaluated. In written discovery, request identification of the following to help aid in your gathering of relevant medical records: (1) all treating providers from the accident through present day; (2) all providers still providing treatment; (3) all providers within a defined timeframe prior to the accident through present day, typically including primary care, emergency or urgent care, chiropractic care, orthopedist, neurologists, pain management, or a surgeon of any kind; and (4) pharmacies for a defined timeframe prior to the accident through present day. Utilize authorizations to request the records, or subpoenas where necessary. Health insurance and pharmacy records can also aid in identifying prior relevant treatment and to assess relatedness of any post-accident complaints. If claims for mental anguish or other psychological or emotional damage are being asserted, be sure that the scope of the requests target providers for such claims.

Employment and Earnings Information

In addition to claims for physical, mental, or emotional injury, plaintiff's claims are likely to involve loss of past or future earnings. To assess such claims, be prepared to gather a detailed history of the plaintiff's employment history and earnings records. Issue requests or subpoenas to all known employment providers and review records received for identification of any other employers not otherwise disclosed. In your requests, you should also obtain records pertaining to promotions or demotions, reprimands or discipline, and official assessments or performance reviews. In addition to the employers' records, independently request tax returns from the IRS[15] or, if unable to provide, from the tax preparer.

Social Media

At times a hot topic issue in discovery litigation, any case should involve a thorough investigation into the social media outlets utilized by any of the parties involved in the case. Written discovery should inquire into the various platforms used, the screen name or username, and a link to the individual's profile. If the profile is set to restricted or private status, inquire as to when it was so restricted, whether before or after the accident. Requests for production should also include social media production requests narrowly tailored based on the relevant jurisprudence in your jurisdiction. For example, some courts allow social media discovery in very limited categories for distinct time frames, such as those posts or content that (1) refer or relate to the accident in question, (2) refer or relate to the plaintiff's alleged emotional distress, (3) that refer or relate to alternative potential emotional stressors or that are inconsistent with the mental injuries plaintiff alleges, (4) that refer or relate to physical injuries, (5) that refer or relate to other physical injuries sustained by the plaintiff, and (6) that reflect capabilities of plaintiff inconsistent with his alleged injuries.[16] Thus,

---

15. The IRS utilizes a specific release, Form 4506, for this purpose. The form is available on its website at: https://www.irs.gov/pub/irs-pdf/f4506.pdf.

16. *See, e.g.*, Wharran v. Morgan, 351 So. 3d 632, 639 (Fla. Dist. Ct. App. 2022) (request for all of plaintiff's cell phone information overbroad and would lead to irrelevant discovery); Cooksey v. Hunt S. Grp., LLC, No. 1:18CV49-LG-RHW, 2019 WL 13128561, at *2 (S.D. Miss. Mar. 22, 2019) (denying requests for login information to social media accounts as overbroad); O'Malley v. Pub. Belt R.R. Comm'n for City of New Orleans, No. CV 17-4812, 2018 WL 733227, at *2 (E.D. La. Feb. 6, 2018) ("Even where discoverable, a defendant is not granted unfettered access to a plaintiff's social networking sites that he or she has limited from public view simply because the plaintiff has put his or her mental and physical conditions at issue."); Farley v. Callais & Sons LLC, No. 14-2550, 2015 U.S. Dist. LEXIS 104533, 2015 WL 4730729 (E.D. La. Aug. 10, 2015); Nucci v. Target Corp., 162

in crafting the discovery requests, be aware of the specific rulings in your jurisdiction on that issue and tailor the requests in such a way that they comply with previous decisions. That way, if you need to move to compel responses, you have solid footing on which to stand in making your arguments.

Requests for Admission

Consider the extent to which a request for admission can be beneficial to your case. While not necessarily "essential," requests for admission can be helpful for narrowing legal issues, authenticating documents, basic fact discovery, and establishing insurance coverage. For a defendant, they can be useful to parse through the scope of claims being made and whether certain treatment has been recommended or performed. In practice, requests for admission often simply draw objections, so be precise and distinct in each request to make it difficult to object and harder to escape a direct answer. Remember that failing to admit a fact later proven correct can open you up to sanctions, which may include attorneys' fees incurred in having to prove that particular fact.

Documentary and Physical Evidence

Authorizations for Records

To obtain health records you will need a Health Insurance Portability and Accountability Act (HIPAA) compliant authorization for medical and billing records. Note there are unique requirements if seeking an authorization that contains mental health records, typically requiring a separate or distinct authorization or disclosure. In addition to a medical authorization, consider including authorizations for Medicare, Medicaid, and/or health insurance records, where applicable. If any type of health insurer is involved, there may be secondary payer obligations to be aware of, and obtaining such records early in the case is important. Further, authorization should be obtained for employment records, IRS/tax returns, and workers' compensation records, where applicable. Consider the potential types of records you may need to defend the case and assess credibility of the plaintiff or other witnesses and be sure to request authorizations for such records. Counsel for the defendant will submit these to counsel for the plaintiff during discovery.

Subpoenaing Records

A plaintiff may object to executing certain authorizations, or perhaps there simply is not an authorization that applies to obtain the records needed. In that event, you will need to issue a subpoena for those records. Such records will include cell phone records/data; bank records or tax preparer/accountant records; and litigation funding schemes that utilize certain doctors, companies, and law firms to connect litigants to treatment for a cut of the fee, many times to the detriment of the defendant who is subject to medical specials for the full

---

So. 3d 146 (Fla. 4th DCA 2015); Mailhoit v. Home Depot U.S.A. Inc., 285 F.R.D. 566, 83 Fed. R. Serv. 3d 585 (C.D. Cal. 2012); Tompkins v. Detroit Metro. Airport, 278 F.R.D. 387 (E.D. Mich. 2012).

billed amount, depending on how your state law handles this issue. Discovery efforts should be targeted to identify who is paying or funding the medical bills and the agreements inherent in such arrangements. In some states, the collateral source rules allow for discovery and perhaps discounted medical specials at trial, depending on who paid the medicals and/or who is ultimately responsible for the balance. Issue subpoenas targeted to those medical providers, medical funding or factoring companies, and similar entities to identify the structure and, more importantly, to vet any potential bias of the treating providers.

Inspections

It is very common in vehicle accident cases that physical evidence must be inspected, recorded, and preserved throughout the litigation. Usually, the first inspection will be of the scene, typically very soon after the accident. For the trucking company, the initial accident response should include inspecting and documenting the scene of the accident as it existed that day, usually through a third-party adjuster. The vehicles should be preserved for inspection, particularly in a catastrophic or multi-vehicular accident. A joint inspection of the vehicles to photograph, measure, inspect, and download electronic data from the vehicle(s) is ideal; however, in many instances the other parties are not represented by counsel. In such event, the trucking company should take care to properly and thoroughly conduct the vehicle inspection and download electronic data stored in vehicle systems and devices using an expert whom it would likely use to present the inspection evidence through the litigation. Similar procedures apply to forensic inspection and downloads of the parties' cell phones. Experts can be utilized to extract the necessary data to help understand the whereabouts of the phone and activities on the phone leading up to and during the accident.

Finally, with a person's medical condition at issue in a personal injury case, most often the inspection that needs to take place is the evaluation of the plaintiff. The defense can and should request an independent medical evaluation of the plaintiff whenever the treatment remains ongoing and is suggestive of more invasive procedures, such as injections or surgery, or perhaps simply a long road to recovery. Early in the case the defense attorney should send a letter to counsel for plaintiff requesting advance notice of any intended surgeries or procedures to afford the opportunity for such an examination. The failure of plaintiff to notify counsel and submit to the exam before undergoing a surgical procedure could be considered spoliation in some jurisdictions. If allowed in your jurisdiction, the plaintiff's attorney should consider attending the independent medical examination or sending a neutral person with the plaintiff to monitor the integrity of the examination. Some defendants resist this practice, and different courts handle discovery disputes arising over it differently.

Depositions

Parties and Fact Witnesses

Once the written and documentary discovery is well under way, depositions of the relevant parties and witnesses need to be conducted. Traditionally, the depositions of the plaintiff, other drivers, and other witnesses pertaining to the facts of the accident are the first to be deposed. These early depositions should include the investigating officers and first responders, as they will be able to testify pertaining to their investigation, photographs, and findings, and can authenticate photographs, videos, and other documents that may be needed in later stages of the litigation and motion practice. Typically, the plaintiff's attorney will take the depositions of the truck driver, the truck dispatcher, the truck company safety manager, and, sometimes, the trucking company hiring manager. Sometimes the plaintiff will take depositions from the freight broker and the shipper, too.

Experts

As the case proceeds, depositions will shift to focus on the extent and nature of damages. If experts have been retained, before they are deposed, subpoena their entire file pertaining to the case so that you have the appropriate documentation available to review and prepare for the deposition. For medical experts, ensure that you have all treatment records and any additional correspondence in the file because the doctor may have sent or received information that is not included in the patient chart but is otherwise relevant for the case. For any expert, be aware of the requirements of the court's rules or scheduling order to determine whether counsel provided all appropriate disclosures and information. For crash reconstruction experts, beware of the fact that they frequently will have been artificially limited by their retaining counsel about the scope of the opinion to be rendered. For example, a party's expert might have been instructed only to identify what the other party did wrong, without analyzing any possible comparative fault by the party who retained that expert. Therefore, it is important to determine the scope of the engagement and test it on cross-examination. Research and review prior testimony and expert retentions for that individual to prepare for the deposition and identify any bias concerns. If available, review prior reports or depositions to assess if the witness took a previous position that is inconsistent with the opinions being offered in the instant case. Lastly, consider any potential challenges that may follow for the expert and be prepared to either pursue or defend against them in the deposition.

Corporate Depositions

In many truck accident cases, the plaintiff will request the deposition of the trucking company through a corporate deposition. If you are representing the plaintiff, consider the scope of the allegations made and the goals of the corporate deposition. For example, pursuant to Federal Rule of Civil Procedure 30(b)(6), the deposition notice "must describe with reasonable particularity the matters for examination."[17] The deposition must also comport with the traditional discovery requirements and rules.[18]

---

17. F.R.C.P. 30(b)(6).
18. F.R.C.P. 26(b)(1).

Thus, in preparing the deposition notice, ensure that the topics are not too numerous and are tailored to the claims at hand, as well as the relevant scope in time and subject matter. Opt for direct, simple language as opposed to long, wordy areas of inquiry. As the defending attorney, carefully review the plaintiff's proposed areas of inquiry and determine whether they meet the requirements of the notice provisions of Rule 30(b)(6) as interpreted in your jurisdiction. Prepare a formal response that outlines any objections. In the response, reorganize the proposed areas of inquiry to fit within the general topics on which the witness will be prepared. For example, if there are multiple topics that touch generally on training drivers, then the response should indicate that the witness will be produced to testify concerning driver training in effect during a specified timeframe, responsive to the enumerated specific corresponding areas listed in the notice. Because a defendant might not have one single person who can handle responding to all topics listed in the plaintiff's deposition notice, the defendant may designate different persons to speak about different topics. Defense counsel and defendants must beware of the fact that the testimony of these witnesses is the testimony of the defendant company. Often defense attorneys do a poor job communicating this fact to the witnesses called to represent the company, and this will disadvantage the defendant company. Thus, it is important to prepare the corporate witness fully for any and all documents, testimony, facts, and evidence that pertain to the case and topics noticed.

Be sure to confirm with counsel the scope of the testimony and topics and, once an agreement is reached on the final scope of the corporate deposition, memorialize same in a writing or letter agreement that is included as an exhibit to the deposition, so there is no confusion later on the agreed upon scope, if different from the original notice. If an agreement cannot be reached, consider whether motion practice is needed before the deposition to appropriately tailor the scope and to prevent issues from arising that deal with prohibited topics or tactics. While not every case will warrant the corporate testimony of the trucking company, both parties need to be aware of the requirements in noticing and responding to a corporate deposition.

CHAPTER 12

Distracted Driving in Commercial Motor Vehicles

Lauren Pilie, Esq.

Prevalence

It is no surprise to anyone that distracted driving is a major problem. In a 2006 study, driver inattention was found to be the leading factor in crashes and near-crashes. The same study found that nearly 80 percent of crashes involved some form of driver inattention in the three seconds prior to the encounter.[1]

The National Highway Traffic and Safety Administration frequently conducts studies on distracted driving. In its most recent study in 2021, "8% of fatal crashes, 14% of injury crashes, and 13% of all police-reported motor vehicle traffic crashes were reported as distraction-affected crashes."[2] "There were 3,522 people killed and an estimated additional 362,415 people injured in motor vehicle traffic crashes involving distracted drivers."[3] "Five percent of all drivers involved in fatal traffic crashes in 2021 were reported as distracted at the time of the crashes. Seven percent of drivers 15 to 20 years old involved in fatal crashes were reported as distracted. This age group has the largest proportion of drivers who were distracted at the time of the fatal crashes."[4]

According to a 2009 study that focused on commercial vehicles, 71 percent of large-truck crashes occurred when the truck driver was doing something besides driving the truck.[5] Imagine how much safer driving could be if

---

1. FMCSA, citing Dingus, T.A., Klauer, S.A., Neale, V.L., Petersen, A., Lee, S.E., and Sudweeks, J., (2006). 100-car naturalistic driving study. Phase 2: Results of the 100-car field experiment. Interim rept. August 2001 to March 2005. Report No. DOT/HS/810-593. National Highway Traffic Safety Administration, Washington, D.C.

2. Nat'l Highway Traffic Safety Admin., Traffic Safety Facts 1 (May 2023), https://crashstats.nhtsa.dot.gov/Api/Public/ViewPublication/813443.

3. *Id.*

4. *Id.*

5. Olson, R.L, Hanowski, R.J., Hickman, J.S., & Bocanegra, J. (2009). Driver Distraction in Commercial Vehicle Operations. Report No. FMCSA-RRR-09-042. Washington, DC: Federal Motor Carrier Safety Administration.

motorists focused on the road instead of the myriad of other things that are constantly competing for a driver's attention.

Types of Distraction[6]

All types of distraction increase risk, and a combination of two or more makes the risk even higher.

- **Physical distraction.** Physical distraction is distraction that causes a driver to divert the driver's eyes from the road or to remove the driver's hands from the steering wheel. Examples of this would include adjusting the temperature or reaching for a drink.
- **Mental distraction.** Mental distractions are distractions that take a driver's mind away from driving. Examples of this would be daydreaming, holding a conversation, or getting lost in an audiobook.
- **Physical and mental distraction.** Physical and mental distractions have the highest risk of resulting in a crash. Examples include holding and talking on a cell phone, sending and receiving text messages, scrolling social media, or reading signs on the side of the road.

Effects of Distracted Driving

While arguably not quite as bad as driving under the influence or fatigued driving, distracted driving shares some common risks with those behaviors. Just as being drunk or sleepy slows a driver's reaction time, distracted driving also slows a driver's perception and delays decision-making.[7] While a drunk driver may be physically incapable of perceiving and responding to a hazard, a distracted driver is likewise incapable of responding, but for different reasons. The driver does not perceive the hazard, and therefore cannot react, simply because of inattention.

Cell Phones and the FMCSR

The Federal Motor Carrier Safety Administration (FMCSA) has enacted regulations to govern and punish both drivers and motor carriers for the use of cell phones while operating a commercial motor vehicle. The rules and punishments for cell phone usage are more strict for the driver of a CMV than for a regular vehicle.

Under the Federal Motor Carrier Safety Regulations (FMCSRs), texting is defined as "manually entering alphanumeric text into, or reading text from, an electronic device."[8] Texting is not limited to strictly sending or receiving text messages. "Texting" also includes emailing, using a web browser, pressing

6. CDL Manual: Types of Distractions; *see* also Delmar's Tractor-Trailer Truck Driver Training, 4th ed.
7. CDL Manual: Effects of Distracted Driving § 2.9.2.
8. 49 C.F.R. § 390.5.

more than a single button to start or end a voice communication, or engaging in any other form of electronic text retrieval or entry.[9] Notably, texting does not include using a GPS system, pressing one button to start or end a phone call, or using a fleet management or dispatch system.[10]

"No driver of a CMV shall engage in texting while driving."[11] "No motor carrier shall allow or require its drivers to engage in texting while driving."[12] Driving includes operating a vehicle with the motor running, even if the vehicle is stopped in traffic or for other delays.[13] The only permissible time that a driver can text while driving under the FMCSRs is when it is "necessary to communicate with law enforcement or other emergency services."[14] The same rules also apply to a driver holding a phone and talking on it.[15] Talking on the phone using Bluetooth is permissible.

If a driver is convicted of texting or using a hand-held phone while driving a CMV two times in a three-year period, then the driver's commercial driver's license (CDL) is disqualified for 60 days.[16] For three convictions in a three-year period, the driver's CDL is disqualified for 120 days.[17] A conviction is defined as "an unvacated adjudication of guilt, or a determination that a person has violated or failed to comply with the law in a court of original jurisdiction."[18] A nolo contendere plea counts as a conviction for purposes of the FMCSRs.[19] The fines for violating these laws are updated regularly, and as of the most recent update in January 2024, a driver could be fined $4,690, and a company could be fined $18,758 for each violation.[20]

Industry Standards on Distracted Driving

Despite laws regulating texting and handheld use of phones, illegal cell phone usage while driving is much more common than cell phone usage convictions. On average, around 18,000 CMV drivers per year are cited for using a handheld mobile phone, and around 1,000 per year are cited for texting while driving.[21] The police are not always around to observe distracted driving behavior, but companies frequently are. Many motor carriers now have sophisticated camera monitoring systems installed (prominent examples include Lytx and Samsara) that have driver-facing cameras. The technology on these systems can detect when a driver's eyes leave the road or when the driver's hands leave the wheel.

9. *Id.*
10. *Id.*
11. *Id.* § 392.80(a).
12. *Id.* § 392.80(b).
13. *Id.* § 392.80(c).
14. *Id.* § 392.80(d).
15. *Id.* § 392.82.
16. *Id.* § 383.51, table 2.
17. *Id.*
18. *Id.* § 390.5.
19. *Id.*
20. *Id.* § 386, Appendix B (a)(3) and (a)(4)
21. https://ai.fmcsa.dot.gov/EnforcementPrograms/Inspections?type=AllViolations&time_period_id=2&report_date=2022&vehicle_type=1%C2%B4_critical=19&state=NAT&domicile=ALL.

Alerts and reports are sent to the motor carrier for review. How those reports are handled varies by carrier.

The Smith System, the industry leader in trucking safety training, encourages all carriers to have a distracted driving policy. Most of the major trucking companies have a policy against cell phone usage. Some carriers have a strict no-texting policy, and a driver who is caught using his phone is immediately terminated (or at least, the policy states that should happen). Other carriers have a graduated system where the driver is fined or suspended and is only terminated after multiple infractions. Some carriers have no cell phone policy at all (these are largely going to be owner–operator situations), although the majority of carriers at least have some sort of manual that includes a cell phone policy.

Having a policy is not enough. How does the company enforce the policy? What methods are in place to detect cell phone usage? Once it is detected, what is done about it? Who is responsible for addressing it with the driver? Many times, a policy turns out to just be lip service.

Practice Pointers Related to Distracted Driving

Always subpoena a truck driver's cell phone records from his carrier. In addition to asking for voicemail records, data usage records, and text messages (both incoming and outgoing), ask for Per Call Measurement Data (PCMD) and Call Detail Records (CDR) with Cell Site Data. PCMD is the time required for the signal to travel from the cell site to the handset and then back to the cell site. PCMD provides an approximate distance of the mobile device from the cell site. This range can narrow the area within the cell site to provide a more accurate estimate of the user's location. CDR will show the date, time, call duration, and numbers involved, but to obtain the first cell site and last cell site used by the call, you must specify "Cell Site Data" in your request. Once you obtain these records, compare them to the truck driver's hours of service logs to detect any overlap or discrepancies.

As a practice pointer, always send a preservation letter immediately, not just for the cell phone records of the driver but also for the actual cell phone itself. In today's world, calling and texting are the least of the activities that we do on our phones. Most of the things we use our phones for do not even appear on a cell phone bill, including imessaging. Cell phone data intricacies go beyond the scope of this chapter but know that to properly investigate a distracted driving case, the cell phone will need to be imaged by a cell phone forensic expert, and there are multiple methods of extraction from which to choose. A cell phone expert can obtain the data, and then a human factors expert or an accident reconstructionist can put the data into more meaningful terms in connection to the wreck. For example, the forensic expert may find that a truck driver was entering text for 26 seconds prior to a crash. A human factors expert can then use that information to discuss the effect on reaction time (increased) and situational awareness (decreased). An accident reconstructionist can apply that information to the facts of the crash, opine on how much distance the driver covered in that time, and how the wreck could have been prevented or lessened had the driver not been texting.

CHAPTER 13
Human Factors: Driver Response

Peter C. Shlanta, PhD

Driving is a dynamic task in which drivers are confronted with numerous stimuli across the roadway environment. At times, these stimuli represent potential hazards that drivers must then respond to. When investigating a crash, determining a reasonable time range for a driver to respond to a perceived hazard is of particular importance to human factors scientists, accident reconstructionists, and other investigators. This time estimate can be used to determine the likelihood that an alert, attentive, and unimpaired driver would have been able to avoid the hazard.

Components of Perception Response Time (PRT)

The interval of time between the potential hazard entering the driver's field of view and the driver's initiation of a response is known as perception response time (PRT). PRT is typically broken down into four stages: detection, identification, decision, and response.

Detection

The detection interval begins when a stimulus becomes available to a driver, and the interval ends when the driver becomes aware of the stimulus.[1] For example, consider a scenario in which a pedestrian begins crossing the street in a location where there are no crosswalks or traffic signals. After the pedestrian has entered the roadway, an approaching driver may notice, or detect, that a moving stimulus is in his or her path of travel ahead.

Identification

The identification stage involves the driver recognizing and identifying whether a stimulus is a potential hazard or not. If the stimulus is moving, the driver must also make predictions about the speed and trajectory of the moving stimulus

1. *E.g.*, David A. Krauss, Forensic Aspects of Driver Perception and Response (Tucson, Arizona: Lawyers & Judges Publishing Company, 2015. Print).

as part of the identification process.[2] In the scenario just mentioned, the driver would need to recognize, or identify, that the moving pedestrian ahead is a hazard. The driver may also appreciate that there is a possibility of an impact, depending on the distance between the driver's vehicle and the pedestrian.

Decision

The decision process requires the driver to choose how to respond to the potential hazard. Typical driver responses include braking, steering, or some combination of both.[3] In our example, the driver may decide to apply the brakes to avoid contacting the pedestrian if the pedestrian is in the same lane of travel. However, drivers may also decide not to respond to a stimulus if that stimulus is not perceived as a threat. Perhaps the driver detected the pedestrian from a great distance, and the driver determines that the pedestrian will finish crossing the roadway before the vehicle reaches the pedestrian's location.

Response

Braking and/or steering requires a driver to respond by performing physical movement, such as turning the steering wheel or moving the foot to the brake pedal. The time that it takes for the driver to move his or her body and initiate the chosen reaction is referred to as the response interval. For example, if the driver decided to brake in response to a hazard, the response interval would include the time that it takes for the driver to move his or her foot from the accelerator pedal to the brake pedal.

Factors That Impact PRT

Since delays in any of the aforementioned stages would result in longer PRTs, the time course of a driver's PRT is dependent on characteristics of the driver and the environment. When evaluating a reasonable PRT range for a particular driver in a particular context, it is essential to consider the factors that might influence that range. The following section includes a summary of several examples of these PRT-relevant factors, but there may be additional factors that are specific to a given scenario and not discussed here.[4]

Driver Factors

At any given time, drivers must attend to a large number of task-relevant stimuli. These stimuli may include traffic signals, surrounding traffic, road signage, lane lines, pedestrians, and more. Attending to this multitude of stimuli in the environment results in a complex visual environment for drivers. To make all of these stimuli more manageable, drivers develop *expectancies* regarding where a given stimulus is likely to be located in the roadway environment. Decades

---

2. *Id.*
3. *Id.*
4. For a more extensive review, see KRAUSS, *supra* note 1.

of scientific literature indicate that these expectancies influence where drivers look in their environment[5] and how quickly drivers react to detected stimuli.[6] Returning to our prior pedestrian example, drivers would likely expect the possibility of pedestrians crossing the street in locations where there are visible crosswalks, signaled intersections, or pedestrian signage. When drivers expect a given hazard or see a hazard in an expected location, studies indicate that driver PRTs are faster.[7] It is unlikely, however, that these same drivers would expect a pedestrian to enter the roadway at a location that lacks pedestrian crosswalks or signage (e.g., mid-block), or at a time when the traffic signals do not permit crossing (e.g., when oncoming traffic has a green traffic light). When hazards are unexpected, drivers have longer PRTs and may fail to detect the hazard entirely.[8]

A driver's PRT for a given hazard is also influenced by whether they are alert, unimpaired, and ready to react. Drivers may be distracted by cognitive (e.g., conversations with a passenger), manual (e.g., interactions with the in-vehicle radio), or visual (e.g., looking at their phone) processes when encountering a hazard.[9] Being distracted can hinder a driver's ability to detect and react to hazards, resulting in longer PRTs.[10] Intoxicated drivers typically also react more slowly to hazards, with studies finding that driver reaction times were longer after alcohol consumption, even at a legal blood alcohol content (BAC) of .05 percent.[11] Additionally, sleepiness and fatigue is associated with generally slower responses to stimuli,[12] which may also affect driver PRTs while driving.

---

5. *E.g.*, Jan Theeuwes, *Visual Search at Intersections: An Eye-Movement Analysis*, 5 Vision in Vehicles 125–34 (1996).

6. *E.g.*, Krauss, *supra* note 1; Jeffrey W. Muttart, *Estimating Driver Response Times*, *in* Handbook of Human Factors in Litigation 14-1–14-25 (CRC Press, 2005).

7. *E.g.*, Krauss, *supra* note 1; Muttart, *supra* note 6.

8. *E.g.*, Krauss, *supra* note 1.

9. *E.g.*, David M Cades, Steven R. Arndt, Joseph B. Sala & David A. Krauss, What You Need to Know about the Distracted Driver, feature article in Ill. Ass'n of Def. Trial Couns. Q. 23 (2013); Centers for Disease Control and Prevention, Distracted Driving | Motor Vehicle Safety | CDC Injury Center (Nov. 3, 2020), https://www.cdc.gov/distracted-driving/about/?CDC_AAref_Val=https://www.cdc.gov/transportationsafety/Distracted_Driving/index.html.

10. *E.g.*, Marco Dozza, *What Factors Influence Drivers' Response Time for Evasive Maneuvers in Real Traffic?*, 58 Accident Analysis & Prevention 299–308 (2013); Zhi Zhang, Yingshi Guo, Wei Yuan & Chang Wang, *The Impact of Cognitive Distraction on Driver Perception Response Time under Different Levels of Situational Urgency*, 7 IEEE Access 184572–4580 (2019); Paweł Droździel, Sławomir Tarkowski, Iwona Rybicka & Rafał Wrona, *Drivers' Reaction Time Research in the Conditions in the Real Traffic*, 10 Open Eng'g 35–47 (2020).

11. *E.g.*, Mary E. Nicholson, Minqi Wang, Collins O. Airhihenbuwa, Beverly S. Mahoney, Robert Christina & Dolores W. Maney, *Variability in Behavioral Impairment Involved in the Rising and Falling BAC Curve*, 53(4) J. Studies on Alcohol 349–56 (1992); Masaaki Tagawa, Michiko Kano, Nobuyuki Okamura, Masatoshi Itoh, Eiko Sakurai, Takehiko Watanabe & Kazuhiko Yanai, *Relationship between Effects of Alcohol on Psychomotor Performances and Blood Alcohol Concentrations*, 83(3) Japanese J. Pharmacology 253–60 (2000).

12. E.g., Ann M. Williamson & Anne-Marie Feyer, *Moderate Sleep Deprivation Produces Impairments in Cognitive and Motor Performance Equivalent to Legally Prescribed Levels of Alcohol Intoxication*, 57(10) Occupational & env'l med. 649–55 (2000).

Environmental Factors

A driver's PRT may also be influenced by environmental factors given that driving occurs under a variety of lighting and weather conditions. Imagine that there is a disabled, unlit SUV on a straight, rural, flat roadway where there are no streetlights. During the daytime, an approaching driver would likely be able to detect the disabled SUV due to the visibility and sight distances afforded by the lighting and roadway conditions. At night, however, an approaching driver would have less visual information available to detect hazards ahead. Recall that the first stages of PRT are *detection* and *identification*. When there is little ambient lighting available, an oncoming driver would not be able to see the disabled, unlit SUV until they are much closer to it, resulting in a later detection of the hazard. Further, the SUV may only appear as a faint, distant shape until the approaching driver is close enough to adequately illuminate the SUV with headlights. Hazards that appear as faint "outlines" or "shapes" may further delay PRT due to an inability to identify the object and determine whether it poses a hazard, increasing the likelihood of an accident.

When lighting conditions are dark, the *conspicuity* of the hazard is especially important for approaching drivers. Conspicuity refers to the likelihood that an object or hazard will come to the attention of an observer who is attentive to the environment based on characteristics such as size, brightness, contrast, color, and location.[13] For example, tractor-trailers are usually lined with red and/or white retroreflective tape, which increases the brightness and contrast of the vehicle. When viewed against a dark environment under nighttime conditions, the brightness and contrast of the retroreflective tape makes the presence of the tractor-trailer more conspicuous to approaching drivers. Scientific literature indicates that vehicle lights are visible for over 3,000 feet under nighttime conditions, and that retroreflective tape or devices are visible for over 700 feet.[14] Similarly, construction equipment and signage (e.g., cones, barrels) are typically designed to be retroreflective and brightly colored, such as fluorescent orange or yellow, to be more conspicuous to approaching drivers. This suggests that headlights, taillights, four-way flashers, retroreflective cones/triangles, or retroreflective tape can be used to increase the conspicuity of a vehicle. Pedestrians walking near travel lanes at night can carry flashlights or wear bright or retroreflective clothing to increase their conspicuity.[15] When drivers can quickly detect and identify an object ahead, they will be able to react more quickly and increase the likelihood of avoiding an incident. When a low-conspicuity hazard

---

13. *E.g.*, KRAUSS, *supra* note 1.

14. David G. Curry,, Edward A. Nielsen, Jason W. Kidd & Matthew R. Tuttle, *Driver Detection of Roadside Obstacles at Night*, 51 PROCEEDINGS OF THE HUMAN FACTORS & ERGONOMICS SOCIETY ANNUAL MEETING 1181–85 (2007).

15. *E.g.*, Joanne M. Wood, Richard A. Tyrrell & Trent P. Carberry, *Limitations in Drivers' Ability to Recognize Pedestrians at Night*, 47(3) HUMAN FACTORS 644–53 (2005); Joanne M. Wood, Nighttime Driving: Visual, Lighting and Visibility Challenges, 40(2) OPHTHALMIC & PHYSIOLOGICAL OPTICS 187–201 (2020); J. Muttart & M. Romoser, *Evaluating Driver Response and Ability to Avoid a Crash at Night*, *in* PROCEEDINGS OF THE 1ST JOINT ITAI-EVU CONFERENCE, HINCKLEY, LEICESTERSHIRE, ENGLAND (2009).

is present under nighttime conditions, drivers may require several seconds to respond—or fail to respond at all. For example, literature indicates that drivers require more time to detect and respond to pedestrians that are wearing dark clothing near unlit roadways.[16]

Weather conditions can also affect driver PRTs by reducing or distorting the visual information available to drivers. If a driver is oriented toward the sun on a clear day, the sun may produce disabling glare effects that obscure the ability to perceive objects ahead.[17] Drivers are also more likely to experience glare effects during rainy conditions. When a roadway surface is wet, it may become reflective and cause the lights from streetlights, the sun, or other vehicles' headlights to be reflected into a driver's eyes and obstruct the ability to see objects ahead.[18] The reflective surface of a wet roadway may also distort the ability to see smaller or darker objects, even without glare effects.[19] Given that hindered visibility can result in longer PRTs, such weather conditions must be analyzed when evaluating driver response times.

Human Factors Analysis of PRT

As described earlier, evaluating reasonable PRT ranges is an important tool to assist in determining whether or not an accident may have been avoidable by an alert, attentive, and unimpaired driver. Using their knowledge, training, experience, and a large body of scientific literature, human factors scientists can assist in providing a range of potential PRTs that reflect the facts and conditions associated with a particular incident. Although some experts may be inclined to assign a singular PRT to the driver involved in an accident, this is not representative of human performance, as there are several different unknowns that make it difficult to assign a singular PRT to a specific individual. In fact, research shows that even a specific individual does not necessarily respond to the same scenario in the same way or in the same amount of time every time.[20] Instead, approaching the analysis by providing a range of PRTs rooted in the facts of the case that would be acceptable for an alert, attentive, and unimpaired driver will better reflect human behavior. For example, imagine a vehicle following scenario in which a lead vehicle slows to make a right turn under daytime conditions on a straight road, and the following vehicle fails to slow or stop, resulting in a collision. In order to determine a range of PRTs for an alert, attentive, and unimpaired driver, a human factors expert would need to consider the factors

---

16. *E.g.*, Wood, Tyrrell & Carberry, *supra* note 15; Wood, *supra* note 15.

17. *E.g.*, Rafael Jurado-Piña & José M. Pardillo Mayora, *Methodology to Predict Driver Vision Impairment Situations Caused by Sun Glare*, 2120(1) Transp. Rsch. Record: J. Transp. Rsch. Bd. 12–17 (2009).

18. Krauss, *supra* note 1; Nicolas Hautière, Eric Dumont, Roland Brémond & Vincent Ledoux, *Review of the Mechanisms of Visibility Reduction by Rain and Wet Road*, *in* 8th Int'l Symposium on Automotive Lighting 445–55 (2009).

19. Hautière, et al., *supra* note 18; Krauss, *supra* note 1.

20. *E.g.*, Paweł Droździel, Sławomir Tarkowski, Iwona Rybicka & Rafał Wrona, *Drivers' Reaction Time Research in the Conditions in the Real Traffic*, 10 Open Eng'g 35–47 (2020).

within this scenario that apply and may impact PRT. In this case, this accident occurred under daylight conditions, on a straight road, and with a highly visible and expected hazard (the lead vehicle slowing at an intersection). Given this scenario, experts can then assign and narrow down a PRT range based on scientific literature, their knowledge, training, and experience.

Once an expert has assigned a PRT range to a particular scenario, the next step would be to determine whether or not an alert, attentive, and unimpaired driver had the time and distance available to avoid the accident. If the driver has more distance and/or time available than they need to avoid a hazard upon braking or steering, then the driver is within the *critical window* (for discussion of the critical window, see Krauss et al., 2012).[21] Calculating the critical window requires the expert to determine the total time available to avoid (i.e., the earliest point the hazard can be identified to the time of impact), as well as the total time the driver needs to avoid, or the *critical stopping distance (CSD)*. The CSD requires the assigned PRT range, as well as the time it takes for the vehicle to make the requested avoidance maneuver (e.g., braking/steering). Human factors experts often work with accident reconstructionists and/or vehicle engineers to provide the vehicle dynamics portion of this equation. If the CSD is less than the total distance available to respond, then it would suggest that an alert, attentive, and unimpaired driver could avoid the incident. When determining whether an accident was avoidable, it is also important that the expert is aware that the earliest point in which a hazard can be identified does not necessarily equate to when the hazard is most likely to be identified. Therefore the expert should make sure to consider all factors before reaching a conclusion.

Conclusion

As outlined here, PRT is the interval of time that it takes for a driver to initiate a response to a hazard after that hazard enters the driver's field of view. PRT is composed of four stages—detection, identification, decision, and response—and each of these stages can be impacted by a variety of different driver and/or environmental factors. Given the complexity of PRT, it is important that human factors scientists assess all relevant facts associated with each incident they investigate and consider how these facts may impact PRT when providing a range of acceptable PRTs for an alert, attentive, and unimpaired driver.

---

21. Krauss, *supra* note 1; David A. Krauss, James Jay Todd & Genevieve M. Heckman, *The "Critical Window," Looming and Implications for Accident Avoidance*, 82(7) Inst. of Transp. Eng'rs. ITE J. 36–41 (2012).

CHAPTER 14

Reliability of Speed and Distance Estimation

Kevin Rider, PhD, PE

Witnesses to motor vehicle collisions have the potential to offer information and insights to events that transpired that may not be available by any other means. Having seen what actually occurred, it would be reasonable to believe that their descriptions would be accurate and useful to understanding what transpired. While the potential usefulness is not in question, eyewitness testimony can also vary widely between observers, and even contradict science and actual evidence at the scene. Separating perception from reality is the challenge. The solution is embedded in understanding how and why certain perceptions may be inaccurate, and which are likely to be more accurate.

Accuracy versus Precision (versus Reliability)

The ability to evaluate the distance and speed of an object depends principally on the amount of time an observer has available to view the object's actual and relative motion, the size and distance to the object, and relevant experience by which the observer can provide accurate estimates. If someone only sees a glimpse of an event or a short portion of a longer sequence, less information is available to that witness to accurately assess what occurred. Similarly, less information is available to that witness to assess the broader circumstances that surrounded the event. Similarly, observers without refined training or experience cannot know if their estimates are accurate. In contrast, police officers are often trained to estimate speeds of vehicles, through repeated training and feedback. Estimations without verification is partially related to the difference between accuracy and precision. Accuracy is a comparison of estimates to an actual value, whereas precision refers to the reliability of repeated estimates (regardless of the actual value). For example, if five people estimate the speed of a vehicle that actually drove past them at 55 mph, their estimates may be 50, 55, 65, 68, and 70. Without knowing the actual driving speed, it would be unknowable if any of the estimates were correct or even close. Various (incorrect) interpretations could be that (1) the variability indicates that none of them are correct, (2) the variability indicates that none of the estimates are reliable, (3) the majority and precision of three guesses (65, 68, 70) indicate that the speed is likely between 65 and 70 mph, and (4) the average and median values indicate the speed was 61.6 or 65 mph, respectively. The variability in estimates does not mean that the estimates are not useful, but the manner in which they are used is the point in question. They are often simply data points in a much broader analysis.

Data, evidence, and testimony often allow crash reconstructionists and other experts to provide scientific estimates of the travel and impact speeds of vehicles, which can also include the angle of collisions, locations of final rest of vehicles (and/or pedestrians), observable damage, debris, and tire marks and gouges on the roadway. In addition, data downloads from vehicles, cell phones, and infotainment systems are often available that can provide a wealth of information, including speed, accelerator use, braking, and steering. Eyewitness testimony is especially useful when some of these data are not available in a forensic analysis, to reach conclusions that are "more likely than not," based on the preponderance of evidence.

In addition to the difficulty of making accurate estimations of speed or distance, the location and perspective of the observer can also cause estimates to vary. When people view an event from different angles, they tend to observe different things. One observer may be able to see that the driver was looking down at his phone, while another observer sees the pedestrian begin to cross the road without looking for approaching vehicles. Each observer could rightly blame the person's actions that each witnessed. Another example is if one observer has a perspective that allows that observer to see that brake lights activated before an impact occurred, while another observer who cannot see the rear of the vehicle may believe that the vehicle did not slow down until after impact. In the first scenario, both observers may be correct in their observations and recollections, as they each had specific vantage points for what they observed. In the second scenario, one observer had a better view of a potentially relevant factor on when the driver responded, which can lead to determining if the driver was attentive to the roadway. A third, albeit unrelated, example regarding the subjective nature of testimony is if five people ate the same meal and then were separately asked to describe the meal. You would invariably get five different descriptions of the meal—each of them accurate in its own way.

Eyewitness Testimony

It is with great caution that eyewitness testimony is used and relied on, and most commonly it is the province of the jury to evaluate the credibility of witnesses. However, that does not mean that attorneys and experts cannot identify testimony that is more consistent with available facts and evidence. Furthermore, while subject matter experts do not typically ignore testimony, there are circumstances in which some testimony can be considered more reliable than others. One example is when one witness "does not recall seeing" something occur and another testifies that second witness saw it occur. These are not equal and opposite opinions. The first individual essentially does not have an opinion, while the second individual has a specific recollection. If a driver operating a vehicle strikes a disabled vehicle in the roadway and then testifies that he or she did not see hazard lights on the disabled vehicle, this does not necessarily mean that the hazard lights were off. It can also mean that the driver was simply inattentive. If a witness in a nearby vehicle testifies that the witness saw the flashing hazard lights and could not understand why the striking driver did not avoid the crash, it may be a reasonable and expert determination that the hazard lights were likely activated prior to the crash. In contrast, when a witness may not be impartial to the events being investigated, testimony must be more carefully evaluated—and this situation is almost entirely within the province of the jury.

Additional considerations for eyewitness testimony include the position, orientation, and movement of the observer. A vehicle operator traveling down the roadway may be accustomed to other vehicles traveling at approximately the same speed, and small differences in speed inherently result in vehicles becoming closer together or further apart. When another vehicle then passes by "at a high rate of speed," it can be difficult to assess the speed of the passing vehicle, except for qualitative and colloquial expressions such as, "it passed me like I was standing still." Without additional information, little more can be known other than the passing vehicle was traveling faster than the vehicle it passed—almost as unhelpful as it reads. Albert Einstein famously derived a "theory of relativity," which can be loosely applied here in that there are often variables that affect one's perception of what is observed, based on where one is located, relative to the positions and movements of other objects. Simply, what one person perceives may be correct from that person's vantage point, while being incorrect relative to all of the movements in the sequence of events. More specifically, what someone believes he or she saw (and attempts to recollect) may not be accurate or sufficiently describe what occurred.[1]

A common debate is whether witnesses have a better recollection at the time of the event or at a later date, sometimes months or years later. The answer is neither obvious nor consistent between seemingly similar circumstances. People tend to recall events based on concepts of primacy and recency—that is, events that have great significance (primacy) or have recently occurred. Traumatic events that occurred months or years prior may be recalled accurately and with great detail, as well as events that may have occurred within the last minute, hour, or day. However, life-altering events (e.g., traumatic brain injuries) may also have distorted an otherwise objective perspective, and recent events may not have been salient enough to commit to memory. However, recollection (without reflection) immediately after an event may not fully capture the broader context of what occurred. Additional time for the witness to recall and process what was experienced can provide a witness with clarity in regard to what happened. While memories and recall cannot typically be verified, they

1. It would be unfair to call the person a liar, because there may be no intent to lie. The person simply may be mistaken or wrong.

remain valuable pieces of complex puzzles of evidence. Understanding the limitations of perception can help one better understand and utilize its benefits.

Difficulty in Perception

Determining whether or not something actually occurred tends to be easier to perceive and recall than the ability to accurately estimate time, distances, and speeds of other vehicles prior to a collision, especially if the collision was sudden and unexpected to the observer. Because witnesses often recollect that a collision "happened so fast," they may not have had sufficient time to comprehend much of the available information. Once the collision occurs, a natural response is to try to understand what happened, including what vehicles and drivers may have been doing in the moments leading up to the collision. If a driver failed to see and avoid a stopped vehicle or pedestrian, an observer may conclude that the driver must have been distracted. However, many other factors may have contributed to the collision, including the estimations of time, distance, and speed and the conspicuity of the struck object.

As a broadly applicable example, a multiple vehicle collision within an intersection typically results when one or more of the drivers (1) failed to see the other vehicle in enough time to avoid or (2) saw the other vehicle and believed that there was enough time to complete the maneuver. Failing to see an approaching vehicle is often a result of inattention or distraction, while the cause of misestimating available time is the predictable result of known perceptual difficulties. It may be difficult for drivers to determine how far away another vehicle is or at what speed it is traveling.

In addition to inaccurate estimations, in general, when vehicles that are moving directly toward or away from an observer, there are limited visual cues to evaluate the vehicle's speed. As commonly understood, objects appear smaller when they are further away and grow in appearance as they get closer. However, when a driver sees another vehicle traveling in the same lane in front of him or her, it may be especially difficult to recognize how fast the lead vehicle is traveling, as it "looms" out front of the observer. This perceptual looming effect can inhibit a following driver from recognizing that he or she is rapidly approaching a stopped or slow-moving vehicle in the roadway. Prior to this recognition, the following driver tends to operate under two assumptions—that the lead vehicle is traveling in the same direction, and that it is traveling at about the speed limit. If either assumption is not correct, additional information is necessary to alert the following driver to the dangerous condition. When there are insufficient visual cues available, the following drivers are often unable to discern that they are approaching the lead vehicle, which is growing in their visual field at a fast enough rate to alert them to the situation. The rate at which the vehicle appears to grow in one's vision—or its visual expansion rate—provides the primary way for drivers to assess the distance, speed, and time of arrival of approaching vehicles. In many scenarios, the following driver may not be alerted to the danger until it is too late to execute successful evasive maneuvers.

A related collision sequence is when drivers are determining whether or not they have sufficient time for their vehicles to cross or enter a roadway before approaching traffic reaches them. This qualitative decision is referred to as "gap acceptance," where drivers decide if there is a large enough gap in traffic for them to successfully complete their intended maneuver. The difficulties discussed earlier in estimating vehicle speeds and distances directly relate to the difficulties in correctly assessing the gap. The decision is based on both the driver's perception and the acceleration capabilities of the vehicle. CMVs typically require more time to accelerate into and across traffic than passenger vehicles, which results in drivers needing larger gaps in order to complete the maneuvers safely. Based on related past experiences, and their perception of the approaching vehicle's time-to-arrival, a driver may choose to accept the gap and attempt the maneuver or reject the gap and wait longer. Drivers tend to assess the time it will take an approaching vehicle to reach the intersection based primarily on how far away it is. However, a common factor in collisions related to gap acceptance is when the approaching vehicle is traveling at a high rate of speed. As a result, another driver may look and see that the approaching vehicle is not near to the intersection (i.e., does not appear to be an imminent hazard), but due to its approach speed it will arrive much sooner than expected.

Due to misestimations of the speed of approaching vehicles, especially when the approaching vehicle is traveling at an unexpectedly high rate of speed, observers may not be able to reliably estimate how much time that they have available. Traveling at high speeds and misestimating the available gap predictably leads to an increased likelihood of a collision. On a practically related issue, many crashes in which vehicles are struck by oncoming trains at railroad crossings occur for similar reasons. Drivers may choose to enter a roadway because they believe they have enough time to complete their maneuvers, or that they expect approaching drivers will see them and slow down or change lanes to avoid a collision. Consistent with state laws nationwide, drivers should not attempt to enter a roadway until and unless that driver can complete the maneuver safely.

Conclusion

Accurately estimating time, speeds, and distances of other vehicles is an inaccurate art, but that does not mean it is unhelpful. Testimony of the events leading up to a collision can provide key insights to the collision sequence, and both the eyewitnesses and the drivers involved in the collision may make the same errors in estimation. Even when testimony is inconsistent, a qualified expert is often able to evaluate the collision sequence and assist the jury in understanding what actually occurred, and why. When investigating a collision, it is essential to understand where drivers and outside observers were located and what was available to be seen from their locations. Ultimately, their decisions may be based on incomplete or inaccurate estimations, and drivers need to ensure that they are not taking actions that are putting themselves and other motorists at risk of injury or death. The human factors of driver perception and response are used to assimilate driver and witness testimony with the time, speeds, and distances of objects and vehicles involved in motor vehicle collisions. This, in turn, allows experts to evaluate the actions (and inactions) of drivers and determine what driver behaviors likely created the dangerous conditions and to what extent collisions may have been avoidable.

CHAPTER 15
On-Board Electronics

John C. Steiner and Peter Doody, Esq.

Abstract

Since the last decade of the twentieth century the development of electronics and electronic controls for medium- and heavy-duty vehicles has rapidly progressed in order for the manufacturers of these vehicles to meet more stringent vehicle emissions regulations in the United States, Canada, the United Kingdom, and the European Union.

As these electronic systems evolved, the number of electronic sensors has grown from an average of about 60 electronic sensors in a class 8 truck-tractor in 1998 to nearly 1,000 sensors on a model year 2024 class 8 truck-tractor.

Today's medium- and heavy-duty vehicles and their foundation of electronic controls (the Electronic Control Unit or ECU), a data network (the Controller Area Network or CAN bus), and sensors are the basis for data recorders.

There is an important distinction between data recorders that are original to the vehicle (OEM) and aftermarket installed devices that must be understood by the investigator. This chapter is an overview of the Original Equipment Manufacturer (OEM) Heavy Vehicle Event Data Recorders (HVEDRs) that can be found on late-model medium- and heavy-duty vehicles operating on North American roads today, as well as aftermarket on-board electronics that can record data.

Introduction

In the realm of commercial, heavy vehicles, HVEDR refers to a digital system—either OEM or aftermarket—that can record, and store data related to specific incidents occurring during the operation of the vehicle. Such incidents could include crashes, abrupt speed variations, both manual and automatic braking events, or anomalies identified in the sensors or systems being monitored by the vehicles Electronic Control Units (ECUs) or aftermarket installed device. These systems are consistently monitoring in real-time sensors measuring the speed of the vehicle, throttle position, engine revolutions per minute (RPM), status of the clutch and brakes, utilization of cruise control, activation of drivetrain retarders, and other crucial operational metrics.

The quantitative and objective information recorded by on-board systems is an invaluable resource for OEMs and Tier 1 Suppliers, collision investigators and law enforcement agencies, government agencies and researchers, as well as fleet managers.

Passenger Vehicle EDR versus Heavy Vehicle EDR

Due to the distinct differences in design of light-duty passenger and cargo vehicles in comparison to the heavy-duty trucks and buses, there are distinct differences between the design and functionality of a light-duty vehicle event data recorder (EDR) found in passenger cars, vans, and pick-up trucks, which are equipped with occupant restraint systems such as airbags and seat belt pretensioners, and heavy vehicle EDRs, which are found in the largest of the medium-duty and most heavy-duty vehicles, which includes straight trucks, truck-tractors, and buses that can carry 19 passengers or more.

The way that the passenger vehicle EDR is triggered to record data, the types of data recorded, and the recording duration are very different from HVEDR, and the two should be treated differently.

EDRs found in passenger vehicles (light-duty vehicles) are technically defined by the Society of Automotive Engineers (SAE) Recommended Practice J1698.[1] The J1698 EDR is typically a software algorithm that is typically incorporated into a light-duty vehicle's Airbag Control Module (ACM) and is programmed to collect and record data from the vehicle's Controller Area Network (CAN) if the ACM detects a crash event that may or may not result in the deployment of occupant protection devices such as seat belt pretensioners and airbags.

When the J1698 EDR is triggered to record data, it only records data for a finite period of time, typically not more than 100 seconds. The J1698 EDR, generally, will capture three categories of data that include (1) occupant protection systems status, including the readiness of the airbag system, seatbelt status, and other diagnostics-related data; (2) crash pulse data, which includes the measured crash pulse in the form of an acceleration-time history and a calculated Delta-V (change in velocity) time history; and (3), the pre-crash data set, which can be the 3 to 100 seconds preceding the crash event and can include data such as vehicle speed, engine speed, steering angle input, accelerator pedal position, brake application, clutch application, engine operating parameters, safety systems parameters and interventions (anti-lock brakes, stability control), and other channels of data.

Most J1698 EDRs will record data to non-volatile memory so that data is not sensitive to data loss issues due to the loss of the vehicle's electrical power during the crash event.

1. SAE J1698, Recommended Practice, Event Data Recorder, 202303, https://www.sae.org/standards/content/j1698_202303/.

Most J1698 EDRs can have their data imaged (downloaded) and saved using a common tool, the Bosch Crash Data Retrieval (CDR) Tool. Most light-duty vehicle OEMs collaborate and have contracts in place with Bosch Automotive so that most vehicles can be accessed with the Bosch CDR Tool.

Three major OEMs who have their own EDR tools are Hyundai, KIA, and Tesla.

In comparison, most of the larger medium-duty and most heavy-duty trucks and buses are not equipped with an occupant protection system such as frontal airbags.

Historical Perspective

Over the last 45 years, advancements in passenger vehicle passive occupant restraint systems and their electro-mechanical controls in the 1970s set the foundation for the development of EDR in North America for passenger vehicles. Initially focused on light-duty vehicles, the functionality of EDRs has now extended to medium- and heavy-duty vehicles. This expansion was prompted by advances in diesel emissions requirements for clean diesel engines as required by the U.S. Environmental Protection Agency (EPA) starting in 2002 and the requirements for lower diesel nitrogen oxides (NOx) emissions. The adoption of electronic engine controls also led to the establishment of standardized on-vehicle serial communications protocols. These protocols defined the physical network (wiring), communications protocols, and messages within vehicles, laying the foundation for HVEDRs. In June 2010, SAE International published a Recommended Practice, J2728 Heavy Vehicle Event Data Recorder, Tier 1,[2] which defined the HVEDR function in vehicles with a Gross Vehicle Weight Rating (GVWR) of 10,000 lbs. (4,536 kg) or more and equipped with a J1587 or J1939 communications data bus.

Interest in HVEDRs has grown due to their ability to record crucial data regarding vehicle dynamics and driver inputs for a short period of time just before and after a triggered event, typically due to a crash or a non-crash event. These recorded event data records provide valuable insights combined with physical evidence, enabling experts to conduct comprehensive vehicle crash reconstruction analysis. The integration of HVEDR data with reconstruction evidence also provides valuable information to enhance our understanding of safety system performance, potentially contributing to safer vehicle designs and more effective safety regulations.

EDR and HVEDR Regulatory Activities

As of the end of 2024, there are no regulatory requirements that any highway vehicles, including medium- and heavy-duty commercial vehicles, be equipped with any kind of Event Data Recorder or Video Data Recorder.

2. SAE J2728, Recommended Practice, Heavy Vehicle Event Data Recorder, Tier 1, 202006, https://www.sae.org/standards/content/j2728-1_202006/.

In 2006, the National Highway Traffic Safety Administration (NHTSA) did publish Part 563 in C.F.R. Title 49 that outlined specifications for uniform, national requirements for equipping EDR. It also provided requirements that vehicle manufacturers were to use when developing commercially available tools and methods for crash investigators and researchers to retrieve EDR data. One important fact to keep in mind, the rule is *voluntary* and applicable to light-duty vehicles of GVWR 3,855 kg (8,500 lbs.) or less manufactured on or after September 1, 2012. It is important to note that the Part 563 rule was revised and reissued in 2009. The Part 563 rule does not apply to medium- and heavy-duty vehicles.

HVEDR Functionality

Light-duty vehicle EDRs and HVEDRs are often compared to Flight Data Recorders (FDR) used in passenger aircraft, which are mandated by the U.S. Federal Aviation Administration (FAA) Part 121.[3] However, there is not much in common between FDRs and EDRs/HVEDRs besides the concept of recording data.

The FDR and the Cockpit Voice Recorder (CVR) are purpose-designed and built with electronic data and audio recorders that independently monitor and record hundreds of channels of data. The data capture engine performance, flight control position, aircraft dynamics, pilot controls inputs, and cockpit audio recordings. These systems have their own dedicated wiring harnesses and power supply to monitor all aspects of the aircraft.

Unlike FDRs, EDRs and HVEDRs rely on preexisting sensors and data networks that are foundational to the vehicle's operation. The data that can be captured, such as engine speed, vehicle speed, and accelerator pedal position data, is generated by sensors that transmit the data for the Engine/Powertrain Control Module to operate the engine and transmission. Similarly, the steering wheel input rate and position are monitored by a sensor that transmits the data to the vehicle's Electronic Stability Control (ESC) system to monitor dynamic situations and assist the driver in maintaining control of the vehicle. The HVEDR algorithm itself monitors the vehicle's sensors and determines when an event of interest has occurred and if that event should be recorded for subsequent imaging. The EDR function, responsible for capturing and recording data, is a function running within an Electronic Control Unit (ECU). This ECU, which contains the HVEDR functionality, also serves other primary functions related to the vehicle's operation, such as engine protection, engine diagnostics, reduced maintenance, engine and road speed governing, fuel economy, emissions control, and other operational tasks. The EDR function is secondary in nature, designed to supplement the primary functions of the ECU.

3. 14 C.F.R. § 121.344.

HVEDR Data

It is important to understand the difference between the recording metrics and triggering protocols of light-duty vehicle EDRs and the triggering mechanics of HVEDRs in heavy-duty vehicles.

In the case of HVEDRs, they are typically triggered by a change in vehicle speed over a period of approximately one second as measured at either the wheel speed sensor(s) or the drivetrain-mounted Vehicle Speed Sensor (VSS).

Historically, early HVEDR functionalities found in the late 1990s and early 2000s leveraged an older, now retired serial data bus network as defined by SAE J1708 (Serial Data Communications Between Microcomputer Systems in Heavy-Duty Vehicle Applications) and J1587 (Electronic Data Interchange between Microcomputer Systems in Heavy-Duty Vehicle Applications).

Today, HVEDR functionalities are built on high-speed Controller Area Networks (CANs) as defined by SAE J1939/13 (Serial Control and Communications Heavy Duty Vehicle Network) and ISO 15765:2011 (Road Vehicles—Diagnostic Communication over Controller Area Network (DoCAN)). Other standardized CAN networks as well as proprietary CAN networks can be used as well.

Some of the key sensors used as primary sources of recorded HVEDR data can include the following:

- **Brake switch.** Used to energize (or command) the activation of the brake lights on the exterior of the vehicle. Also used as a source of analog data for simple service brake applications (ON/OFF).
- **Clutch switch.** Primarily used to disengage the cruise control system (if engaged) when the driver applies the clutch. Can provide analog clutch position (APPLIED/NOT APPLIED).
- **Engine camshaft and crankshaft position sensors.** The source of engine speed (RPM).
- **Steering wheel position sensor.** Primary input to vehicle Electronic Stability Programming (ESP) functionality and provides steering wheel position in degrees positive and negative depending on the definition of values per the OEM or Tier 1 supplier.
- **Throttle position sensor (TPS).** Position of the accelerator pedal (in percent) as applied by the driver.
- **Vehicle speed sensor (VSS).** The source of vehicle road speed.
    - Can be dedicated VSS mounted on the tail shaft of transmission and measures output shaft rotations
    - Anti-Lock Brake System (ABS) wheel speed sensors can be leveraged. Either a singular sensor or, in most cases, two sensors on the same axle can be used and averaged.

Please note that this list is just a sampling of data elements that are available. There are additional data elements captured by HVEDRs in trucks and buses today. For a complete list of data elements, it is recommended to refer to SAE J2728 (Heavy Vehicle Event Data Recorder Recommended Practice).

HVEDR Triggers

There are two main triggers that are defined around the braking and stopping of a heavy vehicle that once activated will result in an HVEDR recording data.

The two different event triggers in HVEDRs can be defined in two distinct categories: acceleration triggers (hard brake/sudden deceleration/quick stop) and last stop triggers. Each heavy-duty vehicle manufacturer implements these event triggers to varying degrees. To promote consistency and standardization, there is a Recommended Practice, SAE J2728 (Heavy Vehicle Event Data Recorder), that describes a common set of performance requirements for recording and storing data related to specific events that can occur during the operation of a heavy vehicle.

These events are triggered and captured differently among the various manufacturers. OEM HVEDR triggers, recording duration, and recording frequency are displayed in Tables 15.1 and 15.2.

Table 15.1 OEM HVEDR-Type Triggers and Recording[4]

	Daimler Trucks North America Detroit Diesel/ Mercedes-Benz	**Volvo Group North America (Mack, Volvo, Volvo Bus/Prevost)**	**Caterpillar**
Engine/ Modules	DDEC 16 (CPC04T) & Mercedes OM471	Mack V-MAC IV+ Volvo Version 3 Controls	CAT C15 EPA 07; ADEM IV Module
Year	2016 to current	2013 to current	2010
Recording Durations	Hard Brake: 1 min (pre), 15 sec (post) Last Stop: 1 min 44 sec (pre),15 sec (post)	Acceleration Triggered: 1 min (pre), 30 sec (post) Last Stop: 90 sec	44 sec (pre), 15 sec (post)
Recording Frequency	1 Hz	4 Hz	1 Hz
Hard Brake Trigger	Factory set to 7 mph/s; configurable by owner	+/– 10 mph/sec	Factory set to 7 mph/s; configurable by owner
Last Stop Trigger	Vehicle speed changes from greater than 1.5 mph to less than 1.5 mph and is stopped for 15 sec.	0 mph/s	N/A
Trigger Conditions	Vehicle speed must be above 10 mph; will not trigger if preceded or followed by acceleration of more than 4 mph/s.	No trigger conditions for acceleration triggered events. Last Stop requires vehicle to exceed 5 km/hr (3.1 mph) for Last Stop to be written.	No special conditions

4. Transport Canada Commercial Bus HVEDR Feasibility Study (File No. T8080-160062) Deliverable No. 6, Commercial Bus HVEDR Feasibility Report; Oxnard, CA, USA; May 11, 2018; https://transcanadahvedr.ca/; https://transcanadahvedr.ca/wp-content/uploads/2022/01/T8080_Deliverable6-HVEDR_Feasibility-KME20180331-FINAL_English.pdf.

Table 15.2 OEM HVEDR-Type Triggers and Recording Continued

	Navistar International	Cummins	PACCAR	Bendix
Engine/ Modules	Navistar A26	X15 Engine; CM2350	MX-11 Engine (EPA 2013)	EC-80 Module
Year Recording Durations	2018 to current 105 sec (pre), 15 sec (post)	2017 to current 59 sec (pre), 15 sec (post)	2010 to 2017 5 sec (pre), 5 sec (post)	2011 and later 10 sec (pre), 10 sec (post)
Recording Frequency	1 Hz	1 Hz	4 Hz	2 Hz
Hard Brake Trigger	7.4 mph/s	9 mph/sec	8.95 mph/sec	0.55 g triggers Bendix Data Recorder log; 0.75 g triggers and locks
Last Stop Trigger	Vehicle comes to a stop and engine is shut down, or vehicle comes to a stop and engine remains idle for more than 2 min.	N/A	N/A	N/A
Trigger Conditions	Minimum vehicle speeds may be required; currently being determined.	9 mph/ sec default; most are not programmable.	N/A	When the magnitude of lateral and/or longitudinal acceleration exceeds 0.5 g in any direction. (acceleration > 0.5 g); when vehicle speed is reduced by 6.9 mph or greater in 1 sec (Hard Brake); when there is a Wingman Advanced system brake intervention; when Active Cruise with Braking (ACB) is set, and the takeover alert (or impact alert) and driver are overriding the system.

Current OEM HVEDR Coverage

OEM HVEDR coverage begins with several makes of heavy trucks and engines starting in the late 1990s. An HVEDR could be found on a North American commercial truck or bus in the vehicle's Original Equipment Manufacturer (OEM) Electronic Control Units (ECUs).

It is important to note that in addition to the OEM HVEDR function, other HVEDR functions may also be found in an aftermarket device (or devices) installed on a commercial truck or bus. These aftermarket devices could include GPS-based telematics devices, Electronic Logging Devices (ELD), or enterprise-level Video Data Recorders (Dashcams). The ELD's primary function is the electronic logging of commercial driver Hours of Service (HOS). There are other digital data sources, such as commercial dashcam systems like Lytx®, Nauto®, Netradyne®, and others.

Heavy-duty trucks and buses typically are equipped with diesel engines manufactured by Caterpillar, Cummins, Detroit Diesel, Mack, Mercedes Benz, Navistar, and Volvo. These engines have been designed and manufactured using OEM ECUs to control the engine's operation. To access the HVEDR functions and any HVEDR data found within the heavy-duty truck or bus, OEM ECUs require a laptop with the appropriate service software and an RP1210-compliant vehicle communications interface to be able to connect, communicate, and image (download) data from the OEM ECUs.

Commercial vehicles manufactured after 1998 may be equipped with HVEDR functionality in the vehicle's engine ECU. Between 1998 and 2007, it was common to see three to four ECUs on a commercial truck or a bus. Typically, they were the Engine ECU, the Vehicle or Cab ECU, and the Anti-Lock Brakes/Traction Control ECU.

Determining which heavy-duty vehicles are equipped with an OEM HVEDR goes beyond solely considering the vehicle's model year, make, and model. For heavy-duty vehicles, it is required that the model year, make, model, and installed engine make/model be known to determine what HVEDR functionality exists on the subject vehicle. Table 15.3 summarizes the available HVEDR functions based on the engine installed in the commercial truck or bus.

Table 15.3 Data-Recording Capabilities[5]

Engine Manufacturer	Data-Recording Capabilities
Detroit Diesel	Two Hard Brake Events (1998–present) One Last Stop Event (1998–present) Three Diagnostic Records (1998–2007 & 2010–present)
Mercedes-Benz	Two Hard Brake Events (2000–2009) One Last Stop Event (2000–2009) Three Diagnostic Records (2000–2009)
Cummins	Three Sudden Deceleration Events (2005–present) Fault Code Snapshots (1998–present)
Caterpillar	Quick Stop Events (2007–2010)* Diagnostic Snapshots (1995–2010) External Triggers (1995–2010) * *Quick Stops not enabled by default*

5. Transport Canada Commercial Bus HVEDR Feasibility Study (File No. T8080-160062) Deliverable No. 2, Database of Highway Safety Research; Oxnard, CA, USA; May 11, 2018.

Engine Manufacturer	Data-Recording Capabilities
Mack	One Acceleration Triggered Event (1998–present) One Last Stop Event (2007–present)** Fault Reporter (1998–present) *** Prior to 2007, it was possible for Mack trucks to record two acceleration triggered events instead of one of each.*
Volvo	One Acceleration Triggered Event (2011–present) One Last Stop Event (2011–present) Freeze Frames (2002–present)
International/Navistar Maxxforce	Two Hard Brake Events (2010–present) Two Last Stop Events (2010–present) Freeze Frames (2010–present)
PACCAR	Three Fast Stop Events (2008–2016) Freeze Frames (2008–present) Fast Stop Recorder (2022–?)

OEM Trip Recorders

Going back to the 1990s, early engine ECUs did not have the capability to include HVEDR functionality. Rather, some engine manufacturers offered an optional instrument-panel mounted trip computer that provided drivers with trip-related information such as travel time, distance traveled, fuel consumption, and fuel economy data. These instrument-panel mounted trip computers also included HVEDR functionality.

When investigating a crash involving an older truck equipped with a Detroit Diesel or Cummins engine, the crash investigator should inspect the instrument panel and the header above the windshield for the presence of trip computer devices.

HVEDR Data Access and Tools

For nearly 20 years, there has been a common, commercially available software and hardware tool that can access almost all makes of passenger vehicles to generate a commonly formatted light-duty EDR report as is defined in 49 C.F.R. part 563 and SAE J1698. This tool is the Crash Data Retrieval Tool (CDR Tool) manufactured and sold by Bosch Automotive®.

As of 2024, there is not a common HVEDR data retrieval tool similar to the Bosch® CDR Tool that can connect to all makes and models of heavy-duty vehicles. Instead, multiple (expensive) OEM diagnostic software tools and hardware are required to image data from the various makes of heavy trucks or buses.

When an expert is working through the process of accessing EDR (including HVEDR) data to save the data from the vehicle, both the SAE J1698 light-duty EDR standards committee and the SAE J2728 Heavy Vehicle Event Data Recorder recommend that, assuming the best forensically neutral methodologies are used, the term "imaging" instead of "downloading" is used to describe the process of copying data from an ECU's physical memory chips. This terminology emphasizes a forensically neutral protocol that ensures data is copied without physically altering, deleting, or clearing those memory chips.

There are some processes of "downloading" data that are more invasive and may not preserve the original data, as it resides on the physical memory chips. Some situations may require these more invasive techniques due to extensive damage to the heavy truck or bus or its ECUs.

In many cases, modern vehicles may have multiple HVEDR functions that can capture data, each requiring specific diagnostics software for access. For example, a 2021 Peterbilt 589 may have a PACCAR® MX13 turbo-diesel engine, an Eaton RoadRanger® Automated Manual Transmission (AMT), and Bendix® ABS, with optional Bendix Wingman Fusion. All of these systems have the capability to record HVEDR events or extensive Diagnostics Trouble Code (DTC)-related snapshot records and would require PACCAR Davie4 software, the Eaton ServiceRanger® software, and Bendix diagnostic software to be able to access, image, and preserve all available data. Failing to use all these software tools could result in an investigator missing a key piece(s) of electronic evidence.

HVEDR Data Quality and Evidentiary Foundation

When reviewing the "digital" data from an HVEDR, it is crucial to validate its accuracy and relevance to the specific vehicle and incident being investigated. Although this chapter does not cover every possible scenario or research paper on data validity, it emphasizes the importance of thorough vehicle component inspections, staying current with HVEDR training, and conducting relevant and necessary practical testing.

Some of the validation points that need to be analyzed are listed here. Failing to document and inspect these areas could result in an inaccurate application of the data.

- Chassis Identification (VIN number, build date)
- Engine Identification (engine serial number, engine model number, engine build date)
- Transmission and Drive Axle Identification (serial numbers, ratios)
- Drive Tires (model, size, load range, condition)
- ECU Identification (ECU serial number, ECU model number, software version)
- Sensors (Vehicle Speed Sensor, Wheel Speed Sensors)

There are typically three foundational questions to answer when analyzing HVEDR data, and they are as follows: (1) establishing that the HVEDR data is from the subject crash or incident, (2) stablishing that the HVEDR data is from the subject vehicle, and (3) establishing the accuracy of the data.

It is important to conduct data imaging (download) of all available data, including odometers and hour meters, to stamp the HVEDR data.

For trucks with real-time clocks, it is important to synchronize the clock on the laptop being used to image data from the vehicle with an accurate time and date. To ensure accurate imaging of HVEDR data, it is recommended to set the laptop's clock to Universal Coordinate Time (UTC) or ZULU Time to prevent introducing any further complications or confusion to the time correction by having to account for different time zones and Daylight Savings Time. Some vehicles can have limited clock functionality, or the internal real-time clock is so far off it may not be usable.

In analyzing the HVEDR reported vehicle speed time history data, the most significant source of error in the reported vehicle speed is from wheel slip as a result of ABS intervention during braking that results in partial wheel lockup leading to a potential underreporting of the vehicle speeds in the range of 7 to 31.5 percent.[6] The second most common source of error in the reported vehicle speed time history data is the calibration of the vehicle speed sensor. Typically, this may result in an error in the reported speed of less than +/− 2 percent.[7] However, greater errors have been observed, especially with trucks that were purchased second or third hand and they have been reconfigured from an over-the-road truck-tractor to a dump truck. It is important for your expert who is imaging data from a heavy-duty vehicle to also properly document what the heavy-duty vehicle physically is and how it is configured, including its drive-train components and installed tire sizes. Build records from the chassis manufacturer can be obtained to show what engine serial number and what other major components and their serial numbers were originally installed in that chassis when the vehicle was manufactured.

It is important to exercise caution when dealing with older vehicles, as there may be instances where the original engine or ECUs may have been replaced. This can lead to discrepancies between the engine data plates and the engine configuration.

Engine ECUs that become no longer serviceable due to internal faults with the circuit board can be replaced with used ECUs. However, it is important to note that replacing faulty ECUs with used ones may require some reprogramming to ensure proper functionality. This reprogramming typically involves matching horsepower output and entering calibration values for the diesel fuel injectors, among other adjustments. Other information, including chassis identification (VIN, Chassis No., Unit No.), might not be updated during this process. If the Vehicle Speed Sensor (VSS) calibration is not updated, the vehicle's speedometer will be incorrect, and any data recorded by the HVEDR may also be incorrect.

Documentation of the truck or bus's powertrain components, such as engine identification, transmission identification, drive axle identification, and drive tire identification, including make, model, load range, size, and condition, is indeed crucial for validating and quantifying the accuracy of the recorded vehicle speed-time history.

---

6. Timothy J. Reust, "The Accuracy of Speed Captured by Commercial Vehicle Event Data Recorders," SAE Technical Paper 2004-01-1199, 2004, https://doi.org/10.4271/2004-01-1199.

7. SAE Course, Accessing and Interpreting Heavy Vehicle Event Data Recorders, Course ID No. C1022, Module 02: Analysis Group, https://www.sae.org/learn/content/c1022/.

It is important to not overlook the passenger vehicle that may be involved in a crash with a heavy-duty truck or bus. The passenger vehicle EDR data is a valuable source of information that can provide accurate and reliable details about the timing, sequence of events, and actions taken leading up to a crash, as well as the performance of occupant protection systems during the crash. Analyzing passenger vehicle EDR data allows for easy correlation with the crash scene, including the actual point of impact (POI).

There can be situations when a crash is between a heavy-duty tractor-trailer weighing over 65,000 lbs. and a small passenger vehicle weighing 3,000 lbs. And the crash event results in no data from an HVEDR because the crash pulse experienced by the heavy-duty tractor-trailer is very low compared to the crash pulse experienced by the passenger vehicle. In these situations, the EDR in the passenger vehicle may be the only source of data.

Completing a traditional investigative reconstruction allows the investigator to understand the sequence of events, compare the traditional crash reconstruction methodologies to the recorded HVEDR data, and validate the recorded HVEDR data.

There is a significant risk of data misinterpretation if the HVEDR data from a heavy-duty truck or bus is solely relied upon to analyze a crash event. As discussed in this chapter, there are data limitations and uncertainties associated with HVEDR (or EDR) data that make it insufficient to stand independently without considering physical evidence and traditional crash reconstruction methodologies that have been utilized and refined over the last 75 years.

To properly address and understand data limitations and the proper analysis of EDR and HVEDR data, continuing technical education on this technology is essential.

Vehicle Data as Evidence

Accessing and imaging data from a commercial vehicle should be completed following forensically neutral practices that have been laid out and taught through internationally recognized standards organizations such as SAE International (Society of Automotive Engineers).

Because most heavy-duty trucks and buses are used in course and scope of a commercial enterprise, that commercial enterprise is obligated to preserve and protect and electronic data that may have been recorded and stored in the commercial vehicle's ECUs.

The imaging of EDR or HVEDR data should be done in a manner that is transparent and well documented by recorded digital video or a detailed series of high-quality digital photographs. This includes the detailed documentation of the vehicle for which data is being imaged and the vehicle's identification plates, drivetrain identification plates and configuration, and drive tires, as previously discussed earlier in this chapter.

The proper documentation of the data imaging process and of the vehicle from which the data is imaged is critical to laying the foundation to validate that the data imaged is from the vehicle in question and from the crash in question, and to validate the accuracy of the data.

The documentation of the foundation for the HVEDR or EDR data and the analysis and interpretation methodologies of the data is important to have well documented and sourced in order to meet the expert witness requirements of *Frye* and *Daubert* and their progeny and related rules of evidence and to allow the data, the analysis, and the expert analyzing the data to be accepted as evidence.

Data Ownership

From the perspective of the expert who is tasked to document a vehicle, whether a private passenger vehicle, a light-duty passenger vehicle used in a commercial operation, or a medium- or heavy-duty bus or truck, there are several open issues surrounding the access of vehicle data and the ownership of such data.

The topic of data privacy has been hashed out in court many years ago in several cases. And to summarize the privacy issue in laymen's terms, essentially the U.S. citizen's expectation of privacy in a vehicle being operated on a public road is greatly diminished. There are several federal- and state-level rules on the books that touch upon data privacy and data ownership but do not address the topic specifically.

U.S. Code of Federal Regulation Title 49, Part 563, does touch upon the topic of data retrieval from a vehicle but does not dive into the topics of vehicle data privacy and ownership.

In January 2015, Congress passed the Fixing America's Surface Transportation (FAST) Act (H.R. 22). Within H.R. 22 is the Driver Privacy Act of 2015.[8] The Driver Privacy Act of 2015 does address vehicle data ownership and the access and consent requirements. The Driver Privacy Act of 2015 states that EDR data is the property of the owner or lessee of the motor vehicle in which the EDR is installed, and the registered owner or lessee has primary ownership rights over the data stored and collected by the EDR.

The Driver Privacy Act also clearly states that no person, except that vehicle's registered owner or lessee can access the EDR data without the registered owner's or lessee's consent. There are several exceptions that allow for access to EDR data without the registered owner's or the lessee's consent and they include court orders, research purposes, emergency situations, or insurance purposes.

8. *Editor's Note:* The Driver Privacy Act of 2015, P.L. 114-94, 129 Stat. 1712, can be found in the notes to 49 U.S.C. § 30101. It also can be found at sections 24301–24303 of the Fixing America's Surface Transportation Act, or the FAST Act. It provides that the data in an "event data recorder," as that term is defined in 49 C.F.R. § 563.5, is the property of the owner of the lessee of the vehicle and that it may not be accessed unless (1) a court authorizes it, (2) the owner or lessee provides "written, electronic, or recorded audio consent," (3) DOT and NTSB investigations are undertaken, or other reasons not relevant here. This editor finds nothing in the Driver Privacy Act of 2015 that indicates any private remedy for violating it.

It is also important to note that at least 19 states have their own regulations regarding EDRs and the ownership of EDR data. Because of the state and federal laws, it is recommended that written consent be obtained from the registered owner (or lessee) of the vehicle. In many cases, it has been acceptable for counsel to sign on behalf of the registered owner (or lessee) of the vehicle, especially if the owner (or lessee) of the vehicle is a corporation or other business entity.

Another situation to be aware of is the transfer of data ownership. Following a crash, there have been a significant number of times that a vehicle is released by an insurance carrier and the vehicle is sold at auction. An individual or a commercial organization who wishes to either part the vehicle out or repair and sell it will purchase these vehicles. And sometimes these vehicles are purchased and taken to other countries, such as Mexico, Guatemala, Colombia, Vietnam, Russia, Saudi Arabia, and other locations around the world. When the vehicle is sold at auction and is owned by someone other than a party to the vehicle crash, it may be necessary to consider the data ownership rights of such person during the discovery process.

Aftermarket On-Board Electronics

A variety of aftermarket electronic devices can be installed or equipped in a commercial vehicle that can capture crucial data before, during, and after a crash. These devices can be categorized into two general categories of semi-pro retail devices that include GPS navigation systems or simple "dashcams" that record video in a loop to a memory card physically installed in the device, and enterprise-level devices that are designed for commercial fleets and will typically have a monthly subscription fee and will be a connected device that is uploading data and imagery to the cloud.

These commercial-grade devices can include the following:

- Electronic Logging Device (ELD), which is a federally mandated electronic device for recording a commercial driver's hours of service. There are many manufacturers of ELDs.
- Commercial-grade GPS-based telematics devices for monitoring and tracking commercial-fleet vehicle operations. Several large GPS telematics service providers include Atlanta Telematics, Azuga, FleetIO, Fleet-Locate, Geotab, Motive, Omnitracs, Samsara, Trimble, Verizon Connect, and Zonar.

Enterprise-level devices that are connected via some kind of mobile data connection will require the vehicle owner (or operator) to access, save, and preserve any data from the device's cloud portal.

The handling and data preservation process for semi-professional retail devices can be completely different from the enterprise-level devices. Semi-professional devices that are not connected to the cloud and are uploading data via some kind of mobile data connection will need to be handled carefully, as the data is being stored internally to some kind of memory chip or internal memory storage. The list of available semi-professional retail devices is too extensive to list in this chapter.

Conclusions

It is important to understand all of the potential sources of data that can be found in today's commercial trucks and buses, and that some of those devices are going to be original equipment manufactured to the truck and installed by the manufacturer. And there are devices that are going to be installed as aftermarket devices. These aftermarket devices, such as GPS telematics, video data recorders ("dashcams"), and Electronic Logging Devices (ELD) can belong to the fleet. And some aftermarket devices can belong to the drivers themselves. Depending on the state you are in, consider the legal ramifications of permission to data access and data ownership.

Additionally, always keep in mind that it is not just the commercial trucks that can have data that should be preserved following a crash. So do the light-duty passenger cars, trucks, and vans that are either being operated in course and scope of a commercial operation or as a private vehicle.

Acknowledgments

The content of this chapter has been referenced from two main sources that are the original work of John Steiner. The SAE Continuing Technical Education Course, *Accessing and Interpreting Heavy Vehicle Event Data Recorders* (Course ID No. C1022) that has been taught by John Steiner and his co-instructors for 14 years.

More information on the SAE Course, Accessing and Interpreting Heavy Vehicle Event Data Recorders (Course ID No. C1022) can be viewed here: https://www.sae.org/learn/content/c1022/.

The second source of information for this chapter is the research conducted by the technical expert team at Mecanica Scientific Services Corp. team on behalf of the Canadian government and Transport Canada. The research specifically into Heavy Vehicle Event Data Recorders (HVEDR) was for two studies requested by Transport Canada. The first is the *Heavy Vehicle Event Data Recorder Feasibility Study* (Contract No. T8080-160062). And the second is the *Heavy Vehicle Event Data Recorders: Best Practices* (Contract No. T8080-210526).

More technical details and more discussions on the functionality of HVEDR can be found in these two research reports, which are public documents available to all and published by Transport Canada. To access, the links are provided here:

- *Heavy Vehicle Event Data Recorder Feasibility Study* (Contract No. T8080-160062)
  - https://transcanadahvedr.ca/
- *Heavy Vehicle Event Data Recorders: Best Practices* (Contract No. T8080-210526)
  - https://tc.canada.ca/en/road-transportation/motor-carriers-commercial-vehicles-drivers/heavy-vehicle-event-data-recorders-best-practices

The authors would like to acknowledge and thank (John Steiner's) co-instructors of the SAE Continuing Technical Education Course, *Accessing and Interpreting Heavy Vehicle Event Data Recorders* (Course ID No. C1022) where much more technical details on HVEDR can be found. Those co-instructors include Timothy Austin (Wisconsin State Patrol), Timothy Cheek (Delta [v] Forensic Engineering, Inc.), Matt DiSogra (Delta [v] Forensic Engineering, Inc.), Wesley Grimes (Mecanica Scientific Services Corp.), Brad Higgins (Mecanica Scientific Services Corp.), David Plant (D.P. Plant & Associates), and Gregory Wilcoxson (Wilcoxson Consulting LLC).

The authors would also like to acknowledge and thank the co-authors of the Transport Canada Feasibility Study and Best Practices Study. They include Wesley Grimes, John Grindey, Bradley Higgins, John Isbister, John Kolter, Kristina Lombardi, Henry Ramirez, and Henry Schmoker of Mecanica Scientific Services Corporation; Steven Anderson; Jean-Louis Comeau.

References

- Data Sources and Analysis of a Heavy Vehicle Event Data Recorder—V-MAC III; Steiner, John C., Cheek, Timothy M., Hinkson, Scott H.; SAE Paper No. 2009-01-0881; SAE World Congress 2009; Detroit, MI
- Unfalldatenspeicher in Nordamerika (Data Recorders in North America); Steiner, John; VKU: Verkehrsunfall und Fahrzeugtechnik; January 2010
- Unfalldatenspeicher für schwere Nutzfahrzeuge in Nordamerika (North American Heavy Vehicle Event Data Recorder (HVEDR); Steiner, John; VKU: Verkehrsunfall und Fahrzeugtechnik; February 2010
- Event Data Recorders & Heavy Vehicle Event Data Recorders, the U.S. Experience / Event Data Recorder & Nutzfahrzeug Event Data Recorder—Erfahrungen aus den USA; 21. Jahrestagung der Europäischen Vereinigung für Unfallforschung und Unfallanalyse e.V./ 21st Annual Congress of the European Association for Accident Research and Analysis; Braşov, Romania; September 2012
- Timing and Synchronization of the Event Data Recorded by the Electronic Control Modules of Commercial Motor Vehicles—DDEC V; Plant, David, Cheek, Timothy, Austin, Timothy, Steiner, John C., Farrell, Michael, Spivey, Heath; SAE Paper No. 2013-01-1267; SAE World Congress 2013; Detroit, MI
- Reust, T., "The Accuracy of Speed Captured by Commercial Vehicle Event Data Recorders," SAE Technical Paper 2004-01-1199, 2004, https://doi.org/10.4271/2004-01-1199
- SAE Course, Accessing and Interpreting Heavy Vehicle Event Data Recorders, Course ID No. C1022, Module 02: Analysis Group
- Steiner., J., Plant, D., Grimes, W., Cheek, T., Austin, T. et al., "Examination of Detroit Assurance® 4.0 Video Radar Decision Unit (VRDU) Records for Use in Crash Analysis," SAE Technical Paper 2023-01-0009, 2023, https://doi.org/10.4271/2023-01-0009
- Steiner, J., Austin, T., Grimes, W., Cheek, T., Plant, D. et al., "Testing of Heavy Truck Advanced Driver Assistance Systems and Crash

Mitigation Systems," SAE Technical Paper 2023-01-0010, 2023, https://doi.org/10.4271/2023-01-0010

- Steiner, J., Cheek, T., Grimes, W., Plant, D., Austin, T. et al., "Examination of Bendix® Data Recording (BDR) Records for Use in Crash Analysis," SAE Technical Paper 2023-01-0012, 2023, https://doi.org/10.4271/2023-01-0012
- Transport Canada Commercial Bus HVEDR Feasibility Study (File No. T8080-160062) Deliverable No. 1, Highway Safety Research Reference List; Oxnard, CA, USA; May 11, 2018
- Transport Canada Commercial Bus HVEDR Feasibility Study (File No. T8080-160062) Deliverable No. 2, Database of Highway Safety Research; Oxnard, CA, USA; May 11, 2018
- Transport Canada Commercial Bus HVEDR Feasibility Study (File No. T8080-160062) Deliverable No. 3, Summary Report of Facts; Oxnard, CA, USA; May 11, 2018
- Transport Canada Commercial Bus HVEDR Feasibility Study (File No. T8080-160062) Deliverable No. 4, All Devices Summary Report; Oxnard, CA, USA; May 11, 2018
- Transport Canada Commercial Bus HVEDR Feasibility Study (File No. T8080-160062) Deliverable No. 5, Summary Report of International Commercial Vehicle EDR Industry Standards and Recommended Practices; Oxnard, CA, USA; May 11, 2018
- Transport Canada Commercial Bus HVEDR Feasibility Study (File No. T8080-160062) Deliverable No. 6, Commercial Bus HVEDR Feasibility Report; Oxnard, CA, USA; May 11, 2018
- Transport Canada Commercial Bus HVEDR Feasibility Study (File No. T8080-160062) Deliverable No. 7, Final Report; Oxnard, CA, USA; May 11, 2018
- Transport Canada Heavy Vehicle Event Data Recorders: Best Practices (File No. T8080-210526); Oxnard, CA, USA; July 23, 2024

CHAPTER 16

Trial Preparation and Strategy

Mark A. Perkins, Esq. and Shari E. Belitz, Esq.

You are now well into this manual, so you know that preparation and strategy actually began when the accident first occurred. Every case should be approached with the assumption it will go to trial even though the reality is that fewer cases actually go through verdict.[1] "Although civil case filings in federal courts, where the data are most reliable, have increased fourfold since the early 1960s, the percentage of civil cases disposed of by jury trial decreased from approximately 5.5% in 1962 to 1.2% by 2002 and to 0.8% by 2013."[2] The reasons for this are complex and incomplete, but for the purposes of this chapter, we bring this to your attention because it's a reality that many lawyers no longer have trial experience, so we will assume that many readers have not had as much experience trying cases as desired.

In order to successfully litigate cases at trial, knowing how and what to look for in the initial investigation and what to ensure is preserved makes your case at trial.

Developing a Plan

As you are preparing the case for trial, there is an assumption that you are organized and have a litigation plan; however, for those of you who like checklists, the following may be of assistance. The guidelines may vary depending on the requirements of the client, but essentially track the following starting from the date of the assignment.

Lists are helpful, but only if you mindfully follow the list. If you gloss over the list without thinking, it is useless. Reminders 15 and 30 days before the deadline should also be set. A good goal is to have every case resolved by trial

1. Shari Seidman Diamond & Jessica M. Salerno, *Reasons for the Disappearing Jury Trial: Perspective from Attorneys and Judges* 81 La. L. Rev. 120 (2020).

2. Marc Galanter, *The Vanishing Trial: An Examination of Trials and Related Matters in Federal and State Courts,* 1(3) J. Empirical Legal Stud. 459 (Nov. 4 2004); Suja A. Thomas, The Missing American Jury: Restoring the Fundamental Constitutional Role of the Criminal, Civil, and Grand Juries (Cambridge University Press, 2016).

or mediation within 18 months of the assignment. Old cases are never good cases to try.

A. Assignment date:
B. Within 7 days of assignment:
    a. Letter to insured driver
    b. Letter to plaintiff's attorney requesting extension
    c. Letter to insured representative (i.e., trucking company)
    d. Letter to claim professional acknowledging receipt of file
    e. Get CAR and budget form
    f. Review for specific instruction from claims professional
    g. Request policy of insurance
    h. Check for affirmative defenses and exceptions
C. Within 15 days of assignment:
    a. Confirm extension granted by adverse party
    b. Review specific instructions by client
    c. Check status of receipt of investigative materials
    d. Confirm who we represent
    e. Litigation holds/preservation letters
D. Within 30 days of assignment:
    a. Review investigative materials
        1. Accident report
        2. Photographs/videos
        3. Statements
        4. Medicals/settlement offers/demands
        5. Property damage appraisals
        6. Driver qualification file
        7. Request health insurance records
        8. Check service
        9. Color photo of front & back of CDL/driver's license & SSN
    b. Review petition, answer, removal, jury request
        1. All defendants served?
        2. Removal to federal court (complete diversity of all parties?)
            i. Jurisdiction amount sufficient ($75,000)
            ii. Requests for admissions of damages
            iii. Prepare corporate disclosure (for LLC, residency of all members disclosed)
    c. Removal to federal court because of federal question preemption?
        1. Carmack Amendment or
        2. FAAAA preemption?
    d. Jury Bond?
    e. Raise comparative fault?
    f. Exceptions/12(b)(6) motions?
    g. Draft discovery specific to the case
    h. Review discovery from adverse party
    i. Evaluate for need for experts (identify)

j. Draft written discovery to other parties
g. Protective order needed?

E. Within 45 days of assignment:
   a. Check with client regarding responses to discovery from adverse party
   b. Draft initial CAR/budget (at same time of answer)
   c. Interview insured driver (at same time of answer)
   d. Load documents online with searchable database

F. Within 60 days of assignment:
   a. Check receipt of responses from adverse attorney to discovery submitted
   b. Issue requests or subpoenas for:
      1. Medical records (issue SDTs to medical providers and to the medical provider CFO/office manager)
      2. Employment records
      3. Academic records (if applicable)
      4. Health insurance records
   c. Review plaintiff's discovery responses (if received)
   d. Set up depositions of:
      a. Plaintiffs
      b. Key witnesses
   e. Review local rules of the venue where the case is being tried. Update the deadlines for any special local rules of the venue. (For example, a local rule about impeachment evidence being presented to the judge 30 days before trial.)

G. Within 90 days of assignment:
   a. Check status of receipt of medical records & health insurance records
   b. Review CAR to see if there are specific things that need to be done
   c. Determine if summary judgment is applicable
   d. Other depositions to set up
   e. All medicals reviewed
   f. Conduct quantum analysis
   g. Experts to be deposed/retained?
   h. Motion to compel?

H. Within 120 days of assignment:
   a. Meds summarized?
   b. Depositions summarized?
   c. Quantum evaluation summarized?
   d. Update CAR/budget
   e. Medical doctors deposed?
   f. Request scheduling conference to set trials
   g. Reports from experts received

I. Within 150 days of assignment:
   a. Trial date should be scheduled
   b. Note local rules
   c. Scheduling order deadlines with reminders?

J. Trial preparation checklist (see all orders) and add:
   a. Mediation scheduled?

b. Subpoenas to be issued
c. Witnesses to be prepared
d. Trial depositions scheduled
e. Exhibits marked and exchanged
f. Jury venire/jury selection analysis
g. Opening statement
h. For exchanged exhibits, bench books/trial binders: (**Be sure** that any documentation has been redacted of address, phone numbers, DOB, social security numbers, bank account numbers, DL number, etc. You could get sanctioned by the court for failing to remove confidential information from the exhibits being filed.)

Also, every trucking case that we open has the following resources for reference:

1. Driver Privacy Act of 2015 § 24302[3] Notice regarding limitations on data retrieval from vehicle event data recorders
2. Emergency response checklist
3. Emergency response guidelines
4. Insured driver interview form
5. DOT recordable accident format
6. Discovery chart
7. List of mandatory documents in driver qualification file
8. Vehicle inspection authorization
9. Forms for letters, such as initial representation, counter-preservation letters
10. Folders created for:
    a. Case assessment reports/budget
    b. Correspondence
    c. Depositions
    d. Discovery
    e. Discovery releases
    f. Exhibits
    g. Experts—defense
    h. Experts—plaintif
    i. Investigation
    j. Legal invoices
    k. Medical information
    l. Medical invoices
    m. Notes, memos, research memoranda, CDL Manual (truck drivers), Office of Motor Vehicle Handbook (automobile drivers)
    n. Pleadings

3. Driver Privacy Act of 2015, Pub. L. No. 114-94 (2015).

Trial Notebook

Once the case is set for trial, create a trial notebook, which may save you from looking silly at trial. Judges and juries do not like wasted time. Although you may not have every document in the trial notebook, you certainly will have a list of pre-marked exhibits listed and organized in a manner for ease of reference. For example, a defendant's trial notebook should have the following items in it:

1. Pretrial reports
   a. Plaintiff
   b. Defense
2. Exhibit list
   a. Plaintiff
   b. Defense
3. Voir dire
4. Opening statement
5. Quick reference objections
   a. Consider the resource created by Jerry Glas, Chair of the Civil Litigation Division of Deutsch Kerrigan, LLP in New Orleans, entitled *The New Science of Trial Advocacy: The Waiter Pivot*.[4]
6. Plaintiff's case-in-chief
   a. List the plaintiff's witnesses in alphabetical order by last name because you do not know the order adversary will call the witness. You do not want to be fumbling about questions/issues and exhibits.
   b. Do **not** bring the entire notebook to the podium when you begin cross examination. Bring only your notes, pre-marked exhibits, and possibly the witnesses' deposition marked for areas that you want to use for prior inconsistent statements.
7. Directed verdict
   a. Be prepared to make an argument for a directed verdict and to counter the anticipated arguments for a directed verdict. It is rare that you will win that motion, but it could happen.
8. Defense case-in-chief
   a. Order your witnesses in the manner that you believe will have the best impact on your case, keeping in mind primacy and recency and that the jurors do not have a long attention span.
   b. Take to the podium only your outline of questions, pre-marked exhibits, and the deposition of the witness.
9. Closing argument
10. Proposed jury instructions/verdict form

4. Jerry Glas, The New Science of Trial Advocacy: The Waiter Pivot 148 (Am. Bar Ass'n 2023).

Themes

There is about as much confusion among lawyers as there is discussion regarding the topic of case themes. When should a case theme be written? Is a case theme the same as a case theory? Can a case theme change over time? What if a case theme cannot be found?

Thematic development is flexible and not time sensitive. It can happen as early as the first client intake call, or as late as a closing argument. Usually somewhere in between, during discovery is most common. Generally, the most effective case themes are often found early in the case, then honed, modified, and tweaked during the course of discovery. Can a theme take a sharp left turn and reverse course during trial? Absolutely, but that is an outlier situation, and if the foundation of a theme is set early, with a mindset toward flexibility, a theme can withstand surprises at trial.

A case theory is often confused with, but qualitatively different than a case theme. A theory is legal in nature and describes your client's position in legal terms. For example, if Y patron was sexually assaulted at X supermarket's dimly lit parking lot, by a sex offender on parole, a case theory would be: X supermarket owner had a duty to Y patron, and by not fixing the broken lighting in its parking lot, caused Y to be assaulted, sustaining physical and emotional injuries. A case theme differs as it takes a common-sense concept and uses the concept to organize the structure of the case. A case theme is like the title of a book, and each witness and piece of evidence is contained in a chapter in that book.

Having a compelling case theme helps jurors mentally organize, understand, comprehend, and remember large chunks of information in a truncated time period. A case theme is generally much shorter than a case theory. An example of a case theme to match our case theory would be, *"This is not a case about broken lights, this is a case about broken justice systems."* The objective of this case theme would be to shift the focus of blame to the violent third-party actor, the sex offender, and remove it from the supermarket owner. This simple theme conveys the concept that parole laws, recidivist sex offenders, and justice systems are the universal problem, not broken lighting.

Universal truths that stand the test of time and are common sense are most compelling to a jury. If you have a case where all of the plaintiff witnesses say, "the light was green," and all of the defense witnesses say, "the light was red," and an accident reconstruction shows the defense witnesses were situated in a better position to see the accident, a common-sense theme might be "who had the vantage advantage?"

In a case involving a plaintiff who felt fine after a car accident, refused medical treatment, then drove himself three hours home and spoke with a lawyer before seeking medical attention, the theme of "putting wealth before health" may be persuasive to a jury. Themes that rhyme are not only more memorable, but rhymes are actually cognitively judged to be more truthful. This is why advertising, and campaigns often use rhyming in their slogans.

Developing a theme may take time. It can be based on something a witness says in their deposition, or a response in an interrogatory. Some of the most compelling themes we have written come from what mock jurors blurt out during the course of a jury research exercise.

A case theme that we used in a recent federal trial was "All Play and No Work," which pertained to a plaintiff who had no documented loss of income or earning capacity, but he wanted the fact-finder to award him past loss of earning and future earning despite that he had no restrictions on his job, and he had chosen to leave a high-paying job before the accident and try to start his own business that didn't pay well. He wanted the defendants to pay for his loss of income unrelated to the accident so that he could continue pursuing his hobby of team steer-roping.

Another theme in a trucking case came from the commercial driver who had been hit by the plaintiff on the side of his trailer. We had a dashcam that clearly showed the plaintiff crossing two lanes of traffic, into the center lane, then into the left lane and hitting the truck while he was lawfully in the right lane and tried to avoid being hit. His comment that became the theme was *"I thought that a picture was worth a thousand words, but this seems like a thousand words is better than a picture."*

Once a theme begins to develop, it is critical to advance it when preparing your witnesses, as well as questioning your adversary's witnesses so you can strategically frame and leverage the strengths of your case. Your witnesses may be a mere chapter in your trial book, but they must know your theme and where they fit in the book.

You may have a good start to a theme, but it may be refuted during discovery. If that happens, it is critical to look at the testimony or evidence refuting it and see if it can be reconciled or incorporated into the theme, or if the theme needs to be changed or disregarded.

Sometimes your theme is a bad idea. You need to know the red flags of a "bad idea theme" to guard against them:

Bad Idea Theme: The facts of your case will allow your theme to be used against you.

Example: Facts indicate the plaintiff has exhibited a high degree of contributory negligence. You decide to use a theme about "personal responsibility." This is risky because in personal injury cases there is a good chance that the theme will be turned right back around on your client.

Bad Idea Theme: Your theme does not comport with the spirit of the times.

Example: If your theme flies in the face of the cultural zeitgeist, at best your jury will disregard it, along with your credibility. At worst, it will offend and anger them. Let's say a ground war breaks out in Europe. You are trying a negligent security (shooting) case that week and planned to use war analogies. Bad idea. Let's say you are defending a municipality, and your theme is "greatest city in the world," and the week before trial there is a transit strike/power outage/mass shooting. Bad idea.

Bad Idea Theme: It is too complicated to understand.

Example: Conventional wisdom says that simplicity favors plaintiffs, while complexity favors the defense. This does not apply to themes! Themes must still be simple to understand. It is perfectly fine for a defense lawyer to say, "Plaintiff wants to make this simple, but it is actually more complicated." You must still offer a simple theme showing why it is more complicated than it appears.

Don't let a bad theme kill a good case.

Witness Preparation

Prepare your witnesses before their depositions are taken. A case is won in preparing your witness for deposition. If they do well, the value of the case shifts in your favor, but if they do poorly, your risk of losing the case increases.

So, what is deposition preparation? It had better be more than coffee and a brief meeting an hour before the deposition. At the very least, deposition preparation should involve the following:

1. Work on psychological obstacles
2. Teaching the case gestalt, which means something that is made of many parts and yet is somehow more than or different from the combination of its parts
3. The theory's objective
4. Body language and nonverbal communication
5. Voice volume, articulation, and cadence
6. Appearance
7. Linguistics
8. How to testify on video
9. Strategies for getting "stuck"

No matter how minor the testimony of a witness to a case, it is critical for the witness to understand the *gestalt* of the case, which is the whole picture as well as the objective of each side. If the witness's testimony is viewed in a vacuum and the witness gets stumped on a question, in other words, if the witness does not know the gestalt of the case, it will be difficult for the witness to recover.

Once you have gauged the witness's understanding of the case, you will know how to educate the witness about how the witness fits into the entire case. Don't get bogged down with every detail. Instead, do exactly the opposite. Make sure the witness understands your overall case theory, the adversary's theory, and the purpose of the deposition. A witness who understands his or her role in the overall case will have a better mental framework for understanding how to respond to questions, and if stuck, will recover more quickly.

When a witness is videotaped for deposition, the witness must face the camera the whole time. If the witness faces the questioning attorney rather than the camera and the video is shown at trial, the witness will look more evasive and less credible.

Although social science shows us that body language is a poor proxy for truth, it does not matter. Jurors don't care what social science says. They use body language as a proxy for credibility.

Always ask the witness to "walk me through the day" of the incident.

Example:

Q: Mr. Jones tell me about your day March 12, 2020, the day of the incident. How did your day start? Walk me through your day.

A: I woke up that morning and turned on the news. I heard that the WHO declared a coronavirus outbreak to be a pandemic. My kids' school was closed so I couldn't work because I didn't have childcare. My wife is a doctor and was at the hospital. She has been working around the clock.

What did we accomplish?

1. We got a snapshot of exactly what was going on in the world the day of the incident. This may not be remembered when the case gets to trial.
2. This gives a clear picture of the state of mind of the witness on the day of the incident.
3. This lends context to the narrative that may be incorporated into the deposition and developed for trial.
4. We are delving into the episodic memory (a component of long-term memory) of the witness so they can more easily recall information.

There is a "cottage industry" on preparing for and defending "reptile questions." For years, plaintiffs' attorneys representing clients injured in motor vehicle accidents involving trucking companies have employed a strategy throughout the litigation process of attacking the company itself as opposed to focusing on the accident. If the plaintiff could find one relevant and admissible thing that the company did improperly, then the plaintiff could try the "out of control" company.

Plaintiffs' attorneys also often attempt to leverage the public's fear of the sheer size of trucks as a means to scare their way to victory. The public's negative impression of the trucking industry as a whole has allowed plaintiffs' attorneys to exploit "the big, bad trucking company" notion at trial.

Defense lawyers are observing with greater frequency an approach by plaintiff attorneys for litigating their trucking cases that has been coined the "Reptile Theory" by Atlanta, Georgia, attorney Don Kennan and jury consultant Dr. David Ball.[5]

5. *See* David Ball & Don Keenan, Reptile: The 2009 Manual of the Plaintiff's Revolution (Balloon Press, 2009).

According to Bill Kanasky, PhD, who authored the article "Debunking and Redefining the Plaintiff Reptile Theory,"[6] the strongest piece of advice for counteracting the Reptile Theory is to prepare your clients for the plaintiff's questions at both their depositions and at trial. According to Kanasky, the best way for drivers and corporate representatives to respond to "reptile" safety questions, which are typically vague and overbroad, is to be honest. The honest answer according to Kanasky is typically some form of "it depends on the circumstances." For instance, the following may be a question and answer during a deposition or trial:

> Q: You would agree that according to your company's safety policy, a driver involved in an accident is required to check on the other drivers, complete an accident report, and take photographs of the scene, correct?
>
> A: Yes.
>
> Q: You would agree that a driver who fails to complete these company-dictated requirements would be violating the company's safety policy?
>
> A: Not necessarily in every situation. There may be instances where a truck driver is too injured to do any of these things. There are also instances where a camera is damaged in an accident so that it is impossible to take photographs. While there are policies and procedures, there are instances where circumstances prevent drivers from performing these tasks.

Much more can be said about preparing witnesses, clients, and experts for deposition, but the focus here is preparing your witnesses for trial.

Let's consider the witnesses who are most likely to testify in the typical liability disputed trucking case:

1. The plaintiff
2. The investigating police officer
3. The defendant driver will likely be called on cross-examination
4. The trucking company representative may be called on cross-examination
5. An accident reconstruction expert for the plaintiff
6. Possibly a biomechanical expert for the plaintiff
7. Eyewitnesses
8. Treating medical doctors
9. Plaintiff's employer about the plaintiff's inability to return to work (before and after witness)
10. Before and after witnesses
11. Possibly an expert on the trucking standards/regulations
12. Neurologist and/or neuropsychologist if traumatic brain injury is alleged
13. Psychiatrist/psychologist may testify about mental/psychological injuries from the accident
14. Life-care planner regarding cost of medical services recommended

---

6. *See* Bill Kanasky, *Debunking and Rede fining the Plaintiff Reptile Theory,* 106 TRUCKING LAW (June 2014).

15. Vocational rehabilitation expert on the plaintiff's vocational ability/skills and job opportunities after the accident
16. Possibly a functional capacity expert
17. The economist assesses the past loss of wages, future loss of earning capacity, and past and future medical expenses discounted to present value
18. A coroner may be called if the case involved a fatality

Depending on the type of case, the defense will likely call the following witnesses for trial:

1. The defendant driver about the facts of the accident
2. Company representative about policies/procedures of the trucking company
3. An expert on trucking regulations/standards
4. An accident reconstruction expert
5. If visibility is an issue, then an expert on conspicuity
6. Forensic medical examiner to testify about the cause of death (this may be disputed if there were multiple collisions) and survival action
7. Biomechanical expert on whether the forces of the accident could cause the alleged injuries
8. Private investigator on surveillance and social media investigation of the plaintiff
9. Various medical experts who may testify about whether the accident caused the plaintiff's condition (these could be orthopedic, neurological, internal medicine, and so on)
10. Experts to counter those retained by the plaintiff, which may involve one or more of the following:
    a. Possibly a neuropsychologist and/or neurologist if traumatic brain injury is alleged
    b. Psychologist/psychiatrist
    c. Functional capacity expert
    d. Trucking regulation/procedures expert
    e. Vocational expert
    f. Life-care planner
    g. Economist

As you can see, the trucking accident trial can be complex, time-consuming, and expensive. You need to be mentally prepared for the long-term of the trial, and you have to coordinate when and how your witnesses will testify.

Typically, this is a bit easier for the plaintiff because the plaintiff gets to go first, obviously, and the defense cannot be certain how long the plaintiff's case will take. Consequently, the coordination of the defense witnesses may require their testimony to be taken by video (not recommended) or by web-conferencing, which absolutely requires an expert in videography. You certainly don't want your $100,000-witness to be expected to testify via Zoom while the courthouse in Podunk, Missouri, does not have sufficient bandwidth.

It is simply not enough to prepare for direct and cross-examination of the witnesses in a trucking case. You also must learn to be a master conductor of a philharmonic orchestra, which requires intense focus and preparation well before the performance. This preparation involves the obvious of knowing their testimony and preparing them for cross examination, but it also involves the following:

- Understanding exactly what to expect in terms of process, standards, and demeanor
- Overcoming poor communication habits (truck drivers typically are not the most social)
- Enhancing the delivery of your theme
- Keeping the jury's attention (and sympathy or anger)
- Responding with calm, confidence, and care throughout their testimony

Unlike the typical automobile accident case, trucking cases are often catastrophic, so the coordination and preparation are much more intense and focused. Of course, there are the standard instructions to your witnesses to tell the truth, speak up, and obey courtroom etiquette. In a trucking accident trial, preparing the witness likely will involve mock trials and focus groups.

If you are not preparing the case with a focus group or mock trial, you are not adequately preparing your witnesses for trial.

A mock trial can be an excellent tool to prepare expert witnesses' complex testimony. Typically lasting either one day or a half-day, mock trials include individuals who play the court roles (plaintiff/prosecution and jury members). They can be used to run through any or all critical elements of a trial to evaluate out specific evidence, arguments, themes, and witness performance. Hiring a jury consultant can be especially helpful during mock trials.

Focus groups are also arranged to gather feedback, though rather than a simulated trial experience, participants are simply asked to review specific aspects of the case that need feedback. Reviewing a recorded deposition testimony of a key witness, for example, can help identify how people who are demographically similar to potential jurors may react to a witness.

In both types of studies, participants can offer real-time reactions, provide detailed feedback, and point out the concerns, questions, or doubts they have encountered.

Lastly, do not forget the practical aspects of timing the witness testimony, housing them if they are coming from out-of-town, instructing them about when to appear, where to park, how to dress, and getting rest. Imagine that you're an event planner for the biggest event of your life and that your professional reputation is dependent on everything going smoothly at the event, and then you will have an idea on how to prepare the witnesses for trial.

Jury Selection

There is perhaps not a more discussed, curious aspect of trial than jury selection. There is also no other area of trial in which the rules and procedures differ from jurisdiction-to-jurisdiction, court-to-court, and even judge-to-judge as much as jury selection.

As a trial consultant who has selected juries in trucking cases across the United States, the only commonality is the trial team must know the rules in order to conduct a meaningful jury selection.

One of the most common misperceptions of jury selection is that it begins in the courtroom. A strategic jury selection begins weeks, months, and sometimes even years before the lawyers see a courtroom. It often starts during discovery when themes are emerging and being fined tuned. Once a theme emerges and begins to set the framework of the case, juror profiles should begin to emerge.

The juror profiles to which I refer are not demographic, but attitudinal. Profiles are not about race, age, or ethnicity, but rather about actual attitudes and worldviews individual jurors hold.

For example, let's take a case where a plaintiff with preexisting back injuries driving a car is in a sideswipe accident with a truck driver who drives for a large corporation. The physical damage to both vehicles appears minor in photographs. The plaintiff refuses medical care, then drives home for three hours and sees a lawyer before a doctor and then proceeds to file a suit claiming he needs back surgery and that he suffers from post-traumatic stress disorder (PTSD).

After a review of these claims, some questions about attitudes should start to emerge as we begin to think about jury selection as early as discovery. Lawyers should focus on the attitudes that they want to use to question their venire. These hypothetical attitudinal measures may include the following:

1. Whether minor accidents can result in major injuries
2. Whether doctors and lawyers work together to profit from the injured
3. Whether doctors inflate their medical bills
4. Whether people target big companies and deep pockets to sue
5. Whether a minor accident could be a financial opportunity to fix a preexisting injury
6. Whether PTSD is a real malady or something that is reserved for those who face combat or severe violent situations

Jerry Glas, in his book, *The New Science of Trial Advocacy: The Waiter Pivot*, offers ideas for voir dire. On pages 18–25, he suggests the following themes:

1. We want smart jurors.
2. We want hard workers.
3. We want fact checkers.
4. We want the best expert to win.
5. We want the treating physician to win.
6. You have one issue to decide.
7. We want jurors to consider care about this one issue.

Once a lawyer identifies the critical issues that can be outcome determinative to their case, then a profile of poor and ideal jurors should emerge.

It is helpful if before a trial a lawyer or consultant makes a list of the critical issues in the trial (like the preceding list) that outlines what good and bad jurors will look like on each issue. For example, in defending a trucking case like the preceding hypothetical case, a good defense juror would hold the following attitudes:

1. Minor accidents cannot result in major injuries.
2. Plaintiffs are pawns of the doctor/lawyer profit process.
3. Doctors inflate medical bills, especially in litigated cases.
4. Big companies are big targets.
5. Small accidents are "jack-pot opportunities" to get medical care for preexisting injuries.
6. PTSD is something combat veterans and sexual abuse survivors get, not people who were in a car accident.

In courts where there is attorney-directed oral voir dire, the questions written are going to be based on the attitudinal profiles constructed in the preceding list. If there is no oral voir dire, juror questionnaires can accomplish the same objective, with the limitation that there may not be follow-up questions.

In an attorney-led oral jury selection, voir dire should generally accomplish a few objectives, which is why it is so important to have a second seat to keep track of responses, take notes, and observe.

During oral voir dire, a lawyer should focus on building rapport by using juror names, making eye contact, and making sure to question each and every person seated in the jury box. One critical observation that should be made is which jurors are the leaders and which are followers.

Leaders often hold leadership positions at work or in the community, have served on a jury previously, or have served in the military. They are usually members with a perceived high-status position. Leaders generally are more talkative members in the jury box, and also appear articulate and confident. Some less obvious leaders may emerge based on subject-matter knowledge. On a 12-person jury, two or three jurors can sway the entire jury, and on a smaller jury, even fewer, which is why it is critical to identify the leaders biased against your case, client, or facts and set them up for a cause strike if possible.

Another objective should be to frame the case by offering some context. This is not done to indoctrinate jurors, or argue the case, but rather to give them a framework and ask the questions geared to the issues central to the case. By using a "looping" technique and taking one prospective juror's response and using it to form a question to another, not only will all jurors be able to offer their opinions about these key issues, but the group dynamic will begin to emerge, and leaders can be identified, as well as subgroups.

Lawyers and consultants should know the standard for a cause strike, so they can begin to build them against jurors who are biased against their case or client. When building a strike, it is important to ask open-ended nonjudgmental questions. "Do you have the ability to be fair?" "Can you be impartial?" are questions which should be reserved to rehabilitate good jurors, but if they are asked when building a strike, they will accomplish the opposite. People do not want their ability for fairness to be questioned, and will often be inhibited by cognitive bias, known as social desirability, and not respond honestly.

Opening Statement

If your jurisdiction, court, and judge has allowed for oral voir dire, then you have had the opportunity to get to know your jurors, start building rapport, and hear some of their concerns voiced in jury selection.

Your opening statement is an opportunity for you to frame your case, introduce your theme more comprehensively than you did in jury selection, and to assuage any lingering concerns your jurors mentioned during jury selection.

In order to make an impression on jurors it is critical to get rid of the robotic tic, "the evidence will show, the evidence will show, the evidence will show." You can still make the same point, but the tone should be more conversational, as part of your objective is to show your jurors you listened to what they said in voir dire, and you will address these concerns at trial.

For example, if jury selection focused on discussion centered around the topic of "truck drivers rushing to meet deadlines," and in your case there is evidence of the exact opposite, you will want to make this part of your opening statement, to put this juror concern to rest.

> Members of the jury, you will hear about how driver X, took his time to get from point A to point B, making sure to take several stops for rest, gas, and a healthy meal.
>
> You will hear testimony about how driver X traveled below the speed limit, as it was snowing, and he wanted to take his time while driving in a poor weather condition.

One underused and underrated technique for opening statements is to use *the present tense* to bring jurors to the scene of the accident. The present tense facilitates learning, memory, comprehension, and cognitive investment of jurors. It "nudges" (a behavior economic concept) jurors into drawing their own conclusions and can shift the plaintiff's reptilian focus off of your client's conduct. Compare these two examples:

Past Tense

On January 5th John picked up the cargo from the factory. He drove down highway X for about an hour. Then at about 6:08 a.m. . . .

Present Tense

It is January 5th. A cold sleet is falling in the mountains of Pennsylvania. John wakes up. He feeds his dog leftovers from last night's burgers. He makes a hot cup of coffee for himself. He places his wife's favorite "My Heart Belongs to a Trucker" mug near the coffeepot. He kisses his baby daughter goodbye. It is so cold John can see his breath. He pulls up to the building and talks to Jim about loading the cargo. John drives down highway X for about an hour. Then at 6:08 a.m. . . .

What happens by using the present tense:

1. The jurors pay attention!
2. You personalized the trucking company through your driver.

3. You keep the focus on the cold January day in Pennsylvania (these conditions will stay in the jurors' minds as plaintiff talks about broken safety rules, and your client's conduct or lack thereof).

Another strategic technique that can be used in opening statements is "warping time." Your adversary wants to make their case simple—X caused Y—by way of examples:

1. Doctor misdiagnosed X (stroke). It caused plaintiff to Y (die).
2. Plaintiff complained to HR about X (company lying on balance sheet). It caused company to Y (fire plaintiff).
3. Bar did X to (overserved) defendant. It caused defendant to Y (break plaintiff's neck) in his car.
4. The trucker was fatigued and didn't pay attention when the plaintiff tried to move into his lane to avoid a head-on collision.

Your adversary's tight timeline (the evidence will show):

1. April 2, 2002, Mr. Driver didn't get enough sleep the night before.
2. He didn't fill out his logbooks accurately.
3. It was raining and he failed to see oncoming traffic.
4. He failed to allow the plaintiff into his lane of travel before the plaintiff was hit head on.

Take this tight timeline and expand it. Defense's expansive timeline (the evidence will show):

1. On April 1, Johnny Brown arrives at truck stop in . . .
2. He performs a post trip inspection of . . .
3. Johnny logs off duty at . . .
4. While off duty, Mr. Brown . . . and then turns over to sleep at . . .
5. On April 1, at 8:00 a.m. Mr. Brown wakes up and . .
6. He conducts a pre-trip inspection of . . .
7. He leaves the truck stop at about . . . which is an hour from where the collision occurs.
8. As he drives from Point A to Point B, Johnny . . .
9. At about 8:50 a.m., meteorology reports indicate that an unseasonable downpour occurs at (location).
10. As Johnny slows down in the right lane traveling at about 55 mph, there is another car to his left ahead of him.
11. Mr. Brown sees another car that appears to be driving in the wrong direction in the left lane.
12. Johnny thinks to himself, "Why isn't that car to my left moving over?"
13. Mr. Brown pulls to the shoulder of the road, but before he can do anything more, the oncoming car slams head on into the driver in the left lane.
14. Immediately, upon impact with the other car driven by a drunk driver, the plaintiff's car veers into his lane causing impact with driver and then the plaintiff's car lands in a deep ditch to driver's right.
15. Driver calls 911 and before the police arrive, driver attempts to rescue the occupants from drowning in the ditch.

Use your opening statement strategically, rather than a recitation of your case. Use it to assuage juror concerns mentioned in jury selection, engage the jury, humanize your client, and create your own timeline.

Presentation of the Evidence

Refer back to the recommendation of the use of a trial notebook regarding the presentation of the evidence by the witnesses and documents. In pretrial conference with the judge, you should have determined the following:

1. The local rules of formatting evidence.
2. If there are no specified local rules (such as providing impeachment documents to the court 30 days before trial), determine what format the court wants evidence submitted and by what date.
3. What kind of technology is available in the court and whether you need to coordinate your own technicians for submission of evidence.
4. How does the court want the evidence to be marked, shared, introduced, and shown (published) to the jury?
5. Before opening, will the court admit evidence that is not objectionable by your adversary?
6. Will the court allow you to show pre-admitted evidence to the jury during the opening statement?
7. When must demonstrative evidence be shared with opposing counsel?
8. May the jury be provided with a binder of pre-admitted documents?[7]

In the presentation of evidence of a trucking case, the following are ideas to consider:

1. Know how to lay foundation for admission of evidence.
2. Allow your experts to correct you as you speak with them in conversational manner.
3. Do not ask your expert leading questions, but allow him or her to educate your jury.
4. Prepare in advance for your expert to explain the most complicated aspects of his or her testimony.
5. With artificial intelligence, you can take the expert's explanation and have it explained to a fifth grader. This is not meant to be condescending of jurors, but if you have a complicated issue that needs to be explained by $100,000-neuroradiologist expert, then it had better be easy to understand.
6. Because jurors have limited attention spans, do what you can with visual aids and get your witnesses out of the witness box when possible and when allowed by the court. For example, if you have a medical doctor testifying about an IME, have him demonstrate what he does to evaluate objective evidence of injury.

7. GLAS, *supra* note 4, at 84.

7. If you can get the MRI images of the plaintiff's produced in three-dimensional format that can be shown and compared to exemplars by a neuroradiologist or orthopedic surgeon, do it.
8. If there is something bad about your witness or expert, control the narrative. Get the unwelcome news out and explain it away.
9. Watch out if the internet might reveal something different than your expert. No matter that jurors are not supposed to investigate independently, they will. They will "Google" whatever they can and if they find something that is bad about your witness or your expert's testimony, they will share it in deliberations.
10. If you have a witness that appears to have gone to school all of her life with no practical experience, it behooves you to allow the expert to explain what she does all day. This may include both the diagnosis and treatment of patients with traumatic brain injury.
11. If your client is "volatile," have second-chair do the direct examination so that any taint from your client won't be directed at you.
12. If you have some great theme, like "I thought a picture was better than a thousand words, but this case seems like a thousand words is better than a picture," it would be amazing if that were to come out during your driver's testimony, and you could use that later in closing. It is hard not to steal the thunder for a theme like that, but let it come out in direct evidence.
13. Be prepared to end your direct examination or cross-examination with a strong point that is not objectionable.

There is so much more than can be said about the presentation of evidence, but this is a "reference manual." If you have or have had the opportunity to work as a state court prosecutor or public defender, you have the golden experience of presenting evidence, cross-examining witnesses without pretrial discovery, while thinking on your feet, creating evidence charts, and more. If you do not have much trial experience, you should go to various courts (criminal and civil) and watch others present evidence, cross-examine witnesses, and conduct direct examination. Watching is not as helpful as doing, but it is critical for those who are not experienced trial attorneys.

Closing Arguments

It is a myth that jurors have their minds made up after openings. Jurors cite closing arguments as second in importance only to the evidence phase of trial. Just as you want to make a fabulous entrance, you must make an even better exit.

Your closing should not be structured like the opening. Your opening lays a foundation for your jurors about what they will hear. It primes their brains by telling a story.

The closing is different! A closing is your last impression, but do not try to be like others. Some of us have tried to impress with Biblical quotes like from the Book of Amos, *"Let justice roll down like a mighty river,"* when the driver of an 18-wheeler is a really great guy, and the trucking company came across as a safe, decent operation.

It has to fit the narrative of your case, so don't just go look in a book of quotes to find something that is catchy. Learn from the mistakes of others.

Here are a few ideas when drafting the closing for the trucking case:

1. Outline your closing at the beginning of trial (if not before).
2. You do not have to comment on every piece of evidence presented (allow the jury to bring up things in deliberation without you pointing it out).
3. Structure the closing around what your verdict sheet will look like.
4. Consider interjecting jury instructions when appropriate.
5. Offer options to the jurors, and if your option on damages, liability, or causation makes more sense, you don't have to tell the jury to accept your option. They will come to that conclusion on their own and they won't feel manipulated.
6. Use one or two visual aids to help the leaders in the jury persuade others. For example, in a civil case the burden of proof is by "preponderance of the evidence," so perhaps you have the "scales of justice" and as defense counsel you explain that even the feather weight of a single piece of paper can tip the scales in your favor and, if so, then the plaintiff has failed to meet the plaintiff's burden of proof. Plaintiff's counsel can do the same thing but instead tip the scales toward their case.
7. If there is a critical piece of evidence, such as dashcam footage, then remind the jury that if they want to review it again, they can ask the judge to review evidence again. If the hours of service are at issue, remind them they can ask to review it again in deliberations.
8. What are the most significant parts of the testimony and exhibits that you want the jurors to recall? Focus on that and don't worry about contesting the testimony of your adversary's experts.
9. If there are many witnesses, as typical in catastrophic accidents where liability, causation, and damages are disputed, you may need to assist jurors with reminding them of the witness with a photo, description, or tagline that may be helpful. For example, a photo of the key eyewitness displayed on a scene diagram from his vantage point. If you learn the doctor for the opposing side glossed over the evidence, you might tag her as "Dr. Gloss-Over-the-Evidence Smith."
10. Offer a realistic, evidence-based verdict range. Imagine what may come up in jury selection as to sympathy or bias, tell the jury that these questions may come up, but they have a duty and an oath to consider all of the evidence (even if it points to an empty chair).
11. End strong. Perhaps, it is with a single phrase or photograph. Tell them what is most important, pause, look each juror in the eyes and say nothing. End the pause with "thank you for your attention."

Conclusion

You will never be fully prepared for a trucking accident trial. The best preparation is from experience, making mistakes, and learning from your mistakes. If you think a case will not go to trial, it will. If you prepare as if it will be tried, it likely will be settled. The tips we give you here are just "tips of an iceberg." What is below the iceberg is what you have to do to prepare; strategize, adapt, and maneuver through the process to reach the best possible result for your client.

PART III

Special Topics Applicable to Truck Accident Litigation

CHAPTER 17

Insurance and Financial Responsibility Requirements

Peter J. Kestner, Esq. and Mary Eliasen, Esq.

Historical Background

The Motor Carrier Act of 1935 was enacted by Congress and signed into law by Franklin D. Roosevelt, in part, because of the hazards presented by large commercial trucks operating on the highways.[1] The act expressly regulated "certification requirements, rates and service requirements, insurance requirements, and requirements for the promotion of public safety."[2] It also vested the Interstate Commerce Commission (ICC), with authority to promulgate a variety of regulations related to motor carriers.[3] In 1936, the ICC created specific regulations requiring motor carriers to carry liability insurance—a requirement that remains in effect today.[4] Current federal law requires motor carriers to file a bond, insurance policy, or other type of security approved by the Secretary of Transportation, in the amounts required by law, sufficient to pay for a judgment against the motor carrier for bodily injury or death resulting from the motor carrier's negligence.[5]

Part of the purpose of the Motor Carrier Act and its subsequent incarnations has always been to protect the motoring public by ensuring that those who operate large trucks for profit in interstate commerce are financially responsible and able to compensate those who were injured as a result of their negligence. Yet, shortly after the Motor Carrier Act of 1935 was passed, motor carriers began taking steps to remove themselves from the liability for the torts of their drivers. The main mechanism motor carriers used to achieve this goal was leasing.[6] In such a situation, the motor carrier, who clearly had to comply

1. 49 U.S.C. § 302 (1935).
2. *Id.* § 304.
3. *Id.*
4. Univ. Overland Express Inc. v. Alsop, 189 A. 458, 460 (Conn. 1936).
5. 49 U.S.C. § 13906 (2010).
6. *See* Am. Trucking Ass'ns v. U.S., 344 U.S. 298, 302–04 (1953).

with the Motor Carrier Act of 1935 and ICC regulations, would lease a tractor and/or trailer from a third party who often was not authorized to operate in interstate commerce and therefore had no reason to comply with federal law.[7] At the time, there was little regulation over the relationship of the motor carrier and the lessor of the tractor and/or trailer.[8] And, the unregulated leasing led to public confusion, made fixing the lessee's responsibility for accidents highly difficult, and often allowed motor carriers to avoid the financial responsibility Congress sought to impose upon them.[9]

As time went by, courts began to recognize that motor carriers were using leasing to avoid the safety and financial responsibility requirements under 49 U.S.C. § 315.[10] In 1956, Congress amended the Interstate Common Carrier Act to require, among other things, that motor carrier lessees be fully responsible for the operation of the leased vehicles as if they were the owners of such vehicles, "including the requirements prescribed [under the Interstate Common Carrier Act] . . . which may include . . . promulgation of regulations requiring liability and cargo insurance covering all such equipment." [11] These amendments were enacted "to ensure that interstate motor carriers would be fully responsible for the maintenance and operation of the leased equipment and the supervision of the borrowed drivers, thereby protecting the public from accidents, preventing public confusion about who was financially responsible if accidents occurred, and providing financially responsible defendants."[12] These requirements have remained largely unchanged since 1956. Current federal law still requires that motor carriers using leased motor vehicles have full responsibility and control to ensure that the leased motor vehicles are operated in full compliance with the law, including the law governing financial responsibility.[13]

Current Laws

Congress passed the Motor Carrier Act of 1980 to impose higher levels of financial responsibility on motor carriers operating under federal permit and intrastate carriers operating under state authority. Table 17.1 is contained in 49 C.F.R. § 387.9; it shows the current minimum required financial responsibility as determined by the type of cargo hauled.[14] For the most part, these "financial responsibility" levels have been in effect, without inflation adjustments, since the law was passed in 1980.

7. *Id.* at 303.
8. *Id.*
9. *Id.*
10. *See* Rediehs Express, Inc. v. Maple, 491 N.E.2d 1006 (Ind. App. 1986).
11. 49 U.S.C. § 304(3) (1956).
12. Morris v. JTM Materials, Inc., 78 S.W.3d 28, 38 (Tx. App. 2002).
13. 49 U.S.C. § 14102.
14. The chart is available online at https://www.ecfr.gov/current/title-49/subtitle-B/chapter-III/subchapter-B/part-387/subpart-A/section-387.9.

Table 17.1 Minimum Financial Responsibility of Motor Carriers

	Type of Carriage	Commodity Transported	Financial Responsibility
1	For-hire[15] (in interstate or foreign commerce, with a gross vehicle weight rating of 10,000 or more pounds)	Property (nonhazardous)	$750,000
2	For-hire and private (in interstate, foreign, or intrastate commerce, with a gross vehicle weight rating of 10,000 or more pounds)	Hazardous substances, as defined in 49 C.F.R. § 171.8, transported in cargo tanks, portable tanks, or hopper-type vehicles with capacities in excess of 3,500 water gallons	$5,000,000
3	For-hire and private (in interstate or foreign commerce: in any quantity; or in intrastate commerce, in bulk only; with a gross vehicle weight rating of less than 10,000 pounds)	Oil listed in 49 C.F.R. § 172.101; hazardous waste, hazardous materials, and hazardous substances defined in 49 C.F.R. § 171.8 and listed in 49 C.F.R. § 172.101, but not mentioned in (2) above or (4)	$1,000,000
4	For-hire and private (in interstate or foreign commerce, with a gross vehicle weight rating of less than 10,000 pounds)	Any quantity of Division 1.1, 1.2, or 1.3 material; any quantity of Division 2.3, Hazard Zone A, or Division 6.1, packing Group I, Hazard Zone A material; or highway route controlled quantifies of a Class 7 material as defined in 49 C.F.R. § 173.403[16]	$5,000,000
5	For-hire fleet including only small freight vehicles under 10,000 pounds GVWR[17]	Commodities not subject to requirements in (1) through (4)	$300,000

Under the act, motor carriers can meet their financial responsibility requirements by showing proof of insurance, surety bonds, or approved self-insurance that meets the minimum public liability requirements. While motor carriers are allowed to self-insure,[18] only a small minority of large carriers do so. Rather, the vast majority of motor carriers meet their financial responsibility obligation by purchasing an auto insurance liability policy and attaching Form MCS-90

15. A "for-hire" motor carrier is a person engaged in the transportation of goods or passengers for compensation, whereas a "private" motor carrier is a person who provides transportation of property or passengers, by commercial motor vehicle, and is not a for-hire motor carrier. *See* 49 C.F.R. § 390.5T. An example of a private motor carrier is a business that transports its own goods by commercial motor vehicle.

16. For an explanation of hazardous materials categories and terminology referred to here, see the chapter in this book about hazardous materials by D.J. Young.

17. Gross vehicle weight rating, or GVWR, refers to the value specified by the manufacturer as the loaded weight of a single motor vehicle. *See* 49 C.F.R. § 390.5T.

18. *See* 49 C.F.R. § 387.309 for the qualifications as a self-insurer.

"Endorsement for Motor Carrier policies of Insurance for Public Liability under Sections 29 and 30 of the Motor Carrier Act of 1980."

Form MCS-90

In an effort to garner the transportation and insurance industry's compliance with the act's mandated levels of financial responsibility, Congress created the MCS-90 endorsement.[19] The act requires the MCS-90 endorsement be attached to any liability policy issued to motor carriers operating commercial motor vehicles that are transporting property in interstate or foreign commerce.[20] When not physically attached to the policy, the terms of the endorsement may be imputed by law.[21] Furthermore, the insurer must file a proof of insurance form (BMC-91x) with the Federal Motor Carrier Safety Administration. The MCS-90 makes the insurer a surety, or guarantor, for the motor carrier's public liability in the event coverage is unavailable under the underlying insurance policy. The endorsement[22] is attached to a Truckers Coverage Form, Motor Carrier Coverage Form, or Business Auto Policy, depending on the coverage form the insurer uses.

Usually, the motor carrier's tractor-trailer is listed in the declarations or is otherwise covered by the insurance policy issued. As such, the insurance contract itself provides the necessary coverage to protect the public. But occasionally, as a result of underwriting errors, policy terms, insolvency, or illegal trucking operations, a tractor-trailer will have no coverage, and the MCS-90 endorsement is triggered.

The purpose of the MCS-90 endorsement is to ensure adequate levels of insurance coverage in the event of a trucking accident involving a member of the public or the environment. The MCS-90 endorsement protects the public by creating a "suretyship by the insurer" when the motor carrier's insurance policy otherwise provides no coverage to the insured.[23] The endorsement effectively shifts the risk away from the public "by guaranteeing that an injured party will be compensated even if the insurance carrier has a valid defense based on a condition in the policy."[24]

The MCS-90 endorsement states:

> [i]n consideration of the premium stated in the policy to which this endorsement is attached, the insurer (the company) agrees to pay,

---

19. The Form MCS-90 is available on the FMCSA's website at https://www.fmcsa.dot.gov/sites/fmcsa.dot.gov/files/2024-05/MCS-90%20Form.pdf.

20. *See* 49 C.F.R. § 387.7(d). As an alternative to proof of insurance by MCS-90 (*see* § 387.7(d)(1)), the motor carrier may provide proof of a surety bond for public liability (Form MCS-82) (*see* § 387.7(d)(2)), or a writing from the FMCSA authorizing it to self-insure (*see* § 387.7(d)(3)).

21. *See* Transport Indem. Co. v. Carolina Cas. Ins. Co., 652 P.2d 134 (Ariz. 1982); Hagans v. Glens Falls Ins. Co., 465 F.2d 1249 (10th Cir. 1972); Travelers Ins. Co. v. Transport Ins. Co., 787 F.2d 1133, 1139 (7th Cir. 1986).

22. *See* 49 C.F.R. § 387.15 for the requirements of the form endorsement.

23. Canal Ins. Co. v. Distribution Servs., 320 F.3d 488, 490 (4th Cir. 2003).

24. Pierre v. Providence Wash. Ins. Co., 784 N.E.2d 52, 53–54 (N.Y. 2002).

> within the limits of liability described herein, any final judgment recovered against the insured for public liability resulting from negligence in the operation, maintenance, or use of motor vehicles subject to the financial responsibility requirements of Section 29 and 30 of the Motor Carrier Act of 1980 *regardless of whether or not each motor vehicle is specifically described in the policy* and whether or not such negligence occurs on any route or in any territory authorized to be served by the insured or elsewhere. . . . It is understood and agreed that *no condition, provision, stipulation, or limitation contained in the policy, this endorsement, or any other endorsement thereon, or violation thereof, shall relieve the company from liability or from the payment of any final judgment, within the limits of liability herein described, irrespective of the financial condition, insolvency or bankruptcy of the insured.*[25]

In cases where the insurer for the motor carrier has cited a coverage defense, a seasoned attorney will immediately sue the motor carrier, driver, and owners of the tractor and trailer. This strategy creates an interesting dilemma for the insurer. Depending on the coverage defense asserted, the insurer is now compelled to either deny coverage and refuse to defend its insured or defend the lawsuit under a reservation of rights and initiate a declaratory judgment lawsuit to determine its duties under its policy. Either choice pits the insurer's interests against its insured's interests. This scenario, if used appropriately, can be used to increase case values.

If the insurer chooses to deny coverage and not answer the lawsuit, it leaves the insured without representation in the lawsuit and the looming possibility of a default judgment.[26] This choice leaves the insurer open to a variety of bad results, including waiver of coverage defenses, bad faith, and a default judgment against its insured. Once a court issues a final judgment against an insured, the injured plaintiff can invoke the MCS-90 endorsement and request payment from the insurer. If the insurer fails to pay the judgment, the injured plaintiff can sue the insurance company to compel payment.[27]

Most prudent insurers choose to defend their insured under a reservation of rights and simultaneously file a separate declaratory judgment action to determine the insurer's duties under the policy. But, under this scenario the insurer's costs and expenses increase exponentially. Furthermore, even if the insurer discharges coverage in a declaratory action, it is ultimately on the hook for any final judgment under the terms of the MCS-90 endorsement. This choice will almost certainly destroy any working relationship between the insured and insurer, and as a result, the insured rarely cooperates in the defense of the plaintiff's claims. Also, the MCS-90 has been held to trump non-cooperation

25. Form MCS-90, p. 2 of 3 (emphasis added), pursuant to 49 C.F.R. § 387.15.

26. For a good example of how this plays out in the real world see Century Indemnity Co. v. Carlson, 133 F.3d 591 (8th Cir. 1998).

27. Form MCS-90, p. 2 of 3 ("[T]the judgment creditor may maintain an action in any court of competent jurisdiction against the insurance company to compel such payment.").

and notice clauses.[28] In effect, the MCS-90 endorsement forces the insurer to pay a premium to get the case resolved because the alternative route is too costly.

No Duty to Defend

The MCS-90 does not create any obligation on the part of the insurer to defend its insured for claims not covered by the underlying liability policy, such as a situation where the insurer disclaims coverage because the tractor-trailer involved in the wreck was not an insured auto. But choosing not to defend can have negative consequences for the insurer. For instance, a failure to defend may result in a default judgment against the insured. Once the judgment is final, the MCS-90 endorsement creates absolute liability on the part of the insurer to satisfy the judgment up to the policy limits listed on the endorsement. And if the insurer fails to satisfy the judgment, the judgment creditor (i.e., injured plaintiff) has a right to pursue a direct action against the insurer for the amount of the judgment. In short, because the MCS-90 endorsement requires insurers to pay any adverse result of a default, insurers are incentivized to choose to defend the underlying tort action or settle the case at a premium.

Subrogation Allowed

As a general rule, a liability insurer cannot receive reimbursement from its insured for losses paid under the policy by subrogation or other means. However, the MCS-90 endorsement contains a subrogation clause that states:

> the insured agrees to reimburse the company for any payment made by the company on account of any accident, claim, or suit involving a breach of the terms of said policy, and for any payment that the company would not have been obligated to make under the provisions of the policy except for the agreement contained in the endorsement.[29]

This provision may give comfort to the insurer, who is ultimately required to pay a judgment where no coverage exists; however, the carrier will have a difficult, if not impossible, time realizing a recovery from its own insured. Assuming the insured has potential assets, the insurer cannot commence recovery efforts against its insured until after it makes payment, which is often years after the loss occurs. Over this timeframe, its insured can file bankruptcy to avoid paying any judgment the insurer receives. In the end, exercising subrogation rights under the MCS-90 endorsement becomes an expensive exercise in futility for the insurer and may not be worth pursuing.

Requires Cancellation Separate from Insurance Policy

The MCS-90 endorsement contains specific cancellation requirements before the insurer extinguishes its obligation to indemnify the public. The endorsement provides:

28. Campbell v. Bartlett, 975 F.2d 1569 (10th Cir. 1992).
29. Form MCS-90, p. 2 of 3, pursuant to 49 C.F.R. § 387.15.

> Cancellation of this endorsement may be effected by the company of the insured by giving (1) thirty-five (35) days notice in writing to the other party (said 35 days notice to commence from the date the notice is mailed, proof of mailing shall be sufficient proof of notice) and (2) if the insured is subject to the FMCSA's registration requirements under 49 U.S.C. 13901, by providing thirty (30) days notice to the FMCSA (said 30 days notice to commence from the date the notice is received by the FMCSA at its office in Washington, D.C.).[30]

So, in instances where an insurer canceled a motor carrier's insurance for any reason, the insurer has the added obligation of notifying the Federal Motor Carrier Safety Administration (FMCSA) and the insured according to the time-frames outlined in the endorsement. A failure to cancel the MCS-90 endorsement properly could result in a continued exposure of the insurer for public liability.

Commonly Litigated Issues

The MCS-90 endorsement has been in use for over 40 years and its terms have been repeatedly litigated. The following is a summary of some of the decisions affecting the MCS-90 endorsement and its application:

Interstate versus Intrastate Commerce

In *Roberts v. Levine*, the Eighth Circuit Court of Appeals concluded that a commodity is deemed interstate or intrastate by examining the facts surrounding the shipment and the "essential character" of the shipment.[31] While the terms of the MCS-90 were not part of the Eighth Circuit panel's analysis, this case is important to an understanding of the MCS-90's application because the endorsement applies to nonhazardous materials loads hauled in interstate—but not intrastate—commerce.

In *Century Indemnity Co. v. Carlson*, the Eighth Circuit, building on its discussion in *Levine*, concluded that whether a shipment is interstate or intrastate is determined by the "essential character of the commerce" and the intent of the parties involved in the transportation transaction.[32] Thus, a farmer who sold his corn to a river terminal in the same state engaged in interstate commerce where he knew the corn would be shipped on the river to a destination outside the state.[33] The court also held that the exempt nature of the commodity being hauled had no bearing on the application of the MCS-90 endorsement.[34] Thus, it is the interstate nature of the load, not the type of property that is being transported (i.e., exempt or non-exempt) that matters for purposes of the MCS-90 application.

30. *Id.* at 1 of 3.
31. Roberts v. Levine, 921 F.2d 804 (8th Cir. 1990).
32. Century Indemnity Co. v. Carlson, 133 F.3d 591, 596–98 (8th Cir. 1998).
33. *Id.* at 598.
34. *Id.* at 599.

Who Is an Insured for Purposes of the MCS-90 Endorsement

In *Pierre v. Providence Washington Insurance Co.*, a New York appeals court held that the motor carrier who purchased the insurance, and thus was the "named insured," need not have been the negligent party for purposes of triggering the MCS-90 endorsement; all that is required is that the accident resulted from negligence (by, for example, a driver employed by the named insured motor carrier) and that a judgment was entered implicating the coverage provisions of the policy and the endorsement.[35]

This rule of law has been upheld when there was a judgment against the employee truck driver and recovery from employer's policy,[36] a judgment against the driver and recovery from the trailer lessee's policy,[37] judgment against the uninsured tractor owner and the uninsured truck driver and recovery from the trailer owner's policy,[38] and judgment against the tractor-trailer driver and the owner of the tractor and recovery from the trailer owner's policy.[39]

In *John Deere Insurance Co. v. Nueva*, the Ninth Circuit determined that the MCS-90 creates a duty to indemnify an insured for the use of noncovered autos that were operated under the motor carrier's authority.[40] Thus, even though the commercial motor vehicle involved in the crash was not scheduled on the underlying liability policy, the permissive drivers of the vehicle were covered under the motor carrier's MCS-90 endorsement.

In *Armstrong v. United States Fire Ins. Co.*, the court held that the motor carrier lessee of a trailer was not an insured under the MCS-90 endorsement attached to the trailer owner's insurance policy.[41] The case arose from the tragic death of a family of four (Armstrong) and the serious personal injury of another party when they were rear-ended at high speed by a tractor-trailer unit operated by World Trucking. World Trucking leased the tractor and trailer involved in the accident from separate entities. The policy at issue in the case was issued to XTRA, the trailer's owner, which was insured by United States Fire Insurance Company.

The court's analysis involved examination of the omnibus insurance clause contained in the policy and the endorsement that modified the omnibus clause. The insurance policy issued to XTRA designated, as an additional insured, "anyone else while using with your permission a covered 'auto' you own, hire, or borrow."[42] However, the insurer eliminated this policy provision by endorsement, thereby excluding coverage for lessees of XTRA's equipment.

35. Pierre v. Providence Washington Ins. Co., 99 N.Y.2d 222, 231, 78 N.E. 2d 52, 57 (2002).
36. Campbell v. Barlett, 975 F.2d 1569, 1581 (10th Cir. 1992).
37. *See* Adams v. Royal Indem. Co., 99 F.3d 964 (10th Cir. 1996).
38. *See* John Deere Ins. Co. v. Nueva, 229 F.3d 853, 860 (9th Cir. 2000).
39. *See* Lynch v. Yob, 95 Ohio St. 3d 41, 768 N.E.2d 1158 (Ohio 2002).
40. 229 F.3d at 853, 860.
41. Armstrong v. United States Fire Ins. Co., 606 F. Supp. 2d 794 (E.D. Tenn. 2009).
42. *Id.* at 798.

The insurer subsequently filed a declaratory judgment action seeking a judicial determination that the motor carrier did not have coverage under the trailer owner's policy. Counsel for the plaintiffs asserted that since the policy contained an MCS-90 endorsement it invalidated any policy exclusions limiting coverage. In a 55-page opinion, the federal court for the Eastern District of Tennessee did a thorough examination of reported MCS-90 cases and the legislative history of the endorsement. Ultimately, the court concluded that the MCS-90 would only trigger when a judgment was rendered against the named insured contained in the insurance policy and would not trigger for judgments against a driver or the lessee of a trailer. In support of its opinion, the court relied on the regulatory guidance issued by the FMCSA regarding 49 C.F.R. § 387.15. Interestingly, the court decided to hear the plaintiff's case despite the fact that plaintiffs did not have a judgment against any defendant as condition precedent to suing the insurer under the MCS-90 endorsement, which is contrary to the explicit terms of the endorsement.[43]

In *Sentry Select Ins. v. Thompson*, the court held that Sentry, the insurer of the trailer, was not obligated to pay under the MCS-90.[44] First, the court relied heavily on the analysis in *Armstrong* that since there was not a judgment against the named insured (trailer owner) the provisions of the MCS-90 were not triggered.[45] Then, the court further rejected the plaintiff's arguments by indicating that since there was $1,000,000 of insurance covering the tractor, the federally prescribed minimum of $750,000 was satisfied; therefore, the MCS-90 was not triggered.[46]

In *Carolina Casualty Ins. Co. v. Yeates*, the *en banc* panel reversed *Empire Fire and Marine Insurance Co. v. Guarantee National Insurance Co.*, and concluded that the MCS-90 only applies where (1) the underlying insurance policy to which the endorsement is attached does not provide coverage and (2) the motor carrier's insurance coverage is either nonexistent or insufficient to satisfy the federally prescribed minimum level of financial responsibility.[47] Critical to the court's analysis was that the endorsement created a suretyship and did not in any way alter the terms of the underlying insurance policy. This analysis was a departure from its previous holdings pursuant to *Empire*, which held that the MCS-90 altered the underlying policy to read out any inconsistent limiting language.[48]

43. *See* Form MCS-90, p. 2 of 3 ("In consideration of the premium stated in the policy to which this endorsement is attached, the insurer (the company) agrees to pay . . . **any final judgment recovered against the insured** for public liability resulting from negligence[.]" (emphasis added).

44. Sentry Select Ins. v. Thompson, 665 S. Supp. 2d 561 (E.D. Va. 2009).

45. *Id.* at 566–67.

46. *Id.* at 567.

47. Carolina Cas. Ins. Co. v. Yeates, 584 F.3d 868 (10th Cir. 2009); Empire Fire & Marine Ins. Co. v. Guar. Nat'l Ins. Co., 868 F.2d 357 (10th Cir. 1989).

48. *Compare Carolina Cas. Ins. Co.*, 584 F.3d at 886–87 *with Empire Fire & Marine Ins. Co.*, 868 F.2d at 362.

"Trip-Specific" Approach

In *Canal Insurance Co. v. Coleman*, the Fifth Circuit Court of Appeals held the applicability of the MCS-90 endorsement is determined with reference to the time of the loss and only covers vehicles when they are "presently engaged in the transportation of property in interstate commerce."[49] Therefore, the MCS-90 endorsement did not apply when a trucker who was employed by the insured was backing a bobtail tractor into his driveway when he collided with another car, and the parties stipulated the trucker was not "engaged in the transportation of property" at the time of the accident. The panel noted, however, that its holding applied only to the facts of the case, including the parties' stipulation,[50] and did not reach the question of whether the trucker was engaged in the transportation of property at the time of the accident, even though the court found it "at least arguable" that the trucker's conduct at the time of the accident "could be termed 'transportation of property.'"[51]

However, in *Prime Insurance v. Wright*, the Seventh Circuit Court of Appeals recently declined to adopt the trip-specific approach endorsed in *Coleman* in determining the applicability of the MCS-90 endorsement when a tractor-trailer was not loaded.[52] The court reasoned that the relevant statutes did not include the qualifier "at the time of the accident," and that carrying freight at the instant of the collision is not essential to the definition of "transportation" under 49 U.S.C. § 13102.[53] As a result, the court found that the empty tractor-trailer was engaged in interstate commerce when it collided with a car during an interstate journey to deliver freight or one of the other services encompassed in the definition of "transportation."[54]

Since its inception, the MCS-90 endorsement has created a wide range of litigation issues that the courts have had to address, which has resulted in some uniformity among the courts. However, the lack of Supreme Court involvement on many issues has created a split of authority in other areas.

Intrastate Requirements

Purely intrastate motor carriers and other interstate motor carriers exempt from the DOT regulations regarding financial responsibility must still comply with state regulations regarding financial responsibility. The minimum insurance requirements vary from state to state, but each state requires that motor carriers operating within their borders provide proof of financial responsibility. Table 17.2 outlines the financial responsibility requirements in each state and

---

49. Canal Ins. Co. v. Coleman, 625 F.3d 244, 249 (5th Cir. 2010).

50. *Id.* at 246 n.1 ("We do not hold today that a 'bobtail' truck can never be engaged in the transportation of property.").

51. *Id.* at 252.

52. Prime Ins. v. Wright, 57 F.4th 597 (7th Cir. 2023), *cert. denied*, 144 S. Ct. 75 (2023).

53. *Id.* at 599.

54. *Id.* at 599–600.

the District of Columbia as of this writing. Similar to the federal MCS-90 filing requirements, individual state governments require solely intrastate motor carrier operations to file a Form E with the state Department of Transportation in each state in which the motor carrier operates. Motor carriers that have a federal MCS-90 filing are exempt from the Form E filing in most states.[55]

Forms E and F are the standard insurance industry forms used for the purposes of meeting financial responsibility requirements set forth by state laws. Form E certifies that the motor carrier named on the form complies with the motor carrier insurance laws in that particular state. Form E, like the MCS-90, applies to all motor vehicles operated by the insured whether or not said vehicles are listed on the insurance policy. Form E is the actual filing made with the states' Department of Transportation.[56]

Form F, on the other hand, is the policy endorsement attached to the motor carrier's insurance policy and constitutes proof of financial responsibility by the motor carrier. Form F also amends the insurance policy "to provide for insurance for automobile bodily injury and property damage liability in accordance with the provisions of such law or regulations to the extent of the coverage and limits of liability required thereby. . . ."[57] The Form F endorsement, like the MCS-90 endorsement, also contains language indicating that the insured agrees to reimburse the insurer for any payment the insurer makes that would not have been otherwise required by the terms of the policy.[58]

Both Forms E and F contain provisions stating that once the forms are in effect, they operate continuously until cancelled.[59] Under most state laws, the insurer must provide "not less than 30 days' written notice to the insured and to the commissioner" that the form is being cancelled.[60] This notice requirement has been held to extend coverage where an insurance policy terminated under its own terms after an expiration of time because the statutorily required notice of cancellation was not given.[61]

55. *See, e.g.*, TEX. TRANSP. CODE § 643.002(1).

56. You can find Form E on many state department of transportation, public utilities, or public service commission websites. For an example, see https://psc.mt.gov/_docs/Transportation/pdf/FORM_E.pdf.

57. Form F is also available online through some state websites. For an example, see https://puc.hawaii.gov/wp-content/uploads/2013/06/FormWC3538.pdf.

58. *Id.*

59. *See, e.g.*, https://psc.mt.gov/_docs/Transportation/pdf/FORM_E.pdf and https://puc.hawaii.gov/wp-content/uploads/2013/06/FormWC3538.pdf.

60. *See, e.g.*, MINN. STAT. § 221.141, subdiv.1a.

61. Great West Cas. Co. v. Christenson, 450 N.W.2d 153 (Minn. App. 1999), noting that even though the result seems absurd, the court had to apply Minn. Stat. § 221.141 as written, and that such an application required an insurer to provide notice of cancellation for a policy that was expiring on its own terms in order to avoid liability because of Forms E and F.

Table 17.2 Intrastate Financial Responsibility Requirements, by U.S. State[62]

State	Minimum Liability Limits
Alabama	26,001 lbs. or more GVWR: $750,000
Alaska	Greater than 26,000 lbs. GVWR: $500,000 bodily injury $200,000 property damage
Arizona	26,001 lbs. or more GVWR: $750,000 21,001 lbs. to 26,000 lbs. GVWR: $300,000
Arkansas	No weight threshold: $50,000 per person/ $100,000 per accident/ $30,000 property damage
California	Greater than 10,000 lbs. GVWR: $750,000 10,000 lbs. or less GVWR: $300,000
Colorado	10,001 lbs. or more GVWR: $750,000 Less than 10,001 lbs. GVWR: $300,000
Connecticut	18,001 lbs. or more GVWR: $750,000
Delaware	26,001 lbs. or more GVWR: $750,000
District of Columbia	Greater than 10,000 lbs. GVWR: $750,000
Florida	26,000 lbs. or more but less than 35,000 lbs. GVWR: $50,000 35,000 lbs. or more but less than 44,000 lbs. GVWR: $100,000 44,000 lbs. or more GVWR: $300,000
Georgia	Greater than 10,000 lbs. GVWR: $100,000 per person $300,000 per accident $50,000 property damage
Hawaii	No weight threshold: $250,000 per person $750,000 per accident $250,000 property damage
Idaho	Greater than 26,000 lbs. GVWR: $750,000
Illinois	10,000 lbs. or more GVWR: $750,000 Less than 10,000 lbs. GVWR: $300,000
Indiana	10,001 lbs. or more GVWR: $750,000 Less than 10,001 lbs. GVWR: $300,000
Iowa	10,000 lbs. or more GVWR: $750,000 Less than 10,000 lbs. GVWR: $300,000
Kansas	10,001 lbs. or more GVWR: $100,000 per person/$300,000 per accident/$50,000 property damage

62. U.S. Dep't of Transp., Fed. Motor Carrier Safety Admin., *Motor Carrier Financial Responsibility Report to Congress*, pursuant to P.L. 114-94 and P.L. 112-141 (Mar. 2018), financial-responsibility-report-final-march-2018.pdf (dot.gov).

State	Minimum Liability Limits
Kentucky	Greater than 18,000 lbs. GVWR: $100,000 per person/$600,000 per accident/$50,000 property damage 18,000 lbs. or less GVWR: $100,000 per person/$300,000 per accident/$50,000 property damage
Louisiana	No weight threshold. Either: CSL of $510,000; or Split limit of $250,000 per person/$500,000 per accident/$10,000 property damage
Maine	Greater than 26,000 lbs. GVWR: $350,000
Maryland	Greater than 26,000 lbs. GVWR: $750,000
Massachusetts	10,000 lbs. or more GVWR: $750,000 Less than 10,000 lbs. GVWR: $300,000
Michigan	10,001 lbs. or more GVWR: $750,000 Less than 10,001 lbs. GVWR: $300,000
Minnesota	Greater than 10,000 lbs. GVWR: $100,000 per person $300,000 per accident $50,000 property damage
Mississippi	10,001 lbs. or more GVWR: $750,000
Missouri	Greater than 6,000 lbs. GVWR: $100,000 per person $300,000 per accident $50,000 property damage
Montana	Greater than 10,000 lbs. GVWR: $500,000 10,000 lbs. or less GVWR: $100,000
Nebraska	Greater than 10,000 lbs. GVWR: $750,000
Nevada	26,001 lbs. or more GVWR: $750,000 10,001 to 26,000 lbs. GVWR: $300,000
New Hampshire	10,001 lbs. or more GVWR: $750,000 Less than 10,001 lbs. GVWR: $300,000
New Jersey	26,001 lbs. or more GVWR: $750,000
New Mexico	10,001 lbs. or more GVWR: $750,000 10,000 lbs. or less GVWR: $300,000
New York	10,001 lbs. or more GVWR: $100,000 per person $300,000 per accident $50,000 property damage
North Carolina	10,001 lbs. or more GVWR: $750,000
North Dakota	Greater than 26,000 lbs. GVWR: $750,000
Ohio	10,001 lbs. or more GVWR: $750,000 Less than 10,001 lbs. GVWR: $300,000
Oklahoma	10,000 lbs. or more GVWR: $750,000 Less than 10,000 lbs. GVWR: $300,000

State	Minimum Liability Limits
Oregon	Greater than 26,000 lbs. GVWR: $750,000
Pennsylvania	Greater than 10,000 lbs. GVWR: $750,000 10,000 lbs. or less GVWR: $300,000
Rhode Island	No weight threshold: $250,000 per person $500,000 per accident $25,000 property damage
South Carolina	10,000 lbs. or more GVWR: $750,000 Less than 10,000 lbs. GVWR: $300,000
South Dakota	Greater than 26,000 lbs. GVWR: $750,000
Tennessee	10,001 lbs. or more GVWR: $750,000 Less than 10,001 lbs. GVWR: $300,000
Texas	Greater than 26,000 lbs. GVWR: $500,000
Utah	10,001 lbs. or more GVWR: $750,000
Vermont	No weight threshold: $25,000 per person $50,000 per accident $10,000 property damage
Virginia	No weight threshold: $750,000
Washington	10,000 lbs. or more GVWR: $750,000 Less than 10,000 lbs. GVWR: $300,000
West Virginia	No weight threshold. Either: CSL of $700,000; or Or split limit of $200,000 per person/$600,000 per accident/$100,000 property damage
Wisconsin	More than 10,000 lbs. GVWR: $750,000 10,000 lbs. or less GVWR: $300,000
Wyoming	Greater than 26,000 lbs. GVWR: $750,000

CHAPTER 18

Trucks and Railroad Crossings

Riley L. Brown, Esq. and Michael A. Vercher, Esq.

Overview

The Federal Railroad Administration reported a decrease in highway–rail incidents between 2019 and 2021. The total number of incidents in 2019 was 2,241, and while this number reduced to 2,154 in 2021, 376 incidents involved tractor-trailer combinations.[1] The states with the highest number of highway–rail incidents are Texas and California, followed closely by Illinois and Georgia.[2] While the number of incidents has decreased over time, collisions between trains and motor vehicles at grade crossings frequently result in very serious or fatal injuries to both the motoring public and train passengers and crew.

Due to the weight, length, and operating characteristics of their vehicles, drivers of tractor-trailers face potential hazards beyond those faced by automobiles while attempting to traverse railroad crossings. Many of the regulations and statutes governing the operation of tractor-trailers at grade crossings are specific to the state where the accident occurred. This chapter provides an overview of both the state statutes and federal regulations applicable to grade crossings and a summary of the unique hazards and potential liabilities presented to drivers of tractor-trailers at grade crossings.

State Statues and Federal Regulations

Drivers Duties

Nearly every state has adopted a version of the Uniform Vehicle Code (UVC). Enacted in 2000, the UVC provides states with recommendations for traffic laws. States are not required to adopt the UVC in whole or in part. However, the UVC provides general guidelines by which each state can model their statutes

1. FRA Safety Analysis Dashboard, 2024, https://data.transportation.gov/stories/s/Highway-Rail-Crossing-Incidents-Landing-Page/9hnw-nt86/.

2. *Id.*

concerning traffic laws.[3] Specifically relating to grade crossings, many states have their own unique statutory requirements concerning a driver's approach to a rail–highway grade crossing. Lawyers can utilize the UVC to understand the general principles and guidelines adopted by nearly every state in the country. The UVC provides, in pertinent part, as follows for obedience to a signal indicating the approach of a train:

> (a) Whenever any person driving a vehicle approaches a railroad grade crossing under any circumstances stated in this section, the driver shall stop within 50 feet; but not less than 15 feet, from the nearest rail of such railroad, and shall not proceed until it is safe to do so. The foregoing requirements shall apply when:
>
> 1. A clearly visible electric or mechanical signal device gives warning of the immediate approach of a railroad train;
> 2. A crossing gate is lowered or when a human flagger gives a signal of the approach of a railroad train;
> 3. A railroad train approaching within approximately 1,500 feet of the highway crossing emits a signal audible from such distance; or
> 4. An approaching railroad train is plainly visible and is in hazardous proximity to such crossing.
>
> (b) No person shall drive any vehicle through, around, or under any crossing gate or barrier at a railroad crossing while such gate or barrier is closed or is being closed.[4]

The Illinois Vehicle Code, Article XII, Section 11-1201(a-1) is a good example of a state that specifically addresses persons operating commercial motor vehicles at grade crossings in a manner similar, but not identical, to the UVC:

> (a-1) Whenever any person driving a commercial motor vehicle, as defined in Section 6-500 of this Code, approaches a railroad grade crossing where the driver is not always required to stop, the person must exercise due care and caution as the existence of a railroad track across a highway is a warning of danger, and under any of the circumstances stated in this Section, the driver shall stop within 50 feet but not less than 15 feet from the nearest rail of the railroad and shall not proceed until the tracks are clear and he or she can do so safely. The foregoing requirements shall apply when:
>
> 1. A clearly visible electric or mechanical signal device gives warning of the immediate approach of a railroad train or railroad track equipment;
> 2. A crossing gate is lowered or a human flagman gives or continues to give a signal of the approach or passage of a railroad track equipment;

3. Uniform Vehicle Code, Nat'l Comm. on Uniform Traffic Laws & Ordinances 2024, https://iamtraffic.org/wp-content/uploads/2013/01/UVC2000.pdf.

4. Uniform Vehicle Code § 11-701.

3. A railroad train or railroad track equipment approaching a highway crossing emits a warning signal and such railroad train or railroad track equipment, by reason of its speed or nearness to such crossing, is an immediate hazard;
4. An approaching railroad train or railroad track equipment is plainly visible and is in hazardous proximity to such crossing;
5. A railroad train or railroad track equipment is approaching so closely that an immediate hazard is created.[5]

Ohio has adopted a more specific version of the UVC in Ohio Revised Code § 4511.62:

> (A)(1) Whenever any person driving a vehicle or trackless trolley approaches a railroad grade crossing, the person shall stop within fifty feet, but not less than fifteen feet from the nearest rail of the railroad if any of the following circumstances exist at the crossing:
>
> (a) A clearly visible electric or mechanical signal device gives warning of the immediate approach of a train.
>
> (b) A crossing gate is lowered.
>
> (c) A flagperson gives or continues to give a signal of the approach or passage of a train.
>
> (d) There is insufficient space on the other side of the railroad grade crossing to accommodate the vehicle or trackless trolley the person is operating without obstructing the passage of other vehicles, trackless trolleys, pedestrians, or railroad trains, notwithstanding any traffic control signal indication to proceed.
>
> (e) An approaching train is emitting an audible signal or is plainly visible and is in hazardous proximity to the crossing.
>
> (f) There is insufficient undercarriage clearance to safely negotiate the crossing.
>
> (2) A person who is driving a vehicle or trackless trolley and who approaches a railroad grade crossing shall not proceed as long as any of the circumstances described in divisions (A)(1)(a) to (f) of this section exist at the crossing.
>
> (B) No person shall drive any vehicle through, around, or under any crossing gate or barrier at a railroad crossing while the gate or barrier is closed or is being opened or closed unless the person is signaled by a law enforcement officer or flagperson that is permissible to do so.
>
> (C) Whoever violates this section is guilty of a misdemeanor of the fourth degree.

The Illinois statute includes a "due care and caution" standard that neither the UVC nor Ohio has included. This example illustrates why it is crucial for lawyers representing clients in actions involving railroad grade crossing

---

5. Ill. Vehicle Code art. XII, § 11-1201(a-1).

incidents to understand the specific statutory requirements and relevant standards in place at the time of the accident to navigate the many liability scenarios that can arise from accidents at grade crossings.

The UVC states that some vehicles must stop at all railroad crossings.[6] Specifically, many states have adopted statutes that require certain commercial motor vehicles, such as those carrying passengers for hire or certain types of hazardous materials, to come to a complete stop with the front of the vehicle within 50 feet, but not closer than 15 feet, of the nearest rail at every grade crossing.[7]

The Federal Motor Carrier Safety Administration (FMCSA) requires that the driver of a commercial motor vehicle that hauls hazardous materials such as poisonous gas, flammable materials, oxygen, or poison stop within 50 feet, but not closer than 15 feet, of the near rail of every railroad crossing, and then listen for a locomotive horn, look in each direction along the tracks for an approaching train, and ascertain that no train is approaching before attempting to proceed across the tracks.[8] When the driver of such a vehicle determines it is safe, he or she must drive the combination across the tracks in a gear that permits it to clear the crossing completely without changing gears.[9] All other commercial motor vehicles "shall, upon approaching a grade crossing, be driven at a rate of speed which will permit said commercial motor vehicle to be stopped before reaching the nearest rail of such crossing and shall not be driven upon or over such crossing until due caution has been taken to ascertain that the course is clear."[10]

Preemption is particularly important when determining whether a grade-crossing lawsuit should be brought under federal law or removed from state court. In the context of adequate warning at a grade crossing, the answer to whether a state tort claim is preempted by federal law depends on the circumstances. The Supreme Court has held that federal regulations governing the adequacy of warning devices apply, and state tort law is preempted, when the Federal Highway Administration approves a crossing improvement project, and the state installs the warning devices using federal funds.[11] This chapter will address the specific issues related to federal preemption of state regulations in a later section. However, it is important to note here that preemption is a common issue in adequate warning claims at grade crossings.

Railroad's Duties

Federal law extensively preempts state regulation of railroad crossings.[12] For this reason, attorneys must look to federal regulations when determining the relevant duty imposed by statute. Federal regulations establishing the requirements

---

6. Uniform Vehicle Code § 11-702.
7. *Id.*
8. 49 C.F.R. § 392.10(a).
9. *Id.*
10. *Id.* § 392.11.
11. CSX Transp., Inc. v. Easterwood, 507 U.S. 658, 670 (1993).
12. 49 C.F.R. § 222.7.

for horn audibility, emergency horn sequence, and training of railroad employees in horn use preempt state law.[13]

Locomotive engineers are required to sound the locomotive horn in a pattern of two long blasts, a short blast, and a long blast at least 15 seconds, but no more than 20 seconds, in advance of a public highway–rail crossing and to continue that horn pattern until the train occupies the crossing.[14] However, this regulation also prohibits sounding a locomotive horn more than one-fourth of a mile (1,320 feet) before a public crossing, even if the horn will be sounded for less than 15 seconds.[15]

Federal locomotive horn regulation expressly preempts state statutes that almost uniformly require the locomotive horn to be sounded for at least one-fourth of a mile before a public crossing.[16] Under this regulation, the locomotive horn of trains traveling at speeds less than 45 miles per hour may be sounded for distances less than one-fourth of a mile, and the locomotive horn of trains traveling at speeds greater than 45 miles per hour may be sounded for less than 15 seconds in advance of public crossings.

This federal regulation also preempts the requirement of most state locomotive horn statutes that the locomotive horn (i.e., a short succession of blasts) be used to alert the motorist and avoid a collision with a vehicle at a public crossing.[17] Instead, the regulation allows, rather than requires, a locomotive engineer to sound the locomotive horn in such an emergency pattern to provide a warning to animals, vehicle operators, pedestrians, or crews of other trains if "in the engineer's sole judgment, such action is appropriate to prevent imminent injury, death, or property damage."[18] Therefore, it is likely that a court will exclude any claim based upon state common law or statute that the locomotive engineer was negligent for failing to sound the "alarm" or "emergency locomotive horn pattern" to alert an inattentive motorist approaching a crossing because this federal regulation provides such an engineer with the sole discretion to decide what is appropriate under the circumstances.[19]

Federal law also permits the establishment of "quiet zones" in which the railroad is not required to sound the horn in applicable circumstances.[20] Quiet zones can only be established by a public authority, which includes public entities such as a city or county responsible for traffic control or law enforcement at the grade crossing.[21] While these quiet zones are regulated by the federal government, they pose safety risks to both the operators of tractor-trailers and railroad employees. Localities wishing to establish a quiet zone must mitigate the

13. 49 C.F.R. § 229.129; Ryder v. Union Pac. R.R. Co., No. CV 15-431-SDD-EWD, 2017 (M.D. La. Sept. 29, 2017).

14. *Id.* § 222.21.

15. *Id.* § 222.21(b)(3).

16. *Id.* § 222.7.

17. *Id.* § 222.23(a)(l).

18. *Id.*

19. *Id.* § 222.7.

20. *Id.* § 222(c).

21. Federal Railroad Admin., 2024, https://railroads.dot.gov/railroad-safety/divisions/highway-rail-crossing-and-trespasser-programs/train-horn-rulequiet-zones.

safety risk caused by the absence of a horn.[22] That said, train horns may still be used in emergency situations or to comply with other federal regulations or railroad operating rules.[23] An emergency situation in which a train operator may be required to sound a horn may create a question of liability where a train and tractor-trailer collision occurs at a quiet zone grade crossing. Additionally, some grade crossings have preexisting "no horn" restrictions, which now may have been qualified as "pre-rule quiet zone[s]."[24] Safety concerns in the quiet zones are high since trains are prohibited from sounding horns as they enter a station to warn commuters and pedestrians of an oncoming train.

Federal Preemption of Railroad Grade Crossing Regulation

The Federal Grade Crossing Program requires state roadway officials to establish a uniform process to improve safety at grade crossings. This includes undertaking projects to install and upgrade warning devices at grade crossings. Federal funds, which are approved through the Federal Highway Administration, are used to implement these projects. Since 2000, fatalities at grade crossings have decreased by 41 percent, largely thanks to the Federal Grade Crossing Program.[25]

From a legal practitioner's standpoint, analysis of the maintenance of the crossing (i.e., whether federal funds have been used to improve the crossing) will determine whether federal law preempts state law at a particular crossing. The program was designed to ensure that states utilize the tools available to them through the federal government in a uniform, rational, and efficient way. No crossing can be treated alike, and the program lays out a process by which the states should evaluate whether federal funding is appropriate.

Passive and Active Crossings

Passive rail–highway crossings are protected only by a crossbuck sign that does not warn a motorist of the approach of a train. Active crossings are protected by warning devices, such as flashing lights or a combination of flashing lights and automatic gates, that, assuming these devices are working correctly, actively warn a motorist that a train is approaching the crossing. Preemption can also be an issue where an accident occurs at a passive crossing. In *Stevenson v. Fort Worth & W.R.R. Co.*, a plaintiff's claim was preempted by federal law where retro-reflective tape on a crossbuck was installed pursuant to a federal safety improvement program.[26] Where federal funds have been used to improve or

---

22. *Id.*
23. *Id.*
24. *Id.*
25. Federal Highway Admin., Railway Highway Crossing Program Overview (2024), https://highways.dot.gov/safety/hsip/xings/railway-highway-crossing-program-overview#:~:text=The%20Railway%2DHighway%20Crossings%20(Section,at%20railway%2Dhighway%20grade%20crossings.
26. Stevenson v. Fort Worth & W. R.R. Co., No. 10-16-00244-CV, 2017 WL 4413445 (Tex. App. Oct. 4, 2017) (unpublished).

reduce hazardous conditions at a passive crossing, preemption may apply to a claim relating to that crossing.

As discussed earlier, unless the tractor-trailer hauls certain hazardous materials, the driver of a tractor-trailer approaching a passive crossing is not required by either state statutes or federal regulations to bring his or her vehicle to a complete stop before proceeding across the tracks, unless a signal from a railroad locomotive horn is audible or an approaching train is visible. However, the locomotive horn is generally considered to be an ineffective warning device, and few motorists know the sight distance they need to be able to see an approaching train in sufficient time to make the correct decision as to whether to stop short of the tracks or to proceed over the tracks. As a tractor-trailer is much longer than a standard passenger vehicle, its driver has less time to decide whether to stop or proceed through a crossing than the driver of a standard passenger vehicle.

Stopping Short of the Tracks

While not all tractor-trailer combinations are required by state statutes or federal regulations to come to a complete stop at every grade crossing, it is sometimes necessary for the driver of a tractor-trailer to stop short of the tracks to listen and look for an approaching train effectively. However, stopping before proceeding across the tracks can, under certain circumstances, also create a hazardous condition. A tractor-trailer that approaches and goes over the railroad tracks at a speed of 25 miles per hour has significantly less "exposure time" (i.e., the time during which it can be hit by a train) than a tractor-trailer that has been brought to a complete stop short of the tracks and is then driven from that stopped position slowly across the tracks at five miles per hour. For that reason, it is critical that a driver of a tractor-trailer who is required to stop or does stop short of the tracks effectively listens and looks for an approaching train to avoid a collision with an approaching train.

Another related problem arises when a roadway traffic-control device on the other side of the tracks at a grade crossing causes traffic to back up and stop on the tracks themselves. In other words, if there is a stop sign or red light close to the tracks, vehicles in front of a tractor-trailer may stop at that traffic control device, forcing the driver of the tractor-trailer to stop before completely clearing the tracks. Therefore, the driver of such a vehicle needs to be sure that there is an adequate "storage area" to pull entirely over and off the tracks before proceeding across the tracks. Much like the previous example, this situation may also expose the trucking company and the driver to liability for an accident resulting from the driver's failure to anticipate the necessary storage area required to clear the tracks in a single maneuver.

The situations discussed here, as well as the many other situations that can arise from a tractor-trailer not fully clearing a railroad-grade crossing, result in accidents and litigation. To avoid injuries resulting from these accidents and the subsequent litigation that often follows, lawyers representing both the trucking companies and plaintiffs injured in accidents should make certain that they are up to date on the applicable federal, state, and local regulations relating to railroad-grade crossings.

Humped Crossings

Statutes or regulations in most states require railroads to construct and maintain smooth, level crossing surfaces. However, as a result of topographical conditions, design, and maintenance factors, some grade crossings become "humped" such that it is possible for commercial motor vehicles, especially trailers that are low to the ground, to become stuck on the tracks.[27] While federal regulations mostly relate to grade crossing maintenance, such a situation would likely be brought under the applicable state law against the entity responsible for maintaining the crossing. At this time, there are no federal regulations requiring states to eliminate humped crossings.

Conclusion

This chapter has addressed a number of liability scenarios concerning accidents involving both the operators of tractor-trailers and railroad companies at high-grade crossings. Liability concerns will almost certainly arise from accidents involving tractor-trailers. Understanding the scenarios in which federal law preempts a particular state statute at the grade crossing is important for legal practitioners to aid and advise their clients. Federal preemption is a common issue, and practitioners should look to the state-specific statutes to determine whether the corresponding federal statute expressly preempts the regulation. Further, lawyers can utilize the UVC as a tool to digest the broad concepts that have been adopted by nearly every state.

---

27. *Accidents That Shouldn't Happen.* A Report by the U.S. Department of Transportation (U.S. DOT) Task Force on Highway-Rail Crossing Safety to Transportation Secretary Federico Pena, March 1, 1996.

CHAPTER 19

Construction Zone Crashes

Danny Ellis, Esq.

The United States boasts an expansive road network, crucial for transportation and economic activity.[1] In 2023, drivers in the United States covered a record-breaking distance, logging over 3.2 trillion miles on roads and streets.[2] With this vast network of roads many crashes take place in construction zones. These crashes require the legal practitioner to engage in multifaceted analysis to determine whether liability exists. This chapter aims to guide lawyers through the essential steps in investigating these crashes and understanding the relevant legal principles.

Investigating Construction Zone Crashes

As with any case, collection of evidence is critical to determining whether liability exists. This section seeks to provide lawyers with an outline of available evidence to assist in the analysis of their case.

1. **Visit the scene and gather evidence.** The immediate aftermath of a construction zone accident is crucial for evidence preservation. If possible, lawyers or their investigators should visit the scene promptly to document it through photographs and videos. This includes capturing the layout of the construction zone, signage, temporary traffic control measures, and any contributing factors like debris or poor lighting.
2. **Interview witnesses.** Eyewitness accounts can provide valuable insights into the events leading to the crash. Lawyers should interview witnesses as soon as possible to obtain their statements while their memories are fresh. These statements can help establish the sequence of events, driver behavior, and the visibility of warning signs or signals. Witnesses will include the following: construction workers, police, EMS responders, firefighters, and independent third-party witnesses.

1. https://highways.dot.gov/public-roads/spring-1994/impact-highway-infrastructure-economic-performance.

2. https://www.ghsa.org/news/Reuters/USdriving/2024#:~:text=Travel%20on%20U.S.%20roads%20in,for%20the%20first%20time%2C%20the.

3. **Obtain official reports.** Police reports, accident reconstruction reports, and any reports filed by the construction company or government agencies involved should be obtained. These reports often contain critical information about the parties involved, contributing factors, and potential violations of traffic laws or safety regulations.
4. **Review contracts and regulations.** Construction zone accidents often involve contractual relationships between various parties, such as the general contractor, subcontractors, and the government entity overseeing the project. Lawyers should carefully review these contracts to determine the responsibilities of each party regarding safety measures and liability. Additionally, applicable federal, state, and local regulations governing construction zones should be examined to identify any potential noncompliance that may have contributed to the accident.
5. **Consult experts.** Depending on the complexity of the case, lawyers may need to consult experts in accident reconstruction, traffic engineering, or construction safety. These experts can analyze the evidence, provide opinions on causation, and assess whether the construction zone met industry standards and safety guidelines.
6. **Freedom of Information/open records request.** Upon receiving the case, lawyers should immediately send a Freedom of Information request or the state equivalent to the following entities:
   a. State Department of Transportation (DOT) if on a state highway or interstate highway
   b. State Homeland Security Department (Highway Patrol)
   c. Emergency responders (fire and EMS)
   d. National Transportation Safety Board (if it performed an investigation)
   e. If applicable, the local city or county government

When contacting the various transportation departments, request the following documents:

a. Statement of Need, which is the justification for repairs or work being performed
b. Design plans plus all DOT communications and consultants' communications relating to plan approval
c. Temporary Traffic Control Plan plus all DOT communications and consultants' communications relating to plan approval
d. Traffic Management Plan
e. Project contract (listing general and subcontractors)
f. Project work schedule (staging plan, critical dates, and changes)
g. Project standards
h. Weekly meeting notes
i. Project-related communications
j. Project change orders
k. Crash history within work zone
l. Citizen complaints made to police or other government agency
m. Public information and media releases

Practitioners may also wish to engage a reconstruction expert to take measurements and secure drone video of the entire work area. Lastly, a thorough search of the internet should be conducted to see what publicity surrounds the crash.[3]

Government Entity as a Defendant[4]

Government entities often enjoy sovereign immunity, which shields them from liability in certain situations. However, this immunity is not absolute and can be waived under specific circumstances, such as those outlined in tort claims acts.[5]

Ministerial versus Discretionary Acts

The distinction between ministerial and discretionary acts is crucial in determining government liability. Ministerial acts are those that are mandatory and involve little to no judgment, whereas discretionary acts involve decision-making and policy considerations. This exception is based on the principle that government employees should be held accountable for their negligence when performing routine tasks that do not involve policy decisions.

Examples of Ministerial Functions

Several cases illustrate the application of the ministerial function exception:

- In *Barree v. Cape Girardeau*,[6] the court held that the city's duty to keep its streets in repair was a ministerial function, and the city was liable for the negligent acts of its employee while making street repairs.
- In *Burns v. Ohio Department of Transportation*,[7] the court determined that while the decision to expand a state route was discretionary (immune),

---

3. This search will reveal if this construction site has had previous issues. In addition, the practitioner may be able to purchase photographs and video of the scene as many of the photojournalists are independent contractors and all too happy to make money.

4. Be aware that many governmental tort liability statutes come with a cap and strict statute of limitation periods with strict notice requirements.

5. This chapter will not address it, but the practitioner must be mindful of the proper place with which to make a claim. For example, in Tennessee, if the Defendant is the State of Tennessee, the practitioner must file a claim with the claims commission, which has its own procedural rules and filing system. Failure to file a claim with the Tennessee Claims Commission could result in the case being dismissed with prejudice. *See* Turner v. State, 184 S.W.3d 701 (Tenn. Ct. App. 2005). That statute, Tennessee Code Annotated section 9–8–307(a)(1), begins by stating that the Commission has "exclusive jurisdiction to determine all monetary claims against the state based on the acts or omissions of 'state employees' falling within one (1) or more of the following categories. . . ." One such category, which applies here, is "[d]angerous conditions on state maintained highways" where, to maintain a suit based on this category, the claimant "must establish the foreseeability of the risk and notice given to the proper state officials at a time sufficiently prior to the injury for the state to have taken appropriate measures" Tenn. Code Ann. § 9–8–307(a)(1)(J). Also of relevance to this dispute is the following directive: "It is the intent of the general assembly that the jurisdiction of the claims commission be liberally construed to implement the remedial purposes of this legislation" Tenn. Code Ann. § 9–8–307(a)(3). *See also* Northland Ins. Co. v. State, 33 S.W.3d 727, 729 (Tenn. 2000).

6. 95 S.W. 330 (Mo. 1906).

7. 529 N.E.2d 1283 (Ohio Ct. App. 1987).

the implementation of that decision, including design, construction, and maintenance, was ministerial (actionable).

- In *Caldwell v. Savannah*,[8] the court distinguished between the maintenance of a public park (governmental function, immune) and the maintenance of a public street (ministerial function, actionable), holding the city liable for injuries caused by negligent street maintenance.
- In *Kyllo v. Panzer*,[9] the court held that driving a motor vehicle was a ministerial function, and state employees were not immune from personal injury actions arising from their negligent driving.
- In *Little v. Mississippi DOT*,[10] the court clarified that road maintenance and repair are ministerial functions, and the Department of Transportation was not entitled to discretionary-function immunity for failing to maintain highways properly.
- In *Myers v. Palmyra*,[11] the court held that the city's snow removal activities constituted street maintenance, a ministerial function, and the city was liable for injuries caused by the negligent operation of snow removal equipment.
- In *Mississippi Transportation Commission v. Adams*,[12] the court held that while the placement of traffic control devices was generally discretionary, certain narrower duties existed that rendered such function ministerial, thus making the government entities liable.

Defining Discretionary Functions

Discretionary functions are those that involve an element of judgment or choice. They are distinguished from ministerial functions, which are acts that are mandatory and involve little to no judgment.

In *City of Tampa v. Fredrick*,[13] the court explained that while the design and construction of a bike lane was a discretionary function, the failure to warn of a dangerous condition created by the bike lane's design could be considered an operational function, not immune from liability.[14]

Factors for Determining Discretionary Functions

Courts consider several factors when determining whether an act is discretionary:

1. **The nature and importance of the function.** Acts involving policymaking, planning, or resource allocation are more likely to be considered discretionary.
2. **The level of judgment involved.** Actions requiring significant judgment, decision-making, and policy considerations are more likely to be discretionary.
3. **The impact on public policy.** If a decision involves balancing competing policy goals or allocating resources, it is more likely to be discretionary.

---

8. 115 S.E.2d 403 (Ga. Ct. App. 1960).
9. 535 N.W.2d 896 (S.D. 1995).
10. 129 So. 3d 132 (Miss. 2013).
11. 355 S.W.2d 17 (Mo. 1962).
12. 197 So. 3d 406 (Miss. 2016).
13. 369 So. 3d 1197 (Fla. 2023).
14. *Id.* at 1199–200.

4. **Guidance from laws and regulations.** The existence of specific laws or regulations that dictate a particular course of action may indicate a ministerial function, but some discretion may still be involved in their implementation.
5. **The nature and severity of harm.** The potential harm resulting from the government's action or inaction is considered. If the risk of harm is high and foreseeable, the court may be less inclined to grant immunity.

Case Law Examples

- In *McKinney v. Gainesville*,[15] the court held that the city's decision not to place barricades along a parade route was a discretionary function, as it involved policy considerations regarding public safety and resource allocation.
- In *Doutre v. Box Elder County*,[16] the court determined that the county's decision not to modify a steep incline in a road was discretionary because it involved evaluating and balancing budgetary considerations and policy factors.
- In *State v. Lucas*,[17] the court held that the state's redesign of a highway was not a discretionary function because a specific provision of the Indiana Tort Claims Act (ITCA) addressed highway design, making the state's actions ministerial.

The Impact of Federal Law and Federal Dollars

On a highway project in which federal funds are used, the project shall comply with the Manual on Uniform Traffic Control Devices (MUTCD).[18] "The MUTCD approved by the Federal Highway Administrator is the national standard for all traffic control devices installed on any street, highway, or bicycle trail open to public travel in accordance with 23 U.S.C. 109(d) and 402(a)."[19] Every state must have a program that provides for the systematic upgrading of substandard traffic control devices and for installation of traffic control devices that meet MUTCD standards.[20] New or reconstructed highways that fall under federal aid projects must conform to the MUTCD.[21] Construction area activities using federal dollars must conform to the MUTCD.[22] This mandatory language may remove sovereign immunity by making compliance with the MUTCD a ministerial function allowing for governmental liability.[23]

15. 814 S.W.2d 862 (Tex. 1991).
16. 548 P.3d 914 (Utah 2024).
17. 223 N.E.3d 253 (Ind. Ct. App. 2023).
18. *See* 23 U.S.C.A. § 109(d).
19. 23 C.F.R. § 655.603.
20. *See id.* § 655.603(d)(1).
21. *Id.* § 655.603(d)(2).
22. *Id.* § 655.603(d)(3).
23. *See* Patterson v. Cowley Cnty., 307 Kan. 616, 633, 413 P.3d 432, 444 (2018) ("'The [discretionary function] exception applies only when no mandatory guidelines exist to govern the defendants' conduct'" quoting Kastendieck v. Bd. of Cnty. Comm'rs, 934 F. Supp. 387, 391 (D. Kan. 1996)).

Basic Design of a Temporary Construction Zone

By design, a construction zone is temporary in nature. Each construction zone must have a Temporary Traffic Control (TTC) plan to help traffic through the construction zone.[24] A TTC has seven fundamental principles:

1. General plans or guidelines should be developed to provide safety for motorists, bicyclists, pedestrians, workers, enforcement/emergency officials, and equipment . . .
2. Road user movement should be inhibited as little as practical . . .
3. Motorists, bicyclists, and pedestrians should be guided in a clear and positive manner while approaching and traversing TTC zones and incident sites . . .
4. To provide acceptable levels of operations, routine day and night inspections of TTC elements should be performed . . .
5. Attention should be given to the maintenance of roadside safety during the life of the TTC zone . . .
6. Each person whose actions affect TTC zone safety, from the upper-level management through the field workers, should receive training appropriate to the job decisions each individual is required to make . . .
7. Good public relations should be maintained . . .[25]

A TTC work zone has four areas.

1. **Advanced Warning Area.** "The advance warning area is the section of highway where road users are informed about the upcoming transition and activity areas or incident area."[26]
2. **Transition Area.** "The transition area is that section of highway where road users are redirected out of their normal path. Transition areas usually involve strategic use of tapers. . . ."[27]
3. **Activity Area.** "The activity area is the section of the highway where the work activity takes place. It is comprised of the workspace, the traffic space, and the buffer space. The workspace is that portion of the highway closed to road users and set aside for workers, equipment, and material, and a shadow vehicle if one is used upstream. Work spaces are usually delineated for road users by channelizing devices or, to exclude vehicles and pedestrians, by temporary barriers."[28]
4. **Termination Area.** "The termination area is the section of the highway where road users are returned to their normal driving path. The termination area extends from the downstream end of the work area to the last TTC device such as END ROAD WORK signs, if posted."[29]

---

24. MUTCD § 6A.01 (11th ed. 2011). Practical note: there are several editions to the MUTCD. Make sure you are using the edition that is relevant to the facts and time frame of your case.
25. *Id.* § 6A.02.
26. *Id.* § 6B.04.
27. *Id.* § 6B.05. Tapers are important and are discussed in detail in the MUTCD.
28. *Id.* § 6B.06.
29. *Id.* § 6B.07.

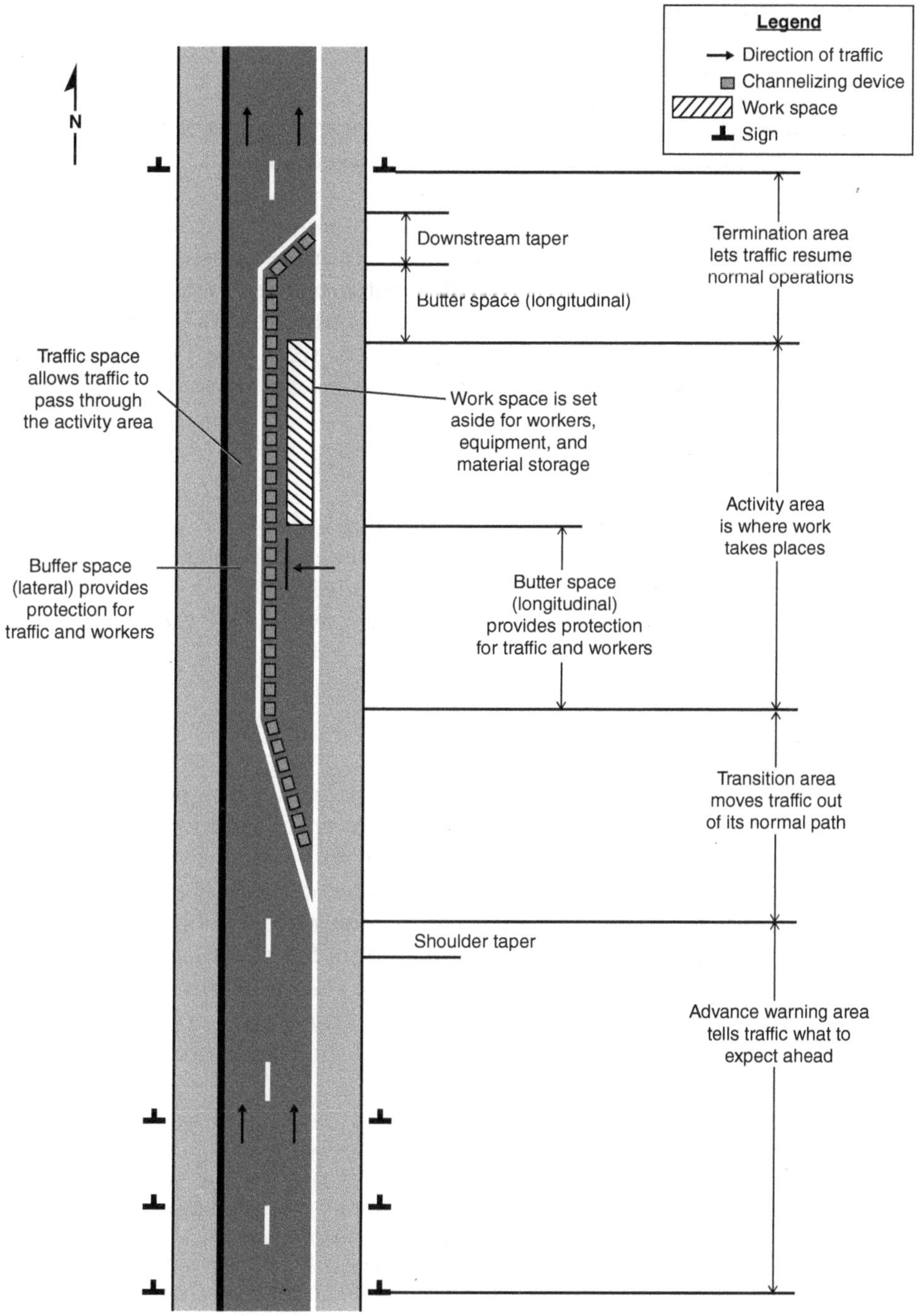

Figure 19.1 Component Parts of a Temporary Traffic Control Zone

Source: MUTCD § 6B.05 (Dec. 2023), p. 772.

Common Problems from a TTC zone

a. Improper signage,
b. Confusing design, and
c. Pavement-edge drop-offs (PEDO) (i.e. "the uneven edge or vertical dropoff between the paved travel lane and the unpaved shoulder. Highway safety experts consider a dropoff of 12.7 centimeters (5 inches) or more to be unsafe, especially if the edge is at a 90-degree angle to the shoulder surface. A dropoff of 5.1 centimeters (2 inches) or more is considered a potential driving hazard. The dropoff along the stretch of highway where the teens' car slipped off the pavement ranged from about 5.1 to 10.2 centimeters (2 to 4 inches), according to two safety engineers from the Federal Highway Administration (FHWA) who visited the site the day after the crash.")[30]

Private Contractors

Many times, governments engage the services of the private sector to perform road maintenance. These private parties may be held responsible for their negligent acts without the benefit of government immunity.[31] The MUTCD, construction standards, and other common law doctrines, will allow the practitioner to establish present negligence claims.

Conclusion

Construction zone accident cases demand meticulous investigation and a thorough understanding of the legal principles governing liability and sovereign immunity. By securing evidence, interviewing witnesses, reviewing contracts and regulations, and consulting experts, lawyers can build a strong case for their clients. Understanding the nuances of contractor liability, government immunity, and comparative negligence is essential for navigating the complexities of these cases and achieving a just outcome for the victims of construction zone accidents. A familiarity with the MUTCD and other applicable standards should help the practitioner navigate and advise the client throughout the case.

---

30. https://highways.dot.gov/public-roads/septoct-2007/low-cost-dropoff-solution.

31. *See* Brown & Gay Eng'g, Inc. v. Olivares, 461 S.W.3d 117, 129 (Tex. 2015) ("a long line of Texas case law recognizes government contractors' liability for their negligence in road and highway construction"); *see also* Showers Appraisals, LLC v. Musson Bros., 2013 WI 79, ¶ 36, 350 Wis. 2d 509, 531, 835 N.W.2d 226, 237 ("the contractor must show both that the contractor was an agent as that term is used in § 893.80(4), i.e., as is expressed in the Lyonstest, and that the allegedly injurious conduct was caused by the implementation of a decision for which immunity is available for governmental entities under § 893.80(4)"); Steinberg v. New York City Tr. Auth., 88 A.D.3d 582, 582, 931 N.Y.S.2d 291, 292 (2011); Sullins v. American Medical Response of Oklahoma, Inc., 23 P.3d 259, 264 (OK 2001) ("A private entity is not an 'agency' of a public trust under the Governmental Tort Claims Act merely because it contracts with the public trust to provide the services which the public trust is authorized to provide"). This is list is not exhaustive but rather a primer to allow research.

CHAPTER 20
Hazardous Materials in Truck Crash Cases

D.J Young, III, Esq.

Introduction

People involved with the transportation of hazardous materials have statutory, regulatory, and common law responsibilities uniquely associated with those circumstances. Environmental law, generally, is an entire academic and practical discipline within the law profession handled by attorneys who concentrate their practices on it. This chapter is not an environmental compliance guide for shippers and motor carriers, and it should not be used that way. Instead, this chapter merely introduces the environmental laws that might be relevant to the truck crash litigator. Even if there is no toxic release during a crash, unique regulations apply to the transportation of hazardous materials that impact matters of documentation, routing, and insurance, which are of interest to the trial lawyer. And, if there is an injury-related hazardous materials release, there are additional legal considerations. This chapter serves as a survey of these issues.

Insurance Requirements

Motor carriers that transport hazardous materials have more strict insurance coverage minimums than do vehicles that do not carry hazardous materials.[1] Depending on the material being transported, minimum insurance can be either \$1,000,000 or \$5,000,000.[2] One must identify the material being hauled and then check the regulations to determine the required level of insurance. If the motor carrier does not carry hazardous materials, then the current minimum coverage required is \$750,000. The point is that because of the higher coverage requirements, the stakes are raised for crashes involving hazardous materials motor

1. Refer to the chapter in this book by Mary Eliasen and Pete Kestner addressing the topic of state and federal insurance requirements generally.
2. 49 U.S.C. §§ 13906, 31139(d).

carriers even if the hazardous material does not have anything to do with the injuries. Bear in mind that in some cases, other parties, like shippers, may have liability and insurance coverage applicable to the motor vehicle crash.

Legal Overview

The major sources of environmental laws and regulations applicable to commercial motor vehicles are discussed in this section. State laws may be applicable, too, but they are beyond the scope of this chapter.

The purpose of the Hazardous Materials Transportation Act, codified at 49 U.S.C. Chapter 51, is to "to protect against the risks to life, property, and the environment that are inherent in the transportation of hazardous material in intrastate, interstate, and foreign commerce."[3] It authorizes the Secretary of Transportation to promulgate regulations for the purpose of the "safe transportation" of hazardous materials that it deems pose an "unreasonable risk to health and safety or property" and those regulations are binding on many different people, including those who (1) transport hazardous materials, (2) cause to be transported hazardous materials, (3) design or manufacture packaging or containers for hazardous materials transportation, (4) prepare or accept hazardous materials for transportation, or (5) are responsible for the safety of hazardous materials transportation.[4]

Notably, the law mandates regulations that impose special training requirements on "hazmat employees" and "hazmat employers"[5]—broadly defined terms in the law.[6] Definitions in this area of the law are specific and detailed.[7] Some carriers of hazardous materials must register that fact, and the records are available to the public.[8] Some carriers of hazardous materials are required to obtain a safety permit depending on the quantity and type of hazardous materials.[9] There is a preemption statute that, in detail, addresses the circumstances when this body of law preempts state law.[10] Whether it preempts any particular negligence claim depends on a careful factual, statutory, and case law analysis.

A special provision of the Hazardous Materials Transportation Act imposes a unique duty on shippers and similarly situated parties: "A person offering hazardous material for motor vehicle transportation in commerce may offer the material to a motor carrier only if the carrier has a safety permit issued under this section authorizing the transportation."[11] Arguably it would be negligent *per se* for a shipper to fail to verify that the motor carrier has the safety permit.

---

3. *Id.* § 5101.
4. *Id.* § 5103; *see also* 49 C.F.R. §§ 171.1, 172.3.
5. 49 U.S.C. § 5107.
6. *Id.* § 5102.
7. *See, e.g.*, 49 C.F.R. § 171.8.
8. 49 U.S.C. § 5108.
9. *Id.* § 5109. *Cf.* 49 U.S.C. § 5117; *see also* 49 C.F.R. §§ 385.403 *et seq.*
10. 49 U.S.C. § 5125; *see also* 49 C.F.R. § 171.1(f) and 49 C.F.R. § 397.3 and 49 C.F.R. pt 397 subpt. E.
11. 49 U.S.C. § 5109(f); *see also* 49 C.F.R. §§ 172.20, 173.22(b).

Such persons also have a duty to provide the "shipping paper" concerning the hazardous material to the motor carrier, and both the shipper and the motor carrier are responsible for keeping that documentation on the motor vehicle that carries the hazardous material.[12] Shippers of hazardous materials have extensive additional duties related to packaging and labeling of the hazardous materials.[13]

The shipping paper must contain a complete description of the hazardous materials or wastes being transported and certifications of legal compliance by the person preparing the shipping paper which, normally, is the one offering the material to be transported,[14] like, for example, the shipper. Lawful transport of "hazardous waste," as that term is defined in the law, requires another document, the "hazardous waste manifest," with its own requirements,[15] discussed more later. All shipping papers must be stored in the transport vehicle within reach of the driver, and, when the driver is not present, in the driver door pocket or on the driver's seat.[16]

Depending on the material being transported, motor carriers are required to provide additional safety rules, accident procedures, and emergency contact information to the drivers of the transport vehicle carrying hazardous materials, and the driver must sign indicating receipt of them.[17] The driver must keep them with the driver, and the motor carrier must retain a copy of the signed receipt for one year.[18]

Any person offering to transport hazardous materials and transporting hazardous materials must prepare the emergency response information required by the regulations and such information must be kept in the transport vehicle with the shipping papers.[19] The shipper is required to keep a copy of the shipping paper for at least two years from the date provided to the carrier, and the carrier is required to keep a copy for at least one year,[20] so it is important to request a copy promptly to avoid the loss of information through a record retention process that authorizes destruction after these short time periods.

Extensive regulations apply to the manufacturers of the packages and containers used to transport hazardous materials, including specifications for the containers used, the flame resistance of such materials, the leak-proofing of such materials, and so on.[21] The identification of the manufacturer must be marked on the package or container, as must other information relevant to that package

12. 49 U.S.C. § 5110.
13. 49 C.F.R. § 173.22.
14. *Id.* pt. 172 subpt. C.
15. *Id.* §§ 172.205, 262.20.
16. *Id.* § 177.817(e).
17. *Id.* § 397.19.
18. *Id.*
19. *Id.* § 172.602. In addition, if the trailer containing hazardous materials is disconnected from the tractor, then the carrier's contact information must be posted on the trailer near the brake hose and electrical connections. Id. § 172.606.
20. 49 U.S.C. § 5110(d); *but see* 49 C.F.R. § 172.201, which requires longer retention periods—two to three years depending on the material. *See also* 49 C.F.R. § 177.817(f).
21. 49 C.F.R. pt. 178.

or container.[22] The regulations have specific requirements related to packaging of hazardous materials.[23]

Packages, containers, and transport vehicles handling hazardous material must be precisely marked, and the transporter may have responsibilities for doing so,[24] as may the shipper.[25] These markings must be quite conspicuous and comply precisely with the regulations.[26] They are required to be in the diamond shape marking with serious-looking symbols and labeling such that they have the warning effect similar to the placement of skull and crossbones on poisons. Examples are shown in Figure 20.1.[27]

CLASS 6 Poison (toxic), poison inhalation hazard, infectious substance: divisions 6.1 and 6.2

Figure 20.1 Examples of markings for vehicles handling hazardous materials.

Anyone who transports or offers to transport hazardous materials is responsible for "placarding" symbols like these on the sides and each end of vehicle transporting the hazardous materials.[28] If the vehicle does not already have the

22. *Id.* § 178.3(a)(2).
23. *Id.* pt. 178.
24. *Id.* §§ 172.300, 172.304, 172.332.
25. *Id.* § 172.400. The shipper's labels must be on the packages or containers of the hazardous materials. *Id.* § 172.406.
26. *Id.* §§ 172.304, 172.516, 172.519.
27. From the Pipeline and Hazardous Materials Safety Administration's website: https://www.phmsa.dot.gov/sites/phmsa.dot.gov/files/2020-07/USDOT%20Chart%2016%20PHH50%200162%201117%20WEB.pdf.
28. 49 C.F.R. §§ 172.500, 172.504, 172.506.

correct placards, the shipper is required to provide them.[29] A motor carrier is prohibited from transporting hazardous materials without complying with the placarding requirements.[30]

Persons loading and unloading hazardous materials from the transport vehicles have additional mandatory regulatory duties. These regulations address matters ranging from placement and securement of the hazardous materials, setting the handbrake while loading and unloading, attendance requirements, use of cargo heaters, and other related subjects.[31]

There are special regulations applicable to the routing of hazardous material transport vehicles.[32] Routes for the transportation of hazardous materials may be restricted by law.[33] The motor carrier is the party responsible for compliance.[34] There are special requirements and prohibitions applicable to the transportation of hazardous materials and passengers in the same vehicle.[35] The applicability of these rules depends upon the type and quantity of materials involved.

In many instances, vehicles containing hazardous materials cannot be left unattended.[36] Whenever a hazardous materials transport vehicle is stopped along the roadway, "special care shall be taken to guard the vehicle and its load or to take such steps as may be necessary to provide against hazard. Special effort shall be made to remove the motor vehicle to a place where the hazards of the materials being transported may be provided against."[37]

Drivers of hazardous materials must have a commercial driver's license endorsement authorizing them to transport hazardous materials.[38] They also must satisfy the security risk procedures of the Transportation Security Administration.[39] In addition to the general training requirements imposed on all motor carriers and their employees, hazmat employers must ensure their hazmat employees are specifically trained for handling of hazardous materials.[40] Training must be recurrent and hazmat employers must retain the training records.[41] In addition, many persons who offer to transport hazardous materials and persons transporting hazardous materials must have written security plans

29. *Id.* § 172.506.

30. *Id.*

31. *Id.* pt. 177, subpt. B. Unique loading and unloading regulations exist for some of the various classifications of hazardous materials. *Id.*

32. 49 U.S.C. § 5112, 49 C.F.R. pt. 397 subpt. C.

33. *Id.*

34. 49 C.F.R. § 397.67.

35. *Id.* § 177.870.

36. *Id.* § 397.5. This regulation mandates that the person attending be awake.

37. *Id.* § 177.854. This regulation also addresses leaking packages and containers. Another regulation governing the stopping of hazardous materials transport vehicles has additional restrictions limiting where they may be parked. *Id.* § 397.7.

38. *Id.* § 383.93(b)(4).

39. *Id.* § 383.141.

40. *Id.* § 172.702(a) and (b); §§ 177.800(c) and 177.816. The employer also is responsible for testing. *Id* § 172.704.

41. 49 C.F.R. § 172.704.

that comply with the regulations.[42] A driver of a hazardous materials transport vehicle must inspect the tires "at the beginning of each trip and each time the vehicle is parked."[43] This is in addition to the general inspection requirements imposed by the Federal Motor Carrier Safety Regulations.[44] It is illegal to drive with an overheated tire until the defect causing the overheating is corrected.[45]

Motor carriers are responsible for compliance with all of the obligations in the hazardous materials transportation regulations.[46]

The Resource Conservation and Recovery Act (RCRA) applies to transportation of regulated hazardous waste.[47] To the extent that RCRA overlaps with the Hazardous Materials Transportation Act, its regulations must be coordinated with those implemented pursuant to the Hazardous Materials Transportation Act.[48] Despite that being the case, some RCRA regulations applicable to transporters are found in 40 C.F.R. Part 263, rather than in Code of Federal Regulations Title 49 where most regulations applicable to motor carriers are found. To transport hazardous wastes, the transporter must obtain an EPA identification number.[49] The transporter is prohibited from accepting hazardous wastes from a generator of such wastes unless it receives a "manifest" form (EPA Form 8700-22, and if necessary, EPA Form 8700-22A) or an electronic manifest form.[50] The manifest form might contain information relevant to a truck crash investigation, as it will contain information identifying the generator, transporter, and designated facility related to the transportation of the hazardous waste.

Under some circumstances, a transporter of hazardous substances to disposal or treatment facilities or sites selected by that transporter can be liable for environmental law violation cleanup costs pursuant to the Comprehensive Environmental Response Compensation and Liability Act (CERCLA),[51] as can shippers and people who arrange for such transport.[52] A statutory private right of action exists to enforce contribution for those costs.[53] It is well-known that the cost to cleanup environmental spills can bankrupt financially responsible persons and entities, and, therefore, the impact of such costs may limit an injured person's recovery solely to available insurance.

---

42. *Id.* §§ 172.800, 172.802.

43. *Id.* § 397.17(a).

44. See the chapter in this book by Amy Papuga about these inspection requirements.

45. 49 C.F.R. § 397.17. There are other regulations related to tires that are generally applicable to all motor carriers regardless of whether they are carrying hazardous materials or not.

46. *Id.* § 177.800(b); *id.* §§ 397.1 and 397.2. They must refuse to transport forbidden materials and improperly packaged materials. Id. § 177.801.

47. 42 U.S.C. § 6923.

48. *Id.* § 6923(b).

49. 40 C.F.R. § 263.11(a).

50. *Id.* § 263.20(a)(1). Each of these is known as the "Uniform Hazardous Waste Manifest." *See also* 49 C.F.R. § 172.205. It should be requested in discovery. There is a three-year recordkeeping requirement. 40 C.F.R. § 263.22.

51. 42 U.S.C. § 9607(a).

52. *Id.*

53. *Id.* § 9613.

Theories of Liability for Crashes Involving Hazmat Transport Vehicles

As already noted, motor carriers are responsible for all of the obligations in the hazardous materials transportation regulations. The permitting, marking, labeling, placarding, training, and security plans are relevant to the truck crash attorney because they are evidence of who is in control of the driver and the vehicle involved in the crash. The persons responsible for compliance with the regulations have significant control and responsibility for the shipment of hazardous materials, and, consequently, such persons are potentially liable for the ensuing injuries and deaths pursuant to direct negligence and/or vicarious liability doctrines.[54]

Some of the rules described earlier are sufficiently specific to form the basis of liability pursuant to negligence *per se* doctrines in states where federal regulations can form the basis for negligence *per se*. This is most likely so when the injury that the regulation was designed to prevent occurs.[55]

If the injury results from the hazardous material being transported, one should consider whether your jurisdiction imposes strict liability for ultrahazardous activities or abnormally dangerous activities. The plaintiff's attorney likely will plead ordinary negligence in the alternative given the narrow applicability of such doctrines. The defense attorney should consider what affirmative defenses might apply if strict liability doctrines are pled. Because of the extreme danger of many hazardous materials, punitive damages are more likely to be an issue in crash litigation involving them.

Practical Considerations

As can be seen from the description of the laws in this chapter, recordkeeping related to hazardous materials transport is extensive. It can contain detailed information about the shipper, the origin and destination of the load, and other parties involved. This information may prove relevant to the analysis of who was really in control of the shipment and, therefore, who likely is liable. This information may prove relevant to the analysis of whether distances can be covered between origin and destination without speeding. This information may prove relevant to the availability of greater amounts of insurance coverage.

Some cases may require the retention of experts in the transportation of hazardous materials and experts in the training of hazmat employers and employees, and if the injuries or deaths stem from the hazardous materials as opposed to the general crash dynamics, or a mix of both, experts knowledgeable about the consequences of exposure to such materials.

---

54. See the other chapter in this book by this author addressing this subject in more detail.
55. See the chapter in this book by Morgan Adams about negligence *per se*.

CHAPTER 21

Oversize and Overweight Vehicles

Gabriela R. Atkisson, Esq., and Michael A. Vercher, Esq.[1]

Introduction

A commercial vehicle must comply with specific federal, state, and local requirements and regulations to ensure it does not fall into an oversized or overweight category. A vehicle is considered *oversized* if it exceeds length, width, or height restrictions, and *overweight* if it exceeds weight requirements. Rules and regulations impose tractor-trailer size and weight limits, and penalties can be enforced on drivers and motor carriers for violating these regulations.

A motor carrier or driver may exceed these specific regulations if they obtain permission from state (and sometimes local) authorities along their route. This is done through a permitting process. However, oversized and overweight permits vary from state to state, with each state having its own requirements for transporting a load, hours of operation, vehicle requirements, and routes.

Size and Weight Limits

Currently, truck size and weight standards are a blend of federal and state regulations and laws. Federal truck length limits are permissive, and federal laws prescribe the minimum dimensions states must allow on the National Network of Highways (NNH), which includes the interstate highway system and designated multilane, divided highways.

Vehicle height is not federally regulated. The states directly and indirectly regulate height. For example, direct regulations include state laws that specify maximum allowable vehicle heights.[2] Indirect regulations include bridge clear-

1. The authors have updated Peter A. Philbrick, Sr.'s work in the 3rd edition of *Truck Accident Litigation.*

2. *See* Compilation of Existing State Truck Size and Weight Limit Laws, U.S. Dep't of Transp. Fed. Highway Admin. (May 2015), https://ops.fhwa.dot.gov/freight/policy/rpt_congress/truck_sw_laws/.

ance, overhead structures, sign heights, traffic structures, permitting processes, and zoning and land use regulations.

Under federal requirements, vehicle combinations are limited to a maximum Gross Vehicle Weight (GVW) of 80,000 pounds.[3] A maximum weight of 20,000 pounds is allowed on any single axle, and a maximum total weight on any two consecutive axles spaced eight or fewer feet apart, like tandem axles, is 34,000 pounds.[4] In addition to the weight restrictions, vehicles are not allowed to exceed the maximum width of 102 inches.[5]

Gross Vehicle Weight Rating (GVWR) refers to the maximum allowable weight a vehicle is engineered to carry safely. The federal government regulates weight ratings, which do not include the weight specs of accompanying trailers.[6] The GVWR of a commercial vehicle is typically found on a label inside the door frame of the vehicle and is determined by factors specific to each manufacturer, including the body of the vehicle, the hitch that connects the trailer to the vehicle, vehicle fluids, the main supporting area of the vehicle, the load being hauled, the driver, passengers, and additional accessories to the vehicle. GVWR is important because the vehicle may not perform as intended if the load passes the recommended GVWR. Gross vehicle weight is the vehicle's actual weight, including cargo, drivers, and passengers.

Trucks and combinations must also stay within weight-to-length limits established by the Federal Bridge Formula. The Federal Bridge Formula is $W = 500 [((LN) / (N - 1)) + 12N + 36]$. W is the maximum allowed total weight in pounds for all axles in the group (when done manually, the pounds are rounded to the nearest 500 pounds and rounded down when right in the middle. L stands for the length or distance in feet (rounded to the nearest foot) between the outer axles of any group of two or more consecutive axles. N is the number of axles under consideration.[7]

It is important to remember that each state may further restrict a vehicle's length, height, or weight. Many states limit the overall length of a combination or vehicle and reduce the maximum weight allowed on certain roads. A state may have a different formula for determining bridge law calculations or restrict vehicle weights during certain times of the year.[8]

3. 23 C.F.R. 658.17.

4. *Id.*

5. *Id.*

6. Weight specifications for trailers typically include Gross Vehicle Weight Rating (GVWR), Gross Trailer Weight (GTW), and Gross Axle Weight Rating (GAWR). For specific regulations for trailers, refer to the National Highway Traffic Safety Administration or the Federal Motor Carrier Safety Administration for commercial trailers.

7. Examples of how the calculation works in practice can be found here: Bridge Formula Weights, U.S. Dep't of Transp. Fed. Highway Admin. (Aug. 2019), ops.fhwa.dot.gov/freight/publications/brdg_frm_wghts/.

8. U.S. Dep't of Transp. Fed. Highway Admin., *supra* note 2.

Permitting

If a driver or carrier accepts a load that exceeds size and weight restrictions, the driver must begin the process of obtaining clearance to transport the load. The federal government does not issue permits for oversized or overweight vehicles; this is a state option. A state can issue permits without regard to the axle, gross, or Federal Bridge Formula requirements for non-divisible vehicles or loads. The term "non-divisible load" has been interpreted differently between states and jurisdictions within a state.

The Code of Federal Regulations, at 23 C.F.R. § 658.5, defines non-divisible as "any load or vehicle exceeding applicable length or weight limits which, if separated into smaller loads or vehicles, would: (i) Compromise the intended use of the vehicle, i.e., make it unable to perform the function for which it was intended; (ii) Destroy the value of the load or vehicle, i.e., make it unusable for its intended purpose; or (iii) Require more than 8 workhours to dismantle using appropriate equipment." A state may issue a divisible load permit based on the historic state "grandfather" rights or congressional authorization for a state-specific commodity or route movement.[9]

The preclearance process, therefore, begins by identifying the trucks, trailers, dollies, and other vehicles to transport the load; this can vary from standard flatbed and lowboy trailers to highly specialized equipment used only for transporting a particular cargo. The carrier needs to calculate weight distribution and axle loads to ensure the trucks and trailers are not carrying more weight than their equipment design limits. Once vehicle and load configurations are determined, the route can be planned. Carriers and drivers of oversized and overweight loads must prioritize planning routes and movements. Due to their size and nature, unexpected road conditions or traffic surprises can present significant difficulties in basic movements such as backing up, turning around, or parking. A detailed planning process will allow drivers to inspect roadway widths and overhead clearances.

Once the load is identified and compliant, vehicle information and route plans are submitted to the state as part of the permitting process.[10] Once the relevant information is submitted, each state will review it to ensure the roads can handle the oversized load. Permits issued by the states typically contain information regarding how the motor carrier and driver should transport the load. States may also require escort or pilot vehicles. Permits are usually only valid for a set number of days. If the route involves travel on major highways, the motor carrier may need to get additional permits from the cities it passes through. Poor planning can lead to alterations to a prescribed route. Motor carriers must then contact the permitting agency to notify them of a change.

---

9. Specific state grandfather rights can be found in Appendix C to 23 C.F.R. pt. 658—Trucks Over 80,000 Pounds on the Interstate System and Trucks Over STAA Lengths on the National Network.

10. *See* Oversize/Overweight Load Permits, U.S. Dep't of Transp. Fed. Highway Admin., https://ops.fhwa.dot.gov/freight/sw/permit_report/index.htm to obtain the contact information for each state agency (last updated Jan. 23, 2024).

Vehicle Marking and Lighting

Most states require vehicles transporting oversized or overweight loads to utilize additional signage, lights, and other conspicuity measures. Typically, the front and rear of the vehicle are marked with banners that indicate the vehicle's oversized condition and alert approaching vehicles to the large cargo that may encroach into the other lanes of traffic.

In addition, the vehicle may be required to use flashing, rotating, or strobe lights on its front, rear, or sides to alert other vehicles on the roadway. Excessively long or wide loads may require additional clearance, brakes, or turn signals to satisfy the permit conditions. These measures may also be required for escort vehicles traveling with the load.

Escort Vehicles and Pilot Cars

Various factors may require the use of escort vehicles or pilot cars. An oversized transport may require the use of escort vehicles or pilot cars. Escort and pilot cars are separate vehicles provided by the motor carrier or a company that travels with the oversized load along the route. A pilot car leads or follows the oversized load to ensure the driver's and other vehicles' safety across the intended path. Pilot cars serve many purposes, including alerting other motorists to the transport, inspecting the road for potential hazards, and monitoring the stability of the load and signage on the vehicle. Pilot car operators may predrive the intended route to identify these potential hazards and clearances.

Pilot cars and operators also assist the driver with spotting the vehicle through turns and other maneuvers as well as securing intersections and roadways so the load can safely pass. The number of escort vehicles depends on the load size and the length of the intended route. Like most things, pilot car requirements vary from state to state. Some states require training, licensing, or certification to operate as an escort vehicle or pilot car, while others require law enforcement to escort an oversized load.

Pilot and escort vehicles play an important role in controlling traffic flow around the load, and may be required to display conspicuity devices, signs, or warning lights while in transit. For example, extremely tall loads may require the lead pilot vehicle to use a height pole. The poles assist the pilot car driver gauge proper overhead clearance as they travel along the route.

Conclusion

Transportation of oversized loads is essential to interstate commerce. With proper planning, preclearance, and permitting, it can be done safely and efficiently across the web of federal, state, and local roads, bridges, and tunnels. Care must be taken at the outset to ensure that the size and weight of the truck or combination complies with applicable federal, state, and local rules and regulations.

CHAPTER 22
Vocational Trucking

Jordan M. Jones, Esq.

Definition of Vocational Trucking

Vocational trucking refers to the use of trucks for specific, job-related tasks other than long-distance freight hauling. These trucks can be designed or modified for the specific task. This includes activities like construction, waste collection, utility work, and local deliveries. Basically, it's about trucks designed and used for specific types of work, usually within a local area or specific industry. These vehicles usually include task-specific equipment to perform a job beyond mere transportation.

Vocational trucking encompasses a variety of specialized vehicles designed for specific job-related tasks. This includes common trucks we see all the time, such as dump trucks, cement mixers, garbage trucks, fire trucks, snowplows, street sweepers, and wreckers. There are also less common specialized trucks like tankers, electrical utility vehicles, aerial lift trucks, and many, many others. Each of these vehicles is uniquely built or modified to efficiently perform their designated vocational tasks.

Training and Knowledge Requirements for Vocational Trucks

The Federal Motor Carrier Safety Regulations (FMCSRs) mandate specific training requirements for commercial truck drivers. According to 49 C.F.R. § 390.3(e)(2), and as adopted by the legislature in most states, trucking companies are obligated to train their employees about compliance with the trucking regulations. Under § 383.111(a)[1] of the regulations, commercial drivers must be knowledgeable in 20 key areas related to safe truck operation. This includes understanding the safety control systems and characteristics of their specific

1. Unless otherwise noted, citations in this chapter are to the Federal Motor Carrier Safety Regulations, found in C.F.R. Title 49.

vehicle.[2] This regulation is often implicated in vocational trucking cases, as there are unique aspects to the vehicles that are simply not implicated when dealing with an "ordinary" semi-truck. These include things like vehicle dynamics, vehicle dimensions, and the safe operation of the specialty vocational equipment with which these vehicles are equipped.

Beyond the aspects of their specific vocational vehicles, operators of these trucks must also be trained and have knowledge in other key areas that apply to all trucks more generally, including things like proper visual search,[3] speed management,[4] space management,[5] extreme driving conditions,[6] hazard perception[7] (§ 383.111(a)(13)), emergency maneuvers,[8] and more.

Standard of Care for Operating Vocational Trucks

Like any negligence case, proving or defending a case begins with establishing the standard of care, and then applying the facts of the case to that standard. In most trucking cases, that standard of care is going to largely come from the applicable state's definition of negligence, but sometimes, in some states, from the FMCSRs and the Commercial Driver's License (CDL) Manual. This is not necessarily the case in specialized vocational trucking cases. In these more specialized cases, we are going to look at, and draw heavily from, the industry custom and practice, as these niche vocational vehicles are generally not addressed in detail by the FMCSRs or applicable CDL Manual.

Role of the CDL Manual

Federal law, in § 383.131(a), requires that the individual states "provide an FMCSA pre-approved driver information manual" to a CDL applicant. The "manual must be comparable to the American Association of Motor Vehicle Administrators' (AAMVA) . . . Model Commercial Driver Manual."[9] Accordingly, every state has a free, publicly available CDL Manual, available from the Secretary of State or Department of Motor Vehicles. While the CDL Manual does not address vocational trucking specifically, it does address general safe driving for all commercial motor vehicles (CMVs), including vocational trucks.

The role of the CDL Manual in vocational trucking cases is usually limited to those more generic rules that apply to all trucking cases. For example, if a truck driver was not properly managing space or speed, in addition to the vocational aspects of the case, the CDL Manual will be implicated. We generally do not find standards and rules specific to vocational trucks in the CDL Manual.

2. 49 C.F.R. § 383.111(a)(3)(i).
3. *Id.* § 383.111(a)(7).
4. *Id.* § 383.111(a)(9).
5. *Id.* § 383.111(a)(10).
6. *Id.* § 383.111(a)(12).
7. *Id.* § 383.111(a)(13).
8. *Id.* § 383.111(a)(14).
9. *Id.* § 383.131(a).

Industry Custom and Practice

Because the standard of reasonableness in most jurisdictions depends upon the circumstances, it is important to recognize that the vocational trucking crash case involves the standard of care that a reasonable person would apply if driving the particular type of vocational truck at the time and place of the crash. The vast majority of safe operation characteristics in vocational trucking cases are going to be found in industry-specific resources and through experts in the field. Professional associations and regulatory bodies are common across various industries, including those active in vocational trucking. These organizations, composed of industry professionals, often develop and publish safety and training materials. These resources are created based on industry research and experience and are generally available to their members and made available to the public. These associations also host industry conferences and presentations that focus on safety and training issues relevant to their field, which can be obtained and relied upon in litigation.

For legal professionals handling vocational trucking cases, these materials are invaluable. They provide comprehensive information that fills in the gaps left by the FMCSRs and the CDL Manual in areas specific to vocational trucking. Obtaining these materials is crucial, as they can be instrumental in building a case, whether representing an injured plaintiff or defending a trucking company and driver. Industry experts often possess these resources, but they can also be ordered online, often without requiring membership in the respective association. These materials are the benchmark to assess the knowledge and actions of vocational drivers. They help determine whether a driver acted appropriately and followed the necessary procedures, making them critical for proving or defending legal cases involving vocational trucking.

The admissibility of these industry materials is complicated, opposed by defendants, and cannot be overlooked. Statements contained in these industry materials are generally considered hearsay. However, statements in a learned treatise, periodical, or pamphlet may be read into evidence if "the statement is called to the attention of an expert witness on cross-examination or relied on by the expert on direct examination," and the publication is established as a reliable authority by an expert's admission or testimony.[10] As you prepare for trial, make sure that an expert in the case has acknowledged or testified that the materials you are relying on are a reliable authority in the vocational area.

Experts in the field can provide insights into what constitutes typical practices in vocational trucking, helping the court or jury understand the expected standards in the context of the case. They will often rely upon and incorporate the aforementioned industry publications and materials in formulating their opinions and articulating the industry custom and practice to explain what reasonable truck drivers do under the circumstances. These materials can provide additional weight to their opinions by showing that their views are consistent with widely accepted standards in vocational trucking, and also support their opinions against any *Daubert* challenge. The experts draw upon their practical

---

10. Rule 803(18)(a)–(b) of the Federal Rules of Evidence.

experience in the industry, in conjunction with industry publications, to flush out the standard of care.

Experts Witnesses in Vocational Trucking Cases

Selection of experts is critical. It's important to choose experts with specific knowledge and experience in the specific field of vocational trucking. This might include former drivers who operated these vehicles, safety managers, association presidents, and so on. The expert's background should be relevant to the specific aspect of trucking at issue in the case. An expert cement truck driver might know little or nothing about operating a milk tanker truck, and vice versa, so choosing one with the right qualifications is necessary. A general trucking expert may not be sufficient to assist in a vocational trucking case.

A strong expert can explain why certain practices are followed in the industry and how they relate to safety and efficiency. This helps the court or jury understand the rationale behind these practices and why deviating from them could be considered negligent. This is especially important because, many times, the exercise of reasonableness in driving a vocational vehicle is contrary to our common sense, or even the CDL Manual. For example, the CDL Manual directs truck drivers to steer to the right to avoid an imminent crash. But in a cement mixer, steering to the right at speed is highly likely to result in a rollover—which often is much worse.

It's also wise to consider if an expert has experience training. Was the expert a driver trainer for the vocational vehicle? Did the expert design training programs that were used in the industry? Does the expert provide private consulting to companies to help them design and implement training? Although closely related, driving the vocational vehicle and training one to drive it are two different things. Although an expert may be qualified to discuss how to safely drive, the expert may not necessarily be qualified to testify regarding training protocols for a reasonably prudent company. In practice, the two qualifications typically go hand-in-hand. But it is something to consider.

But beyond the vehicles themselves, it's important to involve experts to explain various aspects of litigation that are implicated when dealing with these vocational trucks. For example, conspicuity arises frequently in vocational truck wrecks. Conspicuity, or the visibility of a truck to other road users, is a crucial aspect of road safety. Despite the large size of vocational trucks, there are numerous instances where other drivers fail to see them due to the environment, leading to serious accidents. This can occur for various reasons, including poor lighting, the truck's color blending with the background, or simply the unique shape and configuration of the vehicle, such as a tow truck at night.

Human factors experts play a vital role in exploring and explaining why conspicuity is a recurring issue. They can analyze how drivers perceive their environment and how visual cues are processed, particularly in low-light conditions or in complex driving scenarios. These experts can also evaluate the effectiveness of existing visibility aids, such as reflective tape, lights, and flags, in any particular case.[11] They can also explain our attention. These experts can explain why it's not "natural" for drivers to account for overhead obstacles. Driving is an activity that requires constant attention to what is directly in front of the vehicle, including other cars, pedestrians, and road conditions. This forward-focused attention can make it easy to overlook potential hazards above, especially in the case of trucks with high loads like a tow truck.

A human factors expert can explain how these considerations and actions are against what we naturally do, which further highlights the need for strong training programs. These experts can also explain why a vehicle was perceptible, and why it should have been visible to other roadway users. Do not forget to account for those factors beyond the vehicle itself when consulting experts in a litigated case.

Environmental Factors and Operating Vocational Trucks

Vocational trucks are distinct not only in their equipment but also in the diverse environments they operate in, contrasting with semi-trucks, which mainly travel on open highways. Vocational trucks navigate a variety of settings including highways, construction sites, and dense urban areas. This diversity requires a careful consideration of both the equipment and its operating environment. Understanding this helps in identifying the unique hazards associated with using such equipment and in determining the appropriate standard of care. This approach is essential for a comprehensive understanding of the risks and responsibilities in vocational trucking.

Accounting for Unique Aspects of the Operating Environment

Good industry materials and good vocational trucking experts contemplate the environment in which vocational equipment is to be predominantly used. When preparing your case, brainstorm independently about what unique challenges the environment may present. Then, obtain and consult industry publications to identify unique environmental challenges. Finally, consult with your retained expert to identify any remaining environmental challenges, as well has the industry standard for accounting for such environmental hazards.

For example, dump trucks elevate the bed of the truck high into the air and operate predominantly on construction sites. This presents a unique and extremely dangerous hazard for striking overhead powerlines. By contrast, an ordinary semi-truck typically is not on a construction site, and rarely if ever is at risk of striking overhead powerlines. Another example is garbage trucks backing up in heavily populated urban areas. While garbage trucks frequently back up in busy areas with high pedestrian traffic, a semi-truck should rarely (if ever) be backing up in a busy pedestrian area. These unique environmental hazards need to be addressed up front. Identifying these unique hazards drives at

11. Refer to the chapter in this book about conspicuity written by human factors expert Kevin Rider.

duty and foreseeability and it is critical to understand these unique challenges when proving or defending your case.

After Market Modifications to Accommodate the Environment

In vocational truck cases, aftermarket modifications play a crucial role in safety and compliance. Vocational trucks face unique hazards due to the environments in which they operate, inherent risks in the design of the vehicles, or a unique risk created by the two in conjunction. Aftermarket modifications, aimed at mitigating these dangers, can significantly alter a vehicle's operation and safety profile. Think about whether aftermarket solutions are available to mitigate these unique risks. And, if so, are these solutions widely available and feasible to implement? And, have these solutions been widely adopted in the industry? There may be a products liability claim in addition to a negligence claim.

For instance, garbage trucks, notorious for their large blind spots while operating in areas with heavy foot traffic, may be equipped with crossover mirrors and backup cameras to enhance the truck driver's visibility and eliminate blind spots. The widespread adoption of such aftermarket solutions in the industry is a critical point of investigation, often explored through expert witness consultation or industry publications.

In litigation, the presence or absence of these modifications on a company's trucks can be pivotal. If a company has implemented these safety enhancements, it could support an argument of compliance with the standard of care, indicating reasonable prudence in mitigating known industry risks. Conversely, the absence of such modifications might be viewed as falling below the industry's standard of care, potentially indicating negligence. This aspect of vocational trucking litigation underscores the importance of thorough examination of vehicle modifications and their alignment with industry practices.

Common Types of Vocational Trucks

Wreckers

Tow trucks play a crucial role in keeping roadways clear by removing disabled or illegally parked vehicles. However, the operation of tow trucks involves unique challenges and responsibilities that distinguish them from other commercial vehicles. These challenges arise from the nature of the work, the equipment used, and the regulatory environment governing tow truck operations. This section of this chapter explores the key considerations and best practices that tow truck operators must follow to ensure safety and compliance with the law.

One of the primary concerns when operating a tow truck is the height of the equipment, particularly when it is carrying a vehicle. Tow trucks are susceptible to overhead strikes, which can occur when the truck or the vehicle it is towing comes into contact with low bridges, electrical wires, or other overhead obstructions. This risk is exacerbated by the varying heights of different vehicles and the additional height added by towing equipment. Tow truck operators must be acutely aware of their surroundings and the height of their loads to avoid these potentially dangerous collisions.

Tow trucks are often called to assist disabled vehicles, which means they frequently operate in high-risk environments, such as busy roadways or accident scenes. In these situations, it is critically important to warn other road users of the tow truck's presence. The FMCSRs mandate that tow truck operators must put out reflective triangles or other warning devices to alert oncoming traffic. According to § 392.22, these triangles must be placed as soon as safely possible but no later than 10 minutes after the tow truck stops. Proper placement and timely deployment of these warning devices are essential to preventing secondary accidents and ensuring the safety of both the tow truck operator and other road users. This rule applies to tow truck drivers and must be observed.

Tow trucks are also subject to specific regulations that address their unique operational needs. One such regulation is § 393.71, which governs various aspects of tow truck operations, including equipment standards and safety practices. Given the distinctive shape and configuration of tow trucks, especially during nighttime operations, conspicuity—how visible the vehicle and its load are to others—becomes a critical issue. Many states require the use of flags or other visual markers on the equipment or the vehicle being towed to enhance visibility. It is essential for tow truck operators to be familiar with these state-specific requirements and ensure they are in compliance. Under federal law,[12] drivers are required to comply with all applicable state laws, making it imperative that tow truck operators stay informed about the regulations in the areas where they operate.

The CDL Manual does not provide specific guidance for tow truck operations, leaving a gap that must be filled by industry sources. Organizations such as the Towing and Recovery Association of America (TRAA) produce excellent training materials and guidelines that help tow truck operators understand industry best practices. These resources are invaluable for ensuring that operators are trained to handle the unique challenges of their work safely and effectively. By adhering to the standards and recommendations set forth by industry bodies like the TRAA, tow truck operators can better navigate the complexities of their job and maintain compliance with both federal and state regulations.

Operating a tow truck involves a range of special considerations that require a thorough understanding of both the risks and the regulatory requirements. From managing the height of towed vehicles to ensuring visibility in challenging conditions, tow truck operators must be vigilant and well informed to operate safely.

Street Sweepers

Street sweepers, operating in populated urban areas, present unique hazards due to dust creation and their slow-moving nature. According to FMCSA guidance, street sweepers are considered CMVs if they exceed 10,000 lbs. and

12. 49 C.F.R. § 392.2.

operate interstate. If the weight exceeds 26,000 lbs., a CDL is required. There are two types of sweepers: mechanical (more common) and vacuum. Mechanical sweepers use a main broom and curb broom to sweep debris onto a conveyor belt, which moves it into a containment hopper. The system uses water to absorb and mitigate dust creation, thereby reducing visibility hazards.

Again, drivers must be knowledgeable about their vehicle's specific operating characteristics, as per § 383.111(a)(3)(i). This includes knowing how to properly manage traffic around slow-moving sweepers, and properly maintain the water levels in the sweeper to mitigate dust.

Resources and standards for safe operation, including dust mitigation and training guidelines, are provided by organizations like the North American Power Sweeping Association (NAPSA), the World Sweeping Association, and Hard Hat Training. Additionally, street sweeper schools certify operators and managers. Finally, the operational guidelines from equipment manufacturers and contract language detailing specific dust mitigation procedures are also crucial for ensuring safe and compliant operation.

Documents are especially important in sweeper litigation. Often there will be a contractual duty to mitigate dust, or to manage traffic. The procedures for doing so are sometimes included in the contract. Understanding how the driver was trained regarding the slow-moving vehicle hazard created by sweepers, and dust mitigation, as well as what measures the company had in place to abate those hazards, is crucial to pursuing and defending street sweeper cases.

Garbage Trucks

Garbage trucks operate in dynamic urban environments, where they encounter dense pedestrian and vehicle traffic. Running the garbage route involves frequent stopping, backing up, and numerous turns. The design of these trucks inherently includes significant blind spots, especially directly behind the vehicle and under the cab doors. These blind spots, coupled with the truck's frequent stopping, backing, and turning, significantly increase the risk of incidents with pedestrians, bicyclists, and other vehicles. This is a known risk in the industry.

The refuse industry is a sterling example of aftermarket modifications. To mitigate operational risks, the industry has widely adopted various safety modifications. Most garbage trucks are equipped with backup cameras, effectively eliminating the blind spot behind the truck. Crossover mirrors are another common addition, designed to provide visibility in areas under the cab doors where pedestrians, children, or pets, might be present after making a brief stop. Additionally, these trucks often feature loud, audible tones during backing up to alert nearby pedestrians and avoid conflicts. Many garbage truck operators also install aftermarket "light bars," which feature oscillating or flashing lights for added conspicuity.

Another crucial aspect of safety is the design of the garbage truck routes. The garbage companies are responsible for planning these routes, and safety considerations should be paramount. It's important to assess the efficiency and safety of these routes, looking for any unnecessary backing, wide turning, or other maneuvers that could increase the risk of accidents. When looking at the route itself, consider whether there was a safer reasonable alternative. Thoughtful route planning can significantly reduce the potential for dangerous situations, making it a key element in the safe operation of garbage trucks.

Working closely with the appropriate expert, consider what industry solutions are widely adopted, versus what was being used by the garbage truck company in your case. Also, focus on the training that was provided to the garbage truck driver. Was the driver made aware of the high potential for traffic conflicts in urban environments? Was the driver trained to check the crossover mirrors before moving after each traffic stop? Was the truck driver trained to keep the backup camera lens clean and free of debris to maintain good visibility? These considerations are critical in pursuing or defending a garbage truck case.

Snow Removal Vehicles

Snow removal equipment, such as snowplows, presents a unique set of challenges that differ significantly from other commercial vehicles. Operating in challenging weather conditions, these vehicles are tasked with the critical job of keeping roadways clear and safe during winter storms. However, the very nature of their work—often conducted in poor visibility and on snow-covered roads—creates a host of operational and safety challenges that demand specialized knowledge and adherence to industry best practices.

A study by the Virginia Tech Transportation Institute found that the majority of snowplow crashes involve collisions with fixed objects. This statistic underscores the need for specialized training and heightened awareness among snowplow operators, as these accidents often occur under challenging conditions where hazards may be concealed by snow.

While the CDL Manual provides comprehensive guidance for many types of commercial vehicles, it does not offer specific best practices for snow removal equipment. As a result, operators and supervisors must turn to industry-specific resources for guidance. One of the most prominent bodies in this field is the Clear Roads Research Program, which conducts extensive research on the safe operation of snow removal equipment and publishes its findings for the industry. In addition to research, Clear Roads offers training programs for both drivers and supervisors, helping to fill the gap left by the CDL Manual.

Clear Roads emphasizes the importance of identifying hazards. Unplowed snow can easily conceal objects, intersecting roadways, or other potential dangers. To address this, the industry emphasizes constantly scanning the roadway and being acutely aware of where the plow is tracking. Snowplow drivers must be able to identify potential conflicts with the plow and react accordingly to avoid accidents. The industry emphasizes SIPDE, an acronym for "Scan, Identify hazards, Predict if those hazards are a threat, Decide on a plan, and Execute." This method encourages a systematic approach to hazard management, which is particularly important in the ever-changing and often unpredictable conditions faced by snowplow operators. This stacks nicely with the requirements in the CDL Manual requiring drivers to look 12 to 15 seconds ahead of their vehicle (AAMVA Model CDL Manual § 2.4.1) and to always have a plan.[13] Because of reduced visibility in snow conditions, snowplow operators must adjust their speed to avoid collisions with vehicles and other objects on the road.

Another challenge faced by snowplow operators is maintaining their lane position on snow-covered roads where lane markings may be obscured. Remember, the whole reason they are out there is to clear the road off. The industry recommends that drivers stay inside the fog line to avoid running off the road or getting stuck on a soft shoulder, and also recommends using delineator posts to mark known hazards and road edges for future reference if it is safe to do so. This practice can help operators avoid dangerous areas in subsequent passes. Additionally, Clear Roads advocates for the creation of a database of known hazards. This database serves as a valuable tool for operators to review and build institutional knowledge about specific risks in their areas of operation, ultimately contributing to safer snow removal practices.

Many snowplows are classified as commercial vehicles and are subject to the FMCSRs. Specifically § 392.14, will apply virtually any time a snowplow is out on the road. This regulation requires drivers to use "extreme caution" when operating in adverse conditions that affect visibility or traction—conditions that are commonplace for snowplow operators.[14] Clear Roads recommends that snowplows should operate according to the conditions but advises that in no event should they exceed 30 miles per hour when plowing.

Backing accidents are a common issue in snowplow operations due to the equipment that extends behind the vehicle, such as a "spinner" or chute, or sometimes a small trailer with lights to alert other drivers. These challenges are exacerbated by the poor visibility that is inherent to operating a snowplow. To mitigate these risks, industry bodies recommend the use of GOAL (Get Out And Look) or using a spotter whenever possible. This advice is echoed in the CDL Manual, which emphasizes the importance of using a helper when backing up.[15]

Finally, don't forget about fatigue. Fatigue is a significant factor and should not be overlooked. According to the Virginia Tech study, between 75 and 80 percent of all snowplow drivers report feeling fatigued during a shift. This is particularly concerning as these drivers often work during the early morning hours when the body's natural inclination is to sleep. Additionally, 28 percent of snowplow drivers report working shifts longer than 12 hours, further increasing the risk of fatigue-related incidents.

Even if a snowplow driver is not subject to hours-of-service regulations, or is otherwise in compliance with them, there is a separate rule under § 392.3 that addresses fatigued driving. This regulation mandates that drivers must stop driving if their ability to operate safely is impaired or likely to be impaired by fatigue. This is separate and distinct from any hours-of-service rule. The test

13. AAMVA Model CDL Manual § 2.8.4.

14. Section 392.14 is important in all hazardous-weather truck crash cases. Defendants will seek to prevent testimony or evidence concerning it. See the chapter by Morgan Adams in this book in which he discusses this section.

15. AAMVA Model CDL Manual § 2.2.4.

is simply how the driver is feeling—not necessarily where the driver is in that driver's total hours of service. Ensuring compliance with this regulation is essential for the safety of both the driver and the public.

Operating snow removal equipment requires a deep understanding of the challenges posed by driving in winter conditions, and observance of industry best practices. With limited guidance available in the CDL Manual, it is imperative that companies and government agencies operating snowplows have strong training and supervision regimens in place. These training programs will be a source of discovery in snowplow crash litigation.

Tankers

Tanker trucks are distinct not only in their design and operation but also in the legal and regulatory requirements that govern their use. One of the most significant differences between tanker trucks and standard semi-trucks lies in the nature of the loads they carry. Unlike a static load in a dry van or flatbed, the liquid load in a tanker is dynamic and constantly in motion. This movement, known as surge, can greatly affect the handling of the vehicle. Surge occurs when a tanker is partially filled, causing the liquid to shift back and forth as the truck accelerates or decelerates. This movement can push the truck in the direction of the wave, which can be particularly hazardous on slippery surfaces like ice. For example, a stopped truck could be pushed into an intersection by the force of the moving liquid. The surge characteristics of a tanker vary depending on whether any surge-reduction devices are installed in the tanker—which, in turn, depends on the kinds of liquids carried in the tanker. A milk tanker may be more prone to surge than a gas tanker because of the different requirements for the interiors of each such tanker.

The differences between tankers and standard semi-trucks start with the qualification process for drivers. While many truck driving qualifications allow employers to rely on a copy of the CDL in lieu of a road test, this is not the case for tanker drivers. According to § 391.33(a)(1), employers are required to conduct a road test for any driver who will be operating a tanker. This additional step ensures that the driver is not only qualified but also capable of handling the unique challenges posed by driving a tanker.

Driving tankers is governed by an entire section of the CDL Manual—Section 8—dedicated specifically to the nuances of operating these vehicles. Among the many considerations is the higher center of gravity that tankers possess, which makes them more prone to rollovers. This is particularly important when navigating curves or turns, where even adhering to posted speed limits may not be sufficient to prevent an overturn.[16]

Drivers must also be proficient in managing the effects of surge.[17] The CDL Manual offers specific instructions on how to control surge, drive around curves, and adjust stopping distances when operating a tanker.[18] Proper training

---

16. *Id* § 8.2.1.
17. *Id.* § 8.2.2.
18. *Id* § 8.3.

in these specific areas is required. Remember, truckers must be trained regarding the specific characteristics of the type of truck they drive.[19]

Vehicle inspections for tanker trucks are more complex than those for standard trucks. Tankers are equipped with specialized equipment that requires careful inspection. This includes checking for leaks, inspecting vapor recovery kits, ensuring the proper functioning of grounding and bonding cables, and verifying that emergency shutoffs are in working order. These checks are vital for maintaining the safety of the vehicle, the driver, and the public.

Finally, there is significant intersection between tankers and hazardous materials. Tankers are frequently used to transport hazardous materials (hazmats), which introduces another layer of complexity and regulation. Hazmats are inherently dangerous and require additional attention and considerations that do not apply to standard loads. Under 49 C.F.R. § 172.300, "each person who offers hazardous material for transportation" (e.g., the shipper) is responsible for marking these materials accordingly. The compounds that must be marked hazardous accordingly are generally found in 40 C.F.R. § 302.4.[20] However, the CDL Manual imposes a duty on the driver to ensure that the shipper has properly identified, marked, and labeled the materials.[21] Moreover, when transporting hazardous materials in a tanker, all valves must be closed before moving the truck, even if it's only being moved a short distance within a yard.[22] There are also stringent parking regulations, especially for explosive hazmats. These regulations dictate that such materials must be parked at specific distances from the road, the vehicle cannot be left unattended, and in the event of a breakdown, the use of flares is strictly prohibited; instead, triangles must be used. Transporting hazardous materials often involves route restrictions that require special permits, further underscoring the need for specialized knowledge and careful planning when operating tankers in these scenarios.

Cement Mixers

Transporting ready-mixed concrete presents a unique challenge for mixer drivers due to the high center of gravity of the vehicle. The load is carried up above the frame of the truck. Further, because the concrete is susceptible to hardening, it has to be constantly moved—or "agitated"—while in transit so that it does not set. This is done by rotating the drum clockwise, which is known as "charging" the drum. But when the drum is charging, because the concrete is thick, it builds up on the inside of the drum. This phenomenon makes the driver side the "heavy side," of the truck, offsetting the center of gravity and making the vehicle exceptionally susceptible to rolling—especially when making right-hand turns.

19. 49 C.F.R. § 383.111(a)(3)(i).

20. *See also* 49 C.F.R. §§ 172.101–172.102.

21. AAMVA Model CDL Manual § 9.2.3. See the chapter in this book by D.J. Young about hazardous materials.

22. AAMVA Model CDL Manual § 9.5.2.

The consistency of the concrete (how thick it is) is called its "slump." The higher the slump is, the thicker and heavier the concrete is. And the thicker it is, the more it builds up on the inside of the drum as it charges. According to some industry safety training documents, when the drum is charging, it concentrates up to 40,000 lbs. of the load on the left side of the truck. When mixers are turning (especially to the right) or driving on soft road edges, the offset weight combined with the high center of gravity make cement mixers particularly prone to tipping. While truck rollovers can occur in any truck, the inherent rollover danger associated with cement mixers is much more prevalent.

Cement mixer rollovers are very common. They are so common that an industry body actually commissioned a study on mixer rollovers in 2017. The CDL Manual is entirely silent as to operating a cement mixer specifically. Instead, safety rules for cement mixers are largely based on industry custom and practice, as well as materials provided by industry organizations such as the National Ready Mixed Concrete Association (NRMCA), Titan America, and others. The NRMCA produces a range of resources and materials to help educate drivers and promote safe driving practices for cement mixer operators. For instance, the NRMCA publishes monthly safety bulletins that contain information on topics such as driver fatigue, defensive driving techniques, and the dangers of turning at speed.

The NRMCA publishes an entire rollover prevention training program that is designed to educate drivers on the specific causes of mixer rollovers, and how to mitigate the risks. The program covers topics such as navigating job sites and urban driving environments, braking techniques, and maneuvering on uneven terrain. It is a series of real-life case studies that breaks down what happened, the root cause of the rollover, and what the mixer driver should have done differently to avoid the catastrophe. The program is a series of PowerPoint slides and is accompanied by a trainer's manual, which is intended to be read as the trainer progresses through the materials.

The NRMCA also publishes a special driver's manual—the Mixer Truck Driver's Manual (Mixer Manual)—which was created to provide general background information for the concrete mixer driver, and specifically addresses safe operations of a ready mixed concrete truck. This driver's manual covers those unique areas that the state CDL Manual does not. This should be a staple in any safe company's training regimen. It covers everything from maintenance and cleaning to safely operating the chute to safe driving. The Mixer Manual emphasizes defensive driving and highlights the importance of anticipating hazards and how to respond appropriately.

CHAPTER 23

Truck Driver Fatigue: A Primer

Jeffrey A. Burns, Esq.

Background

The connection between over-the-road trucking and driver fatigue is not new. For as long as drivers have had to make certain delivery times and shippers have paid to have their products delivered by truck, drivers have been falling asleep at the wheel. As early as 1935, the National Safety Council issued its report on the problem, "Too Long at the Wheel."[1] Since then, our society has developed into a 24-hour society, and fatigue, in general, has become a broad societal problem. The National Sleep Foundation's annual "Sleep in America" poll in 2013 showed, on average, Americans feel daytime sleepiness three times a week, while more than one-third of adults suffer from daytime sleepiness at least half the week or more, and that sleepiness interferes with their activities. Given the demands of the job, this has to be worse for truck drivers. "Just-in-time" delivery and "rolling warehouse logistics" have made trucking truly a round-the-clock endeavor, not to mention the huge increase in "next day delivery" on internet sales. Yet, even today, certain trucking groups downplay driver fatigue and portray it as a relatively minor problem, with some continuing to cite the industry's old and discredited position that fatigue plays a role in less than 2 percent of fatal truck crashes.[2]

The Large Truck Crash Causation Study (LTCCS) put the prevalence of fatigue-related crashes in the range of 13 percent, but did not have a uniform or generally accepted protocol across all cases to determine the extent to which

1. Nat'l Safety Council, Too Long at the Wheel—A Study of Exhaustion and Drowsiness as They Affect Traffic Accidents (1935).

2. This position cites the 2002 study *Estimates of the Prevalence and Risk of Fatigue in Fatal Accidents Involving Medium and Heavy Trucks*, by Kenneth L. Campbell, which internally admits that "the overall proportion [of fatigue involvement] in fatal accidents . . . underestimates the true value." *See also* CMV Driver Fatigue, Long Term Health and Highway Safety, National Library of Medicine, Aug. 12, 2016.

fatigue had been a factor.[3] The LTCCS also put significant separate percentages on driver errors that are commonly found in fatigued drivers, including but not limited to failure to perceive or react to hazards, leaving the travel lane, performance and response errors, inattention, and following too closely, which combined accounted for more than 80 percent of crashes in the study. The world's leading sleep experts agree that fatigue is the largest identifiable and preventable cause of accidents in the transportation operation. They further point to official underestimation of the problem as part of the problem.[4]

The year 1995 appears to have been the watershed year for taking driver fatigue seriously in trucking. In that year, Secretary of Transportation, Federico Pena, called for the first National Truck and Bus Safety Summit, to be held in Kansas City, Missouri. Trucking industry representatives met with researchers, safety advocates, and government representatives, with the goal of developing a list of the most pressing safety issues facing the trucking industry. The list would be used to guide research, regulation, and training efforts to try to reduce truck crashes, fatalities, and injuries. After several days of meetings, sessions, workshops, and speeches, the summit participants developed a list of 17 safety issues facing the trucking industry and ranked them in priority order. Number one on the list was driver fatigue. However, almost immediately that number was buried at the Office of Motor Carriers (the predecessor to FMCSA), and the listing of "driver fatigue" was relegated to be simply a subcategory under "Driver Health and Wellness." Nonetheless, in the years following, more emphasis has been put on the fatigue issue: fatigue training videos have been offered by all major industry training suppliers, train-the-trainer sessions have been developed, dozens if not hundreds of research projects have been undertaken, and technological advancements have given us gadgets and algorithms to help detect when a driver might be getting too tired to drive safely.

In spite of the additional focus and attention on the issue, and in spite of the Department of Transportation's announced 1999 goal of reducing truck-crash fatalities by 50 percent in ten years (which disappeared almost immediately without notice or announcement), we still have no litmus test or generally accepted protocol to determine whether a driver was fatigued when he or she has been involved in a crash. We are now suffering more than 6,000 fatalities a year due to truck crashes in the United States, and the numbers have been steadily increasing. We still have no solid statistics regarding how many or what percentage of truck crashes are caused or contributed to by driver fatigue, because of lack of documentation and poor investigation into the role of fatigue in crashes (partly because there is no "breathalyzer" or other easily administered test after a crash to determine a driver's fatigue level). Figures as low as

3. https://www.fmcsa.dot.gov/safety/research-and-analysis/large-truck-crash-causation-study-analysis-brief.

4. Consensus Statement: Fatigue and Accidents in Transportation Operations (Blackwell Publishing 2000).

2 percent[5] and as high as 58 percent[6] of particular types of crashes have been given. The fact of the matter is that driver fatigue is a significant cause of losses in the trucking industry and should be investigated as a possible factor in every catastrophic truck crash case.

Fatigue and the Fatigue Regulations

The investigation into whether fatigue played a part in a particular crash will depend upon the type of crash and the information available. What is considered by some to be the classic "fall asleep" case involves a crash with little or no braking with one vehicle running into another vehicle or object (or running straight off the road when the road turns) when there was clear visibility and no obstructions to the driver's view. Not all fatigue-related crashes, however, share these characteristics. A driver does not need to fall asleep to have his or her driving impaired by fatigue. Fatigue impairs drivers in much the same way that alcohol intoxication does: a driver's ability to perceive and react becomes increasingly diminished as the level of fatigue increases. Indeed, even "relatively moderate levels of fatigue impair performance to an extent equivalent to or greater than is currently acceptable for alcohol intoxication."[7]

49 C.F.R. section 392.3 prohibits a driver from operating a commercial motor vehicle while his or her ability to operate the vehicle safely is so impaired (or likely to become impaired) due to fatigue (or illness or any other reason) as to make it unsafe for the driver to begin or continue to operate the vehicle. However, the regulation *also* prohibits a motor carrier from requiring *or permitting* the driver to operate the commercial vehicle under such conditions. Nonetheless, the FMCSA has not interpreted this regulation to mean what it says. During compliance reviews, much attention is paid to a motor carrier's attention to auditing logs and hours of service, but there is no current requirement (other than through a fair reading of section 392.3) for a motor carrier to have in place a fatigue management program that effectively prohibits its drivers from driving fatigued. Take for example, the Walmart/Tracey Morgan crash. It was reported that, at the time of the crash, the truck driver had been awake for more than 25 hours because, before going on-duty driving the truck, he had driven many hours from his home to his assigned starting truck terminal. That is a clear example of an operator whose ability was likely to become impaired by fatigue before the end of his assigned trip. However, the company's failure to have in place a fatigue management program was not focused on by the press (or from news accounts, by the plaintiffs' lawyers) or by FMCSA. It is clear that a driver can be legally compliant with the hours-of-service regulations while, at the same time, being so fatigued the driver is an "accident waiting to happen."

---

5. Kenneth L. Campbell, Estimates of the Prevalence and Risk of Fatigue in Fatal Accidents Involving Medium and Heavy Trucks from the 1991–2002 TIFA Files (2005) (J.A. 1712).

6. Nat'l Transportation Safety Board, Factors That Affect Fatigue in Heavy Truck Accidents, NTSB Number SS-95/01.

7. Dawson & Reid, *Fatigue, Alcohol and Performance Impairment*, Nature 288 (July–Aug. 1997).

Despite this reality, most motor carriers still have no effective fatigue management program in place. This is true even though they can review the contents of the North American Fatigue Management Program (NAFMP),[8] which is fairly comprehensive, and could be used to save hundreds if not thousands of lives, at no cost.

When what we know about fatigue is superimposed over what we know about the economics of the trucking industry since it was deregulated in 1980,[9] it becomes clear that our highways are literally full of "accidents waiting to happen." Accordingly, an evaluation of a crash requires an understanding of the interplay among some or all of the following: the economics of the industry, how the crash occurred, the driver's sleep/wake pattern in the days preceding the crash, time on task, time of day, the driver's training, the driver's health, company policies, and the fundamentals of the science of sleep.

Within the confines of this chapter it is not possible to identify and explore every factor necessary to determine whether driver fatigue caused or contributed to a crash. Each case will bring its own individual facts that will require its own approach. The basics of the science of sleep, against which the facts may be analyzed, however, can be stated and are set forth next.

The Science of Sleep: The Basics

Most of what we know about the science of sleep has been developed in the last 50 years. Although we continue to learn more every year, what we have learned so far indicates that a person's need for sleep grows in direct proportion to that person's lack of sleep (sleep debt) and that, ultimately, sleep is the only safe countermeasure for fatigue.

What Is Sleep?

It has been said that the fundamental essence of sleep in contrast to wakefulness (in which we "perceive and are conscience of the external world") is a

> [D]isengagement from the outer world, accompanied by an engagement with the inner world and the dream world. . . . This disengagement from the outer world is an active process in which sensory input is blocked or modified to effect a complete perceptual shutdown; to all intents and purposes, we are blind and deaf. Even if our eyelids are taped open during sleep, we do not see. We know that signals are received by the retina, transmitted to the thalamus and to the visual cortex; likewise, sound is processed by the auditory system. Yet, we have no idea why, the second before sleep descends, we see an object in the real world, are conscience of it, perceive it; while the seconds afterwards, we are subjectively blind and do not see it at all. Nor can we explain why, during

8. https://nafmp.org/.
9. Michael Belzer, Sweatshops on Wheels (Oxford Univ. Press 2000).

> REM [rapid eye movement] sleep stimuli may enter the brain to be "misperceived" in strange and interesting ways.[10]

This definition, however, does not really "define" sleep, but rather describes it. The description implies that the brain requires rest. This definition, however, is much too simple in that it appears to define sleep as simply being "not awake." Sleep, however, is more complex and involves different stages.

The Stages of Sleep

A healthy person first drops off into non REM sleep, which has four successively deeper stages. Non-REM sleep is regularly broken by a period of REM sleep, the characteristics of which are similar to the patterns of alert wakefulness, with the key exception that the body is immobilized.[11] Stage one non-REM sleep lasts for about five minutes. Stage two sleep is

> still a fairly light sleep, but with reduced mental activity. After about 20 minutes at stage two, the sleeper passes into the deep sleep of stages three and four. Left undisturbed, the first deep sleep of the night will continue for another 30 to 45 minutes. Then, at about an hour of sleep onset, the sleeper passes briefly through the lighter stage two non-REM and into REM sleep. During the first REM period, which lasts for about 10 minutes, dreaming is apparently continuous. There are usually about five such cycles in an eight-hour period, occurring at roughly 90-minute intervals.[12]

According to the National Sleep Foundation, both non-REM sleep and REM sleep are important to experiencing quality sleep; getting the right mix and enough of both REM and non-REM sleep helps one maintain one's natural sleep architecture and have restful and restorative sleep.

Exploring the type and degree of interruptions to this type of quality sleep architecture is part of the inquiry into how and whether fatigue played a role in causing a particular crash. A variety of interruptions may be present, from environmental to inherent (sleep disorders).

Circadian Rhythm

Having regular times for the onset and ending of sleep helps promote quality sleep. The human body has a "circadian clock" that tends to promote sleep at particular times of the day:

> The circadian clock controls the timing of physiological activity (e.g. thermoregulation, immune function, digestion), performance, alertness, and mood. Daily, the circadian clock is programmed for its lowest point around 3 A.M. to 5 A.M. This is the period of lowest activity across physiological systems and human functioning. Performance reductions

10. William C. Dement, M.D., The Sleepwatchers 39 (Nychthemeron Press, 1996).
11. *Id.* at 48.
12. *Id.* at 49–50.

> can occur in a larger window from about 12 A.M. to 6 A.M. A second programmed period of sleepiness occurs at about 3 P.M. to 5 P.M. These windows of circadian lull are associated with decreased performance, alertness, and mood and are especially relevant in an accident investigation when a critical phase of operation occurs during one of them. However, just operating during these periods is associated with physiological changes that reduce performance and alertness.[13]

The irregularity of a driver's schedule frequently presents the danger of causing fatigue. Drivers frequently change schedules and may have very irregular sleep patterns.[14]

Sleep Debt

On average, human adults physiologically require about eight hours of sleep. However, there is a range of sleep need, from about six to ten hours of sleep. Therefore, the average adult will need about eight hours of sleep for optimal waking performance and alertness. Sleep loss can be considered in two ways: acute and cumulative. Acute sleep loss involves the total amount of sleep obtained in a 24-hour period. An average person that obtains only five hours of sleep one night has an acute sleep loss of three hours. Sleep loss that occurs over several days builds into a cumulative sleep debt. An average person who obtains only five hours of sleep for three consecutive nights has a cumulative sleep debt of nine hours. Recovery from a cumulative sleep debt typically involves more deep sleep and not an hour-for-hour payback of lost sleep that requires extended sleep.

Calculating an individual's acute sleep loss or cumulative sleep debt should be based on the person's usual sleep requirement and pattern. Scientific studies have found that even two hours of sleep loss can result in "impairment of performance and levels of alertness."[15]

There appears to be some disagreement with regard to recovery from chronic or extended sleep debt. Some scientists have indicated that generally, two nights of usual sleep, at a person's regular bedtime, can reduce the cumulative sleep debt to nil.[16] However, other studies of operational alertness have found that, even after three nights of extended sleep, the effects of extended sleep debt are not ameliorated.[17]

Microsleeps

Microsleeps are brief, unintended episodes of loss of attention associated with events such as blank stare, head snapping, prolonged eye closure, and so on,

---

13. Mark R. Rosekind, Examining Fatigue Factors in Accident Investigations: Analysis of Guantanamo Bay Aviation Accident, 2–3.
14. *Id.* at 2.
15. *Id.*
16. *Id.*
17. T. Balkin, Effects of Sleep Schedules on Commercial Motor Vehicles Driver Performance (Federal Motor Carrier Safety Ass'n 2000).

which may occur when a person is fatigued and trying to stay awake to perform a monotonous task like driving or watching a computer screen.[18] "Microsleeps are most likely to occur after sleep deprivation."[19] "People who experience these episodes may doze off without realizing it. Some may have an episode in the middle of performing an important task."[20] "Microsleeps are especially dangerous for drivers because of the short time it takes to make a serious mistake at the wheel."[21] During a microsleep episode, one's eyes may be wide open even though one's brain is shut down.[22]

The dangers of microsleeps are readily apparent. At 65 miles an hour, a driver who suffers a three-second microsleep is "driving" a truck the length of a football field while effectively being unconscious. Although a driver may not be able to predict when he or she will experience a microsleep or even know afterwards that he or she has experienced a microsleep, this ignorance is not an excuse . . . by the time a driver experiences a microsleep, they have been very drowsy for some time and yet they *continued to drive* in direct violation of 24 C.F.R. section 392.3.

Sleep Disorders

Almost 90 different sleep disorders exist and are described in a diagnostic classification system. The primary presenting complaint from many of these disorders is excessive sleepiness. A broad range of physiological and psychological causes exist for these sleep disorders and individual sufferers might be unaware of their existence. Most of these sleep disorders can be diagnosed and treated successfully by a credited sleep medicine specialist. This factor is a consideration because an operator may have a sleep disorder that predisposes the individual for excessive sleepiness. Altered circadian rhythms (such as those caused by shift work or time zone crossings) and other factors could further exacerbate the preexisting sleepiness. One example is sleep apnea, a condition in which an individual has breathing pauses throughout sleep. This causes waking sleepiness and performance decrements, as well as other related health problems. Studies of individuals with sleep apnea have shown up to seven times increased risk for car accidents. Sleep disorders, such as sleep apnea, put individuals at increased risk for sleepiness and potential performance reductions.

Sleep apnea is a condition in which a narrowing or closure of the upper airway during sleep causes repeated sleep disturbances, and possible complete awakenings, leading to poor sleep quality and excessive daytime sleepiness. An obstructive apnea occurs when the muscles in the back of the throat are not able to keep the throat open to breathe. This process makes the person literally

18. Martin Moore-Ede, Alertness & Fatigue: Microsleeps, http://www.circadian.com.

19. Dr. Anis Rehman & Jay Summer, *Microsleep: What Is It, What Causes It, and Is It Safe*, Sleep Foundation (Jan. 6, 2023), https://www.sleepfoundation.org/how-sleep-works/microsleep.

20. *Id.* (medically reviewed by Dr. Stacy Sampson, D.O., 10/17/2018), accessed Sept. 2, 2024.

21. *What to Know about Micro Sleep*, WebMD, https://www.webmd.com/sleep-disorders/what-to-know-microsleep (medically reviewed by Dr. Sabrina Felson, MD, 7/17/2023).

22. *What Is a Microsleep?*, Jacksonville Sleep Center, https://jaxsleepcenter.com/what-is-a-microsleep/ (last visited Sept. 9, 2024).

"wake up to breathe," and interrupts the opportunity to obtain restorative sleep. From 1996 to 1998, the University of Pennsylvania Center for Sleep and Respiratory Neurobiology collected data for a study on the prevalence and consequences of obstructive sleep apnea among commercial vehicle drivers. Their study found that 36 percent of commercial truck drivers suffered mild to severe sleep apnea, which the study concluded was approximately the same percentage as found in the general population.[23] Some researchers say the problem is much more serious among commercial truck drivers.[24] Indeed, two indicators that a person may suffer from sleep apnea are obesity (a neck size of 17 inches or greater) and if the person snores loudly. Increased risk factors include smoking and being more than 40 years old.

Given what we know about the dangers of drivers who suffer from sleep apnea, and the relatively simple treatment for it, a nationally known sleep expert has said it is "absolutely indefensible" that Federal Highway Safety officials do not have commercial truck and bus drivers screened for sleep disorders.[25] Indeed, the FMCSA, at one point, proposed required screening of truck drivers for sleep apnea, but due to political pressure, failed to implement a rule. The FMCSA now tries to cover this failure by pointing out that its medical certification regulations require that "a person with a medical history of clinical diagnosis of any condition likely to interfere with their ability to drive safely cannot by medically qualified to operate a commercial motor vehicle." However, since DOT examiners and motor carriers are not required to screen for this condition, this "fig leaf" rings hollow.[26]

Fatigue Countermeasures

Although there are many stories or "myths" about ways to combat fatigue, such as opening a window, turning up the radio, turning down the air conditioner, walking around the truck, and so on, the only real countermeasure against fatigue is adequate sleep. Caffeine can help overcome drowsiness for short periods, but it cannot replace sleep. Its effect may be to compound a sleep debt because the caffeine is keeping the subject from falling asleep when the body wants to. When the caffeine wears off or it loses its effect, the person will be even more sleep deprived. Part of an effective fatigue management training

---

23. Fed. Motor Carrier Safety Admin., Sleep Apnea Crash Risk Study (2004).

24. William DeMent, M.D., *Sleep Apnea and Hypertension in Commercial Truck Drivers*, Sleep (1993).

25. Bus Department News, quoting Dr. Mark Mahowald, director of the Minnesota Regional Sleep Disorders Center and past president of the American Academy of Sleep Medicine.

26. *Driving When You Have Sleep Apnea*, FMCSA Website (reviewed Jan. 30, 2024). https://www.fmcsa.dot.gov/driver-safety/sleep-apnea/driving-when-you-have-sleep-apnea and https://www.fmcsa.dot.gov/sites/fmcsa.dot.gov/files/docs/Driving-Sleep-Apnea_508CLN.pdf. There are no medical screening requirements in the FMCSRs for sleep apnea. *See* section 4.8.3.6 of the 2024 edition of the FMCSA Medical Examiner's Handbook, https://www.fmcsa.dot.gov/regulations/medical/driver-medical-requirements/medical-examiners-handbook-2024-edition and https://www.fmcsa.dot.gov/sites/fmcsa.dot.gov/files/2024-01/Medical%20Examiner%27s%20Handbook%202024%20Edition_0.pdf.

program is to teach drivers that other methods of combating fatigue are simply not effective and should not be relied on.

Industry Pressures and Fatigue Awareness

Although a truck driver's job has never been easy, competitive forces since the industry was deregulated in 1980 have created an environment in which most if not all of the variable costs involved in trucking are attempted to be placed directly on the backs of the individual drivers. The situation has been described by one expert as follows:

> Imagine a world in which there is no effective minimum wage and no 40-hour workweek or time-and-one-half for overtime.
>
> Imagine a world in which most people work more than 60 hours per week—not to "get ahead" but just to make ends meet.
>
> Imagine a world in which most of us compete to offer our services at the lowest possible price but which is so competitive that we get what we want—and end up working longer hours just to earn enough to subsist.
>
> Imagine a world in which people work like this with no regular schedule—irregular days and irregular hours, switching from day to night and back again with little predictability.
>
> Imagine a world in which production workers' wages stop abruptly with every hiccup in the assembly line.
>
> Imagine a world in which employers decide which work to pay you for and which you have to perform for free—and that work comprises 25 percent of your day! Imagine no further, because that is the life of the truck driver today in the hyper-competitive trucking industry.[27]

The number of authorized motor carriers in the United States exploded after deregulation, from less than 30,000 to more than 500,000 by the turn of the century.[28] Today, no exact figure is available, but it is believed to be between 600,000 and 700,000 motor carriers. The resulting unfettered competition has been effective in keeping rates (and driver pay) low. Throughout the long-haul industry, the most common method of payment is still pay "by the mile." This means that the longer and farther the driver travels, the more pay he or she can earn. Because the per-mile rate has been kept relatively stagnant, drivers feel a great deal of pressure to continue driving when they know they should stop to rest. Add this to the fact that most drivers are not paid for time they spend waiting to load and unload, and you have great pressure to drive as many miles as possible to make up for lost time.

Many drivers have left the industry and many drivers who stay in the industry change jobs frequently. The annual driver turnover rate for large truckload

27. Michael Belzer, Sweatshops on Wheels, preface (Oxford Univ. Press 2000).

28. American Trucking Trends 2002 (Economics & Statistics Group, American Trucking Associations).

companies varies wildly but is always staggeringly high over long periods of time. For example, during the second quarter in 2005 the turnover rate jumped to 129 percent, the second highest on record,[29] and in 2019, the rate was 91 percent. The turnover rate (or "churn" rate) at smaller truckload companies is similarly high, but frequently a bit lower on average, and the turnover rate for less-than-truckload (LTL) carriers is much lower, frequently below 20 percent.[30] For decades, the industry has referred to there being a "driver shortage." The reality, however, is that there is no shortage of workers in this country, as is frequently shown by national unemployment statistics. The fact is, there is a shortage of people who want to work 70 to 100 hours per week, be gone from their families for extended periods of time, put their lives on the line in a vocation in which more than 1,000 truck drivers were killed on the job last year, and make an average hourly rate that would be approximately equivalent to a senior fast-food service job.[31] Truck drivers are not protected by the overtime provisions of the Fair Labor Standards Act so there is no requirement to pay truck drivers "overtime" rates.

The result is that well-run, safe companies have been challenged by companies willing to cut corners to obtain or keep business. As carriers compete for the shrinking profit margin, working conditions for many drivers have worsened, leading to these high attrition rates and attracting more poorly qualified drivers into the industry. With this downward spiral, the biggest question is why there are not even more truck crashes on our highways.

When a truck crash is caused by driver fatigue, the claims that arise from the crash will focus on whether the driver and the carrier complied with the regulations regarding the hours the driver can work, and whether they otherwise took reasonable steps to minimize this ever-present danger of fatigue. While hours-of-service violations due to drivers cheating on their logs and driving far beyond the times allowed were once commonplace, since the implementation of required Electronic Logging Devices (ELDs), that kind of cheating has become more rare. The current "cheats" involve the classification of hours as "off duty" instead of "on-duty-not-driving," and fraudulent use of the triggers that cause an ELD to switch to "off-duty" and/or back to "on-duty-not-driving." Safety directors can no longer claim that they did not realize fatigue is a problem. The world's foremost experts who have looked at the fatigue problem have formulated a "consensus statement" and have concluded that fatigue "is the largest identifiable and preventable cause of accidents in transport operations (between 15 percent and 20 percent of all accidents), surpassing that of alcohol- or drug-related incidents in all modes of transportation."[32] The expert consensus statement also identified poor government statistics as one of the contributing

29. *Driver Turnover Gains at-Large Fleets*, Transport Topics 1 (Oct. 3, 2005). *See also Many Cite Driver Turnover Rates, but Few Understand What They Measure*, American Trucking Associations (Mar. 25, 2022).

30. *See, e.g., id.*

31. Bendel, *Op-Ed*, Wash. Post, Apr. 29, 2000.

32. Consensus Statement: Fatigue and Accidents in Transport Operations, compiled by Dr. Torbjörnakerstedt (2000).

factors: "Underestimation of the impact of fatigue can lead to the underutilization of important countermeasures."[33]

Although a wide variety of fatigue training materials are available from all truck industry general supply companies, most trucking companies do not screen their drivers for sleep disorders and do not provide training to their drivers about problems associated with fatigue. Only relatively recently have the federal regulations provided specifically (and vaguely) for any driver training related to "fatigue countermeasures," and this applies only to entry-level drivers.[34] Nonetheless, as indicated earlier, the regulations do provide, albeit somewhat indirectly (and not enforced by the FMCSA), that a motor carrier must provide effective training regarding fatigue to all of its drivers. This requirement is found in 49 C.F.R. § 392.3, which provides:

> No driver shall operate a commercial motor vehicle, and a motor carrier shall not require or permit a driver to operate a commercial vehicle, while the driver's ability or alertness is so impaired, or so likely to become impaired, through fatigue . . . as to make it unsafe for him/her to begin or continue to operate the commercial motor vehicle.

This requirement clearly states that the motor carrier shall not permit a fatigued driver to continue driving when it is unsafe for him or her to do so. Unless that company has someone sitting in the seat next to the driver, monitoring the driver's alertness and telling him when to pull over, the motor carrier must have in place a training system to comply with this directive. Interpretations for the federal regulations published in the Federal Register of April 1997 by the Office of Motor Carriers (predecessor to the FMCSA) confirmed that "carriers are liable for the actions of their employees. Neither intent to commit, nor actual knowledge of, a violation is a necessary element of that liability. Carriers 'commit' violations . . . of . . . regulations by their employees if they fail to have in place management systems that effectively prevent such violations."[35]

Accordingly, in order to comply with the terms of this regulation, a motor carrier should have to have in place a management system that effectively prevents a driver from continuing to drive when he or she is too fatigued to do so. Merely informing drivers that they should pull over when they are too tired to drive would be similar to a motor carrier merely telling drivers not to violate the hours-of-service provisions, without having an audit system in place, and clearly would be indicative of irresponsible and incompetent management.

Many times, the safety department of a trucking company is interchangeably called its "compliance" department. Sometimes it may be referred to as the "safety and compliance" department. Too often, its focus is on compliance

---

33. *Id.*

34. 49 C.F.R. pt. 380, app. A, unit A1.5.4 includes the requirement that entry level instruction must include training on "the issues and consequences of chronic and acute driver fatigue and the importance of staying alert."

35. This official "guidance" was specifically drafted with regard to § 395.3, which provides that no motor carrier shall require or permit any driver used by it to drive in excess of the allowable hours of service. This regulation uses the same "require or permit" language as found in § 392.3.

rather than safety, and the two are not the same thing. The regulations provide for the minimum standards and framework that must be met by a motor carrier. "Compliance" is too often focused on making sure that the motor carrier does not violate the specific terms of the regulations, which is frequently viewed as a matter of pencil-whipping and safekeeping the right papers in a file cabinet (or on a hard drive). A focus on safety, however, should involve an assessment of the risk of a particular operation and the implementation of measures to reduce the risk. The difference, especially in the area of truck driver fatigue, is the difference between life and death. Consider, for example, a driver who drives 11 hours straight followed by ten hours off duty for four continuous cycles. That driver is absolutely compliant with the regulations but is nevertheless at imminent risk of causing serious injury and death because the driver will have been subjected to a rearward rotating schedule with a dangerous alteration of sleep cycles and, in the next driving period, he will be driving throughout the period of time at which he was sleeping at the beginning of his tour of duty. "Compliance" seeks to avoid a literal violation of a regulation. "Safety" seeks to prevent crashes, serious injuries, and deaths. Compliance is simply not sufficient.

Every motor carrier, large or small, should have in place a Fatigue Management Training Program that is customized to its particular operation. The resources are readily available, and, at this point, there is no excuse for any motor carrier not to take steps to ameliorate this ubiquitous risk to life and limb.

Conclusion

The danger of driver fatigue is obvious. Long before a fatigued driver falls asleep, he or she suffers from degraded judgment and decision-making capabilities, cognitive fixation, decreased coordination, impaired reaction time, perseveration, decreased memory and mental functioning, and indifference to normal stimuli. The degradation in performance capability is directly comparable to the degradation found in alcohol impairment and should be considered every bit as dangerous. It is the responsibility of every motor carrier to provide its drivers with the tools necessary to perform the job demanded of them and to prohibit them from driving while fatigued. Since 1995, the industry has been flooded with information about the dangers of driver fatigue, educational and training materials for drivers, and more information for management. Companies that do not provide their drivers with adequate information, training, and supervision to ensure that the drivers do not drive while they are fatigued are the greatest risk to the public that their operations present. Such conduct demonstrates an indifference to and disregard for the safety of others and should be dealt with accordingly.

CHAPTER 24

An Examination of the Hours of Service Rules

Ashley N. Baker, Esq., LL.M.

The Hours of Service (HOS) regulations promulgated by the U.S. Department of Transportation (USDOT) determine when a commercial driver can and cannot operate a commercial vehicle. This chapter will explore these rules and how they work to accomplish the USDOT's goal of increasing truck safety. As a lawyer, these rules might remind you of the logic games that were on the LSAT. While the rules themselves are easy to understand individually, they become more and more difficult as you begin to think about how the rules work together in their application to a practical scenario.

Application

There are different HOS requirements for drivers who operate passenger vehicles and those that operate vehicles carrying property. For the purpose of this book, we will only be discussing the HOS rules as they relate to property-carrying vehicles. Not every driver of a commercial vehicle is subject to the HOS rules. Only drivers and motor carriers who operate commercial motor vehicles over 10,000 lbs. or vehicles that must be placarded for hazardous materials are required to adhere to the HOS regulations.[1] Generally, placards are required when a vehicle contains over 1,000 lbs. (454 kg) of hazardous cargo, and sometimes are required in other circumstances.[2] However, drivers who operate within a 150-mile radius of their home terminal may not be required to follow the logging and supporting evidence portions of the HOS rules.[3] There are limitations on this exemption.[4] The number of drivers that qualify for this exemption is very limited.

1. 49 C.F.R. § 395.1(e)(2)(i). To understand this exemption, it is important to understand who is required to have a commercial driver's license. For that, see 49 C.F.R. pt. 383.
2. 49 C.F.R. § 172.504.
3. *Id.* § 395.1(e)(1). The logging mandate is found at § 395.8 and the supporting documents requirements are found at § 395.11.
4. *Id.* § 395.1(e)(2).

Recording Time

Drivers log their time using a logbook or Electronic Logging Device (ELD) and utilizing four duty statuses.[5] A duty status is simply how the driver spent his or her time. The FMCSA has allotted four duty statuses.[6] Any time a driver is working, and not driving, he is considered to be "on-duty."[7] A person is working "on-duty" when he or she is in possession of freight, under instruction to retrieve a load but has not started driving, while loading or unloading the truck, fueling, or doing a pre-trip or post-trip inspection.[8]

The next duty status is "driving." While this may seem obvious, a driver is considered to be driving when he or she is operating the commercial vehicle or any time he or she is sitting behind the steering wheel of the vehicle.[9] The vehicle does not need to be in motion for the driver to be required to utilize the driving status.

The next duty status is "off duty."[10] A driver may log their time in this duty status anytime he or she is not working, not in the sleeper berth, or is not under a load. The final duty status is "sleeper."[11] Only drivers that operate a vehicle equipped with a sleeper berth can utilize this duty status.[12] A sleeper is a bed that is usually located in the rear of the cab behind the driver and passenger seats. Drivers that operate a day cab, for instance, cannot use this duty status.

Drivers record their duty statuses in what is called a logbook or on their ELD. Each page of a logbook records one day, or 24 hours, of duty statuses. The driver must record the driver's duty status in the logbook or the ELD (whichever is required by the regulations for that driver and truck) for each 24-hour period.[13] This means that no matter how much time a driver spends in each duty status, the total amount of hours must add up to 24 hours, no more and no less. There are five things to remember when recording duty statuses: (1) time is recorded according to the time zone of the driver's home terminal; (2) when there is a change in duty status, there must be a note in the remarks section recording the city and state of the duty change (every time a driver changes duty status, the driver must notate the location (city, state) in the remarks section of the log sheet;[14] (3) drivers must keep logs on hand for the previous seven days, at all times; (4) logs must be submitted to the driver's motor carrier within

5. *Id.* § 395.8(a)(1).
6. *Id.* §395.8(b).
7. *Id.* §§ 395.2 (definitions of driving time and on-duty) and 395.8(b)(4).
8. *Id.*
9. *Id.* §§ 395.2 (definition of driving time) and 395.8(b)(3).
10. *Id.* § 395.8(b)(1).
11. *Id.* §§ 395.2 (definition of sleeper berth) and 395.8(b)(2).
12. *Id.* and 49 C.F.R. § 3939.76.
13. *Id.* § 395.8(a).
14. If a change of duty status occurs at a location other than a city, town, or village, show one of the following: (1) the highway number and nearest milepost followed by the name of the nearest city, town, or village and state abbreviation; (2) the highway number and the name of the service plaza followed by the name of the nearest city, town, or village and state abbreviation; or (3) the highway numbers of the nearest two intersecting roadways followed by the name of the nearest city, town, or village and state abbreviation. *See* Note section of 49 C.F.R. § 395.8.

13 days; and (5) if the driver is using an ELD, the driver must keep a logbook on hand to recreate logs from the current day and the previous seven days if there is an equipment failure with their logging device.[15]

The 11- and 14-Hour Rules

The 11-Hour Rule is very simple. After 11 hours of driving, the driver must complete ten consecutive hours off-duty or in the sleeper berth before the driver can drive again.[16] The 14-Hour Rule works in conjunction with the 11-Hour Rule. The 11 hours a driver is permitted to drive must be completed within a 14-hour period.[17] This means, if 14 hours has expired since the driver went on-duty at the beginning of his shift, he must stop driving. He is still allowed to perform work on-duty, but simply cannot drive. It is best to think of the 14-hour clock as a timer that is always counting down once the driver has been on-duty for any length of time. It is important to note that even if the driver has not used all of his 11-hour drive time, he or she still cannot drive if the 14-hour clock has expired. This 14-hour clock runs consecutively and may not be divided or extended, except in regard to the split sleeper berth provision, which we will discuss later in this chapter.

The Ten-Hour Rule

A driver needs ten hours off-duty or in the sleeper to restart the 11- and 14-hour clocks. These ten hours can be achieved by any combination of time in both the sleeper and off-duty that equals ten hours. Utilizing a combination of time in the sleeper berth and off-duty requires that the two periods be consecutive. If the ten hours is interrupted by going on-duty or driving, the driver must restart accumulating the ten hours as if they never started.

The Split Sleeper Berth Provision

A driver may regain any time not utilized under the 11- and 14-hour rules after spending ten hours in either the sleeper berth or off-duty. However, the Split Sleeper Berth Provision allows the driver to split the ten-hour break into two rest periods instead of one consecutive ten-hour period, where the driver has a long break of at least seven hours in the sleeper and a short break. The driver must spend seven hours of the ten in the sleeper berth, but the total time must add up to ten hours.[18]

---

15. 49 C.F.R. § 395.34(a). Most drivers are required to use USDOT approved electronic logging devices. *See* 49 C.F.R. §§ 395.20–395.38 and Appendix A to Subpart B of Part 395 for the specifications of approved ELDs.

16. 49 C.F.R. § 395.3(a)(3)(i).

17. *Id.* § 395.3(a)(2).

18. *Id.* § 395.1(g)(ii).

Think about it like this, the seven hours in the sleeper pauses the 14- and 11- hour clocks. When the driver wakes up from the seven hours in the sleeper, the driver will have the same amount of time available that he or she had when he or she went into the sleeper berth. With an additional two hours in the sleeper berth and/or off-duty, a driver will regain the 14-hour time in which to drive, which starts at the end of the first seven-hour rest period. The driver will also regain the previously used driving time from the previous 11 hours. The provision is considered split because the driver is doing a traditional ten-hour break, but it may be split into two breaks. The first break is at least seven hours and must be done in the sleeper. The second break is two+ hours and can be completed either in the sleeper berth or off-duty or a combination of both, but both must total ten hours.[19] Thus, day cab drivers cannot utilize this provision. This is best used when the driver has a time-sensitive pickup or delivery. The difference between this and the ten-hour break is that the Split Sleeper Berth Provision allows the driver to drive between the two rest periods if the driver still has time on the 11- and 14-hour clocks.[20]

This rule is meant to provide more flexibility to drivers, especially in circumstances where, for example, they are near their delivery or pickup point but because of the other HOS rules, they would be unable to get to their destination on time. This rule allows them to stop and rest briefly, then continue to the destination, and take another rest period.[21] It is worth noting that this provision is the most difficult to understand, as the driver needs to know how much time is left on both the 11- and 14-hour clocks, as well as balancing their delivery time, and the "split" rest period. On a paper log sheet, and some ELDs, this provision would appear to be a violation. It is important to check all of the rules to determine whether a violation actually occurred.

---

19. A driver that spends only seven hours in the sleeper berth must spend three hours off-duty or in the sleeper berth to complete the requirements of the rule. A driver who spends eight hours in the sleeper berth, only needs two hours in the sleeper berth or off-duty to complete the rule.

20. Per FMCSA guidance, if a driver is stopped for a roadside inspection after taking only one rest period that qualifies for the Split Sleeper Berth Provision, if there is a rest period under that provision that can be taken at some point in the future that would allow the driver to be in compliance, then the roadside inspector should not cite a violation of the HOS rules based on the 11-Hour Rule, 14-Hour Rule, and ten-hour break. See Frequently Asked Question 03 on the FMCSA website. https://www.fmcsa.dot.gov/sites/fmcsa.dot.gov/files/2020-11/FMCSA-HOS-2020-395-FAQ03.pdf. The USDOT's regulatory guidance website on the topic of hours of service can be helpful to understanding the nuances of the HOS rules. https://www.fmcsa.dot.gov/guidance?keywords=&issued_date_from=11/19/2020&field_issued_date_value_1=11/19/2020&page=0.

21. A driver could opt to make the second longer rest period of the Split Sleeper Berth Provision, a ten-hour break, at which point the driver would reset the 11- and 14-hour clocks.

Restarting The Clock
(Quick Reference Guide)

	10-Hour Break (general rule)	Split Sleeper Berth Provision	34-Hour Restart
When the Rule Is Used	To reset the 11- and 14-hour clocks	When the driver has not used all 11 driving hours, or all 14 on-duty hours, and has a pickup or delivery that the driver would not be able to make during the regular 14-hour clock	When the driver's 60/70-hour clock has expired or is about to expire, or anytime
How to Use the Rule	Spend 10 hours in the sleeper berth or off-duty	Spend at least 2 hours either off-duty or in the sleeper berth and another rest period of at least 7 hours in the sleeper berth. The total rest time must equal 10 hours.	Spend 34 hours off-duty and/or in the sleeper berth

The 30-Minute Break

No driver can drive beyond eight hours without taking a 30-minute break, either off-duty, on-duty, or in the sleeper berth. The eight hours is reached when the driver has driven eight hours without a 30-minute break.[22] The 30-minute break does not apply to eight hours of on-duty time.

The 60- and 70-Hour Rules

The 60- and 70-hour rules are two distinct rules. This means that the driver will not need to comply with both rules. These rules provide how many hours a driver may spend driving per week. The first rule is the 60/7 Rule. This rule is for drivers that work for a company that does not operate commercial motor vehicles every day. Under this rule, a driver may not drive and/or be on-duty more than 60 hours in a seven-day period.[23] After the 60 hours is reached by either being on-duty or driving or any combination of the two, the driver may no longer drive. The driver can be on-duty after 60 hours; he or she simply cannot drive.

The second rule is the 70/8 Rule. This rule is for drivers that work for a company that operates commercial vehicles every day. Most motor carriers will fall under this provision. Under this rule, a driver may not drive and/or be on-duty more than 70 hours in an eight-day period.[24] After the 70-hour limit is reached by either being on-duty or driving or any combination of the two, the driver may no longer drive. The driver can be on-duty after the 70-hour limit is reached.

22. 49 C.F.R. § 395.3(a)(3)(ii).
23. *Id.* § 395.3(b)(1).
24. *Id.* § 395.3(b)(2).

The 34-Hour Restart

The 34-Hour Restart is another provision that allows the driver to restart their time. Under this provision, spending 34 hours off-duty and/or in the sleeper berth will allow a driver to restart his or her 60- or 70-hour clock.[25] This can be done at any point, and not simply when the 60- or 70-hour clock has expired.

Exceptions to the Rules

There are some exceptions to the HOS rules. The first applies when the driver is experiencing "adverse driving conditions."[26] During extreme driving conditions or extreme weather, a driver is allowed to drive an additional two hours, past the 11 hours of driving, to reach a safe stopping point.[27] Note that a driver may not drive past the 70/8-hour clock. Driving conditions are sufficiently adverse when a driver did not know or could not reasonably have known about the condition prior to the workday or immediately prior to beginning driving after a rest break, nor to a motor carrier immediately prior to dispatching the driver.[28] In other words, a driver could not have known or have reason to know that it would be that bad. The driver also must have been able to complete the trip without the extension had the extreme driving condition not occurred.

The second exception is for drivers that are needed to operate during emergency declarations.[29] For this exception to apply, first there must be either a federal, state, or local emergency declaration, and, second, the driver must be delivering goods or supplies to aid in the relief. This exception from the HOS rules only exists while the driver is providing relief. Once the load is delivered, the driver must continue following the HOS rules.

Conclusion

The HOS rules help to promote safety in the trucking industry. Whether these rules are too complex for the driver to fully understand, either because there are insufficient educational requirements related to HOS for drivers studying to earn their commercial driver licenses or because they are too complicated, is a conversation that is needed as industry professionals seek to increase safety. This chapter was an overview of each rule and does not include every exception to these rules. A resource containing a deeper explanation of these rules along with practical scenarios a truck driver might encounter is *The Art of Commercial Trucking™: Hours of Service,* 2nd Edition (Modeerf Holdings LLC, 2021) by Ashley N. Baker.

---

25. *Id.* § 395.3(c).

26. *Id.* §§ 395.1(b)(1) and 395.2 (definition of "adverse driving conditions"); *see also* § 395.1(b)(2).

27. The driver will appear in violation of the HOS rules if this exception is used.

28. 49 C.F.R. § 395.2. Extreme driving conditions could include inclement weather, whether or not foreseeable. As a practical matter, a driver should trip plan effectively to avoid delays caused by foreseeable weather events.

29. *Id.* § 390.23(a)(1).

CHAPTER 25

Negligence *Per Se*

Morgan Adams, Esq. and Jamie Guerrette[1]

In most states, violation of a safety regulation or statute is considered negligence as a matter of law, or negligence *per se*. If, after reading the chapters in this book, you are convinced that one or more of the safety regulations governing trucking, the Federal Motor Carrier Safety Regulations (FMCSR), were violated by the driver, the trucking company, or both, and that this violation was a cause of the wreck, the doctrine of negligence *per se* will be an issue in your case. Whether representing the plaintiff or the defendant, if a judge or jury is likely to find the defendant negligent *per se*, the liability in your trucking case changes dramatically.

The basis for a negligence *per se* claim in a trucking case is a violation of one or more of the FMCSR. Nothing beats reading the FMCSR for yourself. Fortunately, the FMCSA makes searching the FMCSR easy with an online database,[2] and it is the most critical area to understand in determining liability in a trucking case.

Negligence *per se* is defined by *Black's Law Dictionary* as: "Negligence established as a matter of law, so that breach of the duty is not a jury question."[3] The first reference to the term "negligence *per se*" appears to have occurred over 150 years ago in *Simpson v. Hand*.[4] By 1889, negligence *per se* was "well-settled" doctrine in American courts of law.[5] Since that time, the concept has become firmly rooted in American jurisprudence.

The Restatement (Third) of Torts: Liability for Physical and Emotional Harm, section 14 on negligence *per se*, states: "An actor is negligent if, without excuse, the actor violates a statute that is designed to protect against the type of accident the actor's conduct causes, and if the accident victim is within the class of persons the statute is designed to protect."[6] One court has explained:

> To prevail on a negligence *per se* theory, the plaintiff may, in certain circumstances . . . rely on a statute or regulation as proof of the applicable

---

1. The author would like to thank Jamie Guerrette, Esq. for assisting the author with updating this chapter.
2. *See* www.ecfr.gov and choose Title 49.
3. Black's Law Dictionary (7th ed. 2001).
4. Simpson v. Hand, 6 Whart. 311, 324 (Pa. 1841).
5. Osborne v. McMasters, 41 N.W. 543 (Minn. 1889).
6. Restatement (Third) of Torts: Liability for Physical and Emotional Harm § 14 (2005).

standard of care. Proof of "[an] unexplained violation of that standard renders the defendant negligent as a matter of law," so long as the violation was the proximate cause of the injuries, and the alleged injuries were of the type which the statute was designed to prevent.[7]

The Restatement (Third) of Torts: Liability for Physical and Emotional Harm, section 38, states: "When a statute requires an actor to act for the protection of another, the court may rely on the statute to decide that an affirmative duty exists and its scope."[8] The Restatement (Second) of Torts defines the negligence *per se* doctrine as follows: "The unexcused violation of a legislative enactment or an administrative regulation which is adopted by the court as defining the standard of conduct of a reasonable man, is negligence in itself."[9]

Under the law, all persons have a duty to exercise reasonable care by "refrain[ing] from conduct that will foreseeably cause injury to others."[10] Failure to exercise reasonable care, under the circumstances, constitutes a breach of this duty.[11] Some minimum duties are established by statute, such that the "failure to perform a statutory duty is negligence *per se*."[12]

Where a driver is found to have violated a statute, ordinance, or regulation intended to protect a class of persons that includes the plaintiff, most courts will hold that said violation is evidence of a defendant's *per se* negligence. "Generally, a claim of negligence *per se* may be supported only by statutes and regulations relating to public safety, such as health regulations and rules of the road."[13]

The effect of establishing negligence *per se* through violation of a statute is to conclusively prove the first two elements of a cause of action in negligence, namely a duty and a breach of that duty.[14] In other words, negligence *per se* lessens the plaintiff's burden on the issue of the "actor's departure from the standard of conduct required of a reasonable man."[15] This is true because the elements of duty and breach are "taken away from the jury."[16] Once proved, however, negligence *per se* does not differ in its legal consequences from

7. King v. Danek Med., Inc., 37 S.W.3d 429, 459 (Tenn. Ct. App. 2000) (quoting McNeil Pharm. V. Hawkins, 686 A.2d 567, 578 (D.C. 1996)).

8. Restatement (Third) of Torts: Liability for Physical and Emotional Harm § 38 (2005); *see* Alex v. Armstrong, 385 S.W.2d 110, 114 (Tenn. 1964) ("In order to found an action on the violation of a statute . . . the person suing must be such a person as is within the protection of the law and intended to be benefitted thereby. . . .") (quoting Carter v. Redmond, 218 S.W. 217, 218 (1919)). *See also* Uithoven *ex rel.* Cook v. Spinnaker's of Rivergate, Inc., 878 S.W.2d 934, 937 (Tenn. 1994) (In order to establish negligence *per se*, it must be shown that the Statute violated was designed to impose a duty or prohibit an act for the benefit of a person or the public.").

9. Restatement (Second) of Torts § 288B(1) (1965).

10. Bradshaw v. Daniel, 854 S.W.2d 865, 870 (Tenn. 1993); *see also* Pittman v. Upjohn Co., 890 S.W.2d 425, 428 (Tenn. 1994).

11. Kellner v. Budget Car & Truck Rental, Inc., 359 F.3d 399, 404 (6th Cir. 2004); Doe v. Linder Constr. Co., Inc., 845 S.W.2d 173, 178 (Tenn. 1992).

12. Tennessee Trailways, Inc. v. Ervin, 222 Tenn. 523, 529, 438 S.W.2d 733, 735 (1969); *see also* Hickman v. Jordan, 87 S.W.3d 496, 499 (Tenn. Ct. App. 2001) (noting that "[t]he statutory requirements help to determine the minimum standard of care").

13. Scarborough v. Brown Grp., Inc., 935 F. Supp. 954, 964–65 (W.D. Tenn. 1995).

14. Slade v. Smith's Mgmt. Corp., 119 Idaho 482, 489, 808 P.2d 401, 408 (1991).

15. Restatement (Second) of Torts § 288B cmt. B (1965).

16. *See* Prosser and Keeton on Torts 230 (5th ed.1984).

ordinary negligence. For example, plaintiff's counsel still may have to prove that his client's negligence, if any, was less than the defendant's negligence in a comparative fault jurisdiction.

Not every statutory violation amounts to negligence *per se*. To trigger the doctrine, the statute must establish a specific standard of conduct. Two additional threshold questions that courts consider in every case involving negligence *per se* are whether the plaintiff belongs to the class of persons the statute was designed to protect and whether the plaintiff's injury is of the type that the statute was designed to prevent. Courts also have considered the following issues: (1) whether the statute is the sole source of the defendant's duty to the plaintiff, (2) whether the statute clearly defines the prohibited or required conduct, (3) whether the statute would impose liability without fault, (4) whether invoking the negligence *per se* doctrine would result in damage awards disproportionate to the statutory violation, and (5) whether the plaintiffs injury is a direct or indirect result of the violation of the statute.

Overview of How States Treat Negligence *Per Se*

The states have adopted three approaches to negligence *per se*. Courts in the majority of states have held that the violation of a statute, ordinance, or safety regulation constitutes negligence *per se*. Courts in a minority of states have disagreed by holding that the violation of a statute, ordinance, or safety regulation does not constitute negligence *per se*, but is mere evidence of negligence. Courts in a few states have combined the two approaches and held that, while a violation of a statute constitutes negligence *per se*, the violation of a regulation is mere evidence of negligence. It should be noted that many states have adopted the FMCSR by statute, and in those states, violation of the FMCSR may in fact be a violation of a statute.[17] Therefore, careful analysis of your state's negligence *per se* law, and how the FMCSR have been adopted in your state, is critical.

Courts in the vast majority of states have held that a violation of a statute, ordinance, or regulation, such as the FMCSR, constitutes, or would likely constitute negligence *per se*. States in this category include Alabama,[18] Alaska,[19] Arizona,[20]

---

17. *See, e.g., Kukla v. Hulm*, 310 F.3d 1046, 1049 (8th Cir. 2002) (citing S.D. Code Laws § 49-28A-3) ("South Dakota has adopted federal regulations regarding motor carriers."); Lands v. Ward, 349 So. 3d 219, 223 (Ala. 2021) ("These regulations have been expressly incorporated into Alabama law by statute.").

18. Woodard v. Transport Magog Express, Inc., 2019 U.S. Dist. LEXIS 15657, 2019 WL 1007112, at *5 (S.D. Ala. Jan. 30, 2019) ("At least two other federal courts in Alabama have indicated, since the passage of § 32-9A-2(a)(1), that violations of the FMCSR, and therefore, the Alabama statute, constitute negligence per se under Alabama law.").

19. Lynden Transport, Inc. v. Haragan, 623 P.2d 789 (Ala. 1981) (finding that the language of 49 C.F.R. § 396.2, requiring systematic inspection and maintenance, not too general and abstract to be incorporated into a negligence per se instruction); HDI-Gerling America Ins. Co. v. Carlile Transp. Systems, Inc., 426 P.3d 881 (Ala. 2018) (endorsing negligence *per se* instruction but finding trial evidence insufficient to establish the same).

20. Orlando v. Northcutt, 103 Ariz. 298, 300, 441 P.2d 58, 60 (Ariz. 1968) ("Violation of a statute created to protect a certain group is negligence per se...."); Brannigan v. Raybuck, 667 P.2d 213, 217 (Ariz. 1983) ("It is the prevailing rule, recognized in Arizona, that a breach of a statute

California,[21] Colorado,[22] Connecticut,[23] Delaware,[24] District of Columbia,[25] Florida,[26] Georgia,[27] Idaho,[28]

---

intended as a safety regulation is not merely evidence of negligence but is negligence *per se*."); Gardner v. Nationstar Mortgage, LLC, 258 F. Supp. 3d 956, 975 (D. Ariz. 2017) ("Where a valid statute, enacted for the public safety, or governmental regulations made in pursuance thereof, provide that a certain thing must or must not be done, if a failure to comply with the regulations is the proximate cause of injury to another, such failure is actionable negligence per se."); Cameron v. Westbrook, 2012 Ariz. App. Unpub. LEXIS 141, 2012 WL 385633, at *7–8 (Ariz. App. Div. 1, Feb. 7, 2012) ("In order to justify instructing the jury on the FMCSR, some testimony or other evidence would be needed as foundation to explain or describe the FMCSR and place it in context."); Hernandez v. Singh, 2019 U.S. Dist. LEXIS 14559, 2019 WL 367994, at *8 (D. Ariz. Jan. 30, 2019) (observing that plaintiffs made only a cursory attempt to establish that FMCSR at issue were enacted to promote public safety and to protect a class of persons that included plaintiffs).

21. Crooks v. Sammons Trucking, Inc., 2001 Cal. App. Unpub. LEXIS 505, 2001 WL 1654986, at *8 (Cal. App. 3 Dist. 2001) (unpublished opinion) ("Here, Regulation 392.14 has the effect of establishing that 'when hazardous conditions, such as those caused by snow, ice, sleet, fog, mist, rain, dust, or smoke, adversely affect visibility or traction,' the standard of reasonable care is 'extreme caution.' . . . This regulation prescribed the proper standard of reasonable care when hazardous conditions undermine visibility."); *see also* Cal. Evidence Code § 669.

22. Lombard v. Colorado Outdoor Educ. Ctr., Inc., 187 P.3d 565, 573 (Colo. 2008) ("A party may recover under a claim of negligence per se if it is established that the defendant violated the statutory standard and the violation was the proximate cause of the injuries sustained."); *See also* Hill v. Western Door, 2005 WL 2991589 (D. Colo. 2005); Connes v. Molalla Transport Systems, Inc., 817 P.2d 567, 572 (Colo. App. 1991); Hageman v. TSI, Inc., 786 P.2d 452, 454–55 (Colo. App. 1989); Leake v. Cain, 720 P.2d 152 (Colo. 1986) (FMCSR 391, 392.21, and 392.22).

23. Bailey v. Bruneau's Truck Service, Inc., 149 Conn. 46, 54, 175 A.2d 372, 376–77 (1961) (dealing with ICC regs) (cited with approval in Pickering v. Aspen Dental Management, Inc., 100 Conn. App. 793, 919 A.2d 520, 524 n.8 (2007)); Nat'l Transp. Co. v. J. E. Faltin Motor Transp. Co., 255 A.2d 606, 609–10 (N.H. 1969)); *see also* Duncan v. Mill Mgmt. Co. of Greenwich, Inc., 308 Conn. 1, 60 A.3d 222, 238 (2013) ("A violation of the statute or regulation thus establishes a breach of duty when (1) the plaintiff is within the class of persons intended to be protected by the statute, and (2) the injury is the type of harm that the statute was intended to prevent.").

24. Nance v. Rees, 161 A.2d 795 (Del. 1960); Taylor v. Pennsylvania R.R. Co., 246 F. Supp. 604, 605 (D. Del. 1965) ("The rule applied repeatedly by the Delaware State Courts in personal injury cases is that the violation of a statute enacted for the safety of others is negligence in law of negligence *per se*.").

25. Otis Elevator Co. v. Tuerr, 616 A.2d 1254, 1259 (D.C. 1992); Liu v. Allen, 894 A.2d 453 (D.C. 2006); Zhou v. Jennifer Mall Rest., Inc., 534 A.2d 1268, 1274 (D.C. 1987).

26. It appears Florida would find a violation of the FMCSR as negligence *per se*. *See* Perlman v. Valdes, 575 So. 2d 216 (Fla. App. 3 Dist., 1990) (negligence *per se* for failing to comply with Federal Maritime Regulations); Underwriters at La Concorde v. Airtech Services, Inc., 493 So. 2d 428 (Fla. 1986) (court permitted negligence *per se* for failure to follow Federal Aviation Authority's inspection regulations); Ritchey v. Florida Power & Light Co., 468 So. 2d 306 (Fla. App. 2 Dist. 1985) (Failure to comply with Federal Safety Regulations regarding lighting in navigable waters constituted negligence *per se*.); and Florida Freight v. Cabanas, 354 So. 2d 1222 (Fla. App. 1978) (court erred in refusing to instruct jury that violation of applicable Federal Aviation Administrative regulations regarding loading of airplanes was negligence *per se*).

27. J.R. Mabbett & Son, Inc. v. Ripley, 185 Ga. App. 601, 365 S.E.2d 155 (1988); Highsmith v. Tractor Trailer Serv., 2005 WL 6032882 (N.D. Ga. 2005) (FMCSR §§ 383, 390, 391, 392, and 396); Parker v. R&L Carriers, 560 S.E.2d 114 (Ga. App. 2002) (The FMCSR violation must be the proximate cause of the wreck.); Lewis v. D. Hays Trucking, Inc., 2011 U.S. Dist. LEXIS 164309 (N.D. Ga. Mar. 16, 2011) (observing that the Eleventh Circuit has adopted as binding precedent that violations of federal law and federal regulations can provide evidence of both negligence and negligence *per se*).

28. Idaho Jury Instruction 2.22; Sanchez v. Galey, 733 P.2d 1234 (Idaho 1986); Ahles v. Tabor, 34 P.3d 1076 (Idaho 2001).

Iowa,[29] Kansas,[30] Kentucky,[31] Mississippi,[32] Minnesota,[33] Missouri,[34] Nevada,[35] New Hampshire,[36]

29. Machmer v. Fuqua, 231 N.W.2d 606, 607 (Iowa 1975); Bangs v. Keifer, 174 N.W.2d 372, 374 (Iowa 1970) (Absent legal excuse, a violation of statutory rules of the road or ordinances constitute negligence *per se* or as a matter of law.); Tim O'Neill Chevrolet, Inc. v. Forristall, 551 N.W.2d 611, 618 (Iowa 1996); Wiersgalla v. Garrett, 486 N.W.2d 290, 292 (Iowa 1992) ("[I]f a statute or regulation such as an OSHA standard provides a rule of conduct specifically designed for the safety and protection of a certain class of persons, and a person within that class receives injuries as a proximate result of a violation of the statute or regulation, the injuries 'would be actionable, as . . . negligence per se.'").

30. Frederick v. Swift Transp. Co., 616 F.3d 1074 (C.A.10 (Kan.) 2010) (The court found that a negligence *per se* instruction for a driver's violation of FMCSR's can be given against the driver as well as his employer.) (FMCSR §§ 383.213(a), 382.501(a), and 392.4(a)).

31. Britton v. Wooten, 817 S.W.2d 443, 447 (Ky. 1991) ("Such violations of administrative regulations, like statutory violations, constitute negligence, *per se*, and the basis for liability if found to be a substantial factor in causing the result."); 601 Ky. Admin. Regs. 1:005 adopts the FMCSR in Kentucky and a violation thereof constitutes a violation of a Kentucky statute. But be careful in your pleading, *see* Alderman v. Bradley, 957 S.W.2d 264, 266 (Ky. Ct. App. 1997) (The negligence *per se* statute is limited to violations of Kentucky statutes and does not extend to federal regulations.); T & M Jewelry, Inc. v. Hicks, 189 S.W.3d 526, 530 (Ky. 2006); Tassin v. BNK Transport, Inc., 2019 WL 2271163, at *2 (W.D. Ky. May 28, 2019) ("'Kentucky courts have held that the 'any statute' language in KRS 446.070 is limited to Kentucky statutes and does not extend to federal statutes and regulations. . . .'").

32. Munford, Inc. v. Peterson, 368 So. 2d 213, 217 (Miss. 1979) ("When a statute is violated, the injured party is entitled to an instruction that the party violating the statute is guilty of negligence, and, if that negligence proximately caused or contributed to the injury, then the injured party is entitled to recover."); *see also* Stong v. Freeman Truck Line, Inc., 456 So. 2d 698 (Miss. 1984) (violations of 49 C.F.R. sections 392.21 and 392.22 are negligence *per se* under Mississippi law.)

33. Minn. Stat. § 169.96 (1990) provides that the violation of a highway traffic regulation (Minn. Stat. Ch. 169) "shall not be negligence *per se* but shall be prima facie evidence of negligence only." *See* Ruhland v. Smith, 1991 WL 257962, at *3 (Minn. Ct. App. Dec. 10, 1991) ("We see no reason to treat federal motor carrier safety statutes different from other traffic regulations."); Soo Line Railroad Co. v. Werner Enterprises, 825 F.3d 413, 419 (8th Cir. 2016) ("Although the statute refers only to violations under Chapter 169, Minnesota courts have extended the rule to violations of FMCSA regulations."). However, if the FMCSR are determined to be regulations other than under Statute § 169, then jury instruction 25.45—Violation of Non-traffic Statute—is negligence *per se*.

34. Monteer v. Prospectors Lounge, Inc., 821 S.W.2d 898 (Mo. App. 1992); *see also* King v. Morgan, 873 S.W.2d 272, 275–78 (Mo. App. 1994) (violation of state statute prescribing width of tractor trailer); Ryno v. Hillman, 641 S.W.3d 385, 392 (Mo. App. 2022) ("[The statute providing for confidentiality of arrest records] is not a public safety statute, does not purport to describe what the conduct of a reasonable person must be, and does not evince any legislative intent to replace the standard of care in a negligence action.").

35. Barnes v. Delta Lines, Inc., 99 Nev. 688, 669 P.2d 709, 710 (1983) ("When a defendant violates a statute which was designed to protect a class of persons to which the plaintiff belongs, and thereby proximately causes injury to the plaintiff, such a violation constitutes negligence per se, unless the defendant can show that the violated was excused."); Brannan v. Nevada Rock & Sand Co., 823 P.2d 291 (Nev. 1992) (same).

36. Mahan v. N.H. Dep't of Admin. Servs., 141 N.H. 747, 754 (1997) ("When an action exists at common law, the negligence per se doctrine may define the standard of conduct to which a defendant will be held as that conduct required by a particular statute, either instead of or as an alternative to the reasonable person standard."); *See also* Yost v. US Airways, Inc., 2011 WL 1655714, at *4 (D. N.H. May 2, 2011) (determining that a federal regulation "does not establish a standard of conduct").

New Mexico,[37] North Carolina,[38] Ohio,[39] Oklahoma,[40] Oregon,[41] Pennsylvania,[42] South Carolina,[43] South Dakota,[44] Tennessee,[45]

---

37. Thompson v. Potter, 2012-NMCA-014, 268 P.3d 57, 66 (2011) (observing that "the regulation or statute at issue must specify a duty that is distinguishable from the ordinary standard of care"); Whitfield Tank Lines, Inc. v. Navajo Freight Lines, Inc., 90 N.M. 454, 564 P.2d 1336, 1341 (N.M. Ct. App. 1977) (FMCSR 392.14); Asbury v. MNT, Inc., 2014 WL 6674475, at *9–10 (N.M. 2014) (permitting expert's testimony concerning alleged violations of 392.14 and 391.25 as relevant to claims of negligence *per se*).

38. Coman v. Thomas Mfg. Co., Inc., 325 N.C. 172, 381 S.E.2d 445, 447 (N.C. 1989) (observing that North Carolina adopted the FMCSR and stating "it is the public policy [of North Carolina] that the safety of persons and property on or near the public highways be protected"); Baldwin v. GTE South, Inc., 335 N.C. 544, 439 S.E.2d 108, 109 (N.C. 1994) ("A safety statute or a safety regulation having the force and effect of a statute creates a specific duty for the protection of others."); McIntyre v. Murphy, 2019 WL 1294645, at *14–15 (E.D. N.C. Mar. 20, 2019) (whether truck driver placed warning triangles as required by FMCSR question of fact for the jury).

39. Pleimann v. Coots, 2003-Ohio-316, 2003 Ohio App. LEXIS 346, 2003 WL 164815 (Ohio Ct. App. 2003); Sikora v. Wenzel, 727 N.E.2d 1277 (Ohio 2000); Shinaver v. Szymanski, 471 N.E.2d 477 (Ohio 1984); Chambers v. St. Mary's Sch., 697 N.E.2d 198, 202 (Ohio 1998) (But note, a violation of an administrative regulation is not negligence *per se*.); *see also* Parker v. Miller, 2018 WL 3743981, at *7 (S.D. Ohio 2018) (observing that the "violation of an administrative rule does not constitute negligence *per se*"); Madera v. KTC Express, Inc., 2022 WL 2916868, at *4 (N.D. Ohio 2022) (same).

40. Howard v. Zimmer, Inc., 299 P.3d 463, 472–73 (Okla. 2013) (Acknowledging the distinction between attempting to enforce a federal regulation and allowing a parallel claim for negligence per se bottomed on violation of the regulation, "[w]e align ourselves with those jurisdictions which would allow a negligence per se claim to proceed."); *see also* Tri-State Cas. Ins. Co. v. Loper, 204 F.2d 557 (10th Cir. 1953); Boyles v. Oklahoma Nat. Gas Co., 619 P.2d 613 (Okla. 1980).

41. Abraham v. T. Henry Constr., Inc., 230 Or. App. 564, 217 P.3d 212, 217–18 (2009); *see also* Martin v. Hannu, 2024 U.S. Dist. LEXIS 45134, 2024 WL 1097625, at *305 (D. Or. Feb. 26, 2024) (finding that section 392.14 not sufficiently specific to fix the standard of care and facts did not establish a violation of section 392.22(a)); Deckard v. Bunch, 358 Or. 754, 370 P.3d 478, 483 n.6 (2016) (distinguishing between statutory violation and negligence *per se* and noting that a statute or rule that sets the standard of care establishes a presumption of negligence).

42. Shamnoski v. PG Energy, 579 Pa. 652, 858 A.2d 589, 601 (2004) (observing that ". . . the statute at issue would have to be so specific as to leave little question that a person or entity found in violation of it deviated from a reasonable standard of care"); Schemberg v. Smicherko, 85 A.3d 1071, 1073–75 (Pa. Super. 2014) (observing that the purpose of the statute or regulation must be, at least in part, to protect the interest of a group of individuals, as opposed to the public generally); Cabiroy v. Scipione, 767 A.2d 1078, 1079 and 1081 (Pa. Super. 2001); McCain v. Beverly Health & Rehabilitation Services, 2002 WL 1565526 (E.D. Pa. 2002).

43. Howard v. South Carolina Dep't of Highways, 538 S.E.2d 291 (S.C. App. 2000); Wise v. Broadway, 433 S.E.2d 857 (S.C. 1993).

44. Engel v. Stock, 225 N.W.2d 872, 873 (S.D. 1975); Stevens v. Wood Sawmill, Inc., 426 N.W.2d 13, 14 (S.D. 1988); Blakey v. Boos, 153 N.W.2d 305, 308 (S.D. 1967) (observing negligence *per se* applies with equal validity to safety rules and regulations); LeVene v. Staples Oil Co., Inc., 685 F. Supp. 3d 791, 809 (D. S.D. 2023) ("Because the South Dakota legislature has explicitly stated that it adopted 49 C.F.R. § 392.14 out of concern for safety and because the federal regulation itself was designed to promote safety in the context of truck drivers operating in hazardous conditions, the court rejects defendants' argument that 49 C.F.R. § 392.14 cannot provide the basis of negligence per se liability.").

45. Fortner v. Tecchio Trucking, Inc., 597 F. Supp. 2d 755 (E.D. Tenn. 2009) (FMCSR 392.9 and 393.122); Darling v. J.B. Expedited Servs., 2006 U.S. Dist. LEXIS 54000, 2006 WL 2238913 (M.D. Tenn.) (FMCSR 395); Ryans v. Koch Foods, LLC, 2015 U.S. Dist. LEXIS 193054 (E.D. Tenn. July 8,

Texas,[46] Utah,[47] Vermont,[48] Virginia,[49] Wyoming,[50] Wisconsin,[51] Fifth Circuit,[52] Sixth Circuit,[53] Seventh Circuit,[54] and the Tenth Circuit.[55]

Courts in a small minority of states have held that a violation of a statute, ordinance, or regulation is mere evidence of negligence.[56] These states include

2015) ("[T]he FMCSR relates to public safety and can form the basis for a negligence *per se* claim under Tennessee law.").

46. Almanzar v. Eaglestar, 2021 U.S. Dist. LEXIS 254678, 2021 WL 7184209, at *3 (W.D. Tex. Dec. 21, 2021) ("Texas courts have recognized negligence per se claims arising from some provisions of the FMCSR, but have held that other FMCSR provisions do not support a negligence per se instruction."); North American Van Lines, Inc. v. Emmons, 50 S.W.3d 103, 123–24 (Tex. App. 2001) (affirming jury instruction on negligence *per se* for driver who drove a commercial motor vehicle without the commercial license required by the FMCSR); Omega Contracting, Inc. v. Torres, 191 S.W.3d 828, 839–41 (Tex. App. 2006) (holding that a "vague" FMCSR provision did not offer "an appropriate standard for applying negligence per se"); Morris v JTM Materials, Inc., 78 S.W.3d 28 (Tex. Ct. App. 2002); Reinicke v. Aeroground, Inc., 167 S.W.3d 385 (Tex. App.-Houston [14th Dist.] 2005, pet. filed) (holding trial court did not err in failing to instruct jury on negligence *per se* when there was no evidence that failure of disabled truck's driver to set out roadside warning triangles as required by FMCSR (see 49 C.F.R. § 392.22(b)(2)(v) (2000)) was proximate cause of collision); Freudiger v. Keller, 104 S.W.3d 294, 297–98 (Tex. App.–Texarkana, 2003) (holding section of FMCSR governing operations during hazardous weather conditions did not create a special standard of care); Yap v. ANR Freight Sys., Inc., 789 S.W.2d 424, 427 (Tex. App.-Houston [1st Dist.] 1990, no writ) (noting without comment trial court's negligence *per se* instruction arising from several FMCSR provisions).

47. Child v. Gonda, 972 P.2d 425, 431–33 (Utah 1998); Cameron v. Spirit Express Trucking, Inc., 2004 WL 1960146 (D. Utah 2004).

48. Bacon v. Lascelles, 678 A.2d 902 (Vt. 1996); Dalmer v. State, 811 A.2d 1214, 1223 (Vt. 2002) ("Violations of safety statutes create rebuttable presumptions of negligence.").

49. Schlimmer v. Poverty Hunt Club, 268 Va. 74, 597 S.E.2d 43, 46 (2004); McKeown v. Rahim, 446 F. Supp. 3d 69, 76 (W.D. Va. 2020) (failure to systematically inspect in violation of § 396.3 may form basis of negligence *per se*); Callander v. Hunter Motor Lines, Inc., 327 F.2d 754 (C.A.4 (Va.) 1964); Virginia Electric & Power Co. v. Savoy Constr. Co., 294 S.E.2d 811 (Va. 1982).

50. Distad v. Cubin, 633 P.2d 167 (Wyo. 1981); Frost v. Allred, 2006 WY 155, ¶ 12, 148 P.3d 17, 21 (Wyo. 2006); Wood v. CRST Expedited, Inc., 2018 WY 62, 419 P.3d 503, 510–14 (2018) (analyzing illegal parking of tractor-trailer in emergency lane of interstate).

51. Locicero v. Interpace Corp., 266 N.W.2d 423, 427 (Wis. 1978).

52. Wallace v. Ener, 521 F.2d 215, 221 (5th Cir. 1975) (FMCSR 392.22 and 393.95).

53. Johnson v. S.O.S. Transport, Inc., 926 F.2d 516 (C.A.6 (Ky.) 1991); Longton v. Burgart, 1990 U.S. App. LEXIS 16478 914 F.2d 257 (C.A.6 (Mich.) 1990) (mere negligence); Myers v. U.S., 17 F.3d 890, 900 (C.A.6 (Tenn.) 1994); Teal v. E. I. du Pont de Nemours & Co., 728 F.2d 799, 802–03 (6th Cir. (Tenn.) 1984).

54. Brandes v. Burbank, 613 F.2d 658, 668 (7th Cir. 1980).

55. Rains v. Bend of the River, 124 S.W.3d 580, 590 (Tenn. Ct. App. 2003).

56. Note however that safety codes and national safety standards are admissible on the issue of negligence. Frazier v. Continental Oil Co., 568 F.2d 378 (5th Cir. 1978); *see generally* AmJur. Evidence § 399. "[S]afety codes and standards are admissible when they are prepared by organizations formed for the chief purpose of promoting safety because they are inherently trustworthy and because of the expense and difficulty involved in assembling at trial those who have compiled such codes." Johnson v. William C. Ellis & Sons Iron Works, Inc., 609 F.2d 820 (5th Cir. 1980) (American Standard Safety Code and other safety publications identified by expert admissible); Frazier v. Continental Oil Co., 568 F.2d 378 (5th Cir. 1978) (Trial court reversed for excluding expert opinion involving industry safety standards, including the NFPA.); *see* FED. R. EVID. 803(18).

Arkansas,[57] Hawaii,[58] Illinois,[59] Louisiana,[60] Maine,[61] Massachusetts,[62] Maryland,[63] Nebraska,[64] New Jersey,[65] North Dakota,[66] Rhode Island,[67] Washington,[68] and West Virginia.[69]

57. Young v. Dodson, 239 Ark. 143, 388 S.W.2d 94, 98 (Ark. 1965) ("[W]e have held, on several occasions, that a law violation *does not constitute negligence per se, but is only evidence of negligence.*"); *see also* Ark. Model Jury Instruction Nos. 901 and 903.

58. Ono v. Applegate, 612 P.2d 533 (Haw. 1980); Michel v. Valdastri, Ltd., 575 P.2d 1299 (Haw. 1978) ("Proof of the failure of the defendant to conform his conduct to standards established by law for the protection of the class to which the injured party belongs, when shown to have a legitimate connection to the issue, is admissible as evidence of the defendant's negligence.").

59. Illinois follows the rule that statutory violations are *prima facie* evidence of negligence, not negligence *per se*. *See, e.g.*, First Springfield Bank & Trust v. Galman, 188 Ill. 2d 252, 720 N.E.2d 1068, 242 Ill. Dec. 113 (Ill. 1999) (improperly parked tanker truck not liable for pedestrian's injury while crossing street); Price v Hickory Point Bank & Trust, 362 Ill. App. 3d 1211, 841 N.E.2d 1084, 299 Ill. Dec. 352 (4th Dist. 2006) (ordinance and EPA violations are evidence of negligence in lead poisoning case); Miller v. Pam Transport, Inc., 2019 U.S. Dist. LEXIS 174577, 2019 WL 4962954, at *4 (S.D. Ill. Oct. 8, 2019) ("[T]he Court finds FMCSR violations are, at a minimum, appropriate evidence to support a claim of negligence.").

60. "The doctrine of negligence *per se* has been rejected in Louisiana. . . . However, statutory violations provide guidelines for civil liability." Galloway v. State ex. rel. Dep't of Transp. & Dev., 94-2747, p. 5 (La. 5/22/95), 654 So. 2d 1345, 1347; Ducote v. Boleware, 216 So. 3d 934, 944 (La. App. 4 Cir. 2/17/16) ("Louisiana does not recognize the negligence *per se* doctrine.").

61. French v. Willman, 599 A.2d 1151, 1152 (Me. 1991) (quoting Dongo v. Banks, 448 A.2d 885, 889–90 (Me. 1982)). Castine Energy Constr., Inc. v. T.T. Dunphy, Inc., 861 A.2d 671, 675 (Me. 2004) ("[v]iolation of a safety statute or regulation is merely evidence of negligence, not negligence per se").

62. Bennett v. Eagle Brook Country Store, Inc., 408 Mass. 355, 557 N.E.2d 1166, 1168 (1990) ("It has long been the rule in [the] Commonwealth that violation of a statute does not by itself establish a breach of duty, for it does not constitute negligence per se.").

63. Absolon v. Dollahite, 376 Md. 547, 831 A.2d 6, 9 (2003) (stating that it is a "long established general rule in Maryland that the violation of a statutory duty is only evidence of negligence, but does not establish negligence *per se*"); New Amsterdam Casualty Co. v. Novick Transfer Co., 274 F.2d 916 (C.A. 4 (Md.) 1960).

64. *In re* Derailment Cases, 416 F.3d 787 (8th Cir. 2005); Ballinger v. Gustafson, 2022 U.S. Dist. LEXIS, 2022 WL 16758558, at *3 (D. Neb. Oct. 19, 2022) ("Under Nebraska law, 'the violation of a regulation or statute is not negligence per se, but [the FMCSR] may be evidence of negligence to be considered with all the other evidence in the case.'").

65. Alloway v. Bradlees, Inc., 157 N.J. 221, 723 A.2d 960, 967–68 (1999) (concluding that a violation of OSHA regulations, that does not constitute the basis for an independent or direct tort remedy, does not constitute negligence *per se* but is nevertheless pertinent in determining the nature and extent of any duty of care).

66. Brandt v. Milbrath, 647 N.W.2d 674, 682 (N.D. 2002) ("The alleged violation of a statutory duty is evidence of negligence, not negligence per se under North Dakota law.").

67. Kurczy v. St. Joseph Veterans Ass'n, 820 A.2d 929, 947 (R.I. 2003) (citing Salcone v. Bottomley, 129 A.2d 635, 637 (R.I. 1957)) ("There is no question that the violation of a statute or an ordinance is not negligence *per se* but is to be used by the trier of the facts merely as an aid in determining that issue on consideration of all the evidence."); D'Agostino v. Yellow Cab Co., 249 A.2d 87 (R.I. 1969).

68. Wash. Rev. Code § 5.40.050. Note there are exceptions to the statute, *see* Yurkovich v. Rose, 68 Wash. App. 643, 847 P.2d 925 (1993).

69. Gillingham v. Stephenson, 209 W. Va. 741, 551 S.E.2d 663, 668 (2001) ("This Court has held that a 'violation of a statute is prima facie evidence of negligence.'") (citing Anderson v. Moulder,

Courts in a very few states have "split the baby" and held that violation of a statute, but not an administrative regulation, constitutes negligence *per se*. These states (Indiana,[70] Michigan,[71] New York,[72] and Montana) are problematic when it comes to a negligence *per se* analysis of the FMCSR. In these jurisdictions, violations of a regulation may nevertheless constitute evidence of negligence. The Montana Supreme Court, for example, has held: "[i]n order to impute liability to a defendant as a matter of negligence per se . . . the defendant must have violated a *statute*, as opposed to merely an administrative regulation, safety code, or professional standard."[73] Thus, the Montana Supreme Court was hesitant "to extend the doctrine of negligence per se beyond the statutory framework[,]" and determined "that violations of administrative regulations that are not specifically incorporated by statute do not constitute negligence per se."[74] While

---

183 W. Va. 77, 394 S.E.2d 61 (1990)); *see also* Waugh v. Traxler, 186 W. Va. 355, 412 S.E.2d 756, 759–60 (1991).

70. Zimmerman v. Moore, 441 N.E.2d 690 (Ind. App. 1982) ("Generally, the violation of a duty prescribed by statute or ordinance is negligence *per se* or as a matter of law, McCall v. Sisson, (1975) 166 Ind. App. 403, 336 N.E.2d 660. . . . However, it has been held in Indiana that the violation of an administrative rule is not negligence *per se.* Town of Kirklin v. Everman (1940) 217 Ind. 683, 29 N.E.2d 206; Second National Bank v. Sears, Roebuck & Company (1979) Ind. App., 181 Ind. App. 1, 390 N.E.2d 229."); Indiana statute, I.C. 8-2.1-24-18, incorporates by reference into Indiana law "49 CFR Parts 40, 375, 380, 382 through 387, 390 through 393, and 395 through 398."

71. "An accurate statement of our law is that when a court adopts a penal statute as the standard of care in an action for negligence, violation of that statute establishes a prima facie case of negligence, with the determination to be made by the finder of fact whether the party accused of violating the statute has established a legally sufficient cause." Zeni v. Anderson, 397 Mich. 117, 143, 243 N.W.2d 270 (1976); *see also* Candelaria v. B.C. Gen. Contractors, Inc., 600 N.W.2d 348, 356 n.5 (Mich. Ct. App. 1999) ("[A] violation of a statute creates a rebuttable presumption of negligence while the violation of an ordinance or administrative regulation constitutes evidence of negligence."); Campbell v. Nationstar Mortg., 611 Fed. Appx. 288, 299 (6th Cir. 2015) ("Michigan does not adhere to the doctrine of negligence *per se*."); Todd v. Rent-A-Ctr., 295370, 2011 Mich. App. LEXIS 145, at *2–3, 2011 WL 240709, at *1 (Mich. Ct. App., Case No. 295370, Jan. 25, 2011) ("violation of an ordinance or an administrative rule or regulation is considered evidence of negligence, but not negligence per se"); *see also* Holcomb v. GWT, Inc., 2016 Mich. App. LEXIS 407, 2016 WL 805635, at *5 (Mich. Ct. App. Case No. 325410, Mar. 1, 2016); Douglas v. Edgewater Park Co., 369 Mich. 320, 328 (1963) ("The rigidity of the negligence per se doctrine should not be extended to administrative rules and regulations."); Malburg v. Grate, 2014 U.S. Dist. LEXIS 125648, at *9, 2014 WL 4473786, at *4 (E.D. Mich. Case No. 11-14856, Sept. 9, 2014) ("violation of [the FMCSR] cannot be offered as evidence of negligence per se [but only as evidence of negligence].").

72. Elliott v. City of New York, 95 N.Y.2d 730 (N.Y. 2001). ("This Court has long recognized a distinction between State statutes on the one hand, and local ordinances or administrative rules and regulations on the other, for purposes of establishing negligence (*see,* Long v. Forest-Fehlhaber, 55 NY2d 154, 160; *see also* Rizzuto v. Wenger Contr. Co., 91 NY2d 343, 349). As a rule, violation of a state statute that imposes a specific duty constitutes negligence per se, or may even create absolute liability (*see,* Van Gaasbeck v Webatuck Cent. School Dist. No. 1, 21 NY2d 239, 243). By contrast, violation of a municipal ordinance constitutes only evidence of negligence (*see,* Martin v. Herzog, 228 NY 164, 169).") *Id.* at 734. *But see Ayala v. Hagemann*, 714 N.Y.S.2d 633, 635–36 (N.Y. Sup. Ct. 2000) (federal regulations have the force of a statute, violation of the regulation is negligence *per se*); Wedlock v. Troncoso, 712 N.Y.S.2d 328, 332 (N.Y. Sup. Ct. 2000) (a violation of a state or federal statute constitutes negligence *per se*).

73. Harwood v. Glacier Elec. Coop., 949 P.2d 651, 656 (Mont. 1997).

74. Thayer v. Hicks, 793 P.2d 784, 792 (Mont. 1990).

"[t]he violation of a non-statutory standard may be used as evidence of negligence," it does not provide sufficient "grounds on which to find the defendant negligent per se."[75]

Logically, the Federal Motor Carrier Safety Regulations should be given greater weight than any state statute because the FMCSR preempts all state statutes seeking to set forth a lower standard.[76] Thus, in *Parrick v. FedEx Ground Package System*, the Montana district court held that the FMCSR, as regulations, were not entitled to the weight of a state statute and that a violation thereof did not constitute negligence *per se* but was instead mere evidence of negligence.[77] However, the *Parrick* court failed to address FMCSR 49 C.F.R. § 392.2, *which states the FMCSR preempts all state law to the contrary*. Therefore, if state law is deemed sufficient for negligence *per se*, federal regulations preempting that same state law should also be deemed sufficient for purposes of negligence *per se*.

Thus, in ascending order of importance in a trucking case, you would have (1) state regulations, (2) state statutes, (3) the FMCSR, and (4) federal statutes. The court should, therefore, find a violation of the FMCSR constituted negligence *per se*. However, because of the word "regulation" in the FMCSR's title, courts occasionally do not give the FMCSR the legal weight they deserve.

How Negligence *Per Se* Works

When requesting a court to apply the negligence *per se* doctrine, plaintiff's counsel must affirmatively demonstrate the following: First, the plaintiff must belong to the group of persons the statute or regulation was created to protect; and secondly, the plaintiff's injury must be the type of injury that the statute or regulation was designed to prevent.

In that regard, Tennessee courts have stated that the negligence *per se* doctrine "is not a magic transformational formula that automatically creates a private negligence cause of action for the violation of every statute. . . . Not every statutory violation amounts to negligence per se."[78] Instead, to invoke the negligence *per se* doctrine, the statute or regulation "must establish a specific standard of conduct."[79] The negligence *per se* doctrine "does not create a new cause of action. . . . Rather, it is a form of ordinary negligence . . . that enables the courts to use a penal statute to define a reasonably prudent person's standard of care."[80]

---

75. Harwood v. Glacier Elec. Coop., 949 P.2d 651, 656; *see also* Lutz v. United States, 685 F.2d 1178, 1184 (9th Cir. 1982) (noting that "Montana law distinguishes between violation of a statute or ordinance and violation of the standard specified in a regulation[,]" with the latter "to be considered as evidence of negligence").

76. 49 C.F.R. § 392.2.

77. Parrick v. FedEx Ground Package System, 2010 U.S. Dist. LEXIS 93232, 2010 WL 3614119 (D. Mont. Aug. 3, 2010).

78. Rains v. Bend of the River, 124 S.W.3d 580, 590 (Tenn. Ct. App. 2003) (citations omitted).

79. *Id.* (citations omitted).

80. *Id.* at 589 (citations omitted).

Is the statutory or regulatory violation the result of an act or omission by the driver, an act or omission of the company/employer, or does the violation relate to the condition of the tractor/trailer? Determining which regulations were violated, and by whom, is important. Remember that the FMCSR establish minimum standards of care for the entire commercial trucking industry.[81] Moreover, "the circumstances relevant to a determination of whether [a truck driver] acted reasonably include the fact that at the time of the collision, [the truck driver] was engaged in a profession or trade (semi-trailer truck driving) and possessed the special knowledge and skill required of semi-trailer truck drivers."[82] Thus, the conduct should be compared to a reasonably prudent truck driver, not a common motorist.

Additionally, nothing in the FMCSR shall be construed to prohibit a trucking company from requiring and enforcing more stringent requirements relating to safety of operation and employee safety and health.[83] Mere compliance with the FMCSR is not a "get out of jail free" card in all circumstances as a reasonable person might do more than the minimum care required by a statute or regulation in some circumstances.[84]

Negligence *per se* "proves" the duty and breach of duty elements in a general negligence claim by allowing the statute or regulation to set forth what is expected of a reasonable person. Since the regulation or statute sets forth what a reasonable person must do, violation of the regulation or statute breaches the standard of care. Negligence *per se* is not a magic bullet, as any plaintiff alleging negligence *per se* still has to prove causation and damages.

The motor carrier is responsible for requiring its drivers to comply with the FMCSR.[85] The FMCSA's driver qualification requirements are minimum standards in addition to any state requirements.[86] Only qualified drivers can be hired to drive an interstate truck.[87] The FMCSR require motor carriers to conduct background checks, road tests, physical examinations, and collect certain records before hiring a driver.[88] These are minimum rules for qualification as a driver.[89] Both the motor carrier and the driver must comply at all times with all FMCSR.[90]

---

81. 49 C.F.R. § 390.3(d) Additional requirements. "Nothing in subchapter B of this chapter shall be construed to prohibit an employer from requiring and enforcing more stringent requirements relating to safety of operation and employee safety and health." *Id.*

82. Dakter v. Cavallino, 866 N.W.2d 656, 673–74 (Wis. 2015).

83. 49 C.F.R. §§ 390.9, 390.3(d).

84. Nichols v. Coast Distrib. Sys., 621 N.E.2d 738 (Ohio 1993) ("[The] statute sets forth a minimum standard to apply to all drivers parking near any intersection. . . . [It] fails to address the potential factual variables which might create additional danger, and which would require a driver to exercise additional care when parking near an intersection."); Morris v. JTM Materials, Inc., 78 S.W.3d 28, 50 (Tex. App. Fort Worth 2002, no pet.) ("Compliance with industry and statutory standards is evidence of the use of reasonable care, but it is not dispositive of that issue.").

85. 49 C.F.R. § 390.1.

86. *Id.* § 390.9.

87. *Id.* §§ 391.1 *et seq.*

88. *Id.*

89. *Id.* § 391.1(a).

90. *Id.* § 391.1(b).

History of the FMCSR

In order to understand how negligence *per se* works in trucking cases, you must also understand the history and purpose of the FMCSR. One of the stated purposes of the Federal Motor Carrier Act of 1984 was to "promote the safe operation of commercial motor vehicles [to protect the public]."[91] In fact, Congress explicitly stated that safety shall be the "highest priority" of the federal agency responsible for promulgating and administering the FMCSR.[92] Congress declared in section 113(b) that the Federal Motor Carrier Safety Administration (FMCSA) "shall consider the assignment and maintenance of safety as the highest priority, recognizing the clear intent, encouragement, and dedication of Congress to the furtherance of the highest degree of safety in motor carrier transportation."[93] The U.S. Department of Transportation Federal Highway Administration (FHWA) has promulgated FMCSR to protect the public.[94] The FMCSR were clearly designed to protect members of the public, a requirement before a statute or regulation can be used to prove negligence *per se.*

FMCSR Preempt State Laws

The Supremacy Clause of the U.S. Constitution provides that any state law that conflicts with a federal law is "without effect."[95] Federal law displaces state law where "(1) Congress expressly preempts state law; (2) congressional intent to preempt is inferred from the existence of a pervasive regulatory scheme; or (3) state law conflicts with federal law or interferes with the achievement of federal objectives."[96] The Supremacy Clause invalidates state laws that "'interfere with or are contrary to'" federal law.[97] Additionally, an FMCSR (i.e., 49 C.F.R. § 392.2) expressly states that the FMCSR preempt all contrary state laws.

While motor carriers must comply with state and local laws and ordinances, the FMCSR establish minimum standards for motor carrier safety, a floor rather than a ceiling, due to the need for a nationally uniform minimum standard of safety in interstate trucking. A state law that sets a lower standard of care for protection of public safety than one expressed or implied by the FMCSR is preempted.[98] In that regard, 49 C.F.R. § 392.2 provides:

---

91. 49 U.S.C. § 31131.

92. *Id.* § 113(b).

93. *Id.; see also* A.D. Transp. Express, Inc. v. United States, 290 F.3d 761, 767 (6th Cir. 2002) (recognizing purpose of statute establishing FMCSA is "promoting safer operation of commercial motor vehicles").

94. *See* 49 C.F.R. pts. 40, 303, 325, and 350–399.

95. Maryland v. Louisiana, 451 U.S. 725, 746 (1981) citing McCulloch v. Maryland, 17 U.S. 316 (1819); *see also* U.S. CONST. ART. VI, cl. 2.

96. Hodges v. Delta Airlines, 44 F.3d 334, 335 n.1 (5th Cir. 1995).

97. Hillsborough Cnty. v. Automated Medical Laboratories, Inc., 471 U.S. 707, 712 (1985) quoting Gibbons v. Ogden, 22 U.S. 1, 211 (1824).

98. *See, e.g.,* Yellow Freight System, Inc. v. Amestoy, 736 F. Supp. 44 (D. Vt. 1990) (holding that the Vermont Drug Testing Act, to extent it precluded subjecting motor carrier drivers to drug test without probable cause, was preempted by Federal Highway Administration's motor carrier

> Every commercial motor vehicle must be operated in accordance with the laws, ordinances, and regulations of the jurisdiction in which it is being operated. *However, if a regulation of the Federal Motor Carrier Safety Administration imposes a higher standard of care than that law, ordinance, or regulation, the Federal Motor Carrier Safety Administration regulation must be complied with.*[99]

However, a state law that sets a higher standard for safety than required by the FMCSR is not preempted.[100]

Did the defendant have more stringent internal operating rules? Since the FMCSR are minimum requirements, simply complying with the regulations may not meet the standard of care required in a given case. Many states hold that a company's own internal guidelines and policies set forth the appropriate standard of care. Discovery and expert development should focus on whether the company (1) actually complied with all relevant FMCSR; (2) whether the relevant state laws, ordinances, and regulations require a higher degree of care; and (3) whether, like similar companies within the industry, the defendant developed more stringent internal criteria for drivers, record retention, inspection, maintenance, and so on, like similar companies within the industry.

FMCSR Apply to All Commercial Motor Vehicles

The U.S. Department of Transportation has promulgated the FMCSR,[101] which applies to all trucks engaged in interstate commerce.[102] The federal government imposes mandatory commercial vehicle safety requirements[103] that "every motor carrier and intermodal equipment provider must systematically inspect, repair, and maintain, or cause to be systematically inspected, repaired, and maintained, all motor vehicles subject to its control."[104] As referenced earlier, in some states, a violation of a FMCSR and/or the parallel state regulation can be a misdemeanor.[105] The FMCSR govern the driving of tractor-trailers and other commercial motor vehicles.[106] The FMCSR set the minimum national standards for all commercial motor vehicles traveling interstate.[107] In that regard, all states

---

safety regulations, which required, inter alia, biennial physical examination to ascertain whether driver was physically qualified in various respects, including absence of drug use).

99. 49 C.F.R. § 392.2 (emphasis added).

100. *See, e.g.*, Specialized Carriers & Rigging Assoc. v. Virginia, 795 F.2d 1152 (4th Cir. 1986) (Virginia statute requiring flashing lights on "overdimensional" load transported by motor vehicle was not preempted as it set a higher rather than lower safety standard).

101. 49 C.F.R. ch. III.

102. *Id.* § 390.3(a).

103. 49 U.S.C. §§ 31301–31504.

104. 49 C.F.R. § 396.3.

105. *See, e.g.*, J.R. Mabbett & Son v. Ripley, 185 Ga. App. 601, 603, 365 S.E.2d 155, 157 (1988) ("Under O.C.G.A. § 46-7-78, failure to comply with the provisions governing motor common carriers constitutes a misdemeanor.").

106. 49 C.F.R. §§ 392.1 *et seq.*

107. *Id.* § 390.3(d). *See* www.fmcsa.dot.gov.

have adopted the FMCSR for intrastate operations as well, whether by regulation or by statute, so the reality is the FMCSR apply in every commercial vehicle case. The FMCSR apply both to motor carriers and to their drivers.[108]

Commercial motor vehicles (CMVs) are defined as

> any self-propelled or towed motor vehicle used on a highway in interstate commerce to transport passengers or property when the vehicle—(1) Has a gross vehicle weight rating or gross combination weight rating, or gross vehicle weight or gross combination weight, of 4,536 kg (10,001 pounds) or more, whichever is greater; (2) Is designed or used to transport more than 8 passengers (including the driver) for compensation; or (3) Is designed or used to transport more than 15 passengers, including the driver, and is not used to transport passengers for compensation; or (4) Is used in transporting material found by the Secretary of Transportation to be hazardous under 49 U.S.C. 5103 and transported in a quantity requiring placarding under regulations prescribed by the Secretary under 49 CFR, subtitle B, chapter I, subchapter C.[109]

All states have adopted all the FMCSR that impact safety for intrastate transportation.

FMCSR Apply to Intrastate and Interstate Transportation

> Interstate commerce means trade, traffic, or transportation in the United States—(1) Between a place in a State and a place outside of such State (including a place outside of the United States); (2) Between two places in a State through another State or a place outside of the United States; or (3) Between two places in a State as part of trade, traffic, or transportation originating or terminating outside the State or the United States.[110] Intrastate commerce means any trade, traffic, or transportation in any State which is not described in the term 'interstate commerce.'"[111]

Thus, in many cases, even when the truck is only traveling between two points in the same state, the truck is involved in interstate transportation.

Do the FMCSR Apply?

Like so many legal questions, the answer is: "It depends." An attorney may use an FMCSR violation to establish a general pattern of negligent conduct or may attempt to prove negligence *per se* based on the same violation. In either case, the attorney should develop a strategy for determining when such violations are

108. *Id.* § 392.1.
109. *Id.* § 390.5.
110. *Id.* (definition of interstate commerce).
111. *Id.* (definition of intrastate commerce).

involved in the case, and as part of the process in selecting venue, by answering the following questions:

1. Was the vehicle in interstate or intrastate transportation?
2. Is the vehicle a commercial motor vehicle as defined by the appropriate FMCSR (either state or federal)?
3. Is the FMCSR violation the result of an act or omission by the driver, by the company/employer, or does it relate to the condition of the tractor/trailer?
4. Did the defendants also violate more stringent internal operating rules, regulations, ordinances, or state statutes?
5. Based on the violations, what are the potential theories of negligence?
6. Were the violations a proximate cause of the collision?
7. Were the violations a proximate cause of the damages?
8. How does the state's law address the use of FMCSR as negligence *per se*?
9. Will experts support the use and violation of the FMCSR as well as proximate cause?

If you fail to prove that the FMCSR apply to the vehicle in your case, the court will likely refuse to consider charging the jury on the violation of same. For example, in *Pleimann v. Coots*,[112] the plaintiff alleged that the defendant driver violated 49 C.F.R. § 392.22(b) requiring near immediate placement of warning devices on the road near the disabled truck, but the court refused to charge the jury that said defendant violated said regulation because plaintiff failed to prove that the driver was engaged in interstate commerce.

Methods of Proving Negligence *Per Se*

First and foremost, attorneys must remember that a failure to amend the complaint to allege a violation of the specific FMCSR as negligence *per se*, or failure to set forth a violation of specific FMCSR prior to the deadline to amend the complaint, can spell doom.[113] In other words, some courts have held that a plaintiff must do more than simply allege "a violation of the FMCSR" to give the defendant fair notice of a claim.[114]

Judicial Notice

Consider having your court take judicial notice of the FMCSR. Specifically, 44 U.S.C. § 1510 states:

---

112. Pleimann v. Coots, 2003-Ohio-316 ¶ 23(Ohio App. Jan. 24, 2003).

113. *See, e.g.*, Huggins v. FedEx Ground Package Sys., 592 F.3d 853, 862 (8th Cir. 2010) ("In his complaint, . . . [plaintiff] did not mention any federal or state law governing authorized motor carriers, nor did he even allege that FedEx was a carrier. Over two years after he filed his complaint, and almost eight months after the deadline passed for seeking leave to amend pleadings, . . . [plaintiff] maintained for the first time in response to FedEx's summary judgment motion that FedEx was liable based on the FMCSR.").

114. *Id.* at 863 (concluding that the complaint did not state a claim under the FMCSR because it did not give defendant fair notice that such a claim was being made).

(a) The Administrative Committee of the Federal Register . . . "may require" . . . the preparation and publication in special or supplemental editions of the Federal Register of complete codifications of the documents of each agency of the Government having general applicability and legal effect, issued or promulgated by the agency by publication in the Federal Register or by filing with the Administrative Committee, and are relied upon by the agency as authority for, or are invoked or used by it in the discharge of, its activities or functions, and are in effect as to facts arising on or after dates specified by the Administrative Committee.

(b) a codification published under subsection (a) of this section shall be printed and bound in permanent form and shall be designated as the "Code of Federal Regulations."

44 U.S.C. § 1507 states: "The contents of the Federal Register shall be judicially noticed and without prejudice to any other mode of citation, may be cited by volume and page number."

Therefore, the contents of the Federal Register and the Code of Federal Regulations are required by law to be judicially noticed. In Tennessee, Rule 202(a) of the Tennessee Rules of Evidence states, "The court shall take judicial notice of . . . (4) any rule or regulation of which a statute of the United States or Tennessee mandates judicial notice." For that reason, Tennessee trial courts are required to take judicial notice of the Code of Federal Regulations and FMCSR.[115] Other states have come to the same conclusion and have taken judicial notice of the FMCSR.[116] "Federal and state regulations are generally subject to judicial notice, whether or not they are binding on a particular party."[117] The rules and regulations of a federal agency promulgated pursuant to congressional authority have the force and effect of law and state courts will take judicial notice of them.[118] Finally, as discussed earlier, the FMCSR preempts state law.

Motion for Summary Judgment

A motion for summary judgment is appropriate if for any reason the case would be better served by focusing on a remaining defendant, to simplify the case, or

115. *See* State v. Jones, 2005 Tenn. Crim. App. LEXIS 1173, 2005 WL 639141, at *12 (Tenn. Crim. App. Mar. 18, 2005) ("A federal statute, 44 U.S.C. § 1507, provides that '[t]he contents of the Federal Register shall be judicially noticed.' Regulations published in the Code of Federal Regulations are part of the Federal Register. *See* 44 U.S.C. § 1510. In consequence, the trial court, in this case, was required to take judicial notice of the regulation in question."); O'Daniel v. PNB Corp., 1988 Tenn. App. LEXIS 567 (Tenn. Ct. App. Oct. 10, 1988) ("We construe 44 U.S.C. § 1507 to mandate that state courts should take judicial notice of federal regulations found in these publications. Our research has not found any case in which a state appellate court ruled that a trial court is free to refuse to judicially notice the contents of the Federal Register and the CFR. In our opinion, the court erred in failing to take judicial notice of the proffered regulations.").

116. *See, e.g.*, Hopkins v. North American Co. for Life & Health Ins., 594 S.W.2d 310, 314 (Mo. App. 1980).

117. Hagan v. Gemstate Mfg., 939 P.2d 141, 147 (Or. Ct. App. 1997), *aff'd*, 982 P.2d 1108 (Or. 1999).

118. Ins. Co. of Pennsylvania v. West Plains Air, Inc., 637 S.W.2d 444, 446 (Mo. App. S.D. 1982)

to prevent a defendant from admitting liability as opposed to the court finding liability. The latter concern may cause a careful defendant to admit liability early in a case in order to be able to state that they have "accepted" liability at trial, as opposed to having a judge find they were at fault.

Submit the Issue to the Jury

A trucking company defendant will often admit fault in a clear case of liability before the issue of negligence is submitted to the jury. There is no question that failing to admit fault in a case involving egregious acts or omissions of negligence by a defendant can cause juror anger driving a verdict higher. A plaintiff's lawyer may therefore want to submit the issue of negligence to the jury in order to get damaging, verdict-driving facts before them.

Causation

A breach of duty or a violation of an FMCSR may not necessarily be a proximate cause of a plaintiff's injury. Although simply violating a statute or regulation may constitute *per se* negligence in some states, in the majority of states this approach "in no [way] dilutes the requirement that for the plaintiff to recover in a negligence action, the defendant's per se negligent act must be shown to have been a proximate cause of the injury."[119]

Additionally, an intervening or superseding cause may break the causal link between a defendant's statutory or regulatory violation and the injury suffered by the plaintiff. Tennessee's "test of liability under the law of intervening cause requires a person to anticipate or foresee what would normally happen; one is not required to anticipate and provide against what is unusual or unlikely to happen[.]"[120] Nevertheless, "[a]n intervening act will not exculpate the original wrongdoer unless it appears that the negligent intervening act could not have been reasonably anticipated."[121]

Furthermore, alleged violations of the FMCSR must be relevant to the plaintiff's claims of negligence involved in the case and must be adjusted to the facts.[122] For instance, the FMCSR violations may involve driving over hours, failing to maintain records of driver competency in the file, or failing to maintain drivers' logs and supporting documentation.[123] However, the plaintiff must present evidence to show not only that the defendants violated those regulations, but also that those violations were a contributing cause of the plaintiff's injury.

---

119. Tennessee Trailways, Inc. v. Ervin, 222 Tenn. 523, 529 (1969) citing Biggert v. Memphis Power & Light Co., 168 Tenn. 638, 80 S.W.2d 90, 92 (Tenn. 1935).

120. *Underwood v. Waterslides of Mid-America, Inc.*, 823 S.W.2d 171, 180 (Tenn. Ct. App. 1991) (citing Ward v. Univ. of the South, 209 Tenn. 412, 354 S.W.2d 246 (Tenn. 1962)).

121. Evridge v. American Honda Motor Co., 685 S.W.2d 632, 635 (Tenn. 1985).

122. Parker v. R&L Carriers, 253 Ga. App. 628, 560 S.E.2d 114 (2002) ("[D]ispositive causal issue in this case was not whether [employee] was negligent in violating the Federal Motor Carrier Safety Regulations, but whether [employee] was negligent in running red light. . . . The running of the red light, and not violation of [the safety regulation], was the proximate cause of accident.").

123. *See* 49 C.F.R. pt. 390.

For example, let's say a driver fails to place his warning triangles. In a case against the driver, none of the violations discussed in the preceding paragraph would be a proximate cause in a case where the plaintiff rear-ended the stopped tractor-trailer. However, if the triangles would have prevented the wreck or lessened its impact, other violations of FMCSR may be evidence that the motor carrier negligently equipped the tractor-trailer (failed to provide the warning triangles), had a negligent safety management program, and/or negligently trained the truck driver (failed to teach him that warning triangles were required), making the company's negligence *per se* a cause of the wreck.

Cases Finding Negligence *Per Se* for Violation of the FMCSR

Load Securement

The majority of courts that have considered the issue have held that a violation of an FMCSR constitutes negligence. For example, in *Fortner v. Tecchio Trucking, Inc.*,[124] the court held that FMCSR relate to public safety[125] because "[t]he authorizing statute, 49 U.S.C. § 31136(a), directs the Secretary of Transportation to establish minimum safety standards to ensure commercial motor vehicles are operated and loaded safely." The Sixth Circuit Court of Appeals determined in an earlier case that the purpose of the FMCSR was, at least in part: "the protection of the public on highways of interstate commerce from the hazards of operation by inexperienced, incompetent and unfit persons, by those engaged in excess of maximum hours, or operating with bad conditioned and dangerous equipment."[126]

Therefore, the *Fortner* court also held that the FMCSR regulation at issue required drivers of commercial motor vehicles to act in a certain way for the benefit of the public and that the plaintiffs clearly fell within the class of people that FMCSR was intended to protect. For those reasons, the *Fortner* court only had to determine if there was a genuine dispute as to whether the defendant driver violated an FMCSR requiring him to ensure the load was properly secured[127] pursuant to FMCSR 392.9 and 393.122,[128] and whether such violation was the proximate cause of the plaintiffs' injuries.[129] The court found it undisputed that the FMCSR was violated and that a finding of negligence *per se* was

124. *Fortner v. Tecchio Trucking, Inc.*, 597 F. Supp. 2d 755 (E.D. Tenn. 2009).

125. *Id.* at 757 (citing Darling v. J.B. Expedited Servs., 2006 WL 2238913 (M.D. Tenn. Aug. 3, 2006)).

126. Commercial Standard Ins. Co. v. Robertson, 159 F.2d 405, 410 (6th Cir. 1947).

127. 49 C.F.R. § 392.9; *see also* Locicero v. Interpace Corp., 266 N.W.2d 423 (Wis. 1978).

128. Fortner v. Tecchio Trucking, Inc., 597 F. Supp. 2d 755, 757 (E.D. Tenn. 2009).

129. *See also* Wallace v. Ener, 521 F.2d 215 (5th Cir. 1975) (violation of 49 C.F.R. §§ 392.22 and 393.95 constituted negligence *per se* under Georgia law); Taylor v. Pennsylvania R.R. Co., 246 F. Supp. 604 (D. Del. 1965) (violation of FMCSR requiring stop before railroad crossing was negligence *per se* under Delaware law); Hageman v. TSI, Inc., 786 P.2d 452 (Colo. App. 1989) (violation of FMCSR requiring driver of disabled vehicle to place warning devices for approaching traffic and to pull onto shoulder of road constituted negligence *per se* under Colorado law); Stong v. Free-

warranted. Other courts have also found that failing to secure cargo (FMCSR 393.100) constitutes a breach of a statutory duty and negligence.[130]

Extreme Caution: Visibility and Traction

49 C.F.R. § 392.14 states:

> Extreme caution in the operation of a commercial motor vehicle shall be exercised when hazardous conditions, such as those caused by snow, ice, sleet, fog, mist, rain, dust, or smoke, adversely affect visibility or traction. Speed shall be reduced when such conditions exist. If conditions become sufficiently dangerous, the operation of the commercial motor vehicle shall be discontinued and shall not be resumed until the commercial motor vehicle can be safely operated. . . .[131]

State tort law generally defines the duty of drivers as ordinary care under an ordinary negligence standard. However, the FMCSR just cited establishes a higher standard of care, requiring "extreme caution," when a professional driver has their visibility or traction adversely affected. A driver's visibility and traction are typically affected by adverse weather, but the regulation is not limited to weather-related problems but applies when *any* hazardous condition exists. The "extreme caution" standard established by 49 C.F.R. § 392.14 preempts any lower state standard. The express preemption requirement is met because the FMCSR imposes a standard higher than state law. Said FMCSR also satisfies the "conflict" test of the preemption doctrine because the lower standard of "negligence" under state tort law would stand as an obstacle to the express requirement of the FMCSR by allowing drivers of commercial motor vehicles to escape liability for injuries resulting from their failure to exercise the required "extreme caution."

A federal judge in the District of South Dakota recently rejected a defense argument that section 392.14 could not provide the basis of negligence *per se* liability.[132] The California Court of Appeals held that it was prejudicial error for a court to refuse to instruct the jury on the section 392.14 "extreme caution" standard and to instead give the usual "reasonable care" instruction under California standard negligence instructions.[133] As explained in *Weaver*,

> The Commercial Motor Vehicle Safety Act (Act) was passed by Congress to promote the safe operation of commercial vehicles and to ensure compliance with safety regulations promulgated under the Act. (49 U.S.C. § 31131(a)(1), (3).) Although the Act does not generally preempt state laws and regulations, of importance here is the following regulation: "Every commercial motor vehicle must be operated in accordance with

---

man Truck Line, Inc., 456 So. 2d 698 (Miss. 1984) (violation of 49 C.F.R. §§ 392.21 and 392.22 were negligence *per se* under Mississippi law).

130. Skeie v. Mercer Trucking Co., 61 P.3d 1207, 1210 (Wash. App. 2003).

131. 49 C.F.R. § 392.14.

132. LeVene v. Staples Oil Co., Inc., 685 F. Supp. 3d 791, 808–09 (D. S.D. 2023).

133. Weaver v. Chavez, 133 Cal. App. 4th 1350, 35 Cal. Rptr. 3d 514 (Cal. App. 2005).

> the laws, ordinances, and regulations of the jurisdiction in which it is being operated. However, if a [federal] regulation . . . imposes a higher standard of care than that [state] law, . . . the . . . regulation must be complied with" (49 C.F.R. § 392.2(2005).).[134]

Courts in other states have also charged the jury on negligence *per se* under the requirement of "extreme caution" set forth in section 392.14.[135]

Hours of Service

Hours of service (HOS) regulations promulgated under 49 U.S.C. Part 395 set forth maximum driving and on-duty time for drivers of motor carriers.[136] Those regulations, imposing restrictions on the number of hours that those engaged in interstate commerce may work in one work week, are intended to prevent accidents due to fatigue.[137] It is clear that these maximum driving and on-duty time regulations were enacted to maintain safety on the highway and protect the public against accidents with drivers of motor carriers. Violation of HOS regulations have been found to constitute "reckless indifference to the rights of others."[138] Courts have held that reasonable juries could find that the imposition of punitive damages is warranted against a motor carrier for failing to monitor its driver's conduct and encouraging drivers to exceed federally proscribed driving time limits.[139] Courts have found a citation for maintaining a false log-book—a violation of 49 C.F.R. § 395.8(e)—to be negligence *per se*.[140]

---

134. *Id.* at 517.

135. Whitfield Tank Lines, Inc. v. Navajo Freight Lines, Inc., 90 N.M. 454, 564 P.2d 1336 (N.M. App. 1977) (syl. 4); Kimberlin v. PM Transp., 264 Va. 261, 563 S.E.2d 665 (2002) (syl. 6) (§ 392.14 creates an expanded duty of care for the operation of commercial motor vehicles; error to rule as a matter of law that truck driver did not violate it); Barrows v. Schneider Nat'l Carriers, 156 F.3d 1235 (9th Cir. 1998) (unpublished opinion) (holding that negligence *per se* instruction based on § 392.14 probably proper under Oregon law, but not harmful where jury instructed negligence *per se* under Oregon law not to drive on right side of road); Asbury v. MNT, Inc., 2014 U.S. Dist. LEXIS 167724, 2014 WL 6674475, at *9 (D. N.M. Aug. 6, 2014) (observing that expert testimony is relevant to negligence *per se* claim alleging violation of section 392.14); Bautista v. MVT Servs., LLC, 2017 U.S. Dist. LEXIS 201683, 2017 WL 6054888, at *8 (D. Colo. Dec. 7, 2017) (same); Dortch v. Fowler, 2008 U.S. Dist. LEXIS 24592, 2008 WL 834091, at *3 (W.D. Ky. Mar. 27, 2008) (contrasting section 392.14 as a provision that "purport[s] to provide civil liability for prohibited conduct"); Lay v. Haskins, 549 Fed. Appx. 707, 710–11 (10th Cir. 2013) (finding no abuse of discretion for negligence *per se* instruction on the basis of section 392.14); *but see* Martin v. Hannu, 2024 U.S. Dist. LEXIS 45134, 2024 WL 1097625, at *4 (D. Ore. Feb. 26, 2024) ("[W]hile the provisions of [section] 392.14 are relevant to the negligence determination. . . , they do not so fix the legal standard of conduct such that there are no issues for the jury to resolve.").

136. *See* 49 C.F.R. pt. 395.

137. *Starrett v. Bruce*, 391 F.2d 320, 323 (10th Cir. 1968), *cert. denied*, 393 U.S. 971, 89 S. Ct. 404, 21 L. Ed. 2d 384; Walling v. Comet Carriers, Inc., 151 F.2d 107, 111 (2d Cir. 1945).

138. *See* Restatement (Second) of Torts § 908(2) (1979).

139. Wang v. Marziani, 885 F. Supp. 74, 79 (S.D.N.Y. 1995).

140. *See, e.g.*, Darling v. J.B. Expedited Servs., 2006 U.S. Dist. LEXIS 54000, 2006 WL 2238913, at *20 (M.D. Tenn. 2006) ("[T]he Court concludes that [driver's] citation for maintaining a false log book—a violation of 49 C.F.R. § 395.8(e)—constitutes negligence per se.").

Other FMCSR

Failure to timely place warning triangles has been found to be negligence *per se* pursuant to FMCSR section 392.22.[141] A driver's use of drugs in violation of FMCSR sections 382.213(a), 382.501(a), or 392.4(a) was similarly found to be negligence *per se*.[142] It was a question for the jury if a company negligently hired an unsafe and unqualified driver in violation of FMCSR sections 391.21 and 391.23.[143]

Cases Not Finding Negligence *Per Se* for a Violation of the FMCSR

A minority of courts that have examined the FMCSR have determined that a violation of regulations does not constitute negligence *per se* for one reason or another. Thus, in *Omega Contracting, Inc. v. Torres*,[144] the court held that FMCSR violations in an accident involving a tractor-trailer whose tire separated and caused a collision between several other tractor-trailers were too vague to constitute negligence *per se*. Plaintiffs alleged violation of numerous regulations including 49 C.F.R. §§ 393.205, 396.3(a), and 396.13. The court refused to consider 49 C.F.R. § 393.205, which requires that "nuts or bolts shall not be missing or loose" as evidence of negligence *per se*.

In that regard, the *Omega* court held that:

> [T]he requirement that lug nuts shall not be "loose" did not put the public on notice by clearly defining the required conduct because the regulations do not define the word "loose" nor specify any particular amount of torque. We agree. In this context, the word "loose" is vague and not susceptible of precise meaning. It does not put the public—or in this case, the owners, operators, and drivers of commercial vehicles—on notice of what conduct is prohibited or required. The [plaintiff] is correct in observing that [the court] must give "loose" its ordinary definition of "not rigidly fastened or securely fastened," but that definition does not make the regulation any more precise.[145]

As for sections 393.3(a) and 396.13, that court stated that those general requirements to "systematically inspect, repair, and maintain . . ." simply require a motor carrier "to maintain motor vehicles 'in safe and proper operating conditions' and

141. Harmon v. Grande Tire Co., Inc., 821 F.2d 252, 255 (5th Cir. 1987); Wallace v. Ener, 521 F.2d 215 (5th Cir. 1975); Hageman v. TSI, Inc., 786 P.2d 452 (Colo. App. 1989); Brandes v. Burbank, 613 F.2d 658 (7th Cir. 1980); Thomas v. McDonald, 667 So. 2d 594 (Miss. 1995); Stong v. Freeman Truck Line, Inc., 456 So. 2d 698 (Miss. 1984).

142. Frederick v. Swift Transp. Co., 616 F.3d 1074, 1080 (10th Cir. 2010).

143. Morris v. JTM Materials, Inc., 78 S.W.3d 28, 49 (Tex. App. (Fort Worth) 2002); Smith v. Tommy Roberts Trucking Co., 435 S.E.2d 54 (Ga. App. 1993); Stephens v. A-Able Rents Co., 654 N.E.2d 1315 (Ohio App. 1995).

144. Omega Contr., Inc. v. Torres, 191 S.W.3d 828, 838–43 (Tex. 2006).

145. *Id.* at 840–41.

a driver to 'be satisfied that the motor vehicle is in safe operating condition.'"[146] Determining what is or is not safe in these circumstances bears practically no difference from what is or what is not reasonable. For those reasons, the court held that sections 393.3 and 396.13 were also not an appropriate basis for a negligence *per se* instruction. The court went on to hold that the trial court erred by submitting the negligence *per se* instruction to the jury.

Private Cause of Action

Historically, in response to injured plaintiffs contending that 49 U.S.C. § 14704(a)(2)[147] authorized a private cause of action for violations of the FMCSR, most courts hold that there is "no federal private right of action allowing personal injury or wrongful death plaintiffs to hold defendants liable for violations of the FMCSR."[148] In a twist, some defendants have tried to generate federal subject matter jurisdiction on that basis, and improperly remove the case to federal court.[149]

More recently, motor carrier defendants have argued that since Congress did not create a private right of action to enforce the FMCSR, the FMCSR cannot properly support a negligence *per se* claim. A federal judge in the Eastern District of Tennessee recently observed that this argument represents ". . . an inaccurate understanding of the current law," noting that Tennessee courts have repeatedly and consistently distinguished between negligence *per se* and a legislatively created private cause of action.[150] Although concluding that a violation of the FMCSR is not negligence *per se* under Kentucky law, a federal judge in the Western District of Kentucky similarly observed:

> As has been established in the Sixth Circuit, the FMCSR does not create a federal private right of action. . . . Without a private right of action, the Defendants are correct, the FMCSR cannot act as a platform for any claim by [plaintiff]. However, the Court does not interpret [the] Complaint as having alleged such a stand-alone claim for violation of the FMCSR. Instead, the Court interprets [the] Complaint as alleging a claim for negligence per se premised upon the Defendants' violation

146. *Id.* at 843.

147. "A carrier or broker providing transportation or service subject to jurisdiction under chapter 135 is liable for damages sustained by a person as a result of an act or omission of that carrier or broker in violation of this part." 49 U.S.C. § 14704(a)(2).

148. *See, e.g.*, Leon v. FedEx Ground Package Sys., 2016 U.S. Dist. LEXIS 30281 (D. N.M. Feb. 16, 2016) (collecting cases).

149. *See, e.g.*, Lopez v. Univ. of the Southwest, 2024 U.S. Dist. LEXIS 3249, 2024 WL 68531, at *3–4 (D. N.M. Jan. 5, 2024) (concluding that the argument lacked merit); *see also* Moody v. Great West Cas. Co., 2017 U.S. Dist. LEXIS 2909, 2017 WL 77417, at *2 (S.D. Ga. Jan. 9, 2017) (quoting Merrell Dow Pharms., Inc. v. Thompson, 478 U.S. 804, 813–14 (1986) ("[T]here is a large difference between a federally based theory and a federal claim. Even when it is an element, 'the mere presence of a federal issue in a state cause of action' does not make it into a federal one.").

150. *See* Nelson v. Werner Enters., Inc., 2023 U.S. Dist. LEXIS 181176 (E.D. Tenn. Sept. 15, 2023).

of the FMCSR. As such, the Defendants [sic] argument concerning the absence of a private right under the FMCSR is immaterial.[151]

"The fact that the FMCSR does not contain a private cause of action does not preclude Plaintiff from using the FMCSR to attempt to establish an applicable standard of care."[152] Common law negligence claims can be predicated on violations of the FMCSR. "Historically, common law liability has formed the bedrock of state regulation, and common law tort claims have been described as 'a critical component of the States' traditional ability to protect the health and safety of their citizens.'"[153] As discussed throughout this chapter, whether a plaintiff can successfully allege a violation of the FMCSR as negligence *per se*, as opposed to arguing that the violations are probative evidence of negligence, depends on the law of the forum state.

In Tennessee and Oklahoma, for example, the FMCSR may be relevant to claims of negligence *per se*.[154] "Kansas negligence law permits plaintiffs to use industry standard safety regulations to demonstrate the degree of care owed by [a] defendant."[155] Conversely, in Nebraska, "'the violation of a regulation or statute is not negligence per se, but may be evidence of negligence to be considered with all the other evidence in the case.'"[156] Regardless, in all states, evidence of industry standards,[157] safety codes, and a company's own policies and procedures[158] can properly serve as a foundation of a negligence case. It would

151. Tassin v. BNK Transp., Inc., 2019 U.S. Dist. LEXIS 88525, 2019 WL 2271163, at *2 (W.D. Ky. May 28, 2019); see also Hejnal v. U.S. XPress, Inc., 2018 U.S. Dist. LEXIS 11304, 2018 WL 534376, at *7 (E.D. Mo. Jan. 24, 2018) ("Plaintiff does not allege a violation of a federal regulation as a cause of action in its own right[;] [r]ather, [the] complaint merely alleges possible violations of federal regulations as an element of state law causes of action.").

152. Nelson v. Werner Enters., Inc., 2023 U.S. Dist. LEXIS 181176, 2023 WL 6444274, at *4 (E.D. Tenn. Sept. 15, 2023).

153. Desiano v. Warner-Lambert & Co., 467 F.3d 85, 86 (2d Cir. 2006) (quoting Cipollone v. Liggett Group, Inc., 505 U.S. 504, 544 (1992)).

154. Fortner v. Tecchio Trucking, Inc., 597 F. Supp. 2d 755, at 757–58 (E.D. Tenn. 2009); Beaber v. Stevens Transp., Inc., 2015 WL 8074312, at *1 (W.D. Okla. Dec. 4, 2015).

155. Kimberly Dionne & Katelynn S. v. Itp W. Express, 2020 U.S. Dist. LEXIS 134205, 2020 WL 4347044, at *4 (D. Kan. July 29, 2020) (rejecting private cause of action argument); *see also* Chavez-Matchie v. Jack Cooper Transp., Co., 2017 U.S. Dist. LEXIS 83756, 2017 WL 2378334, at *4 (D. Kan. June 1, 2017) (same).

156. Ballinger v. Gustafson, 2022 U.S. Dist. LEXIS 190974, 2022 WL 16758558, at *3 (D. Neb. Oct. 19, 2022) (quoting Scheele v. Rains, 874 N.W.2d 867, 872 (Neb. 2016); *see also* Hejnal v. U.S. XPress, Inc., 2018 U.S. Dist. LEXIS 11304, 2018 WL 534376, at *7 (denying motion to strike the plaintiff's references to the FMCSR in connection with his allegations of negligence).

157. *See, e.g.*, Pierce v. Platte-Clay Electric Cooperative, Inc., 769 S.W.2d 769, 772 (Mo. 1989) ("[E]vidence of industry standards is generally admissible as proof of whether or not a duty of care was breached.").

158. *See, e.g.*, Louisiana-Pacific Corp. v. Andrade, 19 S.W.3d 245, 247 (Tex. 1999) ("Corporate safety policies, or the lack of them, can serve as the basis for a gross negligence finding."); Luckie v. Piggly-Wiggly Southern, Inc., 173 Ga. App. 177 (1984) (company rules are admissible to illustrate negligence); Dogan v. Buff, 329 Ga. App. 499, 501 n.5 (2014) ("Rockwell's trucking manual and safety guidelines are not imposing a heightened standard of care. . . . These corporate guidelines are relevant because they may be illustrative of ordinary negligence under the circumstances presented in this case, even though the violation of such a rule is not negligence in and of itself.").

be ridiculous to argue that the trucking industry, much less a trucking company, contends that the FMCSR does not represent a minimum standard of care. If the FMCSR are not followed commercial vehicles are not allowed to drive on public highways and will be placed OOS (Out of Service)[159] by the DOT/FMCSA. If CDL drivers or commercial vehicles are placed OOS they are not allowed to move, and thus can't make money. Clearly the FMCSR set forth a minimum industry and company standard of care that everyone must comply with.

Conclusion

A court's finding of negligence *per se* as a result of a defendant driver's or trucking company's violation of a FMCSR can dramatically change a trucking case. Counsel must continually assess the possibility that one or more of the FMCSR apply to the facts of the case. It is not unusual for a driver to indicate one violation of the FMCSR in his answer to interrogatories, but blame the collision on a second, previously unrevealed, violation at his deposition. Counsel must be able to deal with such surprises by having a thorough understanding of the FMCSR.

A lawyer with a deep familiarity of the FMCSR has a huge advantage in a commercial motor vehicle case. However, every lawyer will need an expert, or concessions from the defendant, to prove the applicability of the FMCSR and how they are used within the industry,[160] the standard of care which they create or require, and how they were violated in a particular case. Critically, how the FMCSR are used within the industry is a matter for expert opinion, otherwise the FMCSR are a creature of law, and the sole source of the law is the judge.[161] For that reason, it is important for lawyers to retain an expert early, investigate the case together, and carefully develop potential theories of regulation-based negligence early in the case.

159. *See* 49 C.F.R. § 395.13 Drivers Ordered Out of Service; 49 C.F.R. § 396.9(c) Motor Vehicles and Intermodal Equipment Declared "Out-of-Service."

160. Roohbakhsh v. Bd. of Trs. of the Neb. State Colleges, 2019 U.S. Dist. LEXIS 190266, 2019 WL 5653448, at *3 (D. Neb. Oct. 31, 2019) ("Expert or fact testimony on industry practice or standards, however, is often relevant and admissible. . . . Testimony about industry standards, or policies adopted by other institutions to comply with applicable regulations, is not generally regarded as a legal opinion or conclusion.") (Collecting cases); Police Retirement System v. Midwest Inv. Advisory Service, Inc., 940 F.2d 351, 357 (8th Cir. 1991).

161. Bammerlin v. Navistar Int'l Transp. Corp., 30 F.3d 898, 900 (7th Cir.1994) ("The meaning of federal regulations is not a question of fact, to be resolved by the jury after a battle of experts. It is a question of law, to be resolved by the court."); Police Retirement System v. Midwest Inv. Advisory Service, Inc., 940 F.2d 351, 357 (8th Cir. 1991) (noting it was error for court to allow expert witness to lecture jury about what statute meant); Specht v. Jensen, 853 F.2d 805 (10th Cir. 1988).

CHAPTER 26

Intermodal and Inland Transport Truck Accident Claims

D.J. Young, III, Esq.

Introduction

When the commercial motor vehicle (CMV) crash involves an international shipment, there are additional considerations for the truck crash litigator. These include the task of identifying the possible parties; laws applicable to intermodal equipment and intermodal equipment providers; leases; interchange agreements; laws applicable to ocean carriers, ocean carrier intermediaries (ocean freight forwarders and non-vessel operating common carriers); and laws applicable to cargo losses, such as the Carmack Amendment, Carriage of Goods by Sea Act, and the Harter Act; the applicability or non-applicability of these to injury and death claims; jurisdiction issues; and international service of process and discovery.

Recognizing International Shipping Defendants

It is important for attorneys handling domestic truck crash litigation involving international shipments to determine whether any of the parties to the international portions of this shipment have liability for the crash. The motor carrier and its driver are not always the sole parties among the parties to the shipment who may be directly or vicariously liable. They may lack sufficient insurance or assets to cover the loss. Thus, attorneys for plaintiffs and defendants must consider whether other parties share in the fault for the loss and decide whether to bring them into the litigation.

The address on the truck driver's commercial driver's license is suggestive of the possibility that the driver is employed by a trucking company that is not organized or headquartered in the United States. This may be true even if the trucking company has registered a corporation or limited liability company in the United States. The attorney must investigate the company. Is the address nothing more than a shared-business address or mere mailing address at someone's residence? What information is available through the applicable state corporation commission or secretary of state? Does that show a non-United States parent company? Does that foreign parent company have sufficient rights of control over the purported American affiliate company to warrant the imposition of vicarious liability? Is the subsidiary company registered with the U.S. Department of Transportation (USDOT) or a state-level equivalent? Is the parent company registered with the USDOT or a state-level equivalent?

Another way to recognize a potential international shipping defendant is to consider the type of motor vehicle equipment involved. The presence of "intermodal equipment" is an indication of the possibility of a foreign responsible party or a domestic responsible party other than or in additional to the motor carrier. "Intermodal Equipment" is "trailing equipment that is used in the intermodal transportation of containers over public highways in interstate commerce, including trailers and chassis."[1] A typical intermodal cargo container is a large, rectangular, metal box, between 20 and 53 feet long, 8 feet wide, and 8 feet 6 inches or 9 feet 6 inches tall that can be stacked like bricks on an ocean-going container ship, stacked on railroad cars equipped to transport them, or stacked onto an intermodal equipment chassis trailer to be towed by another type of commercial motor vehicle (CMV)—a tractor—on the highway. The word "intermodal" refers to the fact that these containers can be transported by multiple modes: ship, railroad, and tractor-trailer. This equipment can be observed all over America, but especially in the vicinity of the major port cities. The motor carrier is unlikely to be the owner of either the cargo container or the intermodal equipment chassis trailer. Those two items are not necessarily owned by the same party, either.

An important way to recognize a potential international shipment defendant is to consider the bill of lading and other shipping papers that may be among the documentary evidence relevant to the investigation of the crash. Ordinarily, the bill of lading must be transported in the CMV with the shipment. It identifies the carrier responsible for the shipment. It sometimes contains other information that can assist in the identification of responsible parties. It also describes the origin and destination of the shipment, which sometimes is helpful for party identification. There are varieties of bills of lading,[2] and, in some cases, more than one bill of lading will be involved, which means that the bills of lading will have to be compared and analyzed to fully understand the roles of the parties identified on them and whether any of them are valid or void. Other documents will include evidence of agreements about who owns the tractor and intermodal equipment.

1. 49 U.S.C. § 31151(f) and 49 C.F.R. §§ 390.5 and 390.5T.

2. For regulatory and statutory examples, *see, e.g.*, 49 C.F.R. pt. 373 and 49 U.S.C. §§ 14706 and 80101.

Background Information Concerning Intermodal Equipment

A note of caution is warranted. International shipping has an entire language of its own that likely will be unfamiliar to many attorneys handling vehicle crash litigation. The terms and abbreviations often have very precise meanings, and it is important to understand and use the terms correctly to avoid problems in the investigation, prosecution, and defense of these cases. The Intermodal Association of North America has a helpful online glossary of such terms, and it is a useful starting point.[3] The statutes and regulations described in this chapter use many statutorily defined terms and those definitions must be considered, too. But, how the important court decisions in your jurisdiction use the terms matters, too, and the attorney must research and understand these terms before pleading the case if the pleadings will need to use any of them. Incorrect usage of terms can be detrimental to the prosecution or defense of the case.

Typically, the intermodal chassis trailer is owned by an intermodal equipment provider (IEP) (discussed later). There are four significant scenarios by which motor carriers obtain use of an intermodal chassis.[4] In the "single chassis provider model," the chassis is owned by an IEP and is supplied to a shipper or motor carrier for rent. In the "motor-carrier controlled model," the motor carrier owns (or long-term leases) the chassis. In the "gray pool model," a manager supervises a pool of chassis supplied by multiple IEPs. In the "pool of pools" model, which is located in Los Angeles and Long Beach, each IEP owns its own pool, but motor carriers can pick up and deliver the chassis trailer to any of their respective pools. The chassis pools are places near ocean terminals, rail yards, and other terminal operations where the intermodal chassis are stored to support the daily usage needs of motor carriers who are hired to haul intermodal containers.[5] According to Consolidated Chassis Management LLC, "chassis pools enable intermodal participants including ocean carriers, motor carriers, leasing companies, shippers, and more to access container chassis under one focused management at the lowest possible cost."[6]

For "gray pools" and "pool of pools" models, usually the ocean carrier contracts with the IEP to make chassis trailers available, and the IEP bills the ocean

3. *Intermodal Glossary* (Intermodal Association of North America, 2017), https://www.intermodal.org/documents/Glossary_0.pdf. Special thanks is due to attorney Morgan Adams for making me aware of this source and the one in the next footnote.

4. U.S. Government Accountability Office report entitled *Commercial Shipping: Information on How Chassis Are Made Available and the Federal Government's Oversight Role*, dated Mar. 8, 2021, p. 9 (hereinafter, "GAO Report"), https://www.gao.gov/assets/gao-21-315r.pdf.

5. Direct ChassisLink, Inc.'s website has a helpful explanation of the different types of chassis pools including competitive pools, third-party operated pools, gray pools, and the "Pool of Pools," https://dcli.com/resource/what-is-a-chassis-pool/.

6. https://ccmpool.com/about/chassis-pools/. The three major chassis providers in the United States currently are Direct Chassis Link, Inc., TRAC, and Flexi Van, according to a filing before the Federal Maritime Commission in Docket No. 20-14, served March 25, 2024, in the case styled, *Intermodal Motor Carriers Conference, American Trucking Ass'n, Inc. v. OCEMA, et al.* (hereinafter, American Trucking v. OCEMA), https://www2.fmc.gov/readingroom/docs/20-14/20-14%20Joint%20Status%20Report.pdf/. Records filed on the dockets of cases before the Federal Maritime Commission can be found at https://www2.fmc.gov/readingroom/.

carrier for "carrier haulage contracts" or the IEP bills the motor carrier for "merchant haulage contracts."[7] The arrangement underlying the movement of shipping containers typically falls under one of these two types of agreements. For "carrier haulage," a shipper contracts with an ocean carrier to provide origin-to-destination transportation for the cargo, including both the oceangoing portion and the inland transport portion to a final destination by a motor carrier, and the ocean carrier contracts with both the motor carrier and the IEP. Under "merchant haulage," the shipper contracts with the ocean carrier to deliver a shipping container over water to a port, but the shipper separately contracts with the motor carrier to provide inland transport from port to final destination, and either the shipper or the motor carrier contracts with the IEP.[8]

Historically, the members of the Ocean Equipment Management Association (OCEMA), which is comprised of 12 major ocean carriers,[9] owned or controlled most of the intermodal chassis used in North America.[10] The ocean carriers included the cost of moving the shipping container from origin to final destination in the full cost of such services.[11] Many ocean carriers have since sold their chassis to IEPs.[12] They eventually coordinated their efforts by way of a process called "chassis pooling." Since that time, the chassis industry has seen significant changes. Presently, familiar names in the chassis industry include CCM, Trac Intermodal, FlexiVan, and DCLI (Direct ChassisLink, Inc.).

Until recently, motor carriers had little to no choice about which chassis pool or chassis to use when retained to haul intermodal containers, but that changed pursuant to a ruling of the Federal Maritime Commission in 2024.[13] Under the 2024 decision, the ocean carriers' practice of designating exclusive chassis providers for merchant haulage denying choice to the motor carriers violates 46 U.S.C. § 41102(c).[14] The Federal Maritime Commission ordered them to cease and desist from such practices in Los Angeles/Long Beach, Chicago, Savannah, and Memphis.[15] The litigation giving rise to this order is not entirely resolved as of the writing of this chapter and further developments may affect these and other locations.[16]

7. GAO Report, *supra* note 4, at 8–9.

8. *Id.* at 6.

9. http://www.ocema.org/members.html.

10. *Chassis Pools: A Brief Background*, Consolidated Chassis Management, LLC, https://ccmpool.com/about/chassis-pools/.

11. GAO Report, *supra* note 4.

12. *Id.*

13. GAO Report, *supra* note 4; American Trucking. v. OCEMA, Order in Docket No. 20-14, served Feb. 13, 2024.

14. American Trucking v. OCEMA, Order in Docket No. 20-14, served Feb. 13, 2024.

15. *Id.*

16. Joint Status Report of the Complainant and the Respondents in Docket No. 20-14, dated August 23, 2024, in *American Trucking v. OCEMA*. A separate docket, Docket No. 24-02 is a "non-adjudicatory investigation" into compliance with the February 13, 2024, order in Docket No. 20-14.

Laws Applicable to Intermodal Equipment Providers

The Secretary of the USDOT is required to "maintain a program to ensure that intermodal equipment used to transport intermodal containers is safe and systematically maintained" and to implement regulations in furtherance of that requirement.[17] The presumed safety function of such laws is to protect road users from injuries and deaths arising out of negligent maintenance of intermodal equipment. In furtherance of that goal, the USDOT has implemented regulations specifically directed to intermodal equipment providers (IEPs).[18] An IEP is "any person that interchanges intermodal equipment with a motor carrier pursuant to a written interchange agreement or has a contractual responsibility for the maintenance of the intermodal equipment."[19] "Intermodal equipment" refers to "trailing equipment that is used in the intermodal transportation of containers over public highways in interstate commerce, including trailers and chassis."[20] As such, intermodal trailers and intermodal chassis satisfy the definitions of "motor vehicle" and "commercial motor vehicle" as those terms are defined in 49 C.F.R. §§ 390.5 and 390.5T.[21] The logical implication of these definitions is that the combination of a tractor and intermodal chassis together satisfies the definition of "commercial motor vehicle."[22]

IEPs are required to register with the Federal Motor Carrier Safety Administration (FMCSA).[23] IEPs must mark their equipment with the USDOT number

---

17. 49 U.S.C. § 31151.

18. 49 C.F.R. § 390.3(h). Notably, IEPs must comply with the Federal Motor Carrier Safety Regulations contained in 49 C.F.R. pt. 390.

19. 49 U.S.C. § 31151(f) and 49 C.F.R. §§ 390.5 and 390.5T.

20. 49 C.F.R. §§ 390.5, 390.5T.

21. Definitions in this area of the law are important. Because "employer" and "employee" in 49 C.F.R. §§ 390.5 and 390.5T are defined in reference to the ownership or leasing and operation of a "commercial motor vehicle" in "interstate commerce," such terms, therefore, include those driving/towing intermodal equipment. "Employee" is defined to include "independent contractors." *Id.* That has significance because the independent contractor defense often does not and cannot work in the context of truck drivers and motor carriers in interstate commerce. The definition of "lease" found in 49 C.F.R. §§ 390.5, 390.5T, and 376.2 includes a "contract or arrangement in which the owner grants the use of equipment, with or without driver, for a specified period to an authorized carrier [under 49 U.S.C. §§ 13901–13902] for use in the regulated transportation of property, in exchange for compensation." "Equipment" as used here includes "semitrailers" which is a "trailer" meeting the definition of "motor vehicle." *Id.*

22. 49 C.F.R. §§ 390.5, 390.5T. The trailer owner's insurance, therefore, may also provide coverage. *See, e.g.,* Ins. Co. of N. Am. v. Royal Indemnity Co., 429 F.2d 1014 (6th Cir. 1970); Contrans, Inc. v. Ryder Truck Rental, Inc., 836 F.2d 163, 166 (3d Cir. 1987) ("It is an accepted principle of insurance law that where an accident arises out of the use of a combined vehicle such as a tractor-trailer and where separate policies cover the tractor and the trailer, all insurance applicable to the combined vehicle comes into play, regardless of which part of the rig was physically involved in the accident."); Carolina Ins. Co. v. Travelers Prop. Cas. Co., 90 F. Supp. 3d 304, 318 (D. N.J. 2014) ("To speak of 'loading' a tractor is almost meaningless. The tractor/trailer rig functions as a unit—articulated, to be sure, but no different in principle from the unitary front and back halves of a straight truck.").

23. 49 C.F.R. § 390.201(b).

assigned to them by the FMCSA.[24] IEPs must "systematically inspect, repair, and maintain" "all intermodal equipment intended for interchange with a motor carrier," and they must do so in accordance with the inspection and record keeping requirements applicable, generally, to motor carriers.[25] Notably, they must "provide intermodal equipment intended for interchange that is in safe and proper operating condition"; "maintain a system of driver vehicle inspection reports"; and "maintain a system of inspection, repair, and maintenance records."[26] In furtherance of these requirements, they must "periodically inspect" their equipment that is intended for interchange with a motor carrier,[27] and "implement procedures to repair any equipment damage, defects, or deficiencies" identified by the CMV driver.[28] IEPs are prohibited from providing their equipment to motor carriers unless it has passed at least one inspection by the IEP within the last 12 months, and it shall cause the "documentation of such inspection [to be] on the vehicle."[29] IEPs are prohibited from "placing intermodal equipment in service on the public highways if that equipment has been found to pose an imminent hazard," which is "any condition" of the intermodal equipment "that substantially increases the likelihood of serious injury or death if not discontinued immediately."[30]

The driver of a CMV hauling intermodal equipment must inspect and make sure that all of the following parts of the intermodal equipment are in good working order before operating it on the road: service brakes, lighting, conspicuity markings, wheels, rims, lugs, tires, air line connections, air hoses, air line couplers, king pin upper coupling device, rails, support frames, tie downs, locking pins, clevises, clamps, hooks, sliders, and sliding frame lock.[31] If the driver operates the intermodal equipment over the road, the driver is deemed to have confirmed that all such equipment is in good working order at the time the driver accepted the equipment.[32] If, during the inspection, the driver finds a problem, the driver must report it to the IEP, and, as noted earlier, the IEP must repair it. If during the driver's operation of the intermodal equipment, the driver discovers damage, defects, or deficiencies in the equipment, the driver must report it to the IEP at the time the driver returns it.[33] Moreover, the trucking

---

24. *Id.* §§ 390.21(g), 390.40(b). Look for identification markings along the curb side of the center beam of the chassis and at the rear of the chassis. If a container is on the chassis, it will have its own identification information on the doors. Using the license plate number of the trailer or the ten-digit code (four letters followed by six numbers) of the equipment, one can search it in the Global Intermodal Equipment Registry to find the party responsible for that intermodal equipment: https://app.gierregistry.com/apps/auth/chassisInquiryPublic.

25. 49 C.F.R. §§ 390.40(c), 396.3.

26. *Id.* § 390.40(d–f).

27. 49 C.F.R. §§ 390.40(g), 396.17. The Intermodal Association of North America has a 300-page equipment inspection and repair guide, *The IANA Guide to Chassis Inspection and Repair: Intermodal Recommended Practices.*

28. *Id.* §§ 390.40(i), 396.11(b).

29. *Id.* § 396.17.

30. *Id.* §§ 390.40(j), 386.72(b)(3), 385.503.

31. *Id.* §S 390.42(a), 392.7(b), 396.9(c), 396.11(b), 396.12.

32. *Id.* § 392.7(b).

33. *Id.* §§ 390.42, 396.11(b).

company and driver in possession of the equipment have independent regulatory obligations to inspect their vehicles and cease operating them if doing so would violate the Federal Motor Carrier Safety Regulations (FMCSRs).[34]

Special requirements apply to the securement of intermodal containers to intermodal container chassis and securement of intermodal containers to vehicles other than intermodal container chassis.[35] Cargo within the containers must be secured in a manner "to prevent shifting upon or within the vehicle to such an extent that the vehicle's stability or maneuverability is adversely affected."[36]

State regulation of intermodal equipment safety is preempted if any such state law "exceeds or is inconsistent with a requirement imposed under or pursuant to [49 U.S.C. § 31151]."[37]

Leases and Interchange Agreements

A motor carrier may obtain the possession of an IEP's intermodal equipment either by way of a "lease" (which is a "contract or arrangement") or by way of an "interchange agreement."[38]

Leases of Equipment

The regulatory structure seems to assume that the typical model will involve the motor carrier obtaining the intermodal equipment from the IEP pursuant to an interchange agreement. This can be seen from the "general exemptions" in the leasing regulations which indicate that such regulations do not apply to "equipment leased without drivers from a person who is principally engaged in such a business" or "any type of trailer not drawn by a power unit leased from the same lessor."[39] Yet, it is conceivable that the authorized motor carrier could lease both the power unit and the trailer from the IEP.[40] A lease may or may not include a "lease" of the driver.[41] To properly comply with the regulations, the motor carrier shall give a receipt to the IEP, the motor carrier shall mark the equipment in accordance with the vehicle identification requirements in the FMCSRs, and the motor carrier shall either keep the lease or a statement concerning the lease in the tractor.[42] The lease is to identify the owner and the motor carrier, state the duration, and provide that "the authorized carrier lessee shall have exclusive possession, control, and use of the equipment for the duration of the lease. The lease

34. Please see the chapter in this book about inspections and maintenance by attorney Amy Papuga.

35. 49 C.F.R. § 393.126.

36. *Id.* §§ 393.126(a), 393.100(b), 393.106.

37. 49 U.S.C. § 31151(d-e); *see also* 49 C.F.R. § 390.46.

38. 49 C.F.R. §§ 376.2(e), 376.11, 376.31, 390.5, 390.5T; *cf.* 49 U.S.C. § 14102.

39. 49 C.F.R. § 376.21(c–d). The exemptions only apply to the "leasing regulations" and not to the "interchange" regulations. *Id.* and § 376.1.

40. The next comments about leasing here are generally applicable regardless of the presence of an IEP or intermodal equipment.

41. 49 C.F.R. § 376.2 definitions of "lease," "lessor," and "lessee."

42. 49 C.F.R. § 376.11.

shall further provide that the authorized carrier lessee shall assume complete responsibility for the operation of the equipment for the duration of the lease."[43] It also must address other items, like which party is responsible for removing identification devices, compensation, "insurance for the protection of the public pursuant to FMCSA regulations," and provision of "any other insurance for the operation of the leased equipment, such as bobtail insurance."[44] It seems obvious that the lease must be in writing.[45] But, not all lessors and lessees reduce their leases to writing. Nonetheless, case law confirms that the failure to document the lease in writing does not negate the obligation of the lessee motor carrier to have "exclusive possession, control, and use of the equipment for the duration of the lease" even when providing it to a third party.[46]

Interchange Agreements

An IEP is "any person that interchanges intermodal equipment with a motor carrier pursuant to a written interchange agreement or has a contractual responsibility for the maintenance of the intermodal equipment."[47] "Interchange" means "[t]he receipt of equipment by one motor carrier of property from another such carrier, at a point which both carriers are authorized to serve, with which to continue a through movement."[48] "Interchange" also means "the act of providing intermodal equipment to a motor carrier pursuant to an intermodal equipment interchange agreement for the purpose of transporting the equipment for loading or unloading by any person or repositioning the equipment for the benefit of the equipment provider, but it does not include the leasing of

43. *Id.* § 376.12(c)(1). Whether the lessor (owner of the equipment) or driver provided by the lessor (which is possible due to the definitions of "lessor" and "lessee" in § 376.2) is an "independent contractor" or "employee" of the "authorized carrier" is not intended to be affected by § 376.12(c)(1), according to § 376.12(c)(4). The regulators' explanation of subsection (c)(4) indicated that it had to do with workers compensation but it is silent about its impact on agency and negligence law. *Ex Parte No. MC-203, Petition to Amend Lease and Interchange of Vehicle Regulations,* 8 I.C.C.2d 559 (June 29, 1992) (referring to 49 C.F.R. § 1057.12, which is the previously codified version of § 376.12). This makes sense, given the fact that other law, regardless of status (independent contractor or employee) covers liability for negligence. Status as employee or independent contractor is addressed in 49 C.F.R. §§ 390.5 and 390.5T. *See also* 49 U.S.C. § 14102(a)(4). And, the motor carrier must have liability insurance covering liability for bodily injury and property damage caused by the motor carrier and driver. 49 U.S.C. § 13906(a) and 49 C.F.R. §§ 387.1, 387.3, 387.5, 387.7, and 387.9. Financial responsibility requirements, therefore, cannot be frustrated by independent contractor relationships. Simpson v. Empire Truck Lines, Inc., 571 F.3d 475, 476 (5th Cir. 2009), Edwards v. McElliotts Trucking, LLC, 286 F. Supp. 3d 867, 879 (W.D. Va. 2017).

44. 49 C.F.R. § 376.12. This section also protects "an agent of an authorized carrier in providing transportation on behalf of that authorized carrier." *Id.* § 376.12(m).

45. *Id.* § 376.11.

46. *See,* Puga v. About Tyme Transp., Inc., 227 F. Supp. 3d 760, 764 (S.D. Tx. 2017) ("no lease—written or oral—is required prior to imposing statutory liability" as an employer) *aff'd on proc. grounds,* 922 F.3d 285 (5th Cir. 2019). *Cf.* Cox v. Bond Transp., 249 A.2d 579, 586–87 (1969) *cert. denied* 395 U.S. 935; Zamalloa v. Hart, 31 F.3d 911, 917 (9th Cir. 1994) (finding that more than one common carrier can be the statutory employer at the same time, and finding that the existence of a written lease in not a condition precedent to imposing statutory employer liability).

47. 49 U.S.C. § 31151(f) and 49 C.F.R. §§ 390.5 and 390.5T.

48. 49 C.F.R. §§ 376.2(c) and 390.5 and 390.5T (third definition of interchange).

equipment to a motor carrier for primary use in the motor carrier's own freight hauling operations."[49] It is important not to confuse which type of interchange is involved. If the equipment is not intermodal equipment, then the definition applicable to two motor carriers applies instead of the definition that involves a motor carrier and an IEP. But the converse is not necessarily so because the two motor carriers may be using intermodal equipment in a transaction that has nothing to do with an IEP.

An "intermodal equipment interchange agreement" is "the Uniform Intermodal Interchange and Facilities Access Agreement (UIFFA) or any other written document executed by an intermodal equipment provider or its agent and a motor carrier or its agent, the primary purpose of which is to establish the responsibilities and liabilities of both parties with respect to the interchange of the intermodal equipment."[50] "Interchange agreement" is defined elsewhere in the regulations to mean "a written contract, lease, or other arrangement providing for the interchange and specifically describing the equipment to be interchanged. This written agreement shall set forth the specific points of interchange, how the equipment is to be used, and the compensation for such use. The interchange agreement shall be signed by the parties or by their authorized representatives."[51]

The "Uniform Intermodal Interchange and Facilities Access Agreement" (UIIA) is a "program" of the Intermodal Association of North America.[52] It is possible that an interchange agreement other than the UIIA agreement might be in place, but the Intermodal Association of North America says that 95 percent of all intermodal equipment interchanges are governed by the UIIA, with 130,000 intermodal trucking companies participating.[53] Thus, it is worth exploring the UIIA here.

The purpose of the UIIA is to define the relationship between the provider of the intermodal equipment, the motor carrier, and the operator of the facility having possession of the intermodal equipment.[54] There may be one provider of the intermodal cargo chassis trailer and another provider of the intermodal cargo container pursuant to this agreement. "Interchange" for purposes of this agreement means "the transfer of physical possession" of things like trailers, chassis, and containers, but excludes tractors.[55] Whenever the event of "interchange" occurs, the parties shall sign and exchange the "Equipment Interchange Receipt"[56] (EIR) which confirms the interchange of the equipment

49. *Id.* §§ 390.5 and 390.5T (first definition of interchange); *see also* 49 U.S.C. § 31151(f)(4).

50. *Id.* §§ 390.5 and 390.5T; *see also* 49 U.S.C. § 31151(f)(2). UIFFA also is sometimes abbreviated UIIA.

51. 49 C.F.R. § 376.31(a).

52. https://uiia.intermodal.org/documents/uiia/newuiia-Home.pdf. This is the link for the Uniform Intermodal Interchange and Facilities Access Agreement, and the identification of the program, parties, and terms are contained within it. The agreement is abbreviated "UIIA."

53. https://intermodal.org/uiia/.

54. UIIA ¶ B(2).

55. UIIA ¶¶ B(12) and B(17).

56. UIIA ¶ D(2).

between the parties and may describe the physical condition of the equipment.[57] The UIIA contractually binds the motor carrier to conduct a pre-trip inspection of the intermodal equipment prior to departure with the interchanged equipment, and it contractually binds the equipment provider to have a valid FMCSA inspection sticker on the equipment.[58] It contractually binds the motor carrier to keep the equipment in the same condition, excepting reasonable wear and tear.[59] The motor carrier is required to return the equipment to the same location where it received the equipment unless the provider directs the motor carrier to return it to a different location within the same local commercial territory.[60] If the equipment is damaged during the motor carrier's possession of it, the motor carrier must pay for the repair.[61] If the tires are damaged before the motor carrier takes possession of the equipment, the repair is the provider's responsibility, but tire damage occurring during the motor carrier's possession is the "sole responsibility of the motor carrier."[62] Exhibit A to the UIIA lists all of the items on the intermodal equipment that the motor carrier contractually agrees to inspect. Exhibit B to the UIIA lists all of the items on the intermodal equipment for which the equipment provider is responsible. Exhibit C allocates responsibility of the listed items to the motor carrier during the motor carrier's possession of the equipment.

The allocation of financial and performance responsibility for maintenance of the intermodal equipment between the provider and the motor carrier is a contractual matter pursuant to the UIIA. It does not necessarily govern the allocation of responsibility for performance of the maintenance for purposes of duties owed to regulatory agencies or tort claimants. The duties to tort claimants may have been contractually assumed by one party pursuant to the agreement, while the other party continues to have the same duty to tort claimants. The UIIA declares that the parties to the UIIA are independent contractors of each other.[63] That contractual declaration, however, is not binding on third-party tort claimants. Instead, that determination is made pursuant to common law and/or statutory law.

The UIIA requires the motor carrier to "defend, hold harmless and fully indemnify" the other parties to the UIIA "without regard to whether the Indemnitees' liability is vicarious, implied in law, or as a result of the fault or negligence of the Indemnities" with respect to property damage, injury, and wrongful death litigation.[64] If the motor carrier lacks the financial ability to satisfy its indemnification obligations, and the loss arises out of something that arguably is the negligence of the IEP, for example, then the IEP (and its

57. *Id.* ¶ B(14). This receipt may be a paper or electronic document.
58. *Id.* ¶ D(3).
59. *Id.* ¶ D(3); ¶ E(1).
60. *Id.* ¶ E(1).
61. *Id.* ¶ E(3).
62. *Id.* ¶ E(4).
63. *Id.* ¶ F(2).
64. *Id.* ¶ F(4). There is an exclusion from the motor carrier's indemnification obligation with respect to certain kinds of defects, as explained here in the UIIA.

insurance company) may be at risk of having to satisfy the tort claimant's judgment regardless of the indemnification clause. The point is, the UIIA's indemnification clause is not binding on tort claimants. If counsel for the motor carrier is concerned about the inability of his or her client to satisfy the tort claim, it may make sense for the motor carrier to bring the equipment provider into the lawsuit if the tort claimant does not do so. Regardless, the UIIA requires the motor carrier to place the other parties to the UIIA on notice of the claim, presumably so they can defend themselves to the extent they believe the motor carrier is unable to protect their interests.[65] To mitigate the risk to the other parties to the UIIA, the motor carrier is required to carry at least $1,000,000 or greater combined single limit insurance coverage that covers the intermodal equipment, and such policy shall name the equipment provider as an additional insured party.[66] Because of inflation in the cost of everything in recent years, $1,000,000 will not be sufficient to cover all casualties.

Impact of the Graves Amendment on Negligence Claims

There is a federal law commonly known as the Graves Amendment, found at 49 U.S.C. § 30106(a), that may provide liability protection to an IEP in circumstances where it was neither negligent nor engaged in criminal wrongdoing. The Graves Amendment protects businesses that are in the business of renting or leasing vehicles.[67] "Although the Graves Amendment prohibits vicarious liability claims against owners of leased vehicles, the Graves Amendment contains a savings clause which allows an owner of a leased vehicle to be found directly liable for the owner's negligence or criminal wrongdoing."[68] "[T]he term 'negligence' as used in the Graves Amendment savings clause is a broad term" and can include direct negligence claims like negligent maintenance.[69] The key is whether the owner of the equipment committed its own direct wrong—direct negligence or criminal wrongdoing. "[I]f a covered owner has done nothing negligent or criminal, it cannot be liable simply for the actions of a renter or lessee. But if a covered owner is itself responsible for some negligent or criminal

---

65. *Id.* ¶ F(5).

66. *Id.* ¶ F(6). The policy is required to have the "Truckers Uniform Intermodal Interchange Endorsement (UIIE-1).

67. It was originally intended to protect typical car rental businesses, like those operating at the commercial passenger airports. Garcia v. Vanguard Car Rental USA Inc., 540 F.3d 1242 (11th Cir. 2008). It has been applied for the benefit of an IEP in circumstances in which direct negligence was alleged against the IEP but there was no evidence of negligence. Holder v. Suarez, 2016 U.S. Dist. LEXIS 17388, at *42–55, 2016 WL 593620 (M.D. Pa. Case No. 3:CV-14-1789, Feb. 12, 2016); *see also* Eisenberg v. Cope Bestway Express, 131 A.D.3d 1198, 1200 (N.Y. App. Div. 2d Dept., 2015) (intermodal chassis); Gruver v. Montesa Express, Inc., 2024 U.S. Dist. LEXIS 79508, at *33, 2024 WL 1913113 (C.D. Ill. Case No. 1:21-cv-1210, May 1, 2024) (intermodal chassis). It has been applied to a case in which a tractor-trailer lessor was sued, because there was no evidence of direct negligence or wrongdoing. Berkan v. Penske Truck Leasing Canada, 535 F. Supp. 2d 341, 343–46 (W.D. N.Y. 2008).

68. *Carton v. GMAC*, 611 F.3d 451, 457 (8th Cir. 2010).

69. *Id.*

conduct, then claims under state law may proceed against it."[70] Thus, a negligent entrustment of a commercial trailer could be actionable against the owner of the trailer if the elements of the state law negligent entrustment claim could be proven.[71] If the owner (lessor) of the vehicle engaged in direct negligence or criminal wrongdoing, then some courts allow a vicarious liability claim against that owner also to proceed, but other courts find an absolute bar on the vicarious liability claim even if there is a direct negligence claim.[72] If the lessor of the equipment qualifies as a lessor for purposes of the Graves Amendment and has retained a motor carrier to deliver the leased equipment to another entity, if the lessor has bound the delivering motor carrier to a lease, then the Graves Amendment protects that lessor from vicarious liability based on FMCSR-related statutory employer liability doctrines.[73] But, the Graves Amendment, by its plain language, provides no protection for liability arising out of the consequence of federal law. Thus, if for example, an IEP is determined by a court or jury to be the "statutory employer" of an independent contractor truck driver as a result of the definitions of "employer" and "employee" in the FMCSRs, then the Graves Amendment is not a valid defense to liability because liability is not based on mere title ownership of the vehicle (covered by the Graves Amendment) but for other liability reasons.[74]

Laws Applicable to Ocean Common Carriers and Ocean Transportation Intermediaries

There are additional parties that may be involved in an international intermodal shipment. Depending on the relationship of these parties to the shipment, they may have responsibility for losses involved in a truck crash.

Ocean Common Carriers and Ocean Transportation Intermediaries

An "ocean common carrier" is a vessel-operating "common carrier" and it operates ships.[75] "Ocean transportation intermediaries" include non-vessel operating common carriers (NVOCCs) and freight forwarders,[76] and they generally must be licensed by the Federal Maritime Commission if they are located in the

70. Rivera v. Convoy, Inc., 2024 U.S. Dist. LEXIS 144068, at *9, 2024 WL 3791183 (D. Conn. Case No. 3:23-cv-01353, Aug. 13, 2024).

71. *Id.* at *9–10.

72. *See,* Parker v. Auto-Owners Ins. Co., 2020 U.S. Dist. LEXIS 16534, at *3–8, 2020 WL 488366 (W.D. Wisc. Case No. 19-cv-374, Jan. 30, 2020) (a case involving a semi-trailer, reviewing the case law).

73. Franklin v. Xtra Lease LLC, 2010 U.S. Dist. LEXIS 16174, 2010 WL 706037 (N.D. Ill. Case No. 08C5042, Feb. 24, 2010).

74. *See, e.g.,* Sentry Select Ins. Co. v. Hosmer, 2011 U.S. Dist. LEXIS 11003, at *22–23, 2011 WL 534353 (WD Mo. Case No. 08-4254, Feb. 4, 2011).

75. 46 U.S.C. § 40102(18) and 46 C.F.R. § 515.2.

76. 46 U.S.C. § 41012(20). This is a different type of freight forward than that which is defined in the motor carrier context under U.S.C. Title 49.

United States or established under the laws of the United States.[77] NVOCCs consolidate cargo from numerous shippers for shipment by an ocean carrier and, in such a circumstance, the NVOCC rather than the ocean carrier issues a bill of lading to each shipper.[78] NVOCCs are distinguished from freight forwarders in that freight forwarders merely facilitate the movement of cargo.[79]

Ocean Common Carrier and NVOCC Responsibilities

Both ocean carriers (aka VOCCs or vessel-operating common carriers) and NVOCCs are "common carriers," which means that they hold themselves out to the public to provide transportation by water between the United States and a foreign country for compensation, they use for "all or part of that transportation, a vessel operating on the high seas or the Great Lakes," and, of most interest here, they "assume responsibility for the transportation from the port or point of receipt to the port or point of destination."[80] An NVOCC is a "common carrier" that does not operate ships in ocean transportation and is a shipper in its relationship with the ocean common carrier.[81]

Note the "all or part" language within the definition of "common carrier"—part of the carriage may occur on land. The service may include "arranging for inland transportation and paying for inland freight charges on through transportation movements."[82] The fact that part of the ocean transport may occur on land is consistent with the principles of Carriage of Goods by Sea Act, described later. An Ocean Transportation Intermediary (an NVOCC or freight forwarder) is "fully responsible for the acts and omissions of any of its employees and agents that are performed in connection with the conduct of the ocean transportation intermediary's business."[83] For any ocean carriers or ocean transportation intermediaries that own intermodal equipment, they may also satisfy the definitions of "employer" or "employee" or both in the FMCSRs depending on the circumstances of their ownership and use of their intermodal equipment.[84] A subset of NVOCCs—registered NVOCCs—"shall be strictly responsible for the acts and omissions of its employees and agents, wherever they are located."[85]

77. 46 C.F.R. § 515.3. Ocean common carriers are not required to be licensed to perform freight forwarding services with respect to cargo under their own bills of lading. 46 C.F.R. § 515.4(c).

78. Prima U.S., Inc. v. Panalpina, Inc., 223 F.3d 126, 129 (2d Cir. 2000).

79. *Id. Compare* 46 C.F.R. § 515.2(h) (freight forwarders) with § 515.2(k) (NVOCCs). Note, while ocean shipping freight forwarders process common carrier bills of lading, freight forwarders registered with the U.S. Department of Transportation must either issue a receipt or through bill of lading to the shipper. 49 C.F.R. § 373.201.

80. 46 U.S.C. § 40102(7) and 46 C.F.R. § 515.2 (identifying an exclusion from the definition of "common carrier" ferry boats, ocean tramps, chemical parcel tankers, and vessels engaged in carriage of agricultural commodities); *see also* Landstar Express Am. Inc. v. FMC, 569 F.3d 493 (D.C. Cir. 2009) (explaining role of NVOCCs and ocean freight forwarders).

81. 46 U.S.C. § 40102(17). NVOCC's may be registered or licensed depending on their location. 46 C.F.R. § 5115.2(r). NVOCC's are financially responsible for inland transportation if they arrange it. 46 C.F.R. § 515.2(v).

82. 46 C.F.R. § 515.2(k)(6) and (l).

83. *Id.* § 515.4(b)(3). *See also* 49 U.S.C. § 40902.

84. 49 C.F.R. § 390.5.

85. *Id.* § 515.21(a)(3).

NVOCCs may use unlicensed "agents" subject to the NVOCC's control and, therefore, the NVOCC retains responsibility for the transportation.[86] "If an agent breaches a contract or commits a tort, the disclosed NVOCC principal in whose name the agent acts is subject to liability."[87]

Impact of Through Bills of Lading

Carriage of freight internationally sometimes involves a carrier's issuance of a "through bill of lading" covering the entire shipment from the originating overseas, foreign location, by ocean carrier to an inland destination in the United States. In this context, a bill of lading identifies the carrier accepting the goods for transport from the shipping party and states basic terms of carriage.[88] "A through bill of lading covers both the ocean and the inland portions of the transport in a single document."[89] For purposes of inland transport using interchanged intermodal equipment, "[t]he traffic transported in interchange service must move on through bills of lading issued by the originating carrier."[90] This is significant because the party that issues the through bill of lading takes on responsibility for the entire carriage, arguably. This sometimes includes the return of the intermodal equipment after the shipment is unloaded because the definition of "interchange" includes "repositioning the equipment for the benefit of the equipment provider."[91]

Responsibility for Damage or Loss to Internationally Shipped Cargo

This section of this chapter involves a complicated subject matter for which significant portions of books have been written.[92] This section of this chapter will introduce the sources of law applicable to the issuance of bills of lading and cargo damage and loss claims arising during motor carrier transport pursuant to those bills of lading. At the highest level, the practitioner must understand that remedies for cargo damage and loss claims often are governed and limited by a combination of statutory and contract law. But, principles of bailment, agency,

86. Landstar Express Am., Inc. v. FMC, 569 F.3d 493 (D.C. Cir. 2009); 49 C.F.R. § 515.4(b)(3).

87. 569 F.3d at 498.

88. Kawasaki Kisen Kaisha Ltd. v. Regal-Beloit Corp., 561 U.S. 89, 94 (2010); *cf.* 49 U.S.C. §§ 80102 *et seq.*

89. *Kawasaki Kisen Kaisha Ltd. v. Regal-Beloit Corp.*, 561 U.S. 89, 94 (2010) *citing* Norfolk Southern Ry. Co. v. James N. Kirby, Pty Ltd., 543 U.S. 14 (2004); *but see* 49 C.F.R. § 373.201.

90. 49 C.F.R. § 376.31(c).

91. *Id.* § 390.5, 390.5T (first definition of interchange); *see also* 49 U.S.C. § 31151(f)(4).

92. *E.g.*, Thomas J. Schoenbaum, Admiralty and Maritime Law 6th Ed. (Thompson West, 2018); George Carl Pezold & William J. Augello, Freight Claims in Plain English 4th ed. (2008). *See also* David N. Nissenberg, The Law of Commercial Trucking: Damages to Persons and Property (4th ed. Vol. 2, Ch. 15 and 17; New York: Matthew Bender, 2023). The author gives special thanks to attorneys David N. Nissenberg and Kenneth L. Shigley for their insights and analysis of some aspects of this subject. For an in-depth explanation of the complexities of these laws, *see* Michael E. Crowley, *The Limited Scope of the Cargo Liability Regime Covering Carriage of Goods by Sea: The Multimodal Problem*, 79 Tul. L. Rev. 1461 (2005).

and negligence are relevant, too. The most that can be done here is to introduce this body of law sufficiently to put practitioners on notice of the complexity of the subject matter and the need for significant case-specific legal and factual analysis. So, the explanation here will start with a focus on domestic freight loss claims pursuant to bills of lading issued by motor carriers, then progress to those issued by rail carriers, followed by those issued by ocean carriers. This is important because the nature of the party (motor carrier, rail carrier, ocean carrier, NVOCC, etc.) will have an impact on the analysis of which statute governs the freight loss claim occurring in a truck crash. While these statutes do not govern personal injury claims, identifying who is responsible for the freight loss claim may prove helpful for discerning which party or parties will be legally responsible for the personal injuries occurring in such a truck crash—and they will not necessarily be the same parties as are liable for the freight loss claim.

Carmack Amendment—Motor Carriers

The law commonly known as the Carmack Amendment applicable to motor carriers[93] requires that a motor carrier or freight forwarders (as that term is defined in 49 U.S.C. § 13102(8)) subject to the jurisdiction of the U.S. Department of Transportation (in interstate commerce)[94] "shall issue a receipt or bill of lading for property it receives for transportation" under such jurisdiction.[95] It makes "that carrier and any other carrier that delivers the property" under such jurisdiction liable for damage or loss caused by the "receiving carrier," the "delivering carrier," or "another carrier over whose line or route the property is transported in the United States or from a place in the United States to a place in an adjacent foreign country when transported under a through bill of lading . . . ."[96] Liability is for the "actual loss or injury to the property,"[97] but the amount of the liability can, in some circumstances be capped in accordance to the terms of agreement with the shipper.[98] "The purpose of the Carmack Amendment [is] to relieve shippers of the burden of searching out a particular negligent carrier from among the often numerous carriers handling an interstate shipment of goods."[99] Jurisdiction for such claims is proper in state or federal court.[100] There is a statute of limitations for such claims.[101] As between the various carriers involved, if one of them satisfies the claim, it may proceed under the statute to recover from the carrier involved in the actual loss.[102]

---

93. 49 U.S.C. § 14706.
94. For purely intrastate transport, state law applies.
95. 49 U.S.C. § 14706(a)(1); *see also* 49 C.F.R. pt. 373, §§ 373.101 (motor carriers) and 373.201 (freight forwarders).
96. 49 U.S.C. § 14706(a)(1).
97. *Id.*
98. *Id* .§ 14706(c).
99. Reider v. Thompson, 339 U.S. 113, 119 (1950).
100. 49 U.S.C. § 14706(d). Read carefully for determining proper venue.
101. *Id.* § 14706(e).
102. *Id.* § 14706(b).

Carmack Amendment—Rail Carriers

The law commonly known as the Carmack Amendment also applies to rail carriers, but it is codified at a different location than the version of the Carmack Amendment applicable to motor carriers and freight forwarders.[103] It works similarly. It mandates that the rail carrier receiving the property "shall issue a receipt or bill of lading for property it receives for transportation" under the jurisdiction of the Surface Transportation Board.[104] "The rail carrier and any other carrier that delivers the property and is providing transportation or service subject to the jurisdiction of the Board" are liable to the person entitled to recover pursuant to the bill of lading "for the actual loss or injury to the property" caused by the "receiving rail carrier," the "delivering rail carrier," or "another rail carrier over whose line or route the property is transported in the United States or from a place in the United States to a place in an adjacent foreign country when transported under a through bill of lading" unless liability is limited by agreement.[105]

For the Carmack Amendment (as to railroads) to apply,

> the journey must begin with a receiving rail carrier, which would have to issue a Carmack-compliant bill of lading. It follows that Carmack does not apply if the property is received at an overseas location under a bill that covers the transport into an inland location in the United States. In such a case, there is no receiving rail carrier that "receives" the property "for [domestic rail] transportation," § 11706(a), and thus no carrier that must issue a Carmack-complaint bill of lading. The initial carrier in that instance receives the property at the shipment's point of origin for overseas multimodal import transport, not for domestic rail transport.[106]

Carmack does not require an ocean carrier to issue bills of lading because an ocean carrier is not a receiving rail carrier, even when it uses the rail carrier for the inland destination portion of the transportation.[107] Nor is the railway required to issue a Carmack-complaint bill of lading in such circumstances because it is not a receiving rail carrier, but merely a delivering carrier.[108] If, however, the bills of lading for the overseas portion of the transportation ended at an American port, then the railway is a receiving carrier and it would have to issue a separate Carmack-compliant bill of lading.[109]

Carriage of Goods by Sea Act—Ocean Carriers

The Carmack Amendment does not apply to water carriers. "If loss or injury to property occurs while it is in the custody of a water carrier, the liability of

103. *Id.* § 11706.
104. *Id.* § 11706(a).
105. *Id.* § 11706(a–c).
106. Kawasaki Kisen Kaisha Ltd. v. Regal-Beloit Corp., 561 U.S. 89, 103 (2010).
107. *Id.* at 103–04.
108. *Id.*
109. *Id.* citing Reider v. Thompson, 339 U.S. 113 (1950). If a through bill of lading had been issued in Argentina, then the result in *Reider* would have been different. *Reider*, 339 U.S. at 117.

that carrier is determined by its bill of lading and the law applicable to water transportation. The liability of the initial or delivering carrier is the same as the liability of the water carrier."[110] The Carriage of Goods by Sea Act (COGSA) governs the terms of bills of lading issued by ocean carriers engaged in foreign trade, requiring certain terms to be included in such bills of lading.[111] "COGSA only applies to shipments from United States ports to ports of foreign countries and vice versa" but allows the parties "to cover 'the entire period in which [the goods] would be under [a carrier's] responsibility, including [a] period of . . . inland transport.'"[112]

COGSA requires that on the demand of a shipper, the owner of the vessel engaged in carriage to or from any port in the United States "shall issue a bill of lading or shipping document."[113] Unlike the damages provisions of the Carmack Amendment, for bills of lading governed by COGSA, liability for damaged shipments is capped, regardless of contract terms at a minimum of "$500 per package . . . or in case of goods not shipped in packages, per customer freight unit . . . unless the nature and value of such goods have been declared by the shipper before shipment and inserted in the bill of lading."[114] COGSA applies from the time the goods are loaded on the ship to the time discharged from the ship unless the carrier extends the scope of the carrier's responsibility for the shipment inland by means of inland transport.[115] The inland portion of the transportation pursuant to an ocean carrier through bill of lading can be provided by rail carrier or motor carrier. "[S]o long as a bill of lading requires substantial carriage of goods by sea, its purpose is to effectuate maritime commerce—and thus it is a maritime contract. Its character as a maritime contract is not defeated simply because it also provides for some land carriage. Geography, then, is useful in a conceptual inquiry only in a limited sense: if a bill's *sea* components are insubstantial, then the bill is not a maritime contract."[116] Thus,

110. 49 U.S.C. § 14706(c)(2).

111. Kawasaki Kisen Kaisha Ltd. V. Regal-Beloit Corp., 561 U.S. 89, 95 (2010).

112. *Id.* (quoting Norfolk Southern Ry. Co. v. James N. Kirby, Pty Ltd., 543 U.S. 14, 29 (2004)).

113. 46 U.S.C. § 30703(a).

114. COGSA § 4(5), 49 Stat. 1207, Pub. L. No. 97-31, 95 Stat. 166, found as a note to 46 U.S.C. § 30701, formerly 46 U.S.C. Appx. § 1304(5). "Congress recodified both COGSA and the Harter Act on October 6, 2006 at 46 U.S.C. § 30701 historical and statutory notes. Act of October 6, 2006, Pub. L. No. 109-304, 120 Stat. 1485." Starrag v. Maersk, Inc., 486 F.3d 607, 610 n.1 (9th Cir. 2007).

115. COGSA §§ 1(e) and 7; Norfolk Southern Ry. Co. v. James N. Kirby, Pty Ltd., 543 U.S. 14, 29–36 (2004).

116. Norfolk Southern Ry. Co. v. James N. Kirby, Pty Ltd., 543 U.S. 14, 27 (2004). There is a federal interest in uniformity of maritime contract and tort law. *Id.* at 25–30. When it is a maritime contract, then federal law controls contract interpretation, due to the Constitution's grant of admiralty and maritime jurisdiction to the federal courts. *Id.* at 22–23; *see also* 28 U.S.C. § 1333(1). When it is a tort, whether the federal court has admiralty jurisdiction depends on whether the tort occurred on navigable waters and whether the wrong bears a significant relationship to maritime activity; both must occur for there to be admiralty jurisdiction over the tort. Baltimore Gas & Elec. Co. v. Coastline Commer. Contr. Inc., 107 F.4th 264, 268–69 (4th Cir. 2024); *see also* Jerome B. Grubart v. Great Lakes Dredge & Dock Co., 513 U.S. 527 (1995); 46 U.S.C. § 30101. The entire subject of admiralty jurisdiction and the federal common law under it is complicated and is beyond the scope of this chapter. For an introduction to this complexity, *see* Hartford Fire Ins. Co. v. Orient

when the transport originates on an ocean carrier's through bill of lading that includes inland transport, and the freight loss occurs on the inland carriage portion of the transport, then it is not the Carmack Amendment that governs the claims for damage or loss to the freight, but the through bill of lading pursuant to COGSA.[117]

Harter Act—Water Carriers

COGSA applies for transport involving foreign ocean ports. Another law, known as the Harter Act, still has some applicability, though most of it was superseded by COGSA. The Harter Act governs once the freight is discharged from the vessel until "proper delivery" of the cargo, which normally occurs at the wharf.[118] Unlike COGSA, which allows contractual cargo loss damage caps, the Harter Act prevents this.[119] Like COGSA, the Harter Act does not compel or prohibit the parties for contracting for the statute's cargo-loss remedies to extend to and apply to losses occurring during inland carriage (inland transport).[120]

Because the remedies are different depending on whether the freight loss claim is governed by the Carmack Amendment, COGSA, or the Harter Act, and the contracts issued pursuant to them, it is no surprise that there is litigation over the subject and there are many reported court decisions related to losses that occur during inland carriage by rail or motor carrier. It is important to understand that the type of bill of lading issued—which is impacted by the applicable law under which it is issued—matters greatly to which parties are potentially responsible for losses associated with a truck crash.

A Few Practical Considerations

There are several practical considerations about truck crashes on inland transport portions of international shipments that should be noted before the close of this chapter. These include some comments about injury claims, jurisdiction, and international service of process and gathering of evidence.

There is the possibility for claims being brought against ocean common carriers, NVOCCs, freight forwarders, and others arising out of injuries sustained in truck crashes involving trucks hauling freight pursuant to through bills of

---

Overseas Containers Lines (UK) Ltd., 230 F.3d 549 (2d Cir. 2000) and the criticism of that case decision in *Norfolk Southern Ry. Co.*, 543 U.S. at 27.

117. Kawasaki Kisen Kaisha Ltd. v. Regal-Beloit Corp., 561 U.S. 89, 111 (2010).

118. Allstate Ins. v. Imparca Lines, 646 F.2d 166, 168 (5th Cir. 1981); Tapco Nigeria, Ltd. V. M/V Westwind, 702 F.2d 1252 (5th Cir. 1983); 46 U.S.C. § 30702(a).

119. 46 U.S.C. § 30704.

120. *See* Mannesman Demag Corp. v. M/V Concert Express, 225 F.3d 587 (5th Cir. 2000); Jagenberg, Inc. v. Georgia Ports Auth., 882 F. Supp. 1065 (S.D. Ga. 1995). The Harter Act presently is codified at 46 U.S.C. §§ 30701–30707. Liberty Woods Int'l v. Motor Vesseel Ocean Quartz, 889 F.3d 127, 129 (3d Cir. 2018). *Liberty Woods* explains the recodification of both COGSA and Harter Act, which is important because cases predating the recodification show each of them at different U.S. Code locations.

lading issued by these types of carriers. In the context of cargo damage claims, courts have deemed truck drivers to be agents of the ocean carriers for inland transport pursuant to the issuer's through bill of lading and, therefore, responsible for the negligence of the truck drivers, as their agents or subcontractors.[121] Under a through bill of lading, the carriers performing it "must be treated, not as independent contracting parties, but as one system; and the connecting lines become in effect mere agents, whose duty is to forward the goods under the terms of the contract made by their principal, the initial carrier."[122] "[W]henever the carrier voluntarily accepts goods for shipment to a point on another line in another State, it is conclusively treated as having made a through contract. It thereby elected to treat the connecting carriers as its agents, for all purposes of transportation and delivery."[123] While the cases tend to be in the context of cargo loss or damage, if the initiating carrier could be deemed the principal for the freight loss claims committed by the negligence of their trucking agents during performance of the inland transport service pursuant to through bills of lading, it follows that they also may be held liable for personal injuries caused by the same trucking agents in the same circumstances.[124] Which liability doctrines might apply depends upon the facts and the applicable law, and might include nondelegable duty doctrines,[125] agency doctrines, *respondeat superior*, statutory employer doctrines,[126] joint employer,[127] and direct negligence claims like negligent selection.[128] Even if negligence doctrines do not apply, one or more of the

121. *See, e.g.*, Philips-Van Heusen Corp. v. Mitsui O.S.K. Lines Ltd., 2002 U.S. Dist. LEXIS 27057, at *28–31, 2003 AMC 2471 (M.D. Pa. Case No. 1:CV-00-0665, Aug. 14, 2002); Agrico Chem. Co. v. SS Atlantic Forest, 459 F. Supp. 638, 647, 1979 AMC 801 (E.D. La. 1978) (because the carrier's duties are "non-delegable" it "may not insulate itself from liability by the use of independent contractors" and "carrier is liable for any negligence of those parties in whose hands it has placed the goods, whether the parties are servants, agents, or independent contractors"). The same has occurred in a personal injury case, but decided under state law principles. Dolan v. Sea Transfer Corp., 398 N.J. Super. 313, 942 A.2d 29 (N.J. App. 2008).

122. Missouri, K&T Ry. Co. v. Ward, 244 U.S. 383, 387–88 (1917). This is a railroad case, but the legal concepts in it are analogous.

123. Galveston, H. & S.A.R. Co. v. Wallace, 223 U.S. 481, 481 (1912). This, also, is a railroad case, but the legal concepts in it are analogous.

124. It is this chapter author's understanding that there are personal injury cases in which such liability claims were made but which were settled pending the litigation.

125. *See, e.g.*, Restatement 2d of Torts, §§ 417, 424, 428 for some types of nondelegable duty doctrines.

126. *See* Puga v. About Tyme Transp., Inc., 227 F. Supp. 3d 760, 764–65 (S.D. Tx. 2017). Not all courts agree about the existence or extent of this doctrine. This is explained in Morales v. OK Trans. Inc., 2024 U.S. Dist. LEXIS 57475, 2024 WL 1348405 (S.D. Tx. 2024). The policy reasons for the federal laws that form the basis of the statutory employment doctrine favor recognition of the statutory employer doctrine in multi-business cases. "By eliminating the common law employee/independent contractor distinction, the definition ['employee'] serves to discourage motor carriers from using the independent contractor relationship to avoid liability exposure at the expense of the public." Consumers County Mut. Ins. v. PW & Sons Trucking Inc., 307 F.3d 362, 366 (5th Cir. 2002).

127. *See Puga*, 227 F. Supp. 3d at 763.

128. One federal court denied federal question jurisdiction even though parts of the truck-crash wrongful death claim were brought on a vicarious liability theory based on 46 U.S.C. § 40102 in

parties involved in ocean shipment may carry an insurance policy that covers the services of its agents and workers inland. Thus, it is important to obtain and analyze those policies.

Which court has jurisdiction over a case involving a truck crash involving international defendants and/or an international shipment can be an interesting consideration. The federal court will have diversity jurisdiction over claims between citizens of a state and subjects of a foreign state (with some exceptions related to legal permanent residents).[129] The federal court has "original jurisdiction, exclusive of the courts of the States, of: (1) Any civil case of admiralty or maritime jurisdiction, saving to suitors in all cases all other remedies to which they are otherwise entitled."[130] Thus, some such claims can be brought in state courts under state law. Whether your claim is an admiralty or maritime claim, or a contract or tort claim for which a state law remedy applies, such that a state court has jurisdiction, obviously depends on the facts, and it is a subject that warrants legal research for cases analogous to your circumstances. It is likely that most, if not all, inland transport truck crash cases can be brought in state court. For Carmack Amendment cases, the federal court has original jurisdiction when the amount in controversy exceeds $10,000.[131] Generally, cases of original jurisdiction in the federal court may be removed to the federal court.[132] Cases for which jurisdiction in federal courts is solely based on diversity cannot be removed "if any of the parties in interest properly joined and served as defendants is a citizen of the State in which such action is brought."[133]

Service of process and discovery with respect to parties outside of America presents its procedural complexities. Any subpoenas that may be needed for purposes of service of process on defendants in other countries must be served pursuant to international treaties, such as the "Hague Convention on the Service Abroad of Judicial and Extrajudicial Documents in Civil or Commercial Matters."[134] As of this writing, many countries are parties to this convention, including the United States. If the Hague Convention does not apply, you will have to determine another treaty or source of law that permits service of process. The Hague Convention procedures are detailed, require communications

conjunction with 49 C.F.R. § 390.5. Moody v. Great West Cas. Co., 2017 U.S. Dist. LEXIS 2909, 2017 WL 77417 (S.D. Ga. Case No. 4:16-CV-276, Jan. 9, 2017). If the claim can be supported purely under state law regardless of an alternative federal law theory of liability, federal question jurisdiction does not attach. Thoele v. Mainfreight Ltd., 2021 U.S. Dist. LEXIS 129469 (C.D. Cal. Case No. 2:21-cv-02813, July 12, 2021); Reichert v. Mendez, 2023 U.S. Dist. LEXIS 21459, 2023 WL 1814293 (D. Az. Case No. CV-22-02163, Feb. 8, 2023). Both NVOCCs and freight forwarders can be held liable for the negligent selection of other businesses that perform services for them, like transportation by truck. *See Prima*, 223 F.3d at 130; Scholastic Inc. V. M/V Kitano, 362 F. Supp. 449, 458–59 (S.D. N.Y. 2005). A defense based on caps on liability may be applicable depending on the nature of the claim. 46 U.S.C. §§ 30704, 30706, 30523, and 30524.

129. 28 U.S.C. § 1332.

130. *Id.* § 1333.

131. *Id.* § 1337.

132. *Id.* § 1441.

133. *Id.* § 1441(b)(2).

134. https://www.hcch.net/en/instruments/conventions/specialised-sections/service.

with the "central authority" of the other country, including following its central authority's rules, may require translation of all documents, and can be very slow. For the gathering of evidence abroad, there is another convention with broad international participation: the "Hague Convention on the Taking of Evidence Abroad in Civil or Commercial Matters."[135] Many countries are parties to this convention, too.

135. https://www.hcch.net/en/instruments/conventions/specialised-sections/evidence.

CHAPTER 27

Truck Accident Litigation in Canada

Robin Squires, Esq. and Sarah Sweet, Esq.

Overview

The importance of motor carriers cannot be overstated on either side of the Canadian–United States border. Due to the importance of cross-border trucking, many readers will be interested to know how the matters covered in this text are addressed in Canada. As in the United States, motor carriers in Canada face regulation in a number of areas, including driver licensing, hours of service, and liability for contracts of carriage. Motor carrier regulation in Canada derives from all levels of government. This chapter provides an overview of Canadian motor carrier regulation and liability. Where there are references to specific laws and regulations, the reader is encouraged to access the full text free of charge using the CanLII service, which can be accessed at www.canlii.org.

Jurisdiction

Jurisdiction over truck transportation and road safety in Canada is shared between the federal and provincial/territorial governments. The federal government addresses construction and importation of new motor vehicles under the Motor Vehicle Safety Act, S.C. 1993, c. 16 and regulates limited operational matters for commercial motor vehicles under the Motor Vehicle Transport Act, R.S.C., 1985, c. 29 (3rd Supp.). The provinces and territories are responsible for the enforcement of safety on their roads and highways, including the enforcement of federal operational matters and operational matters that are the subject of provincial or territorial law.[1]

1. Transport Canada, *Road Safety in Canada 2020*, https://tc.canada.ca/en/road-transportation/publications/road-safety-canada-2020 (last visited Feb. 2, 2025).

In terms of the motor carrier industry, the level of government with jurisdiction depends mainly on the nature of the operator, and whether the operator operates only within a province or territory or the operator crosses provincial/territorial borders. Transport Canada's Motor Carrier Division oversees federally regulated (extra-provincial) motor carriers and commercial vehicle drivers operating outside a single province or territory, while provincial and territorial regulations govern operations within each province or territory. The key pieces of federal legislation relevant to the Canadian trucking industry include the Canada Transportation Act, S.C. 1996, c. 10; Motor Vehicle Safety Act, S.C. 1993, c. 16; and the Transportation of Dangerous Goods Act, 1992, S.C. 1992, c. 34. In some cases, the federal government may delegate authority back to the provinces and has elected to do so in a number of cases. For example, under the Motor Vehicle Transport Act, R.S.C. 1985, c. 29 (3rd Supp.), the federal government grants provinces the authority to issue extra-provincial licenses or safety fitness certificates.

Some federal regulations, particularly safety focused legislation such as hours of service, can also apply concurrently with provincial/territorial regulations. There are a number of provincial/territorial jurisdictions that do not have their own legislation or regulations for the trucking industry. Consequently, those jurisdictions are subject only to the federal regime. These provinces/territories are Prince Edward Island, the Yukon and Northwest Territories, and Nunavut.

Despite the jurisdictional division and overlap just outlined, the federal scheme is not intended to oust provincial authority. Section 7(3) of the Federal Motor Vehicle Transportation Act, RSC 1985, c 29 specifically provides that "laws of a province respecting the safety of motor carrier undertakings apply to an extra-provincial motor carrier undertaking to the extent that those laws are not inconsistent with this Act." The federal government works with the provinces and territories on regulation, but generally leaves the enforcement of the commercial vehicle rules and regulations to the provincial and territorial authorities.

Provincial / Territorial Legislation

Table 27.1 identifies the generally applicable key legislation for each Canadian jurisdiction and those provinces and territories that have repealed their motor carrier safety legislation:

Table 27.1 Provincial Commercial Trucking Legislation

Jurisdictions with provincial commercial trucking legislation	Jurisdictions without provincial commercial trucking legislation
Alberta: *Traffic Safety Act*, RSA 2000, c. T-6	**Prince Edward Island:** *Motor Carrier Act*, RSPEI 1988, c. M-10 [repealed]
British Columbia: *Commercial Transport Act*, RSBC 1996, c. 58 and *Motor Vehicle Act*, RSBC 1996, c. 318	**Yukon:** *Motor Transport Act*, RSY 2002, c. 152 [repealed].

Jurisdictions with provincial commercial trucking legislation	**Jurisdictions without provincial commercial trucking legislation**
Manitoba: *Highway Traffic Act,* CCSM c. H60	**Northwest Territories:** *Public Service Vehicles Act,* RSNWT. 1988, c. P-18 [repealed]
New Brunswick: *Motor Carrier Act,* RSNB 1973, c. M-16 and *Motor Vehicle Act,* RSNB. 1973, c. M-17	**Nunavut:** Nunavut inherited the trucking regime of Northwest Territories, and consequently does not regulate conditions of carriage for trucking.
Newfoundland & Labrador: *Motor Carrier Act,* R.S.N.L. 1990, c. M-19	
Nova Scotia: *Motor Carrier Act,* RSNS 1989, c. 292 and *Motor Vehicle Act,* RSNS 1989 c. 293	
Ontario: *Highway Traffic Act,* RSO. 1990, c. H.8	
Quebec: *Civil Code of Québec,* CCQ-1991 and (QC) *Transport Act,* CQLR, c. T-12.	
Saskatchewan: *The Traffic Safety Act,* SS 2004, c T-18.1	

Notably, for the provinces that continue to regulate the commercial trucking industry intra-provincially, there has been an effort to keep the regulatory conditions of carriage essentially consistent and avoid a patchwork legislative scheme.

Federal Legislation

The Motor Carrier Division of Transport Canada aims to improve commercial motor vehicle safety and reduce the instances of motor vehicle accidents involving large commercial trucks and buses in Canada. The Motor Carrier Division works in consultation with the Canadian provinces/territories and industry members to establish rules and regulations governing the safe operation of commercial vehicles, drivers, and operators.[2]

Licensing, Safety, and Fitness

National Safety Code

The government of Canada has created one nationally approved regulatory safety code, the National Safety Code, which sets 16 performance standards for commercial truck operators (Table 27.2). The minimum performance standards set out in the National Safety Code are aimed at the safe operation of commercial vehicles and cover a wide range of areas, from driver licensing and vehicle safety to cargo securement and facility audits.[3]

---

2. Transport Canada, *Motor Carriers, Commercial Vehicles and Drivers,* https://tc.canada.ca/en/road-transportation/motor-carriers-commercial-vehicles-drivers (last updated Mar. 25, 2024).

3. Transport Canada, *National Safety Code,* https://tc.canada.ca/en/road-transportation/motor-vehicle-safety/national-safety-code (last updated Aug. 17, 2023).

Table 27.2 National Safety Code Performance Standards

Standard 1	Single Driver License Concept
Standard 2	Knowledge and Performance Tests (Drivers)
Standard 3	Driver Examiner Training Program
Standard 4	Driver Licensing Classification
Standard 5	Self-Certification Standards and Procedures
Standard 6	Determining Driver Fitness in Canada
Standard 7	Carrier and Driver Profiles
Standard 8	Short-Term Suspension
Standard 9	Commercial Vehicle Drivers Hours of Service
Standard 10	Cargo Securement
Standard 11	Maintenance and Periodic Inspection
Standard 12	CVSA On-Road Inspection
Standard 13	Trip Inspection
Standard 14	Safety Rating
Standard 15	Facility Audits
Standard 16	Entry Level Training (Class 1)

The National Safety Code has been adopted by all jurisdictions in Canada and applies to all individuals who are responsible for the operation of commercial vehicles, which includes trucks, buses, power units, and trailers.[4] For example, in Ontario, many requirements of the National Safety Code are codified in the Highway Traffic Act, R.S.O. 1990, c. H.8.

The National Safety Code contains many of the same driving and operation requirements as the U.S. Federal Motor Carrier Safety Regulations. Some similarities include hours of service regulations, security load standards, and trip inspection report guidelines. Commercial drivers in Canada, like the United States, can generally refer to the National Safety Code since most provinces have adopted its requirements in their motor vehicle legislation. Generally, any local differences in the provinces' motor vehicle legislation will not be in conflict with the requirements of the National Safety Code.

Commercial Licensing

Canada requires commercial vehicle drivers and operators to hold specific licenses. The National Safety Code sets forth standards for knowledge and performance tests for drivers.[5] All Canadian provinces and territories have authority to establish their own knowledge and performance testing for drivers who receive their license from that jurisdiction. Most provinces legislate when a commercial vehicle license is required, the type of license required, and the

4. Canadian Council of Motor Transport Administrators, *National Safety Code*, www.ccmta.ca, 2024.

5. National Safety Code, Standard 2: Knowledge and Performance Tests (Drivers), Jan. 2020.

procedures for obtaining the appropriate license.[6] The National Safety Code establishes a Classified Driver Licensing System comprised of seven distinct classes, each designating a certain type of vehicle in accordance with the degree of capability necessary for its operation.

While many of the provinces have adopted the Classified Driver Licensing System, others have elected to modify the requirements. The type of license required may differ among provinces and territories and is generally determined by gross vehicle weight.[7] As such, the requisite knowledge and training required of a driver depends on the province or territory administering the license and the characteristics of the commercial vehicle. Carriers conducting extra-provincial transport must take care to comply with local legislation regarding permits and licensing.

Safety Fitness Certificates

The Canadian Motor Vehicle Transport Act, RSC 1985, c. 29 requires that each commercial truck driver obtain a safety fitness certificate to operate a commercial vehicle. Safety fitness certificates are administered by individual provincial transport boards. There are strict prerequisites to obtaining the certificate, including proof of minimum liability insurance coverage and an acceptable safety rating.[8] The provinces and territories in which a carrier operates can dictate the need for additional qualifications, including commercial vehicle permits, under the applicable provincial/territorial legislation.

Inspections and Maintenance

In Canada, inspections are required in more frequent intervals than 12 months. Instead of distinguishing between annual and periodic inspections, Canadian provinces refer to required inspections more generally as Mandatory Periodic Motor Vehicle Inspection (PMVI). Standard 11 of the National Safety Code contains the standards required for commercial vehicle inspections in Canada. For example, the inspections must be completed by an authorized technician at an authorized facility at a scheduled frequency.

Canadian commercial truck drivers are also required to complete trip inspection reports. The general requirements of these reports are included in Standard 13 of the National Safety Code. Many provinces have adopted Standard 13 as a baseline and made additional modifications as they see fit.[9] In Ontario

---

6. See, for example, the (AB) Traffic Safety Act, R.S.A. 2000, c. T-6, (BC) Commercial Transport Act, R.S.B.C. 1996, c. 58 and (BC) Motor Vehicle Act, R.S.B.C. 1996, c. 318, (MB) Highway Traffic Act, C.C.S.M. c. H60, (NB) Motor Carrier Act, R.S.N.B. 1973, c. M-16 and (NB) Motor Vehicle Act, R.S.N.B. 1973, c. M-17, (NL) Motor Carrier Act, R.S.N.L. 1990, c. M-19, (NS) Motor Carrier Act, R.S.N.S. 1989, c. 292 and (NS) Motor Vehicle Act, R.S.N.S. 1989 c. 293, (ON) Highway Traffic Act, R.S.O. 1990, c. H.8, (QC) Civil Code of Québec, CCQ-1991 and (QC) Transport Act, CQLR, c. T-12.

7. See, for example, (ON) Drivers' Licences Regulation, O. Reg. 340/94, s. 2.

8. See, for example, Motor Carrier Safety Fitness Certificate Regulations, SOR/2005-180, ss. 6-8.

9. NSC Standard 13: Trip Inspections (Mar. 2009). See, for example, O. Reg. 199/07: Commercial Motor Vehicle Inspections under Highway Traffic Act, R.S.O. 1990, c. H.8.

for example, the Commercial Motor Vehicle Inspections regulation[10] under the Highway Traffic Act requires vehicle operators to perform daily, annual, and semi-annual safety inspections. There must be records of these inspections and these records must be accessible and kept up to date. There are significant penalties for noncompliance with these regulations in Ontario, such as fines up to $20,000, impounding the noncompliant vehicle, or prohibiting individuals from operating the vehicle until repairs are made.

Provinces and territories may adopt the National Safety Code and/or modify it as they deem fit. Table 27.3 summarizes the inspection intervals of each province and territory in Canada. Most notably, Nunavut does not currently have a mandatory inspection regime. Accordingly, operators there would be subject to the provisions of the National Safety Code without modification.

Table 27.3 Inspection Intervals for Canadian Provinces

		Inspection Interval (months)		
Jurisdiction	**Weight Threshold (kg)**	**Truck**	**Trailer**	**Bus**
BC	8, 201	6	6/12	6
AB	11,794	12	12	6
SK	11,794	6/12	12	6/12
MB	4,500	12	12	6
ON	4,500	12	12	6
QC	4,500	12	12	6
NB	4,500	12	12	6
NS	4,500	12	12	6
PEI	4,500	12	12	6
NL	4,500	12	12	6
YT	11,794	6	12	6
NT	4,500	12	12	6
NU	*PMVI Regulation yet to be implemented*			

For vehicles plated in the United States, Canadian jurisdictions will accept inspections conducted to the U.S. Federal Motor Carrier Safety Administration (FMCSA) standard, or an inspection conducted in a state that meets or exceeds the FMCSA standard.

One notable difference between the United States and Canada inspection requirements is that Canada does not require a post-trip inspection. Nevertheless, post-trip inspections are an industry best practice[11] and many motor carriers still include them in their maintenance regimes.

10. O Reg. 199/07.

11. G. Fontana, *The Importance of Post-Trip Inspections*, FLEETOWNER (Aug. 31, 2021), https://www.fleetowner.com/safety/roadside-inspections/article/21173933/the-importance-of-post-trip-inspections.

Mirrors, Visibility, and Conspicuity

In Canada, the design of all motor vehicles sold or imported in Canada is regulated federally through the Motor Vehicle Safety Regulations, C.R.C., c. 1038. As a result, mirrors, visibility, and conspicuity are regulated federally. Much of the regulation of motor vehicle design in Canada can be found in the *Motor Vehicle Safety Regulations*. These federal regulations delegate certain responsibilities to the provinces to ensure the safety of commercial vehicles. Each province also has its own regulations dealing with vehicle design and maintenance, including, for example, the Highway Traffic Act in Ontario,[12] the Vehicle Equipment Regulation in Alberta,[13] and the Motor Vehicle Act Regulations in British Columbia.[14]

Transport Canada has also introduced the Canadian Vehicle Lighting Regulation, which requires all new vehicles, including heavy trucks, sold in Canada to have at least one of the following features: (1) tail lights that come on automatically with daytime running lights and (2) headlights, tail lights, and side marker lights that turn on automatically in the dark, or a dashboard that stays dark to alert the driver to turn on the lights.[15]

Hours of Service and Driver Fatigue

Like in the United States, driver fatigue is of serious concern in Canada, and hours of service are heavily regulated. These regulations are an effort to ensure driver rest and safety, and thereby reduce the risk of accidents caused by fatigue or exhaustion. Given the extended hours that commercial truck drivers typically spend on the road, coupled with the significant volume of commercial truck traffic, driver fatigue has become a pressing concern in the carrier industry. According to the Canadian Centre for Occupational Health and Safety, approximately one in five collisions can be attributed to fatigue-related factors.[16] This underscores the critical importance of addressing and mitigating driver fatigue to ensure road safety.

There are federal and provincial regulatory schemes for hours of service. The hours-of-service regulations for commercial motor vehicle operators in Canada is a coordinated effort between federal and provincial authorities. Provincial and territorial regulatory bodies govern the operation of commercial vehicles inside their provincial boundaries.

Most of the hours of rest requirements for commercial trucking across Canada are uniform. The provinces and territories generally follow the National Safety Code, which requires ten hours off-duty per day, and eight consecutive

12. RSO 1990, c H.8.

13. Alta Reg 122/2009.

14. BC Reg 26/58.

15. Transport Canada, *Using Your Vehicle Lights to See and Be Seen* (Dec. 12, 2018), https://tc.canada.ca/en/road-transportation/safety-standards-vehicles-tires-child-car-seats/using-your-vehicle-lights-see-be-seen.

16. Trucking Safety Council of BC, *Driver Fatigue Can be Fatal*, https://safetydriven.ca/resource/driver-fatigue-can-be-fatal/#:~:text=When%20you%20are%20fatigued%2C%20you,collisions%20is%20related%20to%20fatigue.

hours off-duty after 13 hours driving or 14 hours on-duty. On-duty time includes all time working, including driving or working as a co-driver, but does not include time in a sleeper berth. In addition, the federal regulation distinguishes between driving north and south of 60° Latitude. North of 60° Latitude, drivers are required to take eight consecutive hours of off-duty time after accumulating 15 hours driving time or 18 hours on duty.[17]

When a commercial vehicle is being operated within a province, that province's hours of service regulations will apply, subject to the qualifications and exemptions therein. When a commercial vehicle is being operated as between two or more provinces, then the hours-of-service application becomes more complex. The application of the federal regime has generally been used to bar drivers from circumventing provincial regulations by crossing the provincial boundaries. For example, if a driver travels ten hours in Ontario and then crosses the provincial boundary into Quebec and drives for another five hours, that driver is in violation of the federal hours of service legislation despite the fact that the driver's driving time in each province independently does not exceed the provincial legislated allowance. In that same example, if the driver crosses the provincial boundary, rests, and then goes on to drive wholly in Quebec to the final destination, the provincial authorities will generally expect the driver to comply with Quebec's provincial hours of service regulations. The federal legislation is intended to prevent such potential gaps and ensure that driving or on-duty time does not "restart" their driving time once a driver crosses a provincial boundary. The provinces have attempted to keep the hours-of-service legislation relatively uniform. As a result, the courts have not been overly concerned with the jurisdictional division.

An example of this concurrent jurisdiction played out in the case of *Ontario (Ministry of Transportation) v. Celadon Canada Inc.*, 2009 ONCJ 465, which involved the question of the constitutionality and constitutional applicability of the Ontario Highway Traffic Act, and Ontario Regulation 555/06, Hours of Service Regulations to a carrier with loads that took it primarily outside Ontario. In this case, Celadon Canada Inc. (Celadon) was a motor carrier incorporated in Ontario with its head office and principal terminal location in Ontario. Charges were laid against Celadon by Ontario Ministry of Transport inspectors under the Ontario Highway Traffic Act, and the Ontario Hours of Service Regulations.

---

17. The federal regulation is at *Commercial Vehicle Drivers Hours of Service Regulations*, SOR/2005-313, section 14. **Ontario:** *Hours of Service Regulations*, O Reg 555/06 at section 6; **B.C.:** *Motor Vehicle Act Regulations*, BC Reg 26/58 at section 37.26; **Alberta:** *Drivers' Hours of Service Regulation*, Alta Reg 317/2002 at section 5(1); **Saskatchewan:** *Commercial Vehicles Hours of Service Regulations*, H-3.1 Reg 12 at section 3; **Manitoba:** *Drivers Hours of Service Regulation*, Man Reg 72/2007 at section 1(1); **Quebec:** *Regulation respecting the hours of driving and rest of heavy vehicle drivers*, C-24.2 r.28 at sections 9 and 13; **New Brunswick:** *Commercial Vehicle Drivers Hours of Service Regulation*, NB Reg 89-147 at section 5; **Nova Scotia:** *Commercial Vehicle Drivers Hours of Service Regulations*, NS Reg 330/2022 at section 7(1); **P.E.I.:** *Commercial Vehicle Drivers Hours of Service Regulation*, PEI Reg EC713/06 at section 14(1); **NFLD:** *Highway Traffic Hours of Service Regulations*, CNLR 1001/96 at section 10; **Nunavut:** *Hours of Service Regulations*, NWT Reg (Nu) 001-92 at section 3; **NWT:** *Hours of Service Regulations*, NWT Reg 099-2008 at section 8(1); **Yukon:** *National Safety Code Regulation*, YOIC 2007/168 at section 3(3)(a).

Caledon argued that as an extra-provincial undertaking, it conducted its business operations under the exclusive jurisdiction of federal laws. As such, Celadon was not subject to the Ontario Hours of Service Regulations. The Provincial Crown argued that the provisions are valid provincial legislation enacted pursuant to the province's exclusive legislative jurisdiction in respect of highway traffic, for the purpose of the safety of highway users. The Crown also argued there was no conflict between the federal and provincial enactments and no inconsistency. In essence, the Crown argued that the provincial and federal enactments serve the same purpose of limiting hours of service in order to reduce driver fatigue.

The court agreed with the Crown's proposition that where provincial law adds requirements that supplement the requirements of the federal law, it will be possible to comply with both laws by complying with the stricter of the two. In such cases, the laws can apply concurrently, and individuals can comply with either of them without violating the other. At paragraph 37 of its reasons (emphasis added), the court commented:

> [S]imultaneous compliance with both enactments is clearly possible in this case. Nothing in the federal regulation requires operators to work hours in excess of those permitted by the provincial regulation, or to refuse to provide daily logs to provincial officers. **There is no conflict in operation between the federal and provincial law. Nor does the provincial enactment frustrate the federal government's purpose.** On the contrary, the provincial and federal enactments serve the same purpose of limiting hours of service in order to reduce driver fatigue.

The court concluded that Celadon and its drivers were bound by Ontario provincial laws and regulations in respect to the use of the province's highways. The court did not accept Celadon's contention that it was subject to the exclusive jurisdiction of federal laws because of the interprovincial nature of their business. Of note, the court also commented that to the extent that there were differences between the federal and Ontario regulations, there is no legal basis to support the proposition that the authority of the inspectors is to apply provincial regulations to all local undertakings and federal regulations to all extra-provincial undertakings.

Commercial drivers who cross interprovincial jurisdictions are expected to adhere to federal hours-of-service regulations. Under the federal regime, commercial motor carriers are prohibited from requesting, requiring, or permitting drivers to operate their vehicles after they have accrued 13 hours of driving time within a single day. In addition, these carriers are restricted from instructing or allowing drivers to drive once they have amassed 14 hours of on-duty time within a day.[18] Off-duty time is also mandatory. Specifically, drivers are not permitted to drive after accumulating 13 hours of driving time unless they have taken a minimum of eight consecutive hours of off-duty time. Furthermore, if a

18. SOR/2005-313 – Section 12: Daily Driving and On-Duty Time; Section 13: Mandatory Off-duty Time.

driver has reached 14 hours of on-duty time, that driver must also take a mandatory eight consecutive hours of off-duty time before driving again. Additionally, drivers are not allowed to drive once 16 hours of on-duty or driving time have elapsed since their last period of eight or more consecutive hours of off-duty time.[19] Electronic logging devices were required as of 2021, although the standard was not enforced until 2023.[20] Notably, these requirements are similar to those provided under the U.S. Federal Motor Carrier Safety Regulations.

Electronic Logging Devices

The implementation of electronic logging devices (ELDs) in the commercial vehicle industry has significantly contributed to the collection, analysis, and preservation of critical evidence in accidents. While the primary function of ELDs is to ensure regulatory compliance with hours-of-service regulations, if they are relevant to the allegations in a proceeding, they will be discoverable, thereby enhancing the investigation and preservation of evidence following accidents.

Trucking Safety as an Employer

Many Canadian provinces have legislation that outlines the legal duties of employers and employees in their work relationship, including where those duties involve motor vehicles. As an example, Ontario's Occupational Health and Safety Act, R.S.O. 1990, c. O.1 (OHSA) provides specific requirements for employers that allow employees to use employer vehicles, equipment, and any materials. Section 25(1)(b) of the OHSA states that employers must ensure that the equipment, materials, and any safety devices provided to employees are maintained in proper condition. Section 25(2)(h) also provides that employers are responsible for the safety of their employees and must take every reasonable precaution in the circumstances to ensure their safety.

Employers also must meet and maintain the safety requirements prescribed by their specific provinces. For example, in Ontario, the Highway Traffic Act, requires vehicle operators to perform daily safety inspections in addition to annual, and semi-annual safety inspections by technicians licensed by the Ministry of Transportation. The records of these inspections must be up to date and available upon request.

In Canada, employers may be liable for their employee's actions when the employee is acting within the scope of their employment duties. Where employees are operating motor vehicles or commercial vehicles as part of their duties, this risk becomes more pronounced. In the decision of *Mustafi v. All-Pitch Roofing Ltd*, 2014 ABCA 265, Alberta Court of Appeal held that an employer can be vicariously liable for an employee's negligence even if the employee

19. Commercial Vehicle Drivers Hours of Service Regulations, SOR/2005-313.

20. Canadian Council of Motor Transport Administrators, *Commercial Vehicle Motor Safety*, 2023, https://www.ccmta.ca/web/default/files/PDF/ELD/ELDs%20-%20Messages%20for%20Industry%20-%20Jan%2023.2023.pdf.

disregarded express instructions from the employer. In *Mustafi,* despite the employer's express instructions not to drive the company truck, the employee was given the keys to the vehicle and allowed to use it to store his tools and supplies. He was also permitted to use the truck to keep warm. Contrary to his instructions, he drove the truck and was involved in an accident. The court relied on section 187(2) of the Alberta Traffic Safety Act ,which provides that he owner of a vehicle liable if, at the time of the accident, the driver was in "possession" of the vehicle with the consent of the owner. The court disregarded the fact of the employer's oral instructions not to drive the vehicle as those instructions were not contained in a written agreement and could easily be revoked.

Any employer operating in the transportation space needs to be wary of which employees are trusted with the use of commercial vehicles and the clear limitations of such vehicles' use. It is important for employers to educate their employees on proper use of their vehicles and have clearly written policies for their possession and use.

Recordkeeping and Reporting

Canada has similar recordkeeping and reporting requirements to the United States when it comes to commercial trucking. Canadian drivers are mandated to retain drivers logs and supporting documents for a minimum of six months.[21] Carriers in Canada may be required to report information related to their assets and productivity to the Minister of Transport on a timely basis under the Canada Transportation Act[22] and Transportation Information Regulations.[23] The purpose of disclosure is for the federal government to consider the economic condition of motor carriers in Canada.

Jurisdictional guidelines for keeping may vary among provinces and territories. Many jurisdictions require proof of maintenance to be kept for four or five years. Many also require at least the following standards set out by the National Safety Code:[24]

(a) Record Keeping Requirements:

(i) Every carrier shall maintain records of the driver licensing qualifications of each person who operates commercial vehicles on its behalf, the hours of service worked by each driver and supporting documents; convictions for traffic offences or criminal driving offences incurred by such drivers, traffic accidents, and training records. The carrier shall obtain a current driver profile from the appropriate government agency and shall review same prior to hiring the driver.

---

21. See, for examples, *the Commercial Vehicle Drivers Hours of Service Regulations,* SOR/ 2005-313, s.81 under the *Motor Vehicle Transport Act,* RSC 1985, c. 29 (3d Supp.). In this book, the chapter by Roberto Ramirez addresses the American recordkeeping requirements.

22. S.C. 1996, c. 10, s. 50.

23. SOR/96-334.

24. Appendix A, Standard 15 *"Facility Audit"* National Safety Code for Motor Carriers (December 2003) at 15-12.

(ii) Every carrier shall maintain, for each of its commercial vehicles, records of vehicle maintenance and inspection procedures carried out in accordance with the commercial vehicle maintenance stands; records as required in NSC Standards #11, 12, and 13; and Notices of Defect received from vehicle manufacturers and proof that such defects have been corrected

(iii) Every carrier shall set out a written program which provides for continuous and regular inspection, maintenance and repair of commercial vehicles

(b) Preservation of Records

The records required to be maintained by carriers in accordance with subsection a) shall be preserved in such a manner as to be accessible for inspection and audit purposes subject to the prescribed retention period as set out by regulation.

(c) Location of Records

The records required to be maintained and preserved under the above-quoted subsections (a) and (b) of the *National Safety Code* shall be kept, or made available, at the carrier's main place of business in the jurisdiction where the carrier's commercial vehicles are base plated or at such other location as may be accepted by the jurisdictional agency responsible for NSC Audits.

Dangerous Goods

In Canada, the transportation of dangerous or hazardous goods is strictly regulated under the Transportation of Dangerous Goods Act, 1992 (S.C. 1992, c. 34) (TDGA). The TDGA and the Transportation of Dangerous Goods Regulations[25] were designed to promote public safety and security during the transportation of dangerous goods. In respect of intra-provincial transport of dangerous goods, provincial regulations generally adopt, by reference, the provisions of the federal TDGR. These regulations are the result of a close cooperation between provincial governments, the federal government, and representatives of the transportation industry. The enforcement of dangerous goods regulations is generally left to the province. The Transportation of Dangerous Goods Directorate (which is responsible for the federal transportation of dangerous goods regulations) has established administrative agreements with each province and territory.[26]

"Dangerous Goods" are defined as a product, substance, or organism included by its nature or by the regulations in any of the classes listed in the

25. Transportation of Dangerous Goods Regulations, SOR/2001-286 (hereinafter TDGR).

26. Transport Canada, *Agreements Respecting Administration of the Transportation of Dangerous Goods Act, 1992* (Nov. 3, 2009), https://tc.canada.ca/en/dangerous-goods/agreements-respecting-administration-transportation-dangerous-goods-act-1992.

schedule.[27] The categories of dangerous goods, as set out in the Schedule to the TDGA, include the following:

- Class 1 — Explosives, including explosives within the meaning of the Explosives Act
- Class 2 — Gases: compressed, deeply refrigerated, liquefied or dissolved under pressure
- Class 3 — Flammable and combustible liquids
- Class 4 — Flammable solids; substances liable to spontaneous combustion; substances that on contact with water emit flammable gases
- Class 5 — Oxidizing substances; organic peroxides
- Class 6 — Poisonous (toxic) and infectious substances
- Class 7 — Nuclear substances, within the meaning of the Nuclear Safety and Control Act, that are radioactive
- Class 8 — Corrosives
- Class 9 — Miscellaneous products, substances or organisms considered by the Governor in Council to be dangerous to life, health, property or the environment when handled, offered for transport or transported and prescribed to be included in this class[28]

Section 5 of the TDGA mandates that in order to import, transport, or handle dangerous goods, a person must comply with the regulations, including providing the appropriate documentation to accompany the goods, properly contain the goods, and label the goods.[29] The TDGR set out the obligations owed by the shipper, carrier, and the consignee.

In general, when transporting dangerous goods the following requirements must be met:

1. The shipping document for the dangerous goods must set out specific information, including identifying the cargo as dangerous goods and provide an emergency phone number.
2. Safety marks must be clearly visible to any person handling the dangerous goods, including on the cargo itself and potentially the commercial vehicle transporting the cargo.
3. The driver who transports the dangerous goods must be trained or under the direct supervision of a trained person.
4. The dangerous goods must be transported in a "proper" container, which must be closed, secured, and maintained so to prevent the accidental release of dangerous goods during the normal rigors of transport.

One of the most critical requirements for the transportation of dangerous goods is adequate safety markings. Hazardous materials must be visibly and legibly marked in accordance with section 4.6 of the TDGR. With respect to carriers, section 4.5 of the TDGR states that the carrier of dangerous goods must

---

27. *Transportation of Dangerous Goods Act*, 1992 (S.C. 1992, c. 34) (hereinafter TDGA), s 2.
28. TDGA, Schedule 1 and 3.
29. TDGA, s 5.

ensure that the required dangerous goods safety marks remain displayed on the small means of containment while the dangerous goods are in transport.[30]

If dangerous goods have been released, resulting in death or injury to a person and/or property or environmental damage, then the TDGA permits the Minister of Transport to order a public inquiry, subject to the *Canadian Transportation Accident Investigation and Safety Board Act* (S.C. 1989, c. 3).[31] The penalties for not complying with the TDGA are substantial. For example, any person who contravenes the act can be fined up to $50,000 for a first offence, subsequent offences of up to $100,000, and up to two years of imprisonment.[32]

Cargo Securement and Loading

Cargo Securement

Standard 10 of the National Safety Code provides specific guidelines for securing loads onto commercial vehicles, ensuring that they remain stable and prevent spills or movement on the road. This standard aims to offer a reference that jurisdictions can adopt, recognizing that some regions may have their own regulations that could overlap with or conflict with the contents of this standard. In such cases, this standard presents optional text for consideration by jurisdictions where necessary.

Under the National Safety Code, cargo securement systems, and each component of a system, used to contain, immobilize, or secure cargo on or within the vehicle must be strong enough to withstand a specified level of force in all directions. These securement components must be in proper working order, be fit for the purpose for which they are used, shall have no knots, damaged or weakened components that will adversely affect their performance for cargo securement purposes, and shall not have any cracks or cuts.

Many provinces have legislated requirements regarding load safety. As an example, Ontario has legislated that any commercially operated vehicle that is transporting cargo must ensure that all the cargo is secured properly as per the Highway Traffic Act, O. Reg. 363/04: Security of Loads. Under the Security of Loads regulation, it is a strict liability offense if the cargo is unsecure and/or causes damage to other vehicles, injury, or death of another driver.

Loading and Unloading Cargo

In addition to cargo securement, Standard 10 of the National Safety Code also provides guidance on loading and unloading cargo from a securement perspective and sets forth the procedures to follow to ensure the load is secured when loading and unloading. Any systems and components of a commercial vehicle involved in the loading and unloading process are also to be inspected and maintained in accordance with Standard 11 of the National Safety Code.

30. TDGR, *supra* note 25.
31. TDGA, *supra* note 27, s 21(1).
32. https://www.ccohs.ca/oshanswers/legisl/tdg/tdg_overview.html; Act, s 33(2).

Loading and unloading of cargo is a notable concern from a worker safety perspective. Due to a number of serious incidents that have occurred involving truck drivers who were fatally injured during the loading and unloading process, Employment and Social Development Canada issued a hazard alert to remind employers of their duty to ensure the health and safety of their employees during the loading and unloading process.[33] The notice highlights that the Canada Labour Code Part II extends beyond the conventional workplace and requires that employers ensure that the health and safety of employees is protected while conducting all work activities.[34] According to the notice,

> To ensure the health and safety of employees on site while loading or unloading a truck, employers must consult the Policy Health and Safety Committee (where they exist) or the Work Place Health and Safety Committee or Representative to:
>
> - identify and assess hazards associated with working in unfamiliar work places
> - identify and assess hazards associated with working with each and every type of load the driver may carry
> - implement adequate control measures to address the assessed hazards, which could include using "no-go" zones during the loading process or simply not being involved
> - train drivers on safe working procedures for loading and unloading the trailer
> - train employees on how to safely operate the necessary equipment[35]

Contracts of Carriage

Most Canadian provinces and territories regulate conditions of carriage and bills of lading for certain goods. Newfoundland, Prince Edward Island, Yukon, Nunavut, and the Northwest Territories currently do not regulate in this area. In the provinces that continue to regulate, the conditions of carriage remain essentially consistent. However, one of the key distinctions among the provincial regimes is the way in which the regulations incorporate the uniform conditions into the contracts of carriage. A consideration in drafting any contract of carriage will be the determination of which province's law will govern. Seven out of ten of the provinces deem their uniform conditions to apply to contracts of carriage made in those provinces as a matter of law. There are three provinces without this language: British Columbia, Saskatchewan, and Prince Edward Island. Those jurisdictions require that the uniform conditions are incorporated into the bill of lading.

33. Employment and Social Development Canada, *Loading and Unloading Flatbed Trucks at Shipping and Receiving Sites*, https://www.canada.ca/en/employment-social-development/services/health-safety/prevention/flatbed-trucks.html (last updated Sept. 9, 2022).

34. *Id.*

35. *Id.*

As an example, in Ontario Regulation 643/05 Carriage of Goods under the Highway Traffic Act sets out what information is required in the contract of carriage for general freight, including the name of the consignor/consignee; the originating and destination points of the shipment; the name of the originating and connecting carriers; a space for the declared value of the shipment; a space to show whether the C.O.D. fee is prepaid or collect; a statement to indicate that the uniform conditions of carriage apply; a statement of the notice of claim requirements in the uniform conditions of carriage; and, if applicable, a statement, in conspicuous form, that the carrier's liability is limited by a term or condition of another agreement.[36]

Regulation 643/05 Carriage of Goods establishes uniform conditions of carriage for general freight, livestock, and animal specialties and household goods. The uniform conditions of carriage include provisions about the carrier's liability, consignees' remedies, limit of liability, and notice periods.

Litigation and Liability

Identifying the Parties Involved

The first step in any litigation involving a motor carrier is ensuring that all relevant parties are identified. The relevant parties will vary depending on the context of the loss. In many cases, separate corporations (or individuals) may own the tractor trailer, the container, the chassis, and the cargo. Equipment may also be leased rather than owned. Drivers may be independent contractors as opposed to employees of the carrier or logistics company. In addition, there may be other parties involved depending on the circumstances, including load brokers (more often called freight forwarders in Canada) or third-party maintenance companies. Where the cause of the loss may be the cargo itself or its securement, relevant parties can also include the cargo owner, supplier, the warehouse or other agents who may have assisted in loading and securing the cargo, as well as any party responsible for declaring the cargo accurately to the carrier.

Freight Forwarders

A significant number of shippers use freight forwarders to handle and arrange the logistics of carriage for their goods. Where there is a claim for cargo damage, shippers will often look to the freight forwarder. A freight forwarder is not automatically liable for the faults of the chosen carrier. However, it is generally accepted that they must use reasonable care in selecting motor carriers to haul their customers' loads. In *Nolar Industries Ltd. v. Freight Transportation Association*, 2005 CanLII 38584, the Ontario Superior Court held that the liability of a freight forwarder is analogous to that of a travel agent in the performance of services by another. The court adopted the comment that if "the carrier defaults

36. *Carriage of Goods*, O Reg 643/05, s. 4.

through no fault of the agent, surely the agent is not responsible."[37] However, there is not a significant abundance of Canadian case law on this issue as of yet. As such, in the absence of statutorily prescribed standard of care and the lack of Canadian case law, it can be expected that Canadian courts will look to American decisions for guidance. General diligence would include reviewing the carrier's insurance certificate, safety fitness certificates, and applicable workers compensation coverage.

One issue of interest is that the uniform conditions of carriage that may apply to limit a carrier's liability do not extend to freight forwarders. There is no legislative presumptive limitation of liability that applies to freight forwarders in Canada. As such, while a carrier may be able to limit its liability vis-à-vis a shipper, there is potentially unlimited liability on the part of the freight forwarder.

Negligence and Liability of the Carrier

A successful claim for negligence in Canada requires the plaintiff to show (1) that the defendant owed the plaintiff a duty of care, (2) that the defendant's behavior breached the standard of care, (3) that the plaintiff sustained damage, and (4) that the damage was caused, in fact and in law, by the defendant's breach.[38]

Notably, while a carrier is subject to significant statutory requirements, many of the licensing and registrations required by statute may be irrelevant to a negligence action. As an example, in *Roy Swail Ltd. v. Reeves* (1956), 2 DLR (2d) 326 (SCC), the Supreme Court of Canada held that the failure to register a truck or obtain a commercial vehicle permit in violation of a statute was not relevant in the negligence action against the driver as the registration and permitting requirement does not have safety as a purpose. The Court commented,

> The absence of an operator's license should only be evidence of lack of skill and thus of negligent driving on the occasion in question where a competency test is a prerequisite for obtaining a license. If a competency test is not required, the absence of an operator's license should always be irrelevant in a negligence action against the unlicensed driver.
>
> * * *
>
> The breach of a licensing statute should be irrelevant in a negligence action, unless the statute provides for a competency test as a condition of obtaining a license. If provision is made for a competency test, then one of the purposes of the licensing statute is safety. It may be, however, that even where safety is a purpose of a licensing statute a breach thereof will not always be relevant in a negligence action.

It's also important to note that allegations of negligent hiring and negligent entrustment have not been readily used against carriers in Canada. To date, there is scarce case law on these causes of action in the commercial trucking context.

37. Nolar Industries Ltd. v. Freight Transp. Ass'n, 2005 CanLII 38584, at para. 22.
38. Mustapha v. Culligan of Canada Ltd., 2008 SCC 27.

Criminal Liability of a Carrier

In Canada an individual can be found to be criminally negligent under s. 219(1) of the Criminal Code where in doing anything or omitting to do anything that is the person's duty the person engaged in wanton or reckless disregard for the lives or safety of others.[39]

In the recent case, *R. v. Matharu*,[40] a truck driver was transporting a perishable load of food in a tractor-trailer from Manitoba to Ontario. The load was required to be at the destination by 10:00 p.m. that day, and the driver was running late. At 9:45 p.m., the driver was stuck in traffic on a busy highway well over an hour from his location if traffic was good.

The driver struck a slow-moving car in front of him causing a chain reaction involving two other cars and another tractor trailer. The accident resulted in four people (one of whom was a five-year-old child) being killed and a fifth being seriously injured. This led to a shutdown of a major highway in Toronto for a 20-hour repair.

Three months later, the driver was charged with four counts of criminal negligence causing death and one count of criminal negligence causing bodily harm. He was ultimately convicted on all five counts.

The court considered evidence including the data recorded in the truck's "black box," which showed that the driver was traveling over 80 km/h (in excess of the posted construction zone limit) and no braking occurred until the moment of impact. In addition, the driver's cell phone records showed that at the time of the incident he was speaking on his phone.

The court also found that the driver had breached the Highway Traffic Act regulations limiting a commercial truck driver's driving time to 13 hours a day, which is required to be followed by an eight-hour off-duty rest before resuming. It was proven that the driver had fabricated his log to show compliance with the regulations. At paragraph 129 the court concluded:

> . . . [the driver] knew that driving on insufficient sleep put public safety (and his own safety) at risk. He simply chose to take the risk, apparently giving his own financial self-interest priority, and he then unreasonably minimized the risk. He also must have known from experience, that lengthy cell phone conversations while driving can lead to a risk of distraction. Once again, he unreasonably minimized this risk. I am also satisfied that he must have known from common sense experience, that exceeding the speed limit in a busy urban construction zone, on a six-lane highway, while approaching a major interchange with another highway, in a large heavy transport truck that requires a longer distance to brake and slow down, puts public safety at risk. Any experienced truck driver would know this. Finally, I am satisfied that he should have known and may have known the risk of continuing to accelerate and exceed the speed limit when the traffic ahead of him in lane 3 was slowing and coming to a stop. In the case of these latter two risks,

39. *Criminal Code*, RSC, 1985, c C-46, RS, c C-34, s 202.
40. 2021 ONSC 3122.

> [the driver] was either willing to take the risks because he was under pressure to deliver the load of meat to Maple Leaf Foods in Hannon by 10:00 p.m. that evening, he was running late, and he thought that he could change lanes at the last moment if necessary. Alternatively, he was unaware of the risks because he was falling asleep and/or he was distracted by his cell phone. Both of these alternative states of mind or fault are culpable. . . .

Standard Carrier Defenses

The defenses available to carriers or truck drivers in Canada are similar to those in the United States. One of the primary defenses available is causation. As a general rule, the defendant's conduct must have caused the plaintiff's loss or else there is no liability. There must be some connection or link between the wrongful act and the damage. The accident must result from or be attributed to the act of the wrongdoer. The Supreme Court of Canada's decision in *Clements v. Clements*, 2012 SCC 32, is the leading case on the test for causation, as follows:

> As a general rule, a plaintiff cannot succeed unless she shows as a matter of fact that she would not have suffered the loss "but for" the negligent act or acts of the defendant. A trial judge is to take a robust and pragmatic approach to determining if a plaintiff has established that the defendant's negligence caused her loss. Scientific proof of causation is not required.[41]

Another defense asserted by carriers is to try to shift liability to another party. This may include other drivers, the owner of or maintenance provider for the equipment, the entity responsible for loading or securing the goods in the trailer that may have shifted and contributed to the accident, and others.

In most of Canada, the time limit for commencing proceedings for negligence is two years. In Quebec, the limitation period is three years.

Personal Injury Claims Involving Commercial Trucks in Canada

Claims for personal injury involving trucks have many similarities to those in the United States. The similarities relate mainly to liability issues, procedure, discovery, and evidentiary matters. There are some significant differences, however. These defenses primarily relate to damages available to plaintiffs.

Pain and Suffering Damages

Canada has a cap on personal injury damages for pain and suffering (non-pecuniary or general damages). The Supreme Court determined in 1978 that the maximum amount that could be awarded was $100,000.[42] This has been indexed to inflation, such that at the time of writing, the maximum amount was $461,823.[43]

41. *Clements v. Clements*, [2012] 2 SCR 181, at para. 46.

42. *Andrews v. Grand & Toy Alberta Ltd.*, [1978] 2 S.C.R. 229, Arnold v. Teno, [1978] 2 S.C.R. 287, Thornton v. School Dist. No. 57 (Prince George), [1978] 2 S.C.R. 267

43. McKellar Structured Settlements, *Statistics*, https://www.mckellar.com/statistics#non-pecuniary-damages-upper-limits.

Punitive Damages

Another significant difference in the calculation of damages in Canada is the availability of punitive damages. Generally speaking, punitive damages are rarely awarded by Canadian courts. "[P]unitive damages should be resorted to only in exceptional cases and with restraint."[44] In addition, the Supreme Court has stated:

> [P]unitive damages may only be awarded in respect of conduct which is of such nature as to be deserving of punishment because of its harsh, vindictive, reprehensible and malicious nature.[45]

Punitive damages are most commonly awarded for intentional torts.[46] As a result, there are relatively few personal injury cases alleging negligence where punitive damages have been awarded. Punitive damages may only be awarded when the compensatory damages are insufficient as a behavior modifier.[47]

The amounts Canadian courts award for punitive damages are relatively low. Even where the defendant is a large corporation,

> the court should relate the facts of the particular case to the underlying purposes of punitive damages and ask itself how, in particular, an award would further one or other of the objectives of the law, and what is the lowest award that would serve the purpose, i.e., because any higher award would be irrational.[48]

The overall award of damages must meet the following objective:

> . . . compensatory damages plus punitive damages plus any other punishment related to the same misconduct, should be rationally related to the objectives for which the punitive damages are awarded (retribution, deterrence and denunciation).[49]

Due to the preceding principles set by the Supreme Court of Canada, we have not seen the same kind of "nuclear verdicts" that are a feature of the U.S. system. Commercial truckers that operate exclusively in Canada may do so without the fear of significant trial verdicts or the accompanying need for extremely high insurance limits. However, Canadian trucking companies that operate on both sides of the border must pay attention to the developments in large verdicts in the United States and prepare accordingly.

---

44. *Whiten v. Pilot Insurance Co.,* [2002] 1 SCR 595 (*Whiten*) at para. 69.
45. Vorvis v. Ins. Corp. of British Columbia, [1989] 1 SCR 1085 at pp. 1107–08.
46. *Whiten,* at para. 67.
47. *Id.* at para. 72.
48. *Id.* at para. 71.
49. *Id.* at para. 74.

Index

E

F

G

I

J

K

L

M

N

O

U

V